The Big Leagues Go to Washington

The Big Leagues Go to Washington

Congress and Sports Antitrust, 1951–1989

DAVID GEORGE SURDAM

UNIVERSITY OF ILLINOIS PRESS
Urbana, Chicago, and Springfield

Manufactured in the United States of America
C 5 4 3 2 1
∞ This book is printed on acid-free paper.

Library of Congress Cataloging-in-Publication Data
Surdam, David G. (David George) author.
The big leagues go to Washington : Congress and sports antitrust, 1951–1989 / David George Surdam.
pages cm
Includes bibliographical references and index.
ISBN 978-0-252-03914-0 (hardback) —
ISBN 978-0-252-09712-6 (e-book)
1. Professional sports—Law and legislation—United States—History—20th century. 2. Antitrust law—United States—History—20th century. 3. Professional sports—Economic aspects—United States—History—20th century. I. Title.
KF3989.S87 2015
344.73'099—dc23 2014034696

Contents

Acknowledgments

As always, I was helped by the kindness of not just strangers but friends (and sometimes strangers, who became friends). Writing a book entails incurring many debts.

I had help from the University of Northern Iowa's Economics Department's assistants, Kayla Gump and Jessy Martin. They cheerfully assembled notecards for the book.

Thomas Drueke of the University of Chicago's D'Angelo Library provided a valuable tip regarding ProQuest's Congressional Publications website.

Professor Ronald Abraham clarified a definition of depreciation allowances. Two anonymous reviewers provided excellent suggestions. One reviewer, in particular, took the time to send ten single-spaced typed pages of valuable comments; on round two, this reviewer sent in fifteen single-spaced pages, clarifying many of the legal intricacies. An author is fortunate to have such a meticulous reviewer, and the readers, too, will benefit from the reviewer's efforts.

My University of Chicago Economics Department dissertation committee of Nobel Prize winner Robert W. Fogel, David Galenson, and D. Gale Johnson encouraged my efforts and emphasized rigor and curiosity.

While at the University of Northern Iowa, I received continued and warm encouragement from Economics Department head Fred Abraham and dean of the College of Business Administration Farzad Moussavi. The university generously funded a summer research fellowship, while the College of Business Administration funded some research trips.

I acknowledge some of the stellar students I've had at the University of Northern Iowa: Charles "Chip" Rank, Travis Buhrow, and Trenton Baker. Chip and I worked on an informal project for a local summer league baseball club, while Travis and Trenton were excellent students in the Sports Economics class. It always is a pleasure to have good, attentive students.

I thank the University of Nebraska Press for their generous permission to reprint table 39 from my book on the National Football League, *Run to Glory and Profits* (table 8 in the current manuscript).

Sarah Statz Cords compiled an excellent index. I have worked with Sarah on several books now, and she is a delightful person with whom to interact.

Darrell Owens has been a long-time friend. College days were always more exciting when Darrell returned from Alaska. We've played many a game on the basketball and racquetball courts and softball diamond.

I also thank the University of Illinois Press's Willis Regier and Tad Ringo for their faith in this work.

This book is dedicated to Professor Louis Cain of Loyola University, who suggested I switch fields from the U.S. Civil War. Several books on professional team sports later, this title is just another ramification of his sagacious advice.

The Big Leagues
Go to Washington

Introduction

Professional team sports were very different in 1951 compared with modern sports. Major League Baseball (MLB) was ensconced as the "National Pastime," while the National Football League (NFL) had recently emerged from a bitter struggle with the rival All-America Football Conference (AAFC). The National Basketball Association (NBA), to those few Americans who cared, was instability exemplified, and its product was all too often a rough and tumble contest devoid of the fluidity and grace, much less the excitement, that would later amaze fans.

All athletes labored under the firm, almost totalitarian, reign of the owners. Baseball and football owners staged games in a collection of aging stadiums, while basketball players performed in converted hockey arenas or high school gymnasiums. Although there are often sickly franchises in sports leagues, the NFL and NBA still possessed dying franchises. For NBA owners, profits seemed chimerical. Some owners could not even give away their debt-ridden franchises.

Owners worried throughout the 1950s. Sportswriter Red Smith wrote: "[Major league owners] are keenly aware that there are men in Washington ready to slam them with antitrust legislation—a vastly more frightful ogre than Khrushchev—if they attempt openly to protect their monopoly."[1] Rather than let the "Khrushchevian shoe" drop upon them, the owners often acquiesced to the legislators' requests.

Why were legislators concerned about antitrust regulations? Americans in the late 1800s worried about the growing concentration of economic power in the hands of large corporations and big trusts such as oil, railroads, steel, meat packing, and tobacco. In response, Congress passed the Sherman Antitrust Act of 1890, which stated that "every combination in the form of trust or otherwise" that resulted in "restraint of trade" was illegal.[2] Owners of professional sports teams may not have resembled industrialists, but they labored under the same antitrust statutes. Major League Baseball owners pioneered league policies covering control of labor, territorial protection, entry of new teams and leagues, and, by the 1950s, the sale of broadcasting rights. These policies triggered antitrust concerns and inspired Congress to investigate.

Congressional committees began investigating professional team sports during the 1950s. These investigations provided glimpses into the leagues' operations. Although the investigations never completely exposed the leagues' activities, such as requesting the minutes of league meetings might have, they provided powerful pieces of evidence. Because of Congress' impact upon professional team sports, its investigations are important toward understanding the development of sports leagues. The owners' cartel-like behavior raised suspicions concerning antitrust violations. Because most cartels are illegal under United States antitrust laws, legislators and economists found and continue to find professional sports leagues of interest.

The congressional hearings raise crucial questions. How did the owners respond to criticisms of their practices? What evidence and theories did the owners employ in defense of their actions? Were their defenses based on sound economic analysis? Did congressional members and their legal counsel identify pieces of information and arguments that were useful in analyzing the owners' actions?

Although the hearings rarely resulted in any legislation, Congress pressured owners to create new teams or relocate to regions without teams, approved national television contracts, and allowed mergers between rival leagues. The legislators notably rarely tampered with the leagues' reserve clauses, reverse-order drafts of amateur players, or territorial rights, despite their concerns about these institutions. Such a system conferred significant advantages for incumbent owners.

Despite the paucity of legislation, professional team sports owners preempted some potentially adverse legislation by voluntarily altering their behavior in the face of Congress' implicit threats. On other occasions, after winning key concessions from Congress, owners performed their own versions of taunting by overstating and boasting about the gains conferred by the legislators.

The relative lack of positive action should not disappoint readers. According to David Truman, government committees served to allow interest groups to provide information and propaganda on causes near and dear to their hearts before government officials and the public, and also to provide an outlet for opposing groups to air out differences and possibly reach a compromise. If any legislation resulted, it was often as an afterthought.[3] The hearings, though, generated material that helped legislators analyze the possible effects of the bills and also led to revisions of the bills. The hearings afforded the legislators a forum by which to gently or not-so-gently persuade sports officials and owners to voluntarily change their operations.

Because of professional team sports' popularity, legislators saw opportunities to garner favorable publicity and perhaps to gain a springboard to greater legislative prominence. Legislators could curry favor with constituents by pressing leagues to place a franchise in their district or by ending unpopular actions by owners, such as blackouts of home games on television. Of course, these opportunities carried some risk. Legislators realized that tampering with professional sports might result in a public backlash. Historian Stephen Lowe argues that legislators were wary of damaging MLB's hallowedness. Rather than pass legislation, legislators were generally willing to issue implicit threats or to remain inert with respect to baseball. Football and basketball did not possess the same reservoir of public goodwill.[4]

No one seemed to note the irony that Congress was investigating monopolistic practices, when the two political parties were duopolists (an industry dominated by two firms). Incumbent congressional members benefited from various barriers to entry, such as seniority and postal franking, to say nothing about being able to deliver goods and services to their constituents. Legislators could teach team owners a thing or two about competitive imbalance, given their 80 percent or higher reelection rate for much of the twentieth century. Congressman Emanuel Celler of Brooklyn, chair of the House subcommittee between 1951 and 1972, won twenty-five consecutive House races before losing his final bid; very few professional sports teams approached such an unbroken streak of success.[5]

Scope and Method of the Book

There has been a marked absence of a comprehensive examination of the congressional hearings dealing with professional team sports, aside from Stephen Lowe's book, *The Kid on the Sandlot*. Lowe described Congress' relationship with professional sports, including boxing. He did not analyze the economics of the antitrust aspects of these leagues or the information presented at the hearings.

Roger G. Noll, a Stanford economist and one of the founders of sports economics, testified during the hearings regarding the proposed merger between the NBA and the upstart American Basketball Association (ABA). He collected a set of articles written by economists and other academics in *Government and the Sports Business*. These authors did not focus on the congressional hearings but established many of the recurring themes in sports economics and sports law. In this book, Lance Davis examined MLB's history of "self-regulation," while Steven B. Rivkin discussed sports leagues and antitrust laws.

Economists James Quirk and Rodney Fort examined professional team sports in two books, *Pay Dirt* and *Hard Ball*. They mentioned the congressional hearings but did not concentrate on them. The authors did, however, use much of the data contained in the 1951 and 1957 hearings.

Historian Robert F. Burk wrote two books detailing the often acrimonious and exploitative relationship between baseball owners and players: *Never Just a Game* and *Much More Than a Game*. He made use of the testimony regarding player and owner relations during several of the hearings.

A number of law professors and economists published books in the intervening decades covering sports and antitrust issues. A representative sample includes Charles E. Quirk, editor, of *Sports and the Law;* Warren Freedman, *Professional Sports and Antitrust;* and Arthur T. Johnson and James H. Frey, editors, of *Government and Sports: The Public Policy Issues*. These authors relied on law cases in building their arguments.

This book focuses on MLB, the NFL, and the NBA. Although National Hockey League (NHL) owners and commissioners testified before some of the investigating committees, their league was a six-team, close-knit group for many years. For antitrust purposes, two of the key issues revolving around hockey concerned the Norris family's interlocking ownership of half the teams in the league and the owners' control of hundreds of players under farm systems.[6]

This book examines hearings and related federal actions. Many of the hearings focused on one or two major topics. For instance, some of the proceedings focused on mergers between rival football and basketball leagues. The hearings are therefore arranged by topics. The topics cover player rights; general antitrust exemptions; territorial rights, franchise relocation and sales; expansion; television policies; and mergers.

The Economy during the Hearings

These hearings took place against the backdrop of a long expansionary period in the American economy until the 1973–1974 recession. The price level (that is, inflation rate) rose sharply right after the war, but by the mid-1950s prices were relatively stable. The Consumer Price Index almost tripled between 1945 and 1975, with rapid increases between 1969–1970 and 1972–1974. Throughout the discussion of franchise appreciation, ticket prices, and other financial matters, readers should recall that changes in the general price level eroded some of the apparent gains.

A Caveat

In considering these hearings, the reader is advised to always keep in mind that the participants—legislators, owners, players, sportswriters, and fans—were self-interested actors.[7] Legislators were interested in pleasing their constituents. Fans wanted new teams, more conclusive championship arrangements, and lower prices, if not free access to games via radio and television. Players wanted more freedom and financial remuneration, including pensions and benefits. Owners, of course, hoped to improve their bottom lines. Sportswriters yearned for exciting and important news to report.

1

A Brief History of Professional Team Sports

An understanding of the history of professional team sports helps place the issues covered in the hearings in the proper context. Player and owner relationships had long been contentious, because the owners held and exploited disproportionate power. The owners' struggles with each other and rival groups were every bit as competitive and cutthroat as those on the playing fields or courts.

Major League Baseball (MLB) established many of the institutions copied by the younger leagues. Baseball owners sought to keep player salaries low and to create price setting, monopoly power by stabilizing league membership. When they succeeded in establishing these goals, they then improved their profitability. Success in these two endeavors, though, meant that other potential owners would envy the profitability of owning a sports team, and these prospective owners would desire to enter the market. Baseball owners, therefore, devised tactics to deter entry. As technology advanced, potentially lucrative opportunities, such as radio and television, arose. Owners realized that under a controlled market, selling broadcasting and telecasting rights could be more valuable. With all of the court cases and antitrust hearings during the twentieth century, owners emerged partially victorious. Their ability to control entry of new teams and to sell broadcast and telecast rights remained largely intact, but they lost much of their power to control the labor market, with the Danny Gardella case being a pivotal event that led to later player successes in whittling down the owners' control.

Although this book focuses on congressional investigations into the actions of professional team sports leagues, court cases have been prominent. The court cases centered upon interpretations of statues and only rarely constitutional issues. The courts often encouraged Congress to enact legislation; on occasion, judicial decisions led to congressional investigations. As an example, Judge Allan K.

Grim's decision disallowing the NFL's national-television contract spurred the NFL to seek congressional action to allow the contract. In this case, Congress responded with legislation; in the main, though, Congress proved hesitant to enact legislation.

Baseball's Rise to National Pastime

In the beginning, there was baseball, a game evolved from other games. Numerous historians have documented baseball's early years.[1]

Harry Wright's Cincinnati Red Stockings were the first overtly professional team. He took the squad around the northeast quadrant of the United States, playing all comers and splitting the gate. Because Wright hand-picked his players, he constructed a powerful club that won more than sixty games in a row.

Though individual unaffiliated clubs could have been the future of professional baseball, the wildly uneven quality of opponents and nebulous way of deciding the champions were unsatisfactory. By 1871, a loose association of ball clubs coalesced into the National Association of Professional Base Ball Players. Any club willing to pay the minimal entry fee could participate. The National Association proved unwieldy, as too many small towns fielded short-lived teams. Some cities fielded multiple teams, usually a viable team and a weak team. The National Association was essentially chaos.

William Hulbert, a Chicago businessman and booster, enticed several of the Boston Red Stockings players to play for his Chicago team in 1876; he did not induce the players to jump their current contracts with Boston but signed them to contracts during the 1875 season. He realized that other teams would be outraged at his audacity and would evict him from the association. To preempt this, Hulbert contacted three or four other teams and invited them to a meeting in Chicago. He also planted stories in the *Chicago Tribune* outlining his plan. After explaining the defects of the National Association, Hulbert suggested a set of rules that included a population requirement of seventy-five thousand or more residents, a $100 membership fee, territorial protection guaranteeing just one team per city, and a more formal structure for scheduling games, including penalties for not completing the schedule.[2] His new league was named the National League of Professional Base Ball Clubs; baseball historian David Pietrusza observed that the new league's title emphasized "Clubs" instead of "Players."[3] In Hulbert's rules lay the genesis of American professional team sports leagues.

The 1876 season was marred by the New York and Philadelphia teams' unwillingness to travel west to complete their schedules. Both clubs offered the western teams inducements to travel east, but the western teams declined. Hulbert and the other owners ultimately kicked the New York and Philadelphia teams out of the league. This disciplinary action, while drastic, emphasized the importance of adhering to league rules.[4]

One key piece was missing from Hulbert's initial set of rules: clear-cut property rights to individual athletes. Owners sought ways to control players.[5] By 1879, they had begun to devise a reserve clause binding a player to the owner. Owners could initially reserve just five players on their rosters. Other owners pledged to honor the reserved players' contracts and not to tempt them with offers. The owners eventually extended the reserve clause to bind all of the players on their rosters.

This initial plan had defects. Owners in the same league might pledge and honor a reserve clause, but owners in other leagues might see little reason to honor such a clause. This reserve system had a second drawback. To fully reap the benefits of owning rights to a player, an owner needed a convenient and safe way to transfer his players to another team. Two owners interested in trading players had to release the individuals and then re-sign them. Such a transaction was risky, as other owners might poach the players upon their temporary release. Initially, owners wanting to trade players sought promises from their fellow owners not to step in. Such gentlemen's agreements were a fragile basis upon which to trade players, and owners gradually created a system whereby they could trade players without the requisite release.[6]

These rules helped owners keep salaries artificially low. The rules worked fairly well, unless a rival league appeared, which occurred frequently. Buoyed by the National League's relative success in the late 1870s, a new set of owners decided to challenge the National League by creating the American Association.

When a lesser league, the Northwestern League, contacted the National League seeking to reach a mutual agreement respecting each other's player contracts in 1883, the National League invited the American Association owners to join in a tripartite agreement, dubbed the National Agreement. The agreement entailed respecting each other's player contracts and reserve lists, while establishing minimum salaries and setting up a grievance board.[7] Over the years, the National Agreement included additional leagues until it dominated organized baseball. The National Agreement also proved handy in combatting new leagues, as the incumbent leagues banded together to fight the interlopers.[8]

After crushing the short-lived Union Association in 1884, National League and American Association owners, while still sparring among themselves, continually sought to suppress player salaries and rights. The players chafed under the owners' power. John Montgomery Ward, a former player turned attorney, suggested a league owned and operated by players, the Players' National League. The players, backed by some businessmen, raided National League and American Association rosters. This was a revolt unlike any before and since. Unfortunately for the players, the resulting losses from having three leagues discouraged their financial backers, and the Players' National League folded after just one season.

Only the National League remained by 1892. The "Gay 90s" were a troubled decade, though, for the National League, even with its newfound monopoly status. Owners were able to tamp down player salaries, but proprietors of stable, wealthy franchises began lending money to and acquiring interests in their weaker brethren, creating a system of interlocking ownership. In some cases, owners with interests in multiple teams would strip one club of its best players to fortify another of its teams in a more lucrative city.

The owners' internecine squabbles and fights led to the revolutionary idea of syndicate baseball, whereby ownership would be centralized and players parceled out under a master plan. Four of the owners favored this dubious idea but four opposed, ultimately dooming the plan.[9]

Professional sports leagues are unique in that while there is competition between teams, teams must also cooperate. In essence, owners are selling competition: competition between independent teams. Although they were selling competition, they feared unbridled competition. As law professor Jeffrey Glick points out, "League members are not economic competitors in the same sense as are individual companies. 'No NFL team, in short, is interested in driving another team out of business, whether in the counting house or the football field, for if the league fails, no one team can survive.' This is certainly not the case in the typical horizontal relationship." He concedes that professional teams could independently arrange games and forego formal ties, but such behavior has been rare since the National Association debacle.[10] Owners were aware of the tension within their leagues. James Hart, owner of the Chicago team, stated: "We are the only paradoxical business institution in the world. My good is your ill; your good is my ill. We compete for players, we compete for points, we compete for games; it is an antagonistic business from start to finish. If it was not, we would not be in business."[11]

A Successful Challenge to the Baseball Monopoly

During the National League's feud, Ban Johnson was dreaming of transforming the Western League into a new major league. By 1901, his association was raiding National League rosters for top-flight talent. Washington owner Clark Griffith recalled that American League owners had to resort to signing "reserve jumpers" to attain parity with National League teams: "We could not have been big league for quite some time. You know, it takes time to develop ballplayers."[12] The American League succeeded in enticing many stars onto its teams, quickly reaching parity with the National League teams. The bidding for players and the invasion of National League territory in five cities infuriated National League owners, whose ongoing internecine strife weakened their resistance. The owners finally declared peace, with two separate leagues sharing the pinnacle of the baseball world.

The two sets of owners revised the National Agreement that dictated rules for governance of the leagues and issues such as player advancement, while maintaining a hierarchy of baseball leagues. The two major leagues set up a governing commission consisting of each league's president and a third member chosen by the presidents. This governing board persisted until the aftermath of the Black Sox World Series gambling scandal of 1919 and owner dissatisfaction with the system. To assuage public confidence in baseball after the 1919 scandal, the owners decided to appoint a commissioner, Kenesaw Mountain Landis, and endowed him with broad powers.[13]

With peace reestablished and player salaries again suppressed, the owners enjoyed a period of prosperity. Several chose to replace their current wooden stands with stadiums constructed of concrete and steel. These stadiums created new barriers to entry: in addition to having to acquire recognized players, potential new leagues needed access to large stadiums. The two leagues also agreed to stage a championship series, the grandiosely named World Series. Having two stable leagues with a total of sixteen teams in the majority of the country's largest cities proved a successful formula.

These actions were so successful that years later, Marvin Miller, head of the MLB Players Association during the 1960s and 1970s, attempted a piece of satire. He summarized the owners' advantages in a mock advertisement, extolling ownership of a MLB team: "You are therefore free to utilize what would otherwise be illegal sanctions to enforce your will in controlling the entire skilled labor complement of the industry, to deprive cities and entire areas of your product when you choose to do so, to maintain with your associates a complete monopoly by barring would-be competitors, to fix prices and to allocate divisions of the market."[14]

The Federal League Challenge

The owners' prosperity throughout the first decade of the twentieth century did not go unnoticed. Other businessmen hungered for their own teams, and because MLB was uninterested in expansion, these nascent owners decided to launch the Federal League. The Federal League had modest success in luring big league stars onto their rosters, and planted franchises in Brooklyn, Chicago, Pittsburgh, and St. Louis in direct competition with existing MLB teams. Both of its pennant races were tightly contested, so the league's competitive balance was not detrimental.

The new owners, though, in addition to obtaining players, scrambled for playing sites. Naturally, the MLB owners combined to battle the interlopers, with the incumbents threatening to stage minor league games in their stadiums, when the big-league team was on the road. Players, though, benefited from the increased competition for their services.

The Federal League presented a serious challenge, but the combined strength of the two established leagues proved sufficient to stymie it. What was the price of peace? The American and National Leagues paid Federal League owners $600,000, allowed Federal League owners in Chicago and St. Louis to purchase the Cubs and Browns, reinstated ineligible players, and allowed the Federal League owners to sell their player contracts to the surviving clubs. One team, however, refused to meekly surrender. The Federal League's Baltimore franchise owners wanted to buy the St. Louis Cardinals and shift them to Baltimore, but were rebuffed. They were offered $50,000 and the Baltimore franchise in the International League.[15] The owners of the Baltimore club disliked the settlement and sued MLB. The established owners, perhaps recalling previous MLB attempts at making Baltimore a successful franchise, disdained the city and the owners of its ball club.

The Baltimore club's lawsuit wended its way to the Supreme Court. During the lawsuit, MLB official Garry Herrman claimed that the owners had not used the reserve clause to injure the Federal League, but rather, "the reserve clause had been used only as a matter of internal protection within organized baseball and, in his opinion, that was the only way it should be used—'to protect yourself.'" He denied that the reserve clause was intended to give MLB owners a monopoly over the player market. In a telling point, the owners filed lawsuits only against players who had jumped their contract, and not those who had jumped their reserve clause.[16]

L. Edwin Goldman, an officer of the Baltimore Federal League Club, made an interesting observation during the team's lawsuit against MLB. When asked, "The fact is, is it not, that in the fall of 1913 there were not enough recognized first-class players to supply both the then existing leagues and also your Federal League, if it should become a major league?" Goldman answered, "No. I will not agree to that at all, for this reason, that if influenza struck every ballplayer in the two major leagues during 1913, you could have taken the next rank of ballplayers, called them major league players and the public would have gone precisely in the same way to see them, because they were the best available." He added, "If you grant that the two major leagues that were then existent had selected the very best talent that existed in baseball, if we wanted to actually compete for public favor by having equal playing strength, undoubtedly we were driven to the ranks of organized baseball for these players."[17]

In 1922, Chief Justice Oliver Wendell Holmes delivered the majority verdict that baseball was not commerce, which thereby squelched the lawsuit. Many later commentators have disagreed with Holmes's ruling, but legal scholar Mitchell Nathanson suggested why Holmes and his fellow judges issued the decision: "In doing so, the Supreme Court skirted around the obvious—that MLB was a business not unlike any other, engaging in interstate commerce—and held that it was somehow different, transcendent, above such mundane acts of legislation as the Sherman Act. To hold otherwise, would be to hold that America's game was no different than a shirt factory, and this simply would not do. The cultural fiction of the baseball creed would not permit it."[18] But another issue simmered: player rights. Prior to the Federal League, MLB players had formed an association to agitate for better working conditions. The Federal League afforded players an opportunity to leverage competing bids into higher salaries. Previously, in *American League Baseball Club of Chicago, 149 N.Y.S.*, a court found that baseball was not interstate trade or commerce under the Sherman Antitrust Act. (Hal Chase signed with the White Sox in March 1914 and then defected to the Federal League.) Employers were using the Sherman Act to battle labor unions, and Holmes opposed this.[19]

A 1977 congressional committee suggested that the Court's ruling that baseball was not interstate commerce was "in harmony with the Court's limited concept of commerce at that time," but that the "narrow view of commerce was shortly abandoned" in *United States v. South-Eastern Underwriters Association.* In comparison, the Shubert brothers and the Klaw & Erlanger theater-booking companies dominated the theater industry; theater groups typically toured the country, similar to professional sports teams. A judge ruled that theater was not commerce and, therefore, was not subject to antitrust law. Steven Rivkin wrote in 1972 that a key analogy used by the majority compared baseball to "'a firm of lawyers sending out a member to argue a case, or the Chautauqua lecture bureau sending out lecturers.' Thus, baseball was originally removed from antitrust coverage by a constitutional rationale quite characteristic of that conservative era but soon to be read out of the mainstream of Supreme Court jurisprudence in the aftermath of New Deal struggles for Federal control of the economy."[20] The Supreme Court's decision would make baseball the envy of its sporting peers, and while many legislators and jurists have bemoaned the ruling, Congress did not step in and clarify the situation.

Other Sports' Treks to Big League Status

At about the same time as the *Federal Baseball* case, the NFL emerged out of the American Professional Football Association (APFA) of 1920.[21] Professional football was a hard, bloody sport with little of today's glamour and excitement. The APFA was centered in the upper Midwest, with Chicago hosting an anchor franchise. Smaller cities and sometimes large cities entered, played, and folded, often within one season. Scheduling was haphazard. Only by the 1936 season did every team play the same number of games. Not until the 1930s did a stable core of franchises in larger cities come to dominate the league. Their main rival, aside from occasional rival professional leagues, was college football. The pros gradually emphasized the passing game and greater scoring in their search for fans. By 1941, the league had attained stability, but a number of the teams barely outlasted World War II.

The National Basketball League (NBL) began in 1937.[22] The majority of teams were located in smaller cities in Iowa, Indiana, and Illinois. Several of the owners were former players or promoters of barnstorming teams. Squads played under primitive conditions, sometimes in high school gymnasiums. However, several of the teams enjoyed a solid fan base.

When the war ended, several owners of hockey arenas and teams hatched the idea of having basketball teams fill in the empty dates of their arenas.[23] Few of these owners knew much about basketball. The nascent Basketball Association of America (BAA) had larger population bases from which to draw fans and larger stadiums than did teams in the NBL, while the latter league possessed a preponderance of the nationally recognized top players, including George Mikan.

Postwar Prosperity and New Challengers

During the 1930s and 1940s, the NFL and eventual NBA were gaining a share of Americans' demand for professional sports. After World War II, with its pent-up demand for consumer spending, owners of existing professional teams hoped an era of prosperity would descend upon sports, but envious entrepreneurs were poised to spoil the good times. Jorge Pasquel and his brothers hoped to create a new baseball major league; they signed a handful of Major League players, but mostly their efforts only helped American players wring higher salaries from the owners.

The NFL found itself combatting a new league, the AAFC. The end results were escalating salaries, and several teams folded. The NFL eventually absorbed three AAFC teams.

In both of these cases, increased competition led to higher player salaries. Immediately after the war, the majority of sports leagues experienced booming attendance and gate receipts. These eventually receded by 1950, but owners, at least in baseball and football, possessed more revenue from which to pay higher salaries. Owner complaints that rising salaries necessarily spurred losses were sometimes, if not usually, dubious.

Initial Player Stands for Their Rights

Because the owners often threatened to blacklist players who switched teams, players began filing lawsuits. Danny Gardella was an obscure MLB player; he had a reasonably good year in 1945, hitting eighteen home runs and batting .272 for the New York Giants. If you look at a baseball encyclopedia, he promptly disappears until 1950. This unsung player, however, proved a key figure in the battle for player rights. Gardella signed with the Pasquel brothers but pleaded to return to MLB. He found himself blacklisted, and later filed suit against MLB. Gardella claimed that he had been "unlawfully deprived of earning a living in retaliation for his acceptance of the Mexican League's offer" and that "baseball is a monopoly, operates across state lines, via the farm systems and the use of radio and television, and that Organized Ball comes under the jurisdiction of the Sherman Anti-Trust Act."[24] A trial judge dismissed Gardella's case believing he "lacked jurisdiction to overturn a Supreme Court ruling." But in 1948, the Second Circuit Court of Appeals reinstated the case. According to Steven Rivkin, two of the appellate judges, Learned Hand and Jerome Frank, were willing to consider the argument that radio and television had transformed baseball into commerce, if it was not commerce before. Rather than let the case proceed, possibly to the Supreme Court, the owners settled with Gardella, and he had a one-game return to the major leagues. Some of the appellate judges' thinking echoed in later sports labor cases, such as *Radovich* and *Mackey*.[25]

St. Louis Cardinals pitcher Max Lanier also jumped to the Mexican League and found himself blacklisted; he, too, filed a lawsuit against baseball. Cardinals' owner Fred Saigh, however, intervened to get Lanier back in MLB, so Lanier dropped his suit. He later testified that baseball needed the reserve clause. Marvin Miller pointed out that Gardella had a stronger case, because he had never signed a contract with a reserve clause, unlike the other players. To avoid a potentially damaging court case, MLB decided to settle. Gardella dropped his suit before trial in return for a cash settlement; he then signed with the St. Louis Cardinals.[26]

By the 1950s, many legal jurists thought that baseball's antitrust exemption in *Federal Baseball* was an aberration; the court upheld it in *Toolson* (where a New York Yankees AAA player fought his demotion to Class A), despite the argument that radio and television had made baseball commerce, while expressing its belief that Congress should address the issue.

In football, players challenged the reserve clause. The *Radovich* case involved a veteran football player, William Radovich, who found himself blacklisted after playing for the AAFC Los Angeles Dons. The court ruled that the NFL was commerce, so the league did not have an antitrust exemption.[27] Both Congress and the Supreme Court hoped the other institution would resolve the inconsistencies in professional sports antitrust status, but neither party took the challenge. For its part, the NFL altered the reserve clause's language to theoretically allow players to play out their option year and then become free agents. Pete Rozelle and owners would bandy their new, gentler reserve clause to impress Congress and the public. When an actual free agent signing occurred in the 1960s, the football owners quickly created a compensation system for owners losing a free agent. Because the compensation system allowed the commissioner to unilaterally impose compensation, the incentive to sign free agents vanished. These machinations allayed players' and Congress' concerns for more than a decade but were overruled by the courts.

The Tottering Birth of Players' Associations

After the turmoil of the immediate postwar years ended, the victorious sports leagues settled into a semblance of stability. Two developments—the disappearance of franchise mortality and the growth of players' associations—gradually transformed professional sports.

After the Dallas Texans folded in 1951, football owners shifted some franchises, but no more franchises went out of business. MLB, of course, had boasted stability, with no franchise casualties and no relocations between 1903 and 1952; six of the original sixteen franchises transferred between 1953 and 1961. The NBA went from seventeen teams to eight teams by the 1954–1955 season; while owners moved several franchises, the eight continue to exist today. No expansion NBA team has folded, although some have relocated. Owners may have lost money and even approached bankruptcy, but they either sold out or had leaguewide backing to continue to play after the mid-1950s.

Aside from the player lawsuits, the players were hesitant to form strong associations. Commentators thought a players' union was unlikely, given the disparity in player salaries. MLB players formed a loose association immediately after the war, with Robert Murphy, a labor attorney, serving as legal adviser. The owners largely ignored Murphy and the association, but did accede to parceling out such crumbs as increased per diem.[28] Later, in a supreme example of owner hubris, the owners appointed and paid Judge Robert Cannon to represent the players. Marvin Miller noted that such a move was patently illegal under labor relations law.[29]

In football and basketball, some owners flatly prohibited their players from joining any union or association. The Fort Wayne Pistons owner, Fred Zollner, reportedly treated his players so well that they felt little need to join an association. George Halas of the Chicago Bears used similar tactics to discourage his players from joining, although he was notorious for pleading poverty and, apparently, lying to his players regarding salaries.[30]

The players associations' initial goals were typically modest: fewer exhibition games and less travel during the season; preseason training money for expenses; and increased per diem. None of the associations agitated for a modification, much less the elimination, of the reserve clause. The owners frequently stonewalled the players' request; over time, the players grew disenchanted and disgruntled with the owners.[31]

NBA players successfully stood up to the commissioner and the owners during a televised all-star contest. Former commissioner Maurice Podoloff had always dithered in responding to the players' request for a pension. Walter Kennedy, being relatively new to the post after Podoloff's death, had sufficient credibility to avert a player boycott of the game and the attendant public relations fiasco; he persuaded the owners to work with the players to create a pension.[32]

When baseball players hired Marvin Miller in the 1960s, they did not envision how effective a labor leader he would be. Miller had experience in the steel industry; he was shocked by the players' naïveté and spent much time educating them. Miller obtained some significant gains for the players, when the players and he negotiated a Basic Agreement with the owners early in 1968. The agreement boosted the minimum salary, spring training meal money, in-season meal money, and Murphy money, among other gains. As Robert Burk points out, "In a less trumpeted but significant provision article 7 included the requirement that the union be formally notified in the preceding off-season of any changes in playing rules and that their consent be secured in the case of any such change potentially affecting player benefits." The players failed to get a grievance process with an independent arbitrator and acquiesced to having the baseball commissioner be the arbiter.[33] In the next round of negotiations, owners agreed to a new grievance board, consisting of a management representative, a player representative, and a third representative chosen by the other two representatives. The 1970 Basic Agreement skirted the issue of the reserve clause, but Miller believed the new arbitration system could interpret the current reserve clause to ascertain its real meaning. Miller needed a test case.[34]

NFL players formed the NFL Players Association in 1957. The owners responded with malign neglect. The players' demands were modest: minimum salary of $5,000; expense money during training camp; $12 a day minimum for board and lodging while on the road; an injury clause guaranteeing a full season's salary; a shorter training season; and formal recognition of the association. Almost every player earned more than $5,000, so the minimum salary demand was not much of a demand, but the owners refused to accede to the request. Many of the owners had already met the players' other demands, and they agreed to standardize these conditions. The owners, though, refused to recognize the Players Association.

Commissioner Bert Bell told the players they could meet with him concerning individual grievances, but that he had no authority to recognize them.[35]

The players persisted in strengthening their association, although their representative Creighton Miller testified before congressional committees regarding the owners' stonewalling tactics. The owners, through Commissioner Bell, did a volte-face during one of the hearings and recognized the association. By the 1972 hearings on a Federal Sports Act, former NFL player-turned New York Congressman Jack Kemp suggested that the NFL Players Association was now solidly established. "I am convinced that the football players . . . are well represented today. They have access to fine legal representation."[36]

Curt Flood Takes a Stand

Marvin Miller believed baseball's reserve clause was a violation of players' civil rights, but he found only one player willing to test it in court. Curt Flood, a longtime St. Louis Cardinals centerfielder, agreed to contest the reserve clause. St. Louis traded Flood to Philadelphia after the 1969 season. Flood did not want to relocate to Philadelphia, for several reasons. Miller emphasized to Flood that he was likely forfeiting his future in baseball by pursuing a lawsuit. Miller also worried that Flood might accept a settlement, as had Gardella, but Flood was determined to press ahead. To Miller the challenge to the reserve clause entailed winning two points. First, Flood and his attorneys would have to show that baseball was covered by antitrust laws. Assuming they established the first point, then Flood and his legal team needed to show how baseball violated the antitrust laws. Miller recalled, "To show that what baseball *did* to Flood was *in violation* of the law would have been the easy part."[37]

Baseball owner Bill Veeck, who was relatively sympathetic to the players' arguments, pointed out that "a ten-year AAA veteran without a dime in future pension claims would have made a more sympathetic victim" than Flood. The player's lawyers launched a general attack on the reserve clause, rather than a personalized "well-focused delineation of an individual litigant's own victimization."[38]

Judge Irving Ben Cooper rejected Flood's argument that baseball was subject to the antitrust laws. In his commentary, Judge Cooper suggested that the players and owners negotiate modifications to the reserve clause.[39]

Nearly contemporaneously, two Yale law scholars, Michael Jacobs and Ralph Winter Jr., were arguing that negotiation was the solution to the reserve clause, now that baseball players had a union to engage in collective bargaining.[40] They pointed out that players' associations changed the legal status of the situation and that grievances were now under the purview of the National Labor Relations Act. Even the Flood lawsuit was based, in their opinion, upon a faulty basis. Because the baseball players had collective bargaining, "the 'right' to exercise individual bargaining power without restraint, which Flood claims, is explicitly denied to employees with a bargaining representative validly recognized under the National Labor Relations Act. Furthermore, the reserve clause in baseball and the common draft in basketball raised questions, not of group boycott of merger law, but of the scope of the duty to bargain and of freedom of contract between parties to collective bargaining."[41]

If players chafed under the reserve clause, Jacobs and Winter held little sympathy: "The reserve clause issue intersects with yet a second fundamental principle of collective bargaining: freedom of contract. We . . . think it is obvious that reserve or option clauses are mandatory subjects of bargaining under the National Labor Relations Act. . . . Because it is a mandatory subject of bargaining, the club owners must discuss the issue in good faith when the players raise it. Freedom of contract, however, is the general rule."[42]

After the court of appeals upheld Judge Cooper's decision, Miller and Flood were down to a faint hope that the Supreme Court would decide to hear their case. The Supreme Court, indeed, decided to do so, a surprise to many observers. The court heard arguments on March 20, 1972.[43]

The Supreme Court voted five to three to uphold the lower courts' rulings regarding whether baseball was subject to antitrust laws; the Court made no ruling on the reserve clause itself. The majority opinion was not the Court's finest hour. Justice Harry A. Blackmun spent much of his opinion writing a paean to baseball, before admitting, "We continue to be loath, fifty years after *Federal Baseball* and almost two decades after *Toolson,* to overturn those cases judicially when Congress, by its positive inaction, has allowed their decision to stand for so long and . . . has clearly evinced a desire not to disapprove them legislatively."[44] Two of the justices had ruled in the *Toolson* case; Justice William O. Douglas said, "While I joined the Court's opinion in *Toolson*, I have lived to regret it, and I would now correct what I believe to be its fundamental error." His fellow dissenter, Justice Warren Burger, added, "Courts are not the forum in which this tangled web ought to be unsnarled."[45] Marvin Miller pointed out that six of the justices held that baseball was commerce, but three of them still chose to uphold the lower courts' rulings.[46]

Although Miller and Flood lost the case, it did help transform the public's attitude toward the players. Legislators and the public alike realized how one-sided the owners' control of the players was. Although there was no groundswell of support for Flood in terms of public demonstrations, at least several prominent sportswriters began to rally around the players.[47]

The Rise of Free Agency

Charles O. Finley was a key figure in baseball's eventual free agency policy. In 1967, he took exception to Ken Harrelson's behavior and cut the player. Harrelson became a free agent, and the Boston Red Sox signed him for a reported $75,000 salary. Given that Harrelson was previously a mediocre batter, the amount paid was eye-opening. Finley later reneged on making payments on an annuity owed pitcher Catfish Hunter; Hunter took the matter to arbitration, and the arbitrator ruled in his favor, creating another free agent. These episodes might have provided owners and players clues that many players were significantly underpaid.[48]

In his account of players gaining free agency by playing out their reserve year, Marvin Miller described the frustration of finding a player willing to challenge the reserve clause. He noticed that the owners after the Flood case decision in the early 1970s appeared none too willing to see a player play an entire season without a signed contract. After the 1974 season, though, Los Angeles Dodgers pitcher Andy Messersmith failed to reach an agreement with the team. The team renewed his contract, but he did not sign it. Messersmith planned to sign a contract, if the Dodgers met his demands, but otherwise he was willing to be a test case for free agency. A second pitcher, aging Dave McNally of the Baltimore Orioles, left baseball after being traded by his longtime team, the Baltimore Orioles, to the Montreal Expos. He had not signed the contract the Expos had sent him for 1975. McNally expressed a willingness to file a grievance and to test the interpretation of the reserve clause.[49]

The arbitration board consisted of John Gaherin, who represented the owners, Marvin Miller, and independent arbitrator Peter Seitz. Seitz had earlier cast the deciding vote in the Catfish Hunter case. Seitz ruled in favor of the two pitchers. Miller believed that Gaherin recognized the weakness of the owners' case and encouraged them to negotiate.[50]

Baseball players won the right to limited free agency. Marvin Miller pointed out that the players association did not want unlimited free agency. He recalled that while owners wanted only a few players to become eligible for free agency at any time, he did not want a flood of free agents. The trick was to correctly choose the eligibility requirement. "With no history of free-agent movement to study, it was impossible to know which eligibility requirement would be best."[51] The owners and players eventually agreed that players completing their sixth season would be eligible for free agency. Not all teams could pursue a given free agent, and a draft was implemented to establish the rights to pursue a particular player. Teams losing a player to free agency would gain a draft pick in a subsequent June draft of amateur players.[52] The players had earlier won the right to salary arbitration. Both of these measures contributed to the breathtaking rise in player salaries after 1976. The rise lent credence, if not proof, to the charge that star players, at least, had been economically exploited in the past. Owners and players alike discovered that even players not yet eligible for free agency could win handsome increases in salaries. Owners later attempted to restore the status quo by trying to negotiate stricter rules governing free agency and arbitration, but the players' hard-won gains proved durable.

Players were no longer docile, with at least three player lawsuits attempting to transform the reserve clause and reverse-order draft: *Oscar Robertson v. NBA; Mackey v. NFL;* and *Smith v. Pro Football.* In the *Mackey* case, the so-called Rozelle Rule stipulating compensation for free agent signings came under judicial review.

NFL owners, finding that they actually had a real free agent signing, quickly and unilaterally implemented a rule, later dubbed the "Rozelle Rule," whereby the commissioner could arbitrarily assess compensation for a team losing a free agent. The uncertainty surrounding any such compensation dampened enthusiasm for signing free agents.

The NFL argued the rule was exempt from antitrust law, because it was part of the collective bargaining agreement. The justices questioned whether the purpose of the Rozelle Rule was truly to redress competitive imbalance or to punish teams for signing free agents. They noted that the rule held not only for the best players but also for average or marginal players. "Only the movement of the better players was urged as being detrimental to football." They pointed out two other flaws: it was unlimited in duration and unaccompanied by procedural safeguard; the rule had also been unilaterally imposed and had not been negotiated. Judge Frank compared the Rozelle Rule to the reserve clause and dismissed the argument that because players were well-paid, they were not being exploited, quoting the opinion expressed in *Gardella v. Chandler:* "If the players be regarded as quasi-peons, it is of no moment that they are well paid; only the totalitarian-minded will believe that high pay excuses virtual slavery."[53] The court believed the player draft and Rozelle Rule needed to be negotiated between the players association and owners and not be unilaterally imposed; by doing so, any such agreement would fall under the labor antitrust immunity exemption.[54]

NBA owners settled the Robertson case and negotiated a limited form of free agency for the players. Players refusing to sign a rookie contract would be placed in the following year's draft. Option clauses were removed, unless agreed upon by both player and owner. Teams had the right to match a free agent's best offer and to receive some compensation for players lost through free agency. The agreement stipulated that the award "may not be punitive." The owners also paid an indemnity of $5.2 million to the players and their attorneys.[55]

Professional Team Sports, Circa 1976

By 1976, television loomed larger for all owners' bottom lines; players enjoyed higher salaries; and attendance was greater. Professional team sports had progressed nicely. The NFL and NBA were experiencing degrees of prosperity much higher than in 1951. Troubles between players and owners persisted, and Congress was no longer so friendly toward sports leagues.

By 1976, players had formed associations or unions and were battling on roughly equal terms with the owners. Legislative and judicial hopes that collective bargaining might resolve labor/management issues did not result in harmony. The bilateral monopoly aspect of their negotiations meant that the outcome depended upon the two sides' respective bargaining strengths and skills. The baseball players' strike in 1972 was a harbinger of future labor and management strife.

The owners took the offensive and claimed that the higher salaries forced them to raise ticket prices.[56] Baseball owners, especially, tried to blame the rising salaries for triggering increases in ticket prices in the late 1970s. However, hikes in ticket prices during the first years of free agency did not greatly surpass the rate of inflation in those years of economic stagflation. Some of the teams raising their prices did so in anticipation of greater demand attendant upon the signing of quality free agents.[57] By 1976, professional team sports presented many features that modern fans take for granted.

In a coda to the struggle to gain free agency, in 1998 both MLB and the Players Association urged Congress to pass the Curt Flood Act, which it did. In essence, Congress codified what the players and owners had already negotiated. The owners' control of players dissipated with just a whimper, and the sky did not fall (nor did the death knell sound). Section 2 read:

"Sec. 2. Purpose. It is the purpose of this legislation to state that major league baseball players are covered under the antitrust laws (i.e. that major league baseball players will have the same rights under the antitrust laws as do other professional athletes, such as football and basketball players), along with a provision that makes it clear that the passage of this Act does not change the application of the antitrust laws in any other context or with respect to any other person or entity."[58]

2

Economics of Antitrust

What is antitrust, and why do we care? How does antitrust law affect professional team sports?

In the late 1800s, Americans worried about the growing concentration of power in the hands of a few producers. Standard Oil, American Tobacco, and other large firms consolidated their holds over industries by merging and acquiring other companies. Other industrial leaders sought to fix prices above those obtained under competition. The Sherman Act, enacted in 1890, states in part:

> Section 1: Every contract, combination in the form of trust or otherwise, or conspiracy, in restraint of trade or commerce among the several States, or with foreign nations, is declared to be illegal.
>
> Section 2: Every person who shall monopolize, or attempt to monopolize, or combine or conspire with any other person or persons, to monopolize any part of the trade or commerce among the several States, or with foreign nations, shall be deemed guilty of a felony.[1]

The act continues by spelling out the punishment for violators. Although the act is brief and seemingly clear-cut, courts would debate the meaning of "contract," "conspiracy," and "trade and commerce" for decades.

Applying the Sherman Act

The Sherman Act remained dormant for years until courts acted to prevent a merger between the Northern Pacific and Great Northern Railroads in the *Northern Trust* case in 1904. Court rulings also broke up Standard Oil and the American Tobacco Company in 1911. The courts found these firms guilty of anticompetitive acts that reduced or eliminated competition. In another case, though, the courts ruled in favor of U.S. Steel, even though Judge E. H. Gary, the chairman of the company, held dinners with leaders of rival steel-producing companies. This being the early 1900s, readers may envision a group of well-fed, cigar-smoking men listening to Judge Gary's admonitions to "follow U.S. Steel's [price] leadership, which they did." After a district court ruled in favor of U.S. Steel, the Department of Justice took the case to the Supreme Court. Two of the justices abstained, because they had previously been critical of U.S. Steel. The remaining justices voted 4–3 in favor of the company. The majority believed that, "since Judge Gary felt compelled to meet with competitors in order to fix and to control steel prices, U.S. Steel had not attained monopoly power." In a rather bizarre twist, competitors, dealers, and customers testified in favor of U.S. Steel.[2]

To demonstrate that a violation occurred, a "rule of reason" operates. Under this concept, courts assess whether the restrictions on competition redound to the net benefit of consumers. There is some debate whether a court should consider the total benefit (both to producers and consumers), rather than a sole emphasis upon consumer welfare. This was not specified in the original act, but over the intervening years, this interpretation evolved.

Looking at Section 1, a leading textbook on industrial organization explains that courts have "interpreted this language as making illegal *per se* all agreements among competing firms to fix prices, to restrict or pool output, or otherwise directly to restrict the force of competition. Such agreements have been singled out for judicial treatment different from under the *rule of reason* approach taken with respect to a variety of other practices."[3]

A classic example of a price fixing violation occurred in the wake of airline deregulation. American Airlines president Robert L. Crandall dialed up his counterpart at the now-defunct Braniff Airlines, Howard Putnam:

> Putnam: Do you have a suggestion for me?
> Crandall: Yes, I have a suggestion for you. Raise your goddamn fares 20 percent. I'll raise mine the next morning.
> Putnam: Robert, we . . .
> Crandall: You'll make more money and I will, too.
> Putnam: We can't talk about pricing.
> Crandall: Oh [expletive], Howard. We can talk about any goddamn thing we want to talk about.

Unfortunately for Mr. Crandall, Putnam recorded the conversation, which was entered as part of a Justice Department's complaint against American.[4] Crandall was duly punished.

In a series of cases, the courts relied upon whether the producers' actions benefited or injured consumers. In *Columbia v. BMI* (ASCAP), the setting of royalty rates was deemed beneficial.[5] Though it fixed prices, the uniformity enabled musicians and radio stations to cheaply settle royalty payments, which ultimately benefited consumers.

Professional team sports would appear to have been violating the Sherman Act. Baseball constitutions contained a clause stipulating a minimum price. Was this a price-fixing violation? Usually there is only one league at the "major league" level, and when there have been multiple leagues, the sparks flew. How have sports team owners avoided being indicted and convicted of violating the proscription on combining? The sports owners' promulgation of controls over players, territorial protection, and national television contracts would be permissible if the owners could demonstrate that these institutions ultimately benefited consumers, and at the least reduction to competition. The owners usually argued that their restrictions created stability—thereby reducing the chance that fans would lose a beloved team—and increased competitive balance, which fans also valued. If these were credible claims, then the owners could avert indictment and conviction.

Economists and lawyers have long recognized professional team sports' peculiar nature. Baseball games could be staged by a single team playing an intrasquad game, but this would be similar to the sound of one hand clapping. College football and basketball teams often stage intrasquad games at the end of training season. Fans attend these games, perhaps because the games are part of a season-ticket package, but no team dares to feed their fans a steady diet of such games.

A game between two rival, independent teams provides more pleasure for fans, especially if the teams are relatively evenly matched. Close, hard-fought games are the acme for sports. (Although Americans did not seem to mind when America's "Dream Team" demolished the basketball competition in the 1992 Olympics.)

Once you have two or more teams, a set of agreements is necessary. When and where will the game(s) be played? Which rules will be used—a critical question in the early days of sports, and one still germane in MLB with its quirky playing fields. Another important issue: How will gate receipts be split?

If State U contracts to play Wossamotta U (from *Rocky and Bullwinkle* fame), is this a contract that would be proscribed under Section 1 of the Sherman Act? If the two teams agree to set a $10 admission fee, is this a case of price fixing? Presumably, the two universities are not primarily in the business of staging ballgames. Suppose we replace State U and Wossamotta U with the New York Mammoths and New York Knights [from *Bang the Drum Slowly* and *The Natural*], two teams (firms) primarily devoted to staging games and earning profits. In a sense, these teams are similar to Ford and Chrysler—competing firms in the same industry. Would these teams violate Section 1 of the Sherman Act by agreeing to play in the Mammoths' stadium on July 6, 1957 at 2:30, with a charge of $2.50 per box seat and $2.00 for reserved seat?

What about sports leagues? Professional team sports could have been comprised solely of independent teams. Fans, though, have an insatiable desire to see a champion crowned, as witness the annual call for an NCAA football playoff system. Professional teams could barnstorm, playing all interested comers, but determining a champion under such haphazard conditions is rife with controversy. A league or leagues comprised of roughly equal teams might produce a champion. The league might need to create and to enforce a rationalized schedule. The early NFL's predecessor, the American Professional Football Association, was an example of a league where the scheduling was so chaotic that the owners had to vote on a champion.

Leagues in America are usually tied with team owners. Owners create the constitution and select league officials. European football (a.k.a. soccer) uses an independent league organization. This firm offers league services, such as scheduling. Stephen Ross argues that "a divestiture of Major League Baseball and the NFL into competing economic entities would best serve the public interest." Ross notes the political difficulty in enacting such a change. The sports leagues' behavior costs individual fans a few dollars here and there, while owners reap millions. Ross laconically notes: "A large body of academic work demonstrates how the legislative process is not conducive to proposals that impose costs upon a few and benefits on many; the owners have a strong incentive to lobby against legislation, while fans and taxpayers feel less intensely and are difficult to organize into a cohesive political force."[6]

A merger of two leagues or a single league's overt attempt to monopolize the market would appear to be violating Section 2 of the Sherman Act. However, what if a firm (or league) dominates or monopolizes the industry because it is more efficient than its rivals? Does monopoly imply just one firm (league) in a market? What market share would indicate a monopoly?

In considering the economics of antitrust, it is important to note that an owner of a professional sports team operates under a set of institutions. An owner of an NFL team in 1950 would have considered the reserve clause, reverse-order draft, territorial rights, and other rights as part of the team's value. If Congress or the courts determined that any of the institutions were illegal, then the value of an owner's franchise in the eyes of prospective buyers would decrease. The owners' intransigence in relinquishing any of their institutions should be seen with this aspect in mind.

Characteristics of Sports Leagues

Scholars differ on the nature of professional sports leagues. Walter Neale argues that "each professional sport is a natural monopoly. The several products which are products joint of legally separate business firms are really the complex joint products of one firm, and this firm is necessarily an all-embracing firm or natural monopoly." He observes that in most cases, multiple leagues eventually become one league. MLB, a seeming exception to his observation, though, is a "joining of economically competing oligopolistic firms into sportingly competitive *natural monopolies* [italics mine]."[7] Part of sports' output is the production of excitement and keen interest in the league standings and eventual determination of a champion.

Gary Roberts believes that sports leagues have a unique economic relationship, which is not "a collection of horizontal competitors whose cooperative activity is inherently unlawful; no court or commentator has ever found or suggested that a sports league is illegal by its very existence." Using the NFL as an example, he continues: "This interrelationship among the 224 regular season and nine playoff games, culminating in the Super Bowl, makes NFL football a distinct and far more attractive product than any individual football game or games. . . . If for any reason one or more member clubs decline to recognize or to accept the results of any league game or games, the entire fabric of the league product would unravel. Only with the total cooperation of every league member on every aspect of league operations can there be a league product, and each individual game is an inseparable part of that indivisible league product."[8]

Roberts's approach differs from Professor Lee Goldman's. Roberts believes, "The ultimate issue here is not whether leagues are single entities or a collection of independent firms; rather, it is whether or not the internal rules and decisions of leagues ought to be immune from case-by-case rule of reason review under section 1. I argue that league governance rules and decisions should be beyond the scope of section 1. I do not claim that they are necessarily lawful. Such rules and decisions might still constitute monopolization, attempts to monopolize, or conspiracies of monopolize, which are all condemned under section 2." He points out that single entity, ancillary restraints, or inherent noncompetition, "achieve the proper result because each recognizes and is premised on the fundamental facts distinguishing a sports league from any other type of business organization in our economy: (1) that the product of a league cannot be produced by any one member team, but rather is only produced by the complete integration and cooperation of each and every member of the league; and (2) that a league member team does not and cannot lawfully have any relevant independent productive function outside its existence as a wholly integrated member of the league." Goldman believes that "member clubs of a sports league have legitimate economic interests of their own, independent of the league and each other," which Roberts does not believe.[9]

In the *Copperweld v. Independent Tube* case of 1984, the Supreme Court ruled that divisions of the same corporation may engage in cooperative actions that independent companies may not engage in under the antitrust laws. These cooperative actions by a single entity may even be per se illegal, with no rule of reason test, if undertaken by independent horizontal competitors (competitors producing similar goods and services), including price fixing. The courts recognize that forcing divisions within the same corporations to make independent decisions may forfeit cost-saving benefits and efficiencies.[10]

American sports leagues are joint ventures, with owners having equal shares in the league. A key question is whether the owners of individual teams are so intertwined that they fall under the *Copperweld* findings and could therefore be seen as divisions of the same company and gain antitrust immunity; or whether the league is simply a joint venture of truly independent businesses for the purposes of cooperating in the minimal activities necessary to operate the league (such as determining the schedule). In the latter case, if the league is used for collusive purposes that do not pass the rule of reason, the owners have antitrust liability. If team owners opt to cooperate in anticompetitive ways that injure consumers—fixing prices or market division—they have to pass a single-entity test. The NFL attempted to use a single-entity argument in its defense, but the courts have never sustained the argument, as will be seen.

Owners acted together to raise profits primarily through two rules that gave them unique advantages. They designated territorial rights for themselves, arguing that having too many teams in one city created ruinous competition.[11] Although it may have been understandable and even justifiable why a league would want only one team in each city, it was less justifiable to extrapolate this desire to one where no other league could place teams in an occupied city. The *Harvard Law Review* questioned the justification of the territorial protection, considering an owner was unlikely to relocate his team to a city incapable of supporting two franchises; in cases where an owner moved his team to a city capable of sustaining multiple teams, the owner and the fans benefited. Of course, the incumbent owner suffered.[12]

Owing to the lack of competition, a baseball owner who had the sole team facing the demand for professional baseball within his city held monopoly power and could set his price. Such power, of course, allowed owners to charge higher prices and earn greater profits than under a competitive market. In addition, an owner's price-setting power meant that he was shielded from the market; in a truly competitive market, owners have to continually scramble to produce quality products at relatively low cost. In the professional sports world, owners could be slovenly, in an economic sense. They could pursue goals other than profit maximization. Owners could avoid carefully studying innovations, and, indeed, baseball owners sometimes seemed behind the times with regard to electric lights and radio broadcasts. On occasion, innovative mavericks such as Bill Veeck Jr. and Charles O. Finley attracted the ire of their fellow owners, who were hesitant, if not downright resistant, to accept their suggested innovations.[13]

Leagues allowed owners to set their prices. However, league constitutions often stipulated a minimum price, thereby preventing some desperate owner from unilaterally slashing prices. Baseball's National League owner William Hulbert stipulated that a fifty-cent minimum admission price would be enacted.[14] A later league, the American Association, decided to establish a twenty-five-cent minimum price. Hulbert set a fairly high minimum to attract a better clientele than many early professional teams had previously drawn.

The second important way owners acted together was in creating the reserve clause. Owners always looked to reduce one of their main expenses: player salaries. Competition for top players created upward pressure on salaries. Owners quickly realized that a free market for players was undesirable.[15] The reserve clause and the player draft bound a player to a single owner. The owner could trade, sell, or release a player at will. This single-employer power (denoted by economists as monopsony—sole buyer—power) gave owners disproportionate bargaining leverage over players and suppressed salaries relative to what players facing a more competitive labor market would pay. But there were limits to how far owners could have exploited their athletes.

The reserve clause alone, though, did not give owners complete immunity from the free market. Until a player signed an initial contract with a team, he was a free agent. Young players, therefore, faced competition for their services. The player draft limited players' bargaining leverage and redounded to the owners' advantage.

The reserve clause and player draft gave owners enhanced bargaining power and were likely to trigger antitrust scrutiny. A reverse-order draft of graduating criminal-law attorneys, based on win-loss records in, say, murder trials, would draw the ire of legislators and the public. People might quickly recognize the unfairness and the flagrant violation of the young graduates' rights to their own labor. Professional team sports owners have been able to deflect criticism of their actions by claiming the rules foster competitive balance and help owners avoid calamity.[16]

Because competitive imbalance has proven persistent, in spite of the reserve clause and the reverse-order drafts, the conclusion is inescapable that the competitive balance argument was a mere fig leaf covering the owners' naked desire for greater profits by suppressing player salaries. Some legal scholars believe that there were alternatives to the reserve clause that would have maintained, or even improved, competitive balance. They suggested remedies such as getting rid of any rule that forced the team signing a free agent to compensate his former team; eliminating the uniform contract provision containing the option and making it negotiable; or drafts of players off other teams' rosters. In addition, they believed owners exaggerated the extent of player movement under free agency, believing that the incumbent team had some built-in advantages for retaining players. Players may have developed ties with the home team community, including lucrative businesses or endorsements.[17]

Earlier in the twentieth century, MLB owners had sold players for cash. As law professor Stephen Ross points out, cash transactions in an economy are more efficient in reallocating assets between owners, because such transactions break the "double coincidence of wants" that economists are fond of discussing. In barter, you have to possess something I want, and I have to possess something you want, or else there can be no deal. Ross concluded that the prohibitions on cash sales created a situation where, "It is ironic that a rule supposedly designed to promote competitive balance actually appears to impede poorer teams' efforts to improve themselves and to become more competitive."[18]

These actions of awarding territorial protection; creating the reserve clause and player draft; setting minimum prices; giving the commissioner power to unilaterally issue edicts; and, later, pursuing national television contracts, were probably all contrary to the spirit if not the letter of antitrust law. Owners could manipulate schedules to increase revenues and profits. Rounds of playoffs to determine championships could curb the benefit of fielding too strong a team, thereby restraining bidding for players. Such manipulations were, however, not necessarily joint-venture cooperation, either, in the sense that controlling players was. The manipulations of the schedule and playing rules only benefited the owners if they appealed to the fans.

These twin advantages of price-setting power from territorial protection and monopsony power from the reserve clause and player draft ensured that, given adequate demand, owners needed to be inept to fail to turn a profit. Modern owners have even more advantages than most business owners. They have been given favorable tax treatment for player "depreciation"; with prudent discretion allowed by generally accepted accounting principles, owners could transform even a healthy profit into a sickly loss. Modern owners no longer tie up large amounts of capital in physical structures. Owners began extorting favorable stadium lease agreements by threatening to relocate their teams if they did not get favorable terms.

Because the owners' advantages were so attractive, they were vulnerable to other owners who were outside the league. MLB owners sought alliances with owners of teams in lesser leagues. Owners in separate leagues could agree to respect the territories, reserve clause, and player draft of each other's leagues in return for similar respect.

Profits, Profits, Where Are the Profits

Sports economists have established one truism: beware of false profits. Owners were and are hesitant to reveal profits and losses. Team owners, though, had plenty of legitimate options in telling the story they wanted. Analyzing professional sports teams' profits and losses is akin to being in Wonderland, where the numbers get "curiouser and curiouser."

Most owners also practiced the art of modesty. Unless they were battling a rival league and wanted to impress the public with their team's popularity, the majority realized that boasting about profits was not only bad manners but poor public relations. Owners might not brazenly lie about their bottom lines but might instead issue some vague statement about "being in the black" or "breaking even." Owners also preferred to exaggerate losses, if they were hoping to get an antitrust exemption, a publicly financed stadium, or a subsidy.

A congressional committee required owners to supply financial data for the mid-1950s. At least for MLB, the Arthur Andersen accounting firm examined the figures and presented them to Congress.[19] Because of the owners' discretion in reporting profits and losses, all such figures should be viewed cautiously. Owners often had other business interests aside from their sports team. In some cases they could shift expenses and revenues between their holdings. They could put relatives on the payroll, or pay themselves a salary, if doing so was beneficial from an income tax standpoint.

For owners purchasing their teams after World War II, the player depreciation allowance rule created paper losses that shrank an owner's income tax liability from the team or from another business interest. Some owners, though, lacked their peers' ability to camouflage profits via the player depreciation allowance. Many owners had not paid anything but a nominal membership fee when a league was formed, or had exhausted their player depreciation allowance. In either case, they could not depreciate the value of their player contracts, except for one of a recently acquired player. Subsequent owners of existing franchises could depreciate the value of the player contracts they acquired when purchasing their franchise. Given the relatively low franchise values of NBA and some NFL teams in the early 1950s, this depreciation allowance would have been relatively small compared with later years.

Were owners of professional sports teams profit maximizers? This is an intriguing question. Owners liked to portray themselves as "sportsmen" or "civic minded." Maurice Podoloff told legislators: "Professional sports is not a business

. . . because if you . . . see the money they have lost, you must be an addict and a bit of a lunatic to stay in professional sports. It is something unusual. . . . But I will tell you one thing; I have seen more than one team owner and manager come off the floor on the verge of tears. He didn't moan and groan because he had lost money. He moaned and groaned because he lost the game."[20] Some owners, of course, had reason to shed real tears over the losses they incurred. Although the owners received some satisfaction from fielding a championship team and may have been willing to sacrifice some profits to do so, there were limits to their pursuit of winning. Some owners had severely limited reserves of capital and could not afford continual losses, so they needed to pay close attention to their ledgers. Owning a professional sports team was sometimes a poor investment for the faint of heart.

In conjunction with the owners' reported profits and losses, franchise values provided clues regarding profitability. When an owner put his team up for sale, prospective buyers assessed the team's past and the expected future profitability. Prospective owners could gauge whether reported losses resulted from use of player depreciation allowances or to other causes. If owners chronically earned losses, they could either get out entirely by folding or by selling their team, possibly at a loss.

Player Salaries and Exploitation

During the years covered by the congressional investigations, almost all of the owners held enhanced bargaining power over their players, thanks to the reserve clause. In a competitive market for labor, the market forces cause employers to pay their employees "what they are worth." Owners would estimate how much additional revenue (marginal revenue product) a player brought to the team, which, in turn, depended on the demand for the team's games. Such calculations were, of course, made under uncertainty. With the enhanced bargaining power emanating from the reserve clause, owners could choose to pay salaries that were below market value.

Fans and envious sportswriters, though, often claimed that athletes were overpaid. Most professional players earned much greater salaries than did the average American. Then again, professional players were not average Americans. Few people would pay money to watch the best plumber at work, but thousands, and eventually millions and billions of people, would pay to see a top basketball player perform.

When businesspeople are losing money, they often focused on trimming costs, especially in this case, player salary costs. Some owners had more leeway in trimming player salary costs than did other owners.

All players had a reservation salary, the minimum necessary to induce them to work at a particular job. If an owner reduced salaries by too much, his players could have opted for their best employment alternatives. If owners had difficulty in trimming salaries, they could have reduced the number of players allowed on a roster. This tactic was limited by the necessity of fielding the requisite number of starters and at least some substitutes, lest quality of play suffer. A tight limit on roster size usually meant cutting lower-paid players, so it would result in only modest savings. Having a limit on the number of players on any team's roster, however, deterred owners of wealthy teams from accumulating too many players; a roster reduction also helped owners resolve the problem of being the first to cut a roster in times of economic downturns and suffering from a competitive disadvantage from having done so.

Fans complained that high salaries drove ticket prices higher, but in fact, it was higher demand for sporting events that tended to raise ticket prices. Salaries generally followed demand for the final product. If a league prospered, then player salaries rose, even under the reserve clause.

If there were rival leagues, such as baseball's Mexican League and football's AAFC during the late 1940s, players could benefit from the competition for their services. Even a little competition could force owners to significantly boost salaries, the reserve clause notwithstanding.

Players could respond to the owners' power by forming a union. Players clearly were not uniformly productive or popular with fans, precluding the desirability and the feasibility of a uniform salary scale, but they could create a monopoly of labor by uniting and thereby strengthening their negotiating power. When owners with single-buyer power confronted a labor union of players, the outcome was unpredictable and depended upon the relative bargaining strength of the opposing groups. Economists describe such a situation as a bilateral monopoly, where each side has an element of monopoly power. The indeterminacy was a crucial reason why negotiations between players and owners were often protracted and acrimonious.

Some Aspects of Competitive Balance

Some professional leagues suffered from competitive imbalance that negatively affected fan interest and profits. Sports economists have difficulty estimating the cost from competitive imbalance, but the New York Yankees' habit of running away with pennants during the late 1930s provided an example. The Yankees' success in clinching the pennant early squelched the gate receipts late in the season. Once the pennant race was over, gate receipts dropped markedly for the remaining games.[21]

Sports fans and observers frequently discuss competitive imbalance. If the New York Yankees were not so successful, much of the interest in the issue might vanish. Many people dislike the Yankees' dominance of baseball, because it highlights the advantage a team playing in a large market has over, say, the Kansas City Royals.

The Yankees' dominance from 1947 through 1964 may have disenchanted American League fans. Even the Yankees experienced stagnating attendance during the early 1960s. The plaint "Break up the Yankees" was well known. That the Boston Celtics and Los Angeles (formerly Minneapolis) Lakers have combined to win half the NBA championships from 1946 to the present did not appear to bother fans, who did not seem as intent on breaking up the two teams. Although the NFL has had dominant teams, many of these were superseded within a decade.

How does one measure competitive balance? Sports fans can judge competitive balance by looking at the day's standings. How wide is the gap between the top and bottom teams? How many games back are the second-place and the last-place teams?

Sports economists often use the standard deviation to measure competitive balance. The idea is simple enough. Suppose you host a group of friends for an exciting evening of flipping coins ("heads you win; tails I win"). You play an eighty-two-game schedule similar to the NBA's. On any given toss of the coin, you have a 50 percent likelihood of winning. Over eighty-two tosses, it is unlikely that you would win exactly forty-one games, but you would have a strong probability of winning roughly forty-one games. The standard deviation measures the spread around the expected number of wins. For the NBA's current eighty-two-game schedule, the expected standard deviation is about 4.5. In other words, a range covering one standard deviation would be 36.5 to 45.5 wins (or .445 to .555 in terms of win-loss percentage). Two-thirds of the teams in your coin-flipping league are expected to have records within this range. About 95 percent of the teams should be within two standard deviations of the mean: .390 to .610. This is not too different from actual league standings, so a coin-flipping league *approximates* a real league.

If you wanted to compare competitive balance across leagues, you need to adjust for the number of games played. Economists use the "idealized" standard deviation as $.5/\sqrt{N}$, where N is the number of games.[22] The idealized standard deviation is largest for the sixteen-game NFL schedule and smallest for the 162-game MLB schedule. Not all sports teams are, of course, created equal. When the Miami Heat play the Toronto Raptors, the odds are rarely even. By comparing the actual standard deviation with the coin-flipping, idealized standard deviation, economists measure the imbalance across professional sports leagues.

There is a second aspect of competitive balance. The ratio between the actual standard deviation and the idealized standard deviation is a snapshot, a particular season. What appears to antagonize fans more than occasional pennant race runaways is the monotony of the same team, such as the Yankees, repeatedly winning pennants.

What affects competitive balance? Economists studying sports pinpoint differences in drawing power among teams. Teams playing in larger cities are likely to draw more people to their games. Sports fans intuitively understand that New York teams are likely to have greater gate and television revenues than do teams in smaller cities.

Economists Roger Noll and Benjamin Okner pointed out that optimal competitive balance did not imply all teams should be equal. Using Memphis and New York City as an example, they suggested, "both Memphis and New York benefit if the two teams are close enough in playing strengths to play an exciting game. New York can win most of the time and still have the balanced competition requirement satisfied." They explained the rationale of trades where the disparity in talent was noticeable: "The team receiving the high-priced player values the net increase in playing skills from the trade more highly than the salary increase it experiences. The other team obviously has the opposite valuation. Sometimes cash is involved in trades. A player's new team is willing to pay his salary plus a cash payment for the right to his services, while the old team obviously values the salary reduction and cash payment more highly than the player's talent."[23]

There are some countervailing forces, though. New York is likely to boast more professional sports teams than Cincinnati or Kansas City, thereby diluting the demand for any particular team. New York currently has at least two teams in each sports league, and this means, for instance, that the basketball Knicks face direct competition not only from the Nets but also indirect competition from baseball and football teams. Portland, Oregon, on the other hand, boasts just the Trailblazers in basketball. New York teams also faced a wider and deeper range of competing entertainment venues, including numerous opportunities for live theater, symphonies, and museums.

Although professional team sports leagues offer entertainment and might be thought to compete with each other (hence the concerns when the NFL pushed its seasons into early September, while MLB extended its playoffs into late October), economic research and antitrust sports cases find this potential competition to be of minor importance, at most. Economists and legal scholars use the concept of relevant market in thinking about competition. The Federal Trade Commission publishes "Horizontal Merger Guidelines" to help define the terms. "Evidence of competitive effects can inform market definition, just as market definition can be informative regarding competitive effects. For example, evidence that a reduction in the number of significant rivals offering a group of products causes prices for those products to rise significantly can itself establish that those products form a relevant market." The guidelines suggest that substitution of rival products can affect the market definition: "Market definition focuses solely on demand substitution factors, i.e., on customers' ability and willingness to substitute away from one product to another in response to a price increase or a corresponding non-price change such as a reduction in product quality or service. The responsive actions of suppliers are also important in competitive analysis."[24] Thus, the introduction of an NFL team into Portland, for instance, would appear unlikely to affect ticket prices and attendance at Portland Trailblazers' basketball games.

What really matters, though, is the marginal effect of winning. Suppose all teams had equal talent and were expected to play .500 ball. A team in New York City that improved to .600 would likely boost its gate revenue by more than a team in Cincinnati experiencing a similar improvement in record. This larger incremental gain in the New York City team's revenue gives that team's owner a greater incentive to improve his team. There are, of course, limitations on how much improvement the owner might profitably garner. Using baseball as an example, at some point, a team winning 80 or 90 percent of its game would turn the pennant race into a farce. Interest in late-season games would fall off and so would revenue. It is possible that improving a team too much would actually reduce its profits, as the costs of additional improvement began to exceed the benefits.

Although incremental changes in revenue from winning more games is important for competitive balance, some forms of revenue may not be very sensitive to changes in a team's win-loss record; the revenue is, in economic parlance, win inelastic.[25] A national television contract that is shared equally is essentially a lump-sum source of revenue and should not affect any team's incremental, marginal revenue from improving its win-loss record, and therefore should not affect competitive balance, aside from the possibility of keeping a weak team from going bankrupt. If a national television contract replaced local television revenues that were affected by teams' win-loss record, then the substitution might affect competitive balance.

What institutional factors affect competitive balance? During the 1950s, baseball, football, and basketball had different institutions affecting player distribution. All three leagues had reserve clauses, albeit with slight differences. The NFL and NBA used a reverse-order draft of graduating college players. Baseball owners faced a free market for signing talented high school and college players until 1965. Baseball owners, though, controlled hundreds of players through their ownership of or agreements with minor league teams. Owners justified these practices by claiming they promoted competitive balance.

Because of the reserve clause and reverse-order player draft, player movement was primarily at an owner's behest during most of the era covered in this book. Only if an owner released a player would a veteran become a free agent. Ronald Coase won a Nobel Prize based on his work studying the effects of property rights. Economists have used the Coase Theorem to study player movement and talent distribution in professional sports leagues. Economist Simon Rottenberg presaged Coase's more general theory with his 1956 paper that focused on baseball's labor market.[26] Coase's basic insight was that it did not matter who possessed the property rights to the resource with respect to the ultimate distribution of a resource. Applying this insight to professional sports, the resource was a player's ability. Rottenberg demonstrated that the property rights to the player's labor could be assigned either to the owner (reserve clause), the player (free agency), or a situation where the owner has the initial rights to a player's talent but with potential free agency after so many years of service. The end result in terms of player distribution, though, would be similar.

To see how the Coase/Rottenberg idea applies to professional sports, consider a hypothetical player: Babe Thorpe. Babe combines the ability to swat a baseball with a trackman's strength and speed. He aspires, as fictional character Roy Hobbs did in *The Natural,* to be the best there ever was. Suppose the St. Louis Browns have the rights to Babe Thorpe. He obviously elevates both the team's record and home attendance. Suppose he raises the Browns' home gate receipts by $100,000 over the course of a season. The covetous owner of the Yankees estimates that Thorpe could increase his team's gate receipts by $500,000 per season. Thorpe is more valuable to the Yankees than to the Browns. There is an incentive for the Yankees' owner to offer sufficient inducement to persuade the St. Louis owner to part with Thorpe. All things equal, Thorpe will land in New York. If Thorpe possessed the property rights to his talent, he could offer himself to any team. New York could sign him by offering more money than St. Louis or any other team. In either case, Thorpe would likely wind up in New York.

The difference in property rights does affect who gets the economic benefit from the player's unique talent, which economists denote as economic rent. Under the reserve clause, the owner reaps much of the benefit from the player's talent; under free agency, the player retains most of the benefit from his talent.

There are two factors to consider. First, the cost of exercising these property rights must be small. Otherwise a friction of sorts may prevent moving players to where they are most valuable. Fan antipathy toward an owner of a team who frequently trades or sells his star players is a potential source of friction. While owners selling star players would usually lose attendance from the accompanying drop in win-loss record, fans might further punish an owner by boycotting the team. Second, if a team becomes too superior, its gate appeal may begin to diminish, so adding an additional star player becomes unattractive. No team is likely to corner the market on all the best talent, because the incremental gain to its win-loss record dwindles and the impact upon gate receipts begins to shrink, if not become negative. Even the Yankees are unlikely to obtain the best player at every position.

A reverse-order draft does not significantly change the conclusion regarding the reserve clause's effect upon competitive balance. Suppose the Browns drafted Babe Thorpe, because their record, as usual, was lackluster. The disparity in Thorpe's value to St. Louis and New York would still exist, and St. Louis would be likely to send him to New York. The Lakers' penchant for getting centers such as Wilt Chamberlain, Kareem Abdul-Jabbar, Shaquille O'Neal, and Dwight Howard exemplifies this prediction. The key difference is that the woebegone teams gain revenue from player sales resulting from a reverse-order draft.

The owners' defense of the reserve clause and the reverse-order draft was likely built on unfounded claims.

Revenue Sharing and Competitive Balance

Sharing of gate revenue has been a feature of professional sports since their inception. The National League implemented a gate-sharing plan in 1877: fifteen cents of every fifty-cent admission price would go to the visiting team.[27]

Many observers of professional sports have claimed that generous revenue sharing improved competitive balance. MLB was often criticized for its alleged stingy revenue-sharing rules relative to the NFL's enlightened policy of "league think." Compared with MLB and the NFL, though, the NBA personified rugged individualism, with no gate sharing at all.

The intuition behind gate sharing was that reducing differences in teams' revenue streams—primarily gate receipts and television revenue—would reduce the edge held by teams, such as those in New York City, in acquiring top talent. This Robin Hood story of taking from the rich and giving to the poor, though, was not straightforward nor was it necessarily effective in promoting competitive parity.

Economists analyzing revenue sharing have gained some insights into such plans' likely effects. They believed that gate sharing could, indeed, shift revenues from teams with strong demand to teams located in cities with weak demand, possibly ensuring the viability of some weak franchises. However, they doubted such plans' ability to improve parity between teams' win-loss records.[28]

In the simplest story, gate sharing reduces the marginal revenue product of acquiring a talented player, because the gains in revenue that he brings to a team is *shared* with visiting clubs. The observant reader will muse, "What about when that team goes on the road, doesn't it gain revenue from the host team?" We will return to this point shortly. The end result may be that gate sharing suppresses the benefits and hence the demand for and the salaries of star players without exerting much effect upon parity. In most cases, competitive balance is unchanged. This story depends, in part, on an assumption that the ability to draw attendance on the road is negatively related to the visiting team' win-loss record. If, instead, a strong team draws well on the road, then revenue sharing's efficacy in redistributing revenue from the teams in larger cities to teams in smaller cities may be reduced and even reversed.

Owners, though, expressed concerns about too generous of a revenue-sharing plan. Those with wealthy teams worried that their less-fortunate fellow owners might be tempted to use their share of the gate not to improve their team but to boost their bottom lines. MLB approved a more generous revenue-sharing plan in the 1990s, but the *Blue Ribbon Panel of Baseball Economics* advised that all teams meet a minimum payroll.[29] Setting a minimum salary for individual players also forces owners to field minimally competitive teams.

Owners sometimes spoke of different rationales for revenue sharing. When Eddie Gottlieb signed Wilt Chamberlain to a hefty basketball contract, he complained that he was going broke. He wanted his fellow owners to share some revenue from the large crowds Chamberlain and the Philadelphia Warriors attracted.[30]

The "Robin Hood" characteristic of most gate-sharing plans, however, assumed having "rich" parties who had adequate revenues to transfer. In a league where there were disparities in gate potential but where all teams were losing money, revenue sharing seemed futile and even detrimental when it threatened the viability of even the teams that only lost only small amounts.

Revenue sharing, then, was not a panacea for promoting competitive parity.

Relocation and Expansion to Greener Pastures

We have seen that gate sharing was not guaranteed to significantly reduce differences in gate receipts between cities. A possible remedy for competitive imbalance was to move teams from smaller to larger cities. Most leagues desired having teams only in the largest cities, because doing so made the league's national television contract more attractive to networks and could potentially create larger crowds and gate receipts. However, too much scrambling for new cities could alienate fans and trigger lawsuits.

Moving to a city more capable of sustaining a team could benefit all members of a league via revenue sharing. The relocation of baseball's Boston Braves to

Milwaukee proved such a lucrative gate bonanza that the Braves' fellow National League owners voted to up the revenue share from 22.5 to 27.5 cents per attendee.[31] Owing to the lack of gate sharing in the NBA, those owners might have focused on transportation costs, because they would not have benefited from any gate bonanza that was achieved by a fellow owner who moved his team to a more lucrative market and, instead, would suffer increased transportation costs if the new city was remote. Although all owners worried about transportation costs, NBA owners might have been more likely than owners in other leagues to vote against an owner's proposal to move to the West Coast.

Once a league attained a measure of prosperity, prospective owners sought teams. The incumbent owners worried that expansion would reduce the number of traditional rivalry games while causing their teams to play unattractive expansion teams. Expansion also meant that incumbent owners faced more competition for players, reaped a smaller share of the national television pie, and experienced diluted voting power. Despite these potential disadvantages, incumbent owners knew that judicious expansion could deter the entry of a rival league.

Law professor Stephen Ross argues, though, that expansion teams increase satisfaction of fans in the cities gaining new teams. He believes this offsets any decreased satisfaction among fans in cities already possessing teams. Ross cites as evidence the increase in attendance when MLB expanded in 1961–1962, 1969, and 1977.[32] He does admit that, "accurately determining the proper balance between adding teams for the benefit of new fans and maintaining player quality for the benefit of current fans, however, is extraordinarily difficult." He quotes economist Henry Demmert, who theorized that someone could bankroll a sandlot team and demand the right to play the New York Yankees: "the legitimacy of athletic competition and thus the very existence of the professional sport would be threatened."[33]

Owners reserved the right to decide which new owners to admit into the league, when an incumbent owner could relocate his team, and to whom an incumbent could sell his team. Most league constitutions and bylaws required supermajorities to approve these transactions. Some legal scholars have pointed out that these normally prohibited actions might be permissible to protect the integrity of the sport by not allowing owners with known gambling interests (although many owners in the past did, in fact, possess such interests); owners with insufficient capital; and owners already possessing teams in the sport. An article in the *Harvard Law Review,* though, disputed the NFL's prohibition on corporate ownership. NFL commissioner Pete Rozelle often argued that when a corporation owned a team, it was difficult to pinpoint a person with the responsibility to make decisions. Owners could also abuse these rules in dealing with maverick owners such as baseball's Bill Veeck or football's Al Davis.[34]

Increasing Demand by Using Technology

Television revolutionized American leisure patterns and culture during the 1950s. The medium's great potential for businesspeople was its ability to eventually create a wide but shallow demand for a product: a demand where many people are willing to pay a small amount of money for the product. In the past, artists and musicians, who were favored by a royal court, faced a narrow but deep demand: a few people willing to pay a considerable amount for their services. With radio and television, hundreds of thousands, millions, or even billions of mildly interested people could now be reached. If these lukewarm fans were only willing to pay twenty-five cents each to watch a game on television, an owner could still reap a handsome amount. Players would ultimately benefit from a wide, shallow demand that boosted revenues, which, in turn, would raise a player's benefit to an owner and, subsequently, the player's salary.

Once television became a lucrative source of revenue, owners began to recognize the wisdom of selling collective rights to televise league games. Selling monopoly rights is an enviable situation—just ask your friendly neighborhood legislator. By selling their collective television rights to a single network, sports owners could reap far more revenue than by each team negotiating individual contracts.

Conclusion: Economics and Sports

Economic analysis does not fully explain owners' or players' actions, but it provides a useful framework in examining the development of professional team sports. Players, owners, fans, and legislators all confronted scarcity; their self-interest compelled them to be careful in allocating their scarce resources, such as time, money, and ability. Their decisions were based upon carefully allocating their scarce resources among the various uses available for such resources, for the purpose of best achieving their goals.

3

An Overview of the Hearings

In the wake of player unrest after World War II and growing demand for new baseball franchises, Congress decided to investigate MLB. When baseball players chafed under the owners' control, with a few filing lawsuits in the wake of the Mexican League raids, Emanuel Celler (N.Y.), chair of the House Subcommittee on Anti-trust and Monopoly, decided to investigate the industry that claimed to be self-regulated.[1] Other committee participants, such as Edwin Johnson and A. S. Herlong had ties with minor league baseball.

1951 Hearings Set the Stage

For the first hearings on MLB in 1951, Celler told reporters that the committee's purpose was to "help baseball against itself." To bolster his point that he was not out to persecute anyone, the committee issued invitations and not subpoenas.[2]

Some of his fellow committee members were unenthusiastic about the investigation. Kenneth B. Keating (N.Y.) wondered why, in the midst of the cold war, Congress was investigating MLB. He pointed out, "I have a feeling, that baseball is pretty clean, the fans like it and want it left alone. We are sticking our necks out for a lot of pop bottles if we interfere too much."[3]

During the hearings, few of the legislators impressed with their savvy. Some did not appear to understand the testimony. On occasion a few made dubious comments. At the height of the cold war, Senator Karl E. Mundt (S.D.) remarked, "I believe baseball has become very definitely a factor in the cold war we are fighting because we have sent baseball teams abroad with universally useful results."[4] Years later, Mundt made up for this silly remark by making one of the more astute observations concerning the granting of a partial antitrust exemption: "We are giving to the fortunate owner an exclusive right which increases vastly his economic investment, and his economic opportunity, and increases vastly the resale value of the investment that he already has." He concluded, "Now I ask you, sir, whether in good conscience we can, by legislative fiat, *make dollar bills out of 50-cent pieces* [italics mine] for the people who own these baseball clubs without assuming some responsibility to be sure that public service is considered by the owners of the club."[5] Readers should remember Mundt's apt turn of phrase, as it applies to much of what follows.

The hearings occasionally lapsed into farce, especially when legislators and sports officials touted sports' benefits in preventing America's potentially delinquent youths from going Red. Senator Alexander Wiley (Wis.): "Public interest is a matter of keeping the youth in action, keeping them mentally alert, particularly now when we are talking about this Khrushchev problem. We can't be diverted from the big issue, which is maintaining the peace." Given this softball of a question, William Shea immediately sent it rocketing into the stratosphere of silliness (to use an alliteration): "You, sir, know that baseball probably constitutes one of the greatest deterrents to juvenile delinquency, because baseball is played, primarily during the summer when the youths are out from school; when they don't have the day-to-day activity of going to school."[6]

Although the hearings did not result in any legislation, committee members made it clear that they wanted more cities to get teams, whether through relocation or by expansion. Celler told Commissioner Ford Frick that in light of population shifts, there were many cities impatient to obtain MLB franchises and that legislators were concerned that baseball was going to ignore the built-up demand. Frick agreed that some cities in California had sufficient population to support a franchise. He also said that Pacific Coast League owners themselves admitted that they were not ready for MLB.[7] His remark did not placate Celler, who pressed the point: "Mr. Frick, that is just a lovely pontifical declaration on which you have not acted. You have not implemented it at all. You have kept the situation in status quo for 50 years. There has been no change."[8]

From an antitrust standpoint, the discussion concerning territorial rights was important. The committee reported that baseball's territorial rights meant that most teams did not face direct competition from another baseball team, but rather, all teams faced competition from other recreational options.[9] Frick tried to encourage such thinking by asserting that ticket prices in baseball were low.

Owners began raising prices after World War II and continued to raise them during the intervening years, although often the increases in ticket prices were similar to increases in the general price level. They did, however, tend to raise ticket prices only every three or four years during the postwar years. Owners of pennant-winning teams often did not raise prices the following year.[10]

Sports Teams' Financial Records

Sports owners are reluctant to release their financial records. Economists studying sports are accustomed to finding their requests for financial information rejected by team owners. Unless a team is publicly held, owners can usually refuse to divulge their finances. The hearings held in 1951 revealed a detailed history of professional baseball and yielded a trove of financial information dating back to 1920. The 1957 hearings contained similar financial data for all four professional team sports.[11]

MLB had much greater attendance than its two younger siblings, football and basketball, during the 1950s. Part of this disparity arose from the differences in the number of home games, because NFL teams had just six home games per season. NFL teams boasted the highest per-game attendance of the three leagues. The NBA was constrained by smaller stadium capacities and lesser popularity. The New York Yankees typically had more attendees for their home games than did the entire NBA. Table 1 shows the attendance figures for the 1946–1964 seasons. The NBA did not have consistent attendance figures for some of the years shown in Table 1. (See Appendix for all tables.)

The NFL showed a steady but not spectacular growth throughout the 1950s. Considering there were twelve NFL teams for most of the 1950s instead of the ten during the immediate postwar years, the league's overall attendance gains were somewhat exaggerated. On the other hand, the NFL's gains contrasted with MLB's attendance doldrums after 1949–1950.

Table 2 shows that, during the mid-1950s, MLB collectively made modest profits, although the profits were unevenly distributed. Some teams still incurred reported losses. The NFL was becoming prosperous, and several teams reported earning profits (see Table 3). The league's weakest franchise—the Chicago Cardinals—consistently reported losses. The NBA still suffered losses, although a few teams earned small net profits before taxes (see Table 4). The league, at least, had stabilized at eight teams and, if not prosperous, members were not hemorrhaging money.

Franchise values buttress the profit and loss figures, although one has to exercise care in interpreting them. Data contained in Quirk and Fort reveals that most professional teams sold to new buyers generated capital gains, although their figures were not adjusted for risk, as some football and basketball teams folded.[12]

A team's profit or loss was also closely correlated to its gross operating income. For instance, the correlation coefficient between the two variables for the NFL was about 67 percent. A team's gross operating income ("gross receipts" in the NBA) was comprised of "games at home" receipts (less visitors' and league's shares), "games away" receipts, exhibition game receipts, concessions receipts, sale of television and radio rights, and other revenue, such as renting stadiums for other events. Because most NFL and NBA owners did not own the stadium or arena they played in, they earned little concessions revenue. NBA teams had roughly one-quarter of NFL and one-ninth of MLB teams' gross operating income; these basketball teams relied primarily upon "games at home" receipts and a trickle of television revenue.

For baseball and football, "games at home" receipts generated roughly half of the teams' gross operating income, while "games away" receipts provided another one-fifth of football's and one-ninth of baseball's. Receipts from the sale of television and radio rights contributed about 13 percent of gross operating income in baseball and football. The "games at home" revenues varied considerably between teams within a league, but the disparities were similar across leagues (see Table 5). The distribution of "games away" receipts was narrower than that for "games at home" receipts.

There was one source of revenue in the NFL where disparities were marked. Few commentators on the NFL's revenue sharing and equity mentioned the disparities in exhibition game receipts. NFL teams played preseason exhibition games. For some teams, the games were quite lucrative.[13] The San Francisco 49ers and Los Angeles Rams dominated this source of revenue, as the two teams often combined for more than one-third of total league exhibition game receipts. The Baltimore Colts and Green Bay Packers were overwhelmed in the quest for exhibition game revenues.

NFL commissioners Bell and Rozelle expressed concerns about widening disparities in television revenues. Although the ratio of television revenues sometimes reached ten-to-one between teams for a particular season, across the five seasons, the distribution had smaller disparities than in MLB. The New York Giants held an advantage over Green Bay, but the disparity was smaller than for the baseball Yankees versus the Baltimore Orioles (formerly St. Louis Browns).

Owners complained about rising costs, even apart from player salaries. The salient question was whether the owners' expenses were rising faster than the general price level. Even if such expenses rose faster than prices in general, such a rise might have reflected prosperity. Teams might have decided to house their players in nicer hotels, taken first-class train travel, provided more uniforms, and other amenities. Owners might have hired additional office workers to help with the increasing ticket sales; innovative owners may have begun hiring publicity and promotion staff to expand gate receipts even more.[14] Gross operating expenses rose by almost 30 percent in MLB and the NFL but only 6.4 percent in the NBA.

If professional sports teams showed disparities in gross operating income, they also had marked but narrower disparities in gross operating expenses (see Table 5). Gross operating expenses included administrative salaries, other expenses, and player salaries. Stadium rental fees may not have appeared in other expenses, as owners may have subtracted them at the end of each game. Although NFL owners complained about salaries—and salaries might have been their largest single expense—they made up just over one-third of the gross operating expenses. Salaries, though, constituted a smaller proportion of NFL teams' expenses in 1956 than in 1952, as other expenses and administrative expenses increased faster. A similar story held for MLB.

Administrative expenses were where owners could opt to adjust net income (see Tables 2, 3, and 4). If an owner chose to take a larger salary, he would reduce his profit or even incur a loss. By paying himself a larger salary, therefore, an owner might try to reduce the tax on team income while raising his personal income tax or, if more beneficial, cut his salary and report more team income and less personal income.

Other expenses comprised more than half the total expenses. These expenses rose by around 30 percent over the five-year period for both baseball and football respectively, rates faster than the change in the general price level (see Tables 2, 3, and 4).

In the NFL, gross operating income and "games at home" receipts increased more rapidly than did salaries. Player salaries as a proportion of gross operating income or "games at home" declined, even though the league began to stabilize and even prosper. Payrolls were remarkably similar between teams. As Table 5 shows, in none of the years shown did the team with the largest payroll exceed the team with the smallest payroll by even 50 percent. Baseball's American League had a somewhat greater proportional spread between the top and bottom payrolls, but the payroll disparities in the American League just before the end of the millennium dwarf the disparities in the 1950s NFL.[15] When the Lions and Browns won league championships, their payrolls, if the highest, were not much greater than that of some other teams in the league.

Baseball payrolls also rose between 1952 and 1956, increasing by 13.7 percent in the American League and 12.6 percent in the National League. Despite these increases, player salaries comprised just 17–21 percent of gross operating income in baseball during the 1950s; this proportion had declined from the Great Depression.[16]

Owners in all three sports would frequently plead poverty throughout the years spanning the hearings covered in this book. Certainly some teams were struggling and perhaps should have gone out of business or relocated. Many baseball and football owners, though, released information suggesting that they were reaping profits. The basketball owners were not so fortunate, but their league was relatively new. Evidence also suggests that these basketball owners simply had not succeeded in generating large enough crowds to offset payroll, arena rental, and other expenses. In whatever way owners might have manipulated their financial figures, the general rate of appreciation in franchise values, even after being adjusted for inflation and risk, suggest that a majority were faring well. As always, there were some owners struggling to survive, but in the two older leagues, such franchises were few in number by 1960.

Sports Leagues' Search for Antitrust Exemptions

Aside from perusing financial data, Celler and his fellow committee members worried that a blanket antitrust law would "be used arbitrarily," although they recognized the potential need for partial exemptions allowing sports to enact rules to promote competitive balance. The legislators concluded, "Legislation is not necessary until the reasonableness of the reserve rules has been tested by the courts."[17]

The committee's hesitance to endorse stronger action began a tradition that baseball exploited. "Baseball's tactic of convincing whatever forum they are before that some other forum is the more appropriate one to handle its particular problem did not begin or end with the Celler Committee-*Toolson* episode." The 1977 committee reflected how baseball argued in *Federal Baseball* that the "States were 'entirely competent to reach and deal with any evil in the field of sport.'" During a 1966 lawsuit dealing with the Milwaukee Braves' attempted relocation to Atlanta, baseball argued that "only Federal law could regulate it adequately. In that case the court overruled a lower state court ruling holding that the 1965 transfer . . . violated antitrust law." Later in that decade, owners claimed, "unsuccessfully, to the National Labor Relations Board that any labor dispute in professional sports would not effect [sic] interstate commerce substantially because it was a local affair." In the *Flood v. Kuhn* case, "baseball argued, among other things, that what was involved was not an antitrust but a labor relations issue which should be properly presented before the National Labor Relations Board. Finally, before this Committee the Commissioner of Baseball strongly urged that the remedies to the problems facing the sport lay at the bargaining table or with its self-regulatory mechanisms."[18]

No legislation ensued as a result of the 1951 hearings and, for the most part, legislators seemed more interested in learning about the mechanics of the sport while inquiring about the possibility of gaining franchises for the burgeoning cities outside the northeastern quadrant of the country. In 1951, ten cities had MLB teams, with five of them possessing multiple teams. Legislators also considered baseball's reserve clause and farm systems; though they expressed concerns about these practices, they made no serious attempt to alter or to eradicate them.

The 1950s witnessed the television boom. MLB and the NFL had policies regulating telecasts and radio broadcasts of games into other teams' territories. The Department of Justice believed these leaguewide rules violated antitrust law and filed suit. Congress investigated MLB's radio and television policies in 1953. The big-league owners claimed that the Department of Justice's ruling that rescinded baseball's ban on radio broadcasts and telecasts injured not only their home attendance but was affecting the minor leagues.

Because courts during the 1950s had ruled that professional football, basketball, and hockey were subject to the antitrust laws, owners of teams in these sports hoped to get congressional approval of an antitrust exemption. Besides the antitrust exemption issue, the issue of more franchises became a focal point for the next set of hearings held annually between 1957 and 1960. By this time, MLB's roster of teams had not expanded, but three cities had lost and three cities gained teams. Throughout 1957, the big news was the rumored shift of the Brooklyn Dodgers and New York Giants to the West Coast. Because Emanuel Celler represented Brooklyn, he was naturally very interested in the rumored relocations.

The hearings also delved into such issues as the extensive farm systems whereby a single MLB team might control hundreds of players on minor league teams. The legislators also subjected the reserve clause to closer scrutiny; the perennial ineptitude of the Washington Senators raised questions concerning the reserve clause's ability to foster competitive balance. The committee also investigated rumors that the Kansas City Athletics were subservient to the New York Yankees, given a series of trades between the two clubs.

The 1959 and 1960 hearings continued to examine the general issues, but new events took center stage. Entrepreneurs decided to launch the Continental League in baseball and the American Football League (AFL). These two prospective leagues promised to bring high-quality professional sports into several cities currently without such entertainment, although the majority of the cities had AAA baseball. The legislators proved sympathetic to such attempts, although they exerted little direct effort in helping the newcomers. The committee also began to express concerns about players and their rights, including the right to form an association or a union.

The 1961 hearings investigated the NFL's proposed national television contract with the Columbia Broadcasting System (CBS). The contract promised to be far more lucrative than the owners' current set of individual contracts. The drawback was the contract's violation of antitrust laws. Instead of waiting for a possible judicial reversal, Pete Rozelle opted to persuade Congress to pass an antitrust exemption for the contract. In this, he was successful.

The issue of franchise relocation recurred during the 1964 and 1965 hearings. Owners of two of the first three MLB teams that relocated during the 1950s—the

Milwaukee Braves and Kansas City Athletics—were getting restless. Wisconsin, Missouri, and Kansas legislators voiced concerns over baseball's game of musical chairs, with their constituents the potential losers. Such antics began to erode the goodwill most legislators had held toward professional team sports. In addition, MLB was implementing a draft of amateur players; such drafts had long existed in the NFL and the NBA and had been examined by previous committees, but baseball's plan drew scrutiny. In the midst of these controversies, the New York Yankees owners dropped a bombshell: They had sold the team to CBS. Although the owners, Del Webb and Dan Topping, were quite wealthy, their wealth was minuscule compared with CBS's financial holdings. The sale also punctured the image of team owners as sportsmen, as corporations began buying franchises. Legislators and the public wondered about the antitrust implications of the most successful television network purchasing the most successful baseball team.

Throughout the early 1960s, the NFL was battling the AFL. Both sets of owners decided that a merger was preferable to the competition, so they petitioned Congress to permit such a merger. The 1966 hearings demonstrated the erosion of congressional support since the 1950s; instead of quickly approving such a deal, the House committee expressed several reservations. Rozelle enlisted powerful supporters in Congress to attach a rider permitting the merger to a popular tax bill, thereby circumventing the committee's potential disapproval of the merger. This would be one of two legislative successes for professional team sports.

Emboldened by the NFL's success in gaining permission for a merger, owners in the two warring basketball leagues—the NBA and the ABA—decided to press Congress to sanction their proposed merger. This time both the Senate and House committees proved more skeptical, although some of the committee members favored the mergers. The tenor of the 1971–1972 hearings was much less cordial than previous hearings. In the end, discontent with the NFL owners' behavior in the wake of their merger and a growing skepticism regarding many of professional team sports' claims led the committee to recommend something quite different than what the owners had asked for.

The NFL's television policies once again generated controversy and ill will. The Senate and House held a series of hearings beginning in 1972 and for several years afterward regarding television blackouts. The hearings pertained to all four sports, but the NFL received the spotlight because the league's blackout policies drew the most public ire. For legislators, the political calculus seemed obvious: Many explicit winners—the public and television networks—and relatively few losers—NFL teams and associated businesses. This time the NFL blinked and adjusted its policies.

Senator Marlow Cook (Ky.) sponsored a bill calling for the creation of a Federal Sports Commission in 1972. The act was designed to protect the public interest.

He denied that the bill was supposed to result in a regulatory agency. Because his hearings occurred simultaneously with the hearings on the proposed merger between the basketball leagues, much of the testimony was similar between the hearings. Cook even had Senator Sam Ervin Jr. (N.C.) as a witness. Ervin expressed his skepticism regarding any attempt to maintain stability; indeed, he even wondered whether stability in itself was a desirable goal. In the end, Senator Cook appeared to doubt the rationale of his own bill, so nothing came of it.[19]

The House convened a special committee on professional sports in 1976 to investigate the instability in the sports industry.[20] The hearing provided a good wrap-up of the issues covered in the first quarter-century of hearings. The members cited strife between labor and management, player but not owner drug usage, player agents, immigration of athletes, tax treatment for owners, antiblackout rules, player and spectator violence, gambling, and player occupational safety.[21] Chair B. F. Sisk (Calif.) pointed out that between the Supreme Court's decisions in *Toolson* and *Flood*, more than fifty sports bill had been introduced, of which two passed the House or the Senate but not both (H.R. 10378 in 1958 and S. 950 in 1965).[22] Of course, the two bills that passed both chambers—the 1961 NFL television bill and the 1966 AFL/NFL merger—were big victories for professional football and gains for the other sports in terms of an exemption covering national television contracts. The 1976 committee believed that baseball's antitrust exemption was not warranted, although it stopped short of advocating rescinding it.[23]

The committee identified one of MLB's arguments for defending the status quo. In the half century after *Federal Baseball*, owners came and owners went. Owners purchasing teams after the 1922 verdict relied upon the belief that they were purchasing, along with the franchise, the rights to an antitrust exemption: "club investments of millions of dollars on player development, long term leases, and new franchises subsequent to, and purportedly in reliance on, *Federal Baseball*, *Toolson*, and now *Flood*. As the Court observed in *Radovich*, 'vast efforts had gone into the development and organization of baseball since the decision (in *Federal Baseball*) and enormous capital has been invested in reliance on its permanence.'"[24] An owner purchasing a team before the 1970s presumed that the reserve clause would remain intact. The advent of free agency theoretically diluted, if not eliminated, one of the property rights he purchased and could reduce the value of his franchise. The committee, though, expressed an opinion that such a change in property rights need not be catastrophic: "it is highly speculative to suggest that chaos would result should baseball's exemption be lifted. All other professional sports have certainly grown and for the most part prospered within antitrust purview."[25] The committee might have also pointed out that payment for a profitable institution that was illegal would not be a morally or legally justifiable argument.

In trying to address antitrust issues, legislators were hindered by the lack of reliable and definitive financial information. The owners frequently resorted to submitting accurate if incomplete and possibly misleading financial information.[26] In retrospect, the wonder is that all of the owners had submitted detailed information to the 1951 and 1957 hearings.

The committee also examined the various tax angles available to owners. They considered the question whether owning a team was a tax shelter. Because the player depreciation allowance lasted for a limited number of years, one might predict frequent turnover once the limit was reached. Baseball's commissioner, Bowie Kuhn, cited the fact that many owners held their teams for decades as evidence against the tax shelter claim.[27] Some owners did, however, overstep the tax rules by claiming an inordinate proportion of their purchase price to player contracts; the courts repudiated many of these tax claims. The Tax Reform Act of 1976 purportedly put a stop to such shenanigans.[28]

Conclusion: Recurring Themes in Sports Antitrust

The hearings covered in this book demonstrate that the past is not even past, so to speak. Legislators returned to another simmering issue with a series of hearings examining franchise relocation and expansion. When Al Davis relocated his Oakland Raiders to Los Angeles in the early 1980s, he ignited a firestorm of litigation with his fellow owners and the two cities. Legislators, still smarting at losing yet another Washington Senators team years earlier, were more willing to consider explicit regulation of professional team sports, although, ultimately, no legislation ensued.

The final hearing covered in this book examined deals with changes in television technology, specifically cable television. Cable and pay television technology dated back to the 1950s, but various factors impeded their growth until the mid-1970s. In some respects, pay television represented a logical step for revenue-seeking owners. Although owners earned revenue from network telecasts, pay television and, to a lesser degree, cable television promised a more direct way to charge customers to watch games. Legislators, though, were loath to let cable and pay television businesses supplant free network television. The legislators' animus and fears were evident during the 1989 hearings. They considered one bill that expressly prohibited cable and pay television from telecasting certain sporting events.

4

Player Rights
1951 and 1957

Throughout the congressional hearings, legislators queried owners, commissioners, players, and others about players' rights. The issue permeated almost every hearing. Team owners in other sports instituted reserve clauses similar to the National League's reserve clause that evolved from 1879. Although baseball held drafts of minor league players, basketball, football, and hockey owners developed player drafts of collegians and graduating high school seniors. The amateur drafts not only reduced a player's bargaining leverage but denied them their rights to decide where and for whom to play. When Congress began examining labor practices in professional team sports, the owners justified these violations of players' rights on the basis of preserving competitive balance. Though congressional committee members and their staff grew more skeptical about the owners' claims, legislators generally remained passive, if sometimes vocal, critics of the evolution in player rights from the reserve clause to free agency.

Because of the reserve clause and the player draft, owners had minimized competition for players and therefore had salary-setting power over their players and could exercise discretion in how much they paid them. The owners rarely commented in polite society that the draft gave the lucky owner leverage versus the young player, as the player's options were to negotiate with the team that drafted him or to sit out a year.[1]

Owners and their commissioners employed novel arguments supporting the necessity of having the reserve clause. Ford Frick, baseball commissioner, made some highly dubious arguments before the House subcommittee in 1951: "Industry also does not have the problem of public confidence in the loyalty of employees to employers. The public buys Lucky Strikes without concern as to whether the employees of American Tobacco Co. are doing their best for that company or are trying to get jobs with Liggett & Myers or Reynolds Tobacco Co. But the public demands that each baseball player have full loyalty to and extend his best efforts for his club." He then employed a non sequitur: "How can public confidence in player loyalty and will to win be maintained if the player, while playing for one club, may seek a job with another or may be pressed with offers from several other clubs, against some of which he is playing?" He then pointed to the hapless St. Louis Browns: "if there were no reserve clause, the St. Louis Browns . . . would have lost practically all of their major-league talent . . . or certainly would have been forced to move to a community better able to support it. There are many such communities."[2] Frick was being too clever. The Browns' owners sold the majority of their best players, and the team would, in fact, relocate to Baltimore. Browns fans could be forgiven, if they doubted the blessings of the reserve clause.

The 1951 House subcommittee also recognized that the reserve clause was a necessary prerequisite for establishing minor league systems: "The farm system could not exist without the reserve clause for it is that device which makes control of the players by any club a practical reality. If clubs could not reserve their players, obviously players could not be controlled through subsidiary organizations."[3]

By the 1950s, though, player resistance to the reserve clause and reverse-order draft was stiffening.

The Sorry State of Player Salaries

After the war, most NFL and basketball players earned less than $20,000 a season, far below salaries of top baseball players. MLB, of course, generated greater revenue streams than football or basketball in the 1950s. Professional wrestlers, too, made far more than the best NFL and NBA stars during the late 1940s and early 1950s, with Lou Thesz reportedly earning $250,000 per season. Even top women professional wrestlers might pull in $30,000 per year.[4]

Basketball and football owners, in particular, were unable to suppress salaries too much, though. The NFL and basketball owners boasted about having college men playing their games, thereby erasing the image of the athletic bum. Because most basketball and football players during the 1950s and 1960s had college degrees, their reservation salaries—the minimum salaries needed to induce them to play pro ball or for a particular employer—were higher than for players in baseball, owing to their college degrees, which provided attractive outside opportunities.

The *Statistical Abstract of the United States* did not list earnings by educational attainment in 1950, but the average weekly earnings for manufacturing workers was $59.33 in 1950 and $64.24 in July 1951. Players who earned $6,000 or more in 1950 put their families well into the top 20 percent of household incomes.[5]

Players earned more playing football or basketball than did the average American in their jobs, but owners were unable to cut salaries by very many thousand dollars before the players would be earning similar amounts as manufacturing workers and entry-level business jobs. Basketball's limited gate receipts established a fairly low ceiling for paying the stars. Basketball owners, therefore, had less leeway with regard to salaries than did their baseball counterparts. If an owner slashed salaries too much, his players could opt for their best employment alternatives. Several NBA-caliber players decided to take jobs with large companies, such as Phillips Petroleum, fielding semipro teams. NBA president Maurice Podoloff told a congressional hearing that some of the industrial leagues were offering between $9,000 and $10,000 in salaries for players in 1957, although he admitted these were rumored prices.[6] The offer of a salary for playing basketball plus a full-time job within an industry proved enticing to some players.

The BAA immediately imposed a salary cap of $5,000 for any player and $40,000 total for a team. The league also tried to enact a $5,000 salary-cap for rookie players, but this quickly failed, because too many rookies had leverage in the form of other offers.[7]

When the NFL was the only national professional football league between 1950 and 1959, collegians who wanted to play pro ball in the United States had to acquiesce to whatever the team drafting them was offering to pay, or go to Canada and play a different style of football. The players themselves realized the negative effect the owners' monopoly had on their salaries, although some did not think it mattered much. When a congressional committee member, citing the tens of thousands of dollars in bonuses untried baseball prospects received to sign with teams, asked Philadelphia Eagles football player Chuck Bednarik, "Don't you think if there were no player draft, the bonuses to football players to sign would be much higher?" Bednarik responded, "Well, I don't think a football player goes into football with the idea of staying in the game for 15 or 20 years, or with the object of making a lot of money. Football is more hazardous than baseball and there is no such thing as bonus." Bednarik testified that he had been lucky in that two teams from different leagues held draft rights to him, so "I could dicker with both, and get that extra buck. A man has to prove himself in football." Bednarik proved himself an exception to his rule by playing fourteen seasons.[8]

After the agreement between the NFL and AAFC, observers predicted that the players' prosperity was over. A *Time* magazine writer quoted Browns' owner Arthur McBride as saying, "players who got $10,000 and $12,000 this year will be playing for half that—or less—next season."[9]

NFL players' real salaries—salaries adjusted for changes in the Consumer Price Index—increased during the second half of the 1950s; however, even better times were coming. The AFL promised to raise salaries in the same way the AAFC had. One report stated the AFL hoped to establish a minimum salary that was 10 percent higher than the NFL's $6,500 minimum.[10]

In the NBA, African American players sometimes received lucrative offers from Abe Saperstein's Harlem Globetrotters. Wilt Chamberlain played one season with the Globetrotters, skipping his senior year at Kansas. Saperstein had earlier offered Bill Russell a reputed $50,000 salary, but Russell turned it down. Russell admitted, "I'll say this—it was a good thing for me and it's a good thing for other Negro basketball players. When the Globetrotters bid for you, it helps you get a better deal with the pros."[11]

After the BAA and NBL combined, there was less competition for players. Owners hoped for a reduction in salaries. Emory Jones, general manager of the soon-to-be defunct St. Louis Bombers, thought the average player earned more than $5,000. Because team rosters were comprised of eleven players, a coach, and a trainer, the payroll might amount to $70,000 or so.[12]

The Explicit Use of the Reserve Clause

There were many examples of owners explicitly using their power from the reserve clause to browbeat players. Ben Kerner's Hawks were among the lowest-paid players in basketball. The low pay stemmed, in part, from the team's lackluster records and sparse attendance. Kerner was a Jekyll-and-Hyde type of owner. He could be ruthless when negotiating salaries, as Rudy LaRusso remembered: "We heard that Kerner would tell you, 'Either you take this or you work at the car wash. Now make up your mind.'" Player Zelmo Beaty confirmed LaRusso's remarks about negotiating with Kerner, "I won't trade you. You'll just sit and get nothing." Clyde Lovellette remarked that Kerner used St. Louis' smaller revenue potential to hammer down salaries: "Ben told me, 'You might be an $18,000 or $20,000 player [elsewhere], but this is what you're worth to me ($12,000).'"[13] Baseball's Senators were also notorious for paying subpar salaries, as the owner, Clark Griffith, used the team's poor attendance as an excuse to tamp down payrolls.[14]

Some league officials also employed the reserve clause as an explicit threat. Ed Macauley reminisced that after his team, the St. Louis Bombers, folded, the league assigned him the rights to Boston. Macauley concurrently received an offer from a team in the American (Basketball) League. While he was discussing the situation with Boston owner Walter Brown, league president Podoloff called and said, "Put Macauley on the phone. If you so much as think of going to the other league you'll be sued, you'll be out of basketball, and your career will come to an end." Macauley was naturally angered by Podoloff's needless outburst and retorted, "Mr. Podoloff, do me a favor. You sue me. Let's go to court. Let's find out whether such things as the reserve clause are legal." Podoloff and the owners did not want a court test of the reserve clause, so nothing came of the commissioner's bluster. In any event, Macauley and Brown had already finalized a deal.[15]

Keeping Mum about Salaries

Owners bemoaned player salaries, but they instilled manners in their players. Along with such topics as politics and religion, they encouraged their players to consider discussing player salaries among themselves to be taboo. The less players knew about what their teammates and rivals were earning, the easier for the owner to keep salaries low. Baseball player, later play-by-play announcer, Tony Kubek urged players to share salary information, considering secrecy only protected the owners.[16] Quarterback Norm Van Brocklin told the antitrust committee that he was paid $21,000 in 1957, but that he had no idea how his salary compared with other players. "The practice in professional ball is, at least with the Rams, not to find out what your teammates are making; they just do not talk about it."[17]

These players were not being paranoid about the owners' desire to keep them ignorant. Bert Bell, years before becoming football's commissioner, suggested a gentlemen's agreement during the league meetings in 1939. Bell bemoaned the publicity given to college all-stars and All-Americans, as such publicity boosted players' bargaining leverage when drafted. He suggested that owners and officials refrain from participating in making up such lists of players. The league's publicity department, though, demurred, believing that the publicity outweighed the reduction in bargaining leverage over salaries. The owners, however, approved a resolution prohibiting officials from taking part in selecting college all-star teams. The Green Bay Packers' owner, Curley Lambeau, wanted to extend the gentlemen's agreement to include prohibiting owners or officials from publishing player salary information.[18]

In addition to often having just one suitor, NFL players were discouraged from employing agents or legal counsel during negotiations. George Halas regaled the antitrust subcommittee with a story. "A player came in and I gave him a pretty substantial increase. It was a salary up to about $12,500. And he said, 'Gee, I would like to have a little more.' Well, I said, 'All right, we will make it $13,000.' Well, he said, 'Gee you know,' he says, 'I think any number with 13 is bound to be very unlucky, and it may affect me.' So I gave him the $14,000. Do you think for a minute that I would grant anything like that to any outside representative or a counsel? No chance."[19] Legislators did not press Halas to elaborate on his rather bizarre anecdote.

A Slow-Moving Rebellion for Rights

The times were changing. In the wake of baseball's Mexican League–inspired competition for players during the 1946 season, some baseball players began challenging the reserve clause. Danny Gardella, a journeyman player, filed a lawsuit against MLB. Sportswriter Dan Parker asked why professional sports needed such a clause, when no other entertainment industry did so, before concluding, "At best, only the outstanding players would be affected to any great extent by the new type of contract." He admitted that, in theory, the richest clubs would get the majority of the best players, but he believed the owners would figure out a way to sufficiently equalize the talent to avoid attendance problems.[20]

Some basketball players, though, were not passive. George Mikan wound up on the Chicago American Gears. Mikan claimed that the Gears did not fulfill their obligations. He asked the circuit court of Cook County to nullify his five-year contract with its salary of $7,000 per season. Mikan believed the contract was one-sided, because it stipulated that he could be terminated at any point. Mikan quit the team on December 12, 1946. The team counterfiled and asked for damages of $100,000 to compensate for the losses incurred when Mikan broke the contract. The team owner said he had spent large sums to promote Mikan, as well as losing revenue at games the star sat out. Circuit Judge Harry Fisher told reporters that the key issue concerned whether the eligibility phase of the contract, the phrase that governed releasing a player, was divisible from the rest of the contract. The reporter noted that MLB had recently altered its ten-day release clause to allow for a thirty-day notice or severance pay. Mikan and the team eventually negotiated a compromise that brought him back on the court by the end of January, although neither party dropped its suit.[21]

NFL owners faced an upsurge in player litigation in the wake of the struggle with AAFC owners. Fullback Ralph Ruthstrom filed suit against George Preston Marshall and the Washington Redskins in 1949. The Redskins had suspended Ruthstrom in 1947, and he requested a release to play with the AAFC Buffalo team. The Redskins did not issue such a release until 1948. Marshall argued that the player left without permission, as though Ruthstrom was a truant schoolboy. Ruthstrom filed suit for $4,100, alleging the Redskins prevented him from making a living playing football. Judge David A. Pine was not convinced and denied the lawsuit via a directed verdict. In addition to turning down his claim, the judge ordered Ruthstrom to pay the Redskins the $41.80 they claimed he owed them from a loan they issued.[22]

New York Giants' player Arnie Weinmeister signed to play for the Vancouver Lions when the Giants informed him in a letter that he would be replaced in the coming season. Weinmeister told owner Wellington T. Mara that he would not return to the Giants for the 1954 season, and signed with Vancouver for $15,000. The Giants promptly sued him. Part of their claim for damages was that Weinmeister was an "indispensable part" of the team. Weinmeister's attorneys tried to demonstrate that fans were primarily interested in watching the backfield men perform, not lowly tackles such as his client. An interesting aspect of Weinmeister's case, in addition to Mara's letter, was Mara's confession that he paid Weinmeister $1,000 above what his contract called for: "Weinmeister contends the contract figure of $11,000 approved by the NFL commissioner, was exceeded, voiding the contract." This novel and dubious legal argument—"Your honor, he paid me too much, so the contract is voided"—did not prevent Weinmeister from prevailing, with Mara's letter proving pivotal.[23]

The league faced a far more serious lawsuit when the Supreme Court agreed to hear William Radovich's case. Radovich was a seven-year veteran of professional football. He had played five seasons with Detroit before finishing his career with the AAFC Los Angeles Dons. The San Francisco Clippers of the Pacific Coast League wanted to hire him for the 1948 season but backed off, because, according to Radovich, NFL owners had blacklisted him. "Radovich sued the Lions and the NFL for $105,000 in damages. He charged attempts to monopolize interstate commerce in the business of professional football."[24]

A Ninth Circuit court cited the Supreme Court baseball judgment in ruling Radovich's case was outside the scope of the Sherman Act. The court further advised, "[I]f Congressional indulgence extended to and saved baseball from regulation, then the indulgence extended to other sports."[25] The Ninth Circuit court's ruling was subject to further scrutiny, which was a judicial form of a play under review.

The Supreme Court ruled that "Radovich is entitled to an opportunity to prove his charges and refused to grant professional football immunity from the antitrust laws. Of course, we express no opinion as to whether or not respondents have, in fact, violated the antitrust laws, leaving that determination to the trial court after all the facts are in."[26] The NFL asked the Court to reconsider, but they were denied. Radovich and his attorney hoped to demonstrate that the NFL differed from MLB, mainly because of the reverse-order draft that stripped the player of most of his freedom of choice.[27]

As an example that no lawsuit was without its potential benefit, Bell and the NFL owners employed the now-plausible argument that without an antitrust exemption, their league was in danger of being bankrupted by litigation or by extreme competitive imbalance that would destroy weaker clubs. Despite these lawsuits, though, the owners still dominated the players.

Congress Examines Player Rights

Congressional committee members expressed shock at the owners' marked lack of regard for player rights. They interrogated the owners and their representatives about playing conditions, the reserve clause, and the reverse-order draft. Although players made above-average incomes, their chattel-like status was clear. Owners in all team sports worked very hard to establish and maintain the fiction that these violations of the players' fundamental rights to their labor were necessary to maintain competitive balance, which benefited fans. The owners were aided by the public's ignorance of the athletes' exploitation, in the sense of being paid below market salaries for their unique talents.

Bell occasionally irritated some of the committee members by his constant referral to the players as "boys" and "kids" and his claims that he sided with the players instead of the owners, because, "they're younger and don't know the angles." Emanuel Celler responded in exasperation, "Are they college graduates?" Bell stuck to his belief that the college graduates did not know the angles.[28]

Bell repeatedly mentioned that players were free to come to him to discuss grievances. Committee members pressed him on his neutrality in such situations, considering the owners paid his salary. Bell professed to favor the players in disputes. He characterized them as callow and unaware of "the different angles and different situations" and that "80 percent of the players do not even read their contract except for the amount of money that is on it."[29] Committee members, many of whom were lawyers, were incredulous. They started asking players whether they had read their contracts and the question, "Have you read your contract?" became de rigueur (instead of that other 1950s question: "Are you now or have you ever been a member of the Communist Party?"). Bednarik confessed that, "I feel that I am fairly intelligent, but I never read the fine print. I just look at the amount of money they are going to pay me." He believed the vast majority of the players acted similarly. Celler was nonplussed, especially when Bednarik said he had a degree from the University of Pennsylvania's Wharton School. He did not read the fine print because, "money was the big thing then. I didn't have a nickel then, and I looked at the figures to see if that was satisfactory to me." Bednarik confirmed Bell's interventions on behalf of players. When Celler commented, "Well I hope Mr. Bell lives for many, many, many years," Bednarik agreed, "I do, too."[30]

Creighton Miller, the players' legal representative, based his explanation of the players' failure to read their contracts on two factors. "They know about it from the veteran ballplayers" and "They cannot do anything about [their contracts]."[31]

One former player, though, had read his contract. George Connor, former Chicago Bears player and now assistant coach, told the committee he had carefully read his contract and consulted with a lawyer. "We had three clauses in the contract crossed out, and we had another thing written on the side, an injury clause, that if I was injured I would get paid for my full contract." He had stricken the "release clause" that meant they had to keep him on the team for all three seasons. He also had the "physical capabilities of the player are not up to standard" and "conduct" clauses crossed out. Connor disputed Bell's claim that teams did not select players who did not want to play for them, citing his experiences with some owners.[32]

MLB players still needed their collective consciousness raised. During the 1958 Senate hearings, Mickey Mantle, Ted Williams, Stan Musial, Robin Roberts, and Ed Yost each testified that the reserve clause was necessary. No journeyman players or disgruntled minor league players testified.[33] Some legislators might have wondered about the selected group of player witnesses; however, the majority of them seemed content with trading pleasantries with the big stars.

Players, of course, had to be leery of publicly criticizing the reserve clause. Bob Friend, National League player representative, asserted that the players backed the reserve clause as necessary for the game's survival. According to him, baseball players were not ready for a union. He thought a union would be divisive: "you immediately make a sharp cleavage between the players and the club executives . . . we immediately will begin antagonizing the owners. . . . It would tend to destroy the image of the baseball star for the youngsters because of the haggling between the players and the owners."[34] Meanwhile, Judge Robert Cannon, legal advisor to the players, testified before the Senate by repeating Gene Woodling's observation about the players and the owners' relationship: "We have it so good we don't know what to ask for next." Cannon added, "I think this sums up the thinking of the average major league ballplayer today."[35] The attitude of Chicago White Sox owner, A. C. Allyn Jr., though, augured ill for future labor-management relations. Allyn defended the reserve clause before the Senate saying, "The players, it is true, either have to sign a contract with us or not at all, but they do have *the privilege of not at all* [italics mine]."[36]

Creighton Miller testified that football deserved exemption from the antitrust laws only if such restraints "foster equal playing competition among league rivals and consequently permit the sport to engage in the operation as a business. Football is unquestionably a unique business because it necessitates cooperation among competitors in order to produce a marketable product. That product is competition." He also supported the reserve clause, because "elimination of the reserve clause with no substitute would remove the abuses attendant thereto and would probably temporarily increase players' salaries, but, if the rich clubs thereby destroyed competition by competitively being too superior, it might act as a cure that killed the patient." Miller, however, cautioned that some safeguards should be enacted to ensure fair treatment of players.[37]

Miller then went on the offensive during his testimony. He bluntly claimed, "The professional football players' contract is a legal monstrosity." He subsequently quoted Judge Jerome N. Frank's opinion in the *Gardella* case: "We have a monopoly which, in its effects on ballplayers like the plaintiff, possesses characteristics shockingly repugnant to moral principles that, at least since the War Between the States, have been basic in America as shown by the thirteenth amendment to the Constitution condemning involuntary servitude."[38] Owners could release players at a moment's notice without compensation, a clear lack of mutuality.[39] Celler wasted no time expressing his disapproval of "paragraph 11" in the standard player contract that concerned a player's automatic waiver of his right to seek redress from the commissioner's decision. "I would say this, gentlemen. I think that section is void as against public policy. You cannot preclude a man from going into the courts to have redress of wrongs. . . . That is a pretty harsh section."[40]

The owners' main defense of the reserve clause rested upon its alleged salutary effects on competitive balance. In a strange coincidence, economist Simon Rottenberg had recently published a seminal article in the *Journal of Political Economy*. Rottenberg described the singular characteristic of professional team sports leagues: such leagues were mixtures of competition and cooperation. He concluded that competitive balance was unlikely to differ greatly under either a reserve clause or a free agency regime.[41] Unfortunately for the players, the congressional committee did not call upon him to testify.

The NFL owners had earlier decided to modify their standard player contract after receiving legal advice. Football owners became aware of the dubious legality of the player contract when Bert Bell introduced attorney Phil Gilbert to the owners at an April 1946 meeting. Gilbert analyzed the validity of the Player Contract: "any Player Contract which had a forty-eight hour release clause, or a reserve clause similar to the same only of longer duration, in all probability would not stand up in court." Bell distributed a new Uniform Players Contract the next day with the suggested adjustments, and the owners unanimously approved it.[42]

The new contract specified "the obligations of the club and of the player and adds to the protection of the player. The contract is for one year, with an option on the player's services for the succeeding season at a specified price." Bert Bell extolled the virtues of the new contract before making an interesting statement: "This contract eliminates 'servitude.'" If he believed this, he was one of the few owners or officials ever to admit that players toiled under conditions of servitude. The owners hoped the adjustments, which turned out to be essentially cosmetic, would persuade the courts not to rule the contracts invalid on the grounds of lack of mutuality, hence Bell's statement, "we have talked about the player. Now we talk about the player and the club, about their responsibilities to one another."[43] A cynical observer might view the owners' action as a response to the AAFC and potential legal battles.

From this point on, football owners boasted that their version of the reserve clause—as a one-year contract with an option year binding a player for a second season at no less than 90 percent of his contract salary—was less restrictive than

MLB's "in perpetuity" interpretation. Bell claimed, "We changed our contract because our players do not play nearly as long in football as the average baseball player does. Pro football is a means to an end to establish a youngster in business. So we can make changes that baseball could not make, and we tried to make them."[44] He took pains to point out that players could easily play out their option year and become free agents.

Bell's testimony impressed Wyoming Senator Joseph C. O'Mahoney, at least. O'Mahoney told Bell and the committee that he was pleased with the NFL's version of the reserve clauses, as it gave players "a real freedom of contract." Bell seized the opportunity to repeat the boast that the NFL's reserve clause was "the greatest bargaining situation in the world for a ballplayer." He claimed that he advised some players deadlocked in negotiations with their owners to use the option year as leverage.[45]

The NFL enlisted compliant players, both former and current, to testify on behalf of the necessity of the reserve clause. Red Grange, Chuck Bednarik, Sid Luckman, Norm Van Brocklin, and George Ratterman testified. While all acknowledged the necessity of the reserve clause and the reverse-order draft, they proved more willing than the baseball players would be the following year in requesting modifications and a right of appeal. Ratterman, especially, was an interesting witness, as he had played in the AAFC and had flirted with playing out his option year.[46] His testimony will be described in greater detail in a subsequent section.

Bell's ebullience disappeared when he was pressed for names of players who had sought free agency. In response, he stammered. He finally mentioned Ed Modzelewski and George Kennard, but these players had either retired for a year or left the team before signing with another team. Kennard returned to his team, while Modzelewski was still negotiating with others. Bell claimed that players usually preferred to stay on their original team.[47]

Committee members, perhaps recalling the Sherlock Holmes story "Silver Blaze" and the importance of "the dog that didn't bark," could have wondered about the free agents who were not signed. Bell later testified that George Ratterman was pursuing free agency. In an example of doublespeak, Bell told Senator O'Mahoney (who later thanked him for his testimony and was clearly sympathetic to the owners): "Ratterman had the bargaining power. This [reserve] clause gives the greatest bargaining power a player can have."[48]

Countering Bell's enthusiasm, Creighton Miller pointed out that originally a player received 100 percent of his original contract during the option year, but that the owners had changed this to 90 percent "to discourage players from becoming so-called free agents, as most players prefer to renegotiate their contract rather than take an automatic 10 percent reduction." Miller agreed with Emanuel Celler, who suggested there might be some "sort of a secret agreement by the owners not to hire a man that becomes a free agent."[49] Players, too, had difficulty naming any colleague who had successfully become a free agent. They cited rumors that the owners maintained a blacklist against any free agents. Bednarik had played in the NFL since 1949, and he could not recall a single player becoming a free agent, although he thought Bud Grant might have been one. However, Grant's free agency entailed playing in Canada and not for another NFL team. Bednarik and fellow NFL player Jack Jennings denied there was a blacklist; Jennings claimed that, hypothetically speaking, if George Halas needed a guard and a free-agent guard was available, "I am sure Mr. Halas would pick [him] up."[50]

Miller explained to the committee that two players had played out their option but no club had signed them, "although many coaches expressed serious interest."[51] A letter from a former player, Jim Sid Wright, expressed his frustration as a free agent in 1949 (apparently he was not one of the players to whom Miller alluded). Wright encountered difficulties with Boston Yank owner Ted Collins, who frequently was involved in such disputes, so he had appealed to Bell. The AAFC New York Yankees signed him for 1949, but the team received a letter from Ted Collins requesting them not to play Wright. The Yankees subsequently said Wright was too slow and placed him on waivers. He did not receive any offers and left football. Wright wrote his letter to Robert Nelson, who also had difficulties dealing with Bell and the NFL, and who went public with his grievances. Bell repudiated Nelson's version of events and pointed out that the player had played with Baltimore in 1950 before being released.[52] These two played in Canada during the 1953 season. They returned to their original teams in 1954.

George Ratterman became the focal point of the free agency discussion. He had played three seasons with Buffalo's AAFC team. When the league disbanded, he played with the New York Yanks. He signed a one-year contract with the Yanks that contained the usual option clause. Then, he waited for the team to exercise its option for his services, but when the May 1951 deadline passed, he believed he became a free agent. Ratterman thought the issue was straightforward, but the team would not admit that he was a free agent. "I was informed by the general manager of the New York Yanks [Frank Fitzgerald] at that time that I could not go any place and play anywhere. I said, 'Why not? I am a free agent.' He said, 'Well, none of the other teams in this league would sign you.'" Ratterman played in Canada, but he settled with the Yanks and finished the season with them because the NFL season extended past the Canadian League season. Then Bert Bell stepped in and informed Ratterman he could not play for the Yanks until he appealed. "The commissioner said he did not care what the judge in New Jersey said, the league rules said he had jurisdiction, and I could not play in the NFL until I sent him a telegram requesting a hearing under [my] existing contract."

Bell fined Ratterman $2,000 for playing in Canada. He came up to Ratterman the next season and said, "Forget the rest of your fine and just be a good boy."[53]

George Halas denied Ratterman's claim of a blacklist against free agents. When told that Fitzgerald claimed there was such a list, Halas tried to discredit him by ridicule: "That is Ted Collins' son-in-law. He did not know very much about football, to be frank with you. He was just a son-in-law, who was put in there—trying to save a buck." Halas stated he would be willing to sign a free agent.[54]

Presaging the future of player movement, San Francisco 49ers receiver R. C. Owens played out his option year and became a free agent. If there was an informal gentlemen's agreement not to sign free agents, the Baltimore Colts must have ignored it by signing Owens (renowned for the "Alley-Oop" pass play) for the 1962 season. The owners, facing a bona fide free agent, promptly enacted a rule stipulating that a team signing a free agent had to render proper compensation to the team losing the player. This rule, later called the Rozelle Rule, naturally made signing free agents less attractive, so players continued to find little benefit from playing out their option.[55]

In 1957, Bell and Miller concluded their testimonies by proclaiming that they would be satisfied if Congress enacted one of four almost identical bills that would explicitly maintain the reserve clause.[56]

Better Times Coming for Players

The reserve clause did not suppress salaries forever. When revenues increased, NBA and NFL owners began paying more.

Signing big-name college stars sometimes significantly boosted a team's revenue. The Minneapolis Lakers, moribund since George Mikan's retirement, signed Elgin Baylor for a $20,000 salary. Baylor raised the team's performance, and revenue jumped by more than $130,000. Oscar Robertson exerted a similar effect upon Cincinnati's fortunes. "Before Oscar had finished his college year, the Royals were $40,000 above previous seasons in advance sales, fired by the anticipation of The Big O romping in Royal pantaloons."[57]

Before the subcommittee, owners and their commissioners frequently boasted about and sometimes bemoaned rising player salaries. Bell testified that the "average income of league players has increased approximately 325 percent." Part of this 325 percent increase, of course, would have been needed to keep pace with the change in the general price level (roughly 48 percent between 1946 and 1958). He went on to slyly demean the players: "The salary of a league football player, who devotes only 2 months full time and 3 months part time to playing football averages over $9,200 per season."[58]

The owners' rosy depictions of salary increases did not go uncontested. Creighton Miller told the antitrust committee that, "the average professional football player's salary from 1946 to 1949 increased from $4,000 to $8,000. . . . The player's average salary at the present time, according to Commissioner Bell, is between $8,500 and $9,000 per season, which means that since 1949, during a period which found the owners enjoying greatly increased revenues, the average player's salary was increased by no more than $1,000 in this 7-year period." Kenneth Harkins, chief counsel for the committee, pointed out that the NFL owners' payroll figures suggested that the average player's salaries rose from $7,458 in 1952 to $9,216 in 1956. Miller himself did not have access to player salary data, and he admitted that his figures of $4,000 to $8,000 originated in a January 3, 1949 article in *Time* magazine.[59] Harkins questioned Miller regarding why player salaries did not keep up with net income and revenues, and Miller attributed it to the lack of competitive bidding owing to the NFL's monopoly position.[60]

Some players received other football income in addition to their salaries. Those who participated in league championship games received a share of the gate receipts and sometimes of the television money. Because the attendance and gate receipts varied considerably for these championship games, players could have only a rough idea of this added income ahead of time. Some players found the added income a proportionally significant boost to their salaries. Football all-star players also received money for playing in the postseason Pro Bowl.[61]

The Player Draft Challenged

Bell and his fellow league officials stoutly defended the reserve clause and the reverse-order draft. Some legislators were willing to put their doubts about the practices into law. One proposed Senate bill stipulated that the reverse-player draft, if given antitrust protection, would require that "no player could be subject to our player selection system unless he had previously given his written consent to be subject to this selection system." Bell opposed this clause if it meant that a player was a free agent if he refused to give consent. Senator Estes Kefauver (Tenn.) asked Bell whether he thought many players would refuse to sign the consent. Bell replied, "It brings about intricate problems. People where they play, coaches and others may say to them, 'Don't allow yourself to be selected because, if you do, you will have to play with that team, and otherwise you might be able to get where you want to and you will get more money and at least you can't lose anything by holding out.'" Bell feared that this would create competitive imbalance, as players would gravitate to wealthier teams. Senator Kefauver disputed Bell's fear, stating, "This doesn't prevent you from trading players and equalizing player strength. All my bill is intended to do is to try to give an individual player some rights by requiring him to give you a written statement that he will be subject to the draft." Bell refused to concede the point and repeated his assertion that the "written consent" would lead to competitive imbalance. He added, "I personally think that large bonuses are a very terrible thing. I think that the ballplayer that plays on that field and puts the fans in the stands is the fellow that should get the increases in salary; not the fellow that you guess may make good in 2 or 3 years while the other fellows that are producing take less money."[62]

Government counsel Paul Dixon, at least, began to strip away the fallacies in Bell's arguments with regard to the efficacy of the player draft and of the reserve clause in promoting parity. Bell boasted about how eight different teams had won championships between 1945 and 1957. He claimed that about sixty rookies made the NFL rosters each season. Dixon asked, "Is it your contention that this equalization is coming through the addition of five ballplayers to each team each year?" Bell said, "The five right ballplayers, the five best college football players. The one first goes to the lowest club and then the next lowest club and so on." Dixon recalled previous testimony of three college football coaches that they did not think they would be able to select the five best players. Bell admitted that "Some of them [highly-touted college players] don't and sometimes your 15th choice of a guy that never went to college will become a great player."[63] Bell eagerly made the claim that pro football was a temporary avocation, as most players stayed a few years, acquired savings, and went into business. He repeatedly told the legislators that the average career was 3.5 years.

Dixon pointed out that, in many cases, drafted players did not receive any money unless they made the team. "Therefore the club isn't taking any gamble. The boy is taking a gamble there, isn't he?" Bell replied, "The club is taking the gamble to the extent that if they pick the wrong player, and he doesn't make the team, they are not going to do very well. . . . But the player isn't taking much of a gamble either when he can find out in 8 weeks if he can make the ball club and establish himself in business in the town where he is playing."[64]

Bell exerted much effort in justifying the player draft and the reserve clause. He said that teams contacted players before the draft and questioned them as to their willingness to play for them. If a player indicated he would not play for a particular team, Bell said the team usually honored his wishes. To buttress Bell's testimony, the Chicago Cardinals owner had several of his players send in testimonials. Some of the testimonials seemed vague. Donald Stonesifer wrote, "I would quit playing football if I could be bought and sold to the highest bidder. . . . I do not care to be bought and sold like a slave."[65] Not every Cardinals player proved enthusiastic about the campaign; one informed the committee, "We were asked to send a reply, and although it wasn't compulsory for us to reply, our chances of staying with the team would probably be very slim. The way pro football is today the players have no chance for collective bargaining, which is an accepted American practice. . . . I don't feel that I can sign my name to this letter because it will definitely hurt my chances of staying with the Cardinals."[66]

George Ratterman argued against the necessity of a player draft by pointing out that MLB did not have a draft of amateur players. He wondered, "If football needs a player draft, why doesn't baseball?"[67] In the aftermath of the controversy regarding the owners' denial of players' basic civil rights inherent in the draft, Bell tried to insert a clause into the league constitution and bylaws dealing with the informal, "don't want to play for you, don't draft" policy.[68] As with many of the NFL's actions to ostensibly grant players more of their civil rights, this rule contained a large loophole—the commissioner had the power to determine whether a request was reasonable.

The Formation of Players Associations

The players were somewhat passive about loosening the owners' control over them. The NFL constitution permitted players to bring labor-related matters to the commissioner. Bell exerted his authority largely to both the owners and the players' satisfaction. He frequently urged owners to placate individual players. Maurice Podoloff would echo Bell's depiction of their use of the commissioner's or president's power with regard to players. Of course, such testimony was somewhat self-serving.

In answering Peter Rodino Jr.'s (N.J.) question about the football players' lack of input in selecting a commissioner, George Connor did not think players could make an intelligent assessment of a candidate for commissioner because they were not in the league long enough to make an informed decision. Connor said he did not even think player representatives should have a vote: "I do not think the players should have anything to do with the commissioner—I mean, electing the commissioner. They have no money involved."[69]

Appealing to the league's commissioner or president was not a satisfactory method for dealing with general labor/management issues. After World War II, a few baseball players tried to form a union. Previous attempts always ended in failure. At that time, they enlisted Robert Murphy to assist them. Some contemporary observers predicted that the effort was futile, as players had disparate skills: "no two ball players are of precisely the same ability, therefore it is impossible to set a maximum wage scale, although a minimum would be feasible."[70] Murphy's efforts proved largely futile, and he failed to organize a union. He did, however, get some small gains for the players, including more per diem expense money for spring training, promptly dubbed "Murphy money"; the owners also granted a minimum salary of $5,000 and a pension. By 1957, Major League players had won an increase in the minimum salary to $7,000. Baseball owners bragged about the players' pension plan. Former Yankees' owner Larry MacPhail persuaded his fellow owners to start the pension in 1947.[71] The pension became a selling point for inducing talented athletes to choose baseball over other opportunities. It improved relations between owners and players, but the pension also provided owners with another deterrent against players considering joining an outlaw league.

Football players hired Creighton Miller, a former Notre Dame halfback-turned attorney, to represent them in negotiations with the commissioner and club owners.[72] The players' chief demand was for a pension, similar to one that baseball players enjoyed. They also sought nominal payment for exhibition games, a minimum salary, and some other concessions. Aside from the pension, their demands were quite modest, which was a similar state of affairs with baseball and basketball players' demands. However, some owners, such as George Preston Marshall, were outraged: "The proposals sound ridiculous and, from a practical standpoint, they don't deserve any recognition from me. It's a matter for Commissioner Bell." Edwin W. Pauley, co-owner of the Los Angeles Rams, heard the news with placidity: "I believe it will help pro football. It's the same as in any business. There is nothing to fear."[73]

NFL players' representative Norm Van Brocklin read a prepared statement to the committee. The players highlighted the NFL's improved economic condition, reflected by increased revenues and profits owing to lower amusement taxes, increased ticket prices, and decreased transportation tax. They argued that their demands were fair and that "Many of our representatives have only one or two years of play remaining and their contributions to our association are not based on selfish motives—but are rather designed to improve the conditions under which future athletes will play."[74]

Whatever Bell's personal beliefs about players' associations, he was the owners' agent, so he delayed recognizing the players' association, although he met for an informal chat with Kyle Rote, Van Brocklin, and Miller. Bell told reporters that, "he was not representing and had no right to represent the club owners."[75] Bell's reactions to player demands were reflective of his peers' actions in baseball and basketball.

The NFL players asked for a minimum salary of $5,000; expense money during training camp; $12 per day minimum for board and lodging while on the road; an injury clause guaranteeing a full season's salary; a shorter training season; and formal recognition of the association. Because few, if any, players had salaries below $5,000, their first request was merely a formality. The owners refused to accept it, though. Bell said, "there is no player in the NFL who does not receive over this minimum. If there is one, and he tells me about it, I'll see that it's corrected." Probably because many of the owners had already fulfilled some of the other requests, all of the owners agreed to adopt them to standardize fringe benefits across teams. The owners, though, refused to recognize the Players Association. Bell reiterated, "It is submitted that if any problems now exist or hereafter arise, the player or players on each club should meet with their individual owners for the purpose of discussing and resolving their particular grievances." Rarely has "divide and conquer" been stated so blandly. The players responded with an immediate show of support for the Players Association by exhibiting 304 member signatures.[76]

Miller also focused on the owners' handling of workmen's compensation ("workmen's" was the contemporary term). Once the regular season began and paychecks began coming in, some football players could not financially afford to become injured. NFL players did not always qualify for benefits under state Workers Compensation laws. Owners did not view player contracts as binding: If the player got hurt, why pay him? Although many, if not most, owners honored the contracts, they did so not out of legal necessity but out of the goodness of their hearts or to placate a star player. Miller said that he did not know of any player who had filed for workmen's compensation, explaining, "He is protected by workmen's compensation, but this does not insure his salary. Few players file for workmen's compensation because many clubs pay them their regular salary anyway, in order not to raise what is already a rather prohibitive premium because of the dangers involved in professional football." Miller continued by testifying that Bell opposed inserting an injury clause into the players' contracts. Bell told him that the insertion would create "a lot of minor [law] cases on our hands if somebody gets a sore thumb."[77] Teams submitted information on Workmen's Compensation costs. The Chicago teams were not covered, while the Pennsylvania teams had been rejected because the benefits were too small and the club paid the full costs resulting from injuries. The other eight teams paid between $1,500 and $18,236 in 1956, with five teams paying less than $9,000 each.[78] Teams indicated how many lawsuits players filed over salaries. Most teams had no lawsuits filed, but the Cardinals (4), Packers (4), Lions (3), Giants (1), and Redskins (1) had lawsuits filed against them. The Lions' lawsuits included the Radovich case.[79]

The football players' next goal was a pension plan. Bell's oft-repeated claim that playing pro football was a temporary avocation and not a career was invoked against implementing a pension: players simply did not stay long enough in the league to make a pension feasible. Such an argument might have been valid if the pension was to fully provide for a player's retirement income. After Bell and the owners delayed, the pension plan moved forward.[80]

Insurance advisor Bill Dudley told owners and reporters that a modest pension could be started for $338,000, of which $125,000 would be from player contributions and the remainder possibly from extra preseason exhibition games.[81]

Dudley persuaded Bell and the owners, so they performed their usual about-face. In the league meeting minutes of April 23, 1959, Bell proclaimed the favorable publicity resulting from initiating a benefits plan. The package included a $5,000 life insurance policy, hospitalization and medical coverage for themselves and their families at league expense, and the pension. To qualify for the pension, a player had to play five seasons in the league, defined as four full seasons and at least one game of a fifth season. The plan was to be financed from the increased television fees for the annual championship playoff game.[82] The owners, though, still refused to recognize the Players Association.

The players were lucky, because a power greater than Bert Bell and the owners was coming to their rescue. The Congressional Antitrust Subcommittee of 1957 showed keen interest in player-management relations throughout sports. If Shakespeare had been writing in the 1950s, he might have written, "Congressional committees doth makes cowards of us all."

Before the subcommittee, Miller detailed his frustration in dealing with Bell. Bell had at first indicated that recognition was forthcoming and implied that he, Bell, had the authority to do so, contradicting his earlier claim that he lacked such authority. Miller claimed that Bell told player representatives that he (Bell) would not take the players' proposals to the owners without the players publicly endorsing the option clause and the player draft. This occurred during the *Radovich* case. He claimed Bell told him, "If you endorse the option clause, you won't have any trouble getting recognized. I'll be able to take this into the owners, and say this is a sign of good faith; the boys have done something for us." Miller and the players refused to sign the endorsement.[83] The congressional committee pressed Bell on this point. Bell recalled that he urged the players to make the public endorsements and that he would do his utmost to get the owners to recognize the association. He also stated that the owners' primary opposition to the association was their fear that it did not have the proper authority, and that "They also believed individually that the players could do much better for themselves dealing individually with their own clubs." Bell told Kenneth Harkins that although he agreed to insert the $5,000 minimum salary clause into the players' proposal, he was against it. "I think it was academic, because there was nobody in 1955 who received less than $5,000."[84]

Baltimore Colts' owner Carroll Rosenbloom testified that some players informed the owners that the association did not represent them. The biggest stumbling block was that the Chicago Bears players had yet to join the association.[85] George Halas testified that his players were unenthusiastic about joining the players association. He referred to an article in the *Washington Post and Times Herald*, dated February 14, 1957, in which Bears player Stan Jones said, "After talking it over, we felt we'd have nothing to gain by belonging to the association. Halas is more than generous with us, we feel. When you're being treated right, I don't think it's any time to be complaining." Jones went on to say that Halas already had given them most of what the association was bargaining for.[86] Miller told reporters that the owners refused to meet with him, even though the association represented more than 90 percent of the players.

Basketball players and owners, too, sparred over a players association. Player representatives from seven teams helped organized a committee to "work for the betterment of basketball in the NBA to the mutual benefit of the owners and the players." Players on the eighth team, the Fort Wayne Pistons, opted not to join the committee, in deference to team owner Fred Zollner, who disliked unions.[87]

The basketball owners performed their own stalling tactics on resolving player requests. Maurice Podoloff blandly remarked that the owners and he had no strong opposition to a players' committee, but he thought players did not need to unionize. "Is it necessary to hire a lawyer who apparently is unfamiliar with basketball to air some complaints? Is it possible that they are trying to capitalize on some free advertising?" Podoloff further said that players were making an average of $7,500 per season.[88] He conveniently forgot that he had known very little, if anything, about basketball, when the owners had appointed him as president.

NBA owners, though, were dealing with a savvier group of athletes than their baseball peers. Almost every basketball player had attended and graduated from a four-year college or university. Several players possessed lucrative outside jobs. Although baseball owners rigged the players' association during the 1950s with their own hired gun as players' counsel for the unwitting players, basketball owners never committed such travesties.

In early 1956, the basketball players again announced a set of demands.[89] When Podoloff and the owners again dithered, Boston Celtics star Bob Cousy and the players considered affiliating with the AFL-CIO. To forestall such an affiliation, Podoloff asked the players to give him three months to arrange some sort of grievance process. He claimed that the owners were thinking about consulting with the players.[90] Cousy and the other player representatives' efforts were also hampered by their fellow players' half-hearted support. By 1958, Cousy was ready to resign as the spokesman, citing insufficient enthusiasm among the players. "Considering all the gains made by the Players Association last spring, there should be more interest and cooperation. If there is not a healthy sign at the All-Star get-together, I'm ready to step down." Cousy said that only forty-one players, or roughly half, had paid their annual dues of $10 for 1957.[91]

Basketball players Cousy, Ed Macauley, and Bob Pettit testified before a congressional hearing in 1957. They all saluted the reserve clause and the reverse-order draft, although Cousy suggested the desirability of altering the draft. All three players thought the two institutions ensured competitive balance and prevented chaos.

Macauley, though, said some interesting things about the ramifications of NBL and BAA competition for players. Because of the competition between the two leagues, he received more money than he otherwise would have if there been just one league, but "this proved disastrous for me because of the financial setup. . . . Most ballplayers, myself in particular, with the [St. Louis] Bombers, were pushed up into an income bracket that the owners possibly could not afford. As a result, I think the salary they paid me in the first year contributed somewhat to the fact that the ball club at the end of the season ended financially. They couldn't continue."[92]

Although the players did not wish to upset the basic institutions of the league, they expressed a desire for a pension; they admitted that the owners had granted their requests to limit exhibition games and to increase the travel money.[93] Macauley again assumed a conciliatory stance, suggesting that the owners eventually create a pension and stating his belief that the owners could afford to finance such a pension.[94]

The league's national television contract for Saturday afternoon telecasts also created friction between players and owners. All-Star Game and television revenue funded the MLB players' pension, and the basketball players hoped owners would designate television money to a similar pension fund. Cousy was doubtful that any such pension would benefit his contemporaries, a prescient belief on his part. Decades later, pioneering NBA players were still petitioning the league for some modest pension for themselves.[95]

The owners naturally claimed in public that they could not afford to fund a player pension. One league official, unnamed by *New York Times* columnist Arthur Daley, echoed Eddie Gottlieb's claim that, "the cost of our payrolls in relation to receipts is close to 60 per cent., while both baseball and football will run 25 to 30 per cent. They also make huge amounts of money from television. We have none." This official further stated, "The owners in this league are not wealthy men and I guess only Fred Zollner of Detroit could be classified as a tycoon. The rest of them amaze me. Why do they take this financial beating, year after year? There's only one answer: They're basketball nuts."[96] The NBA owners, apparently, hoped to deflect pressure to create a player pension by pleading penury and insanity.

Podoloff's dilatory responses and the owners' intransigence eventually culminated before the nationally televised 1964 All-Star Game. The players demanded definite action on creating a pension plan and issued an ultimatum: a promise on moving forward on the pension or no game. At that point, new commissioner Walter Kennedy begged the players not to boycott the game, with the ensuing disastrous publicity.[97] Some legislators had grilled Podoloff about a rule in the standard player contract that forbade striking before a nationally televised game, which proved how prescient the owners were in inserting the clause, not that it prevented the players from threatening to strike in 1964.[98] Kennedy promised that he would relay the players' concerns to the owners and come up with solutions. He apparently retained sufficient credibility and goodwill to persuade the players to trust him.

The Outcome of the Hearings

Under congressional pressure, Bert Bell made his big announcement, his "long bomb" if you will, at this point. Bell did a volte face and told the committee he was willing to begin meeting with the Players Association's officials and that he had the authority to recognize it.[99] "Accordingly, in keeping with my assurance that we would do whatever you gentlemen consider to be in the best interest of the public, on behalf of the NFL, I hereby recognize the NFL Players Association and I am prepared to negotiate immediately with the representative of that association." After Celler and the other members of the committee congratulated him, Bell repeated the owners' stance that prior recognition had been lacking because they were not sure the association "was truly representative of the players in the league." After a couple of skeptics asked whether Bell had authority for his statement, he replied, "Mr. Chairman, I do not think there is anyone against this association. I think what they have to do is find out, exactly what it is and what it means, and so forth; and that is my job." While not quite Casey Stengelese, Bell's last sentence was sufficiently vague to allay concerns for the moment.[100]

Fortunately for Bell, George Preston Marshall provided him cover when he told reporters that recognition of the Players Association had been "a matter for the clubs to decide and not the commissioner."[101] Several days later, the Players Association told Bell to "put in writing his verbal agreement to recognize the league's new player association."[102]

At the next set of hearings in 1958, the committee pressed Bell as to the owners' actions. Bell reported that an injury clause had been attached to the players' contracts, as of January 1958, although he admitted the owners had not consulted with the players in writing the clause.[103]

Some players still did not trust the owners. The Senate committee received a letter from "Unnamed Prominent Football Player." He urged the committee to give careful consideration to its decision on the reserve clause. With the exemption, owners would leave players no recourse in grievance cases except to appeal to Bert Bell. The player asked the relevant question, "Why shouldn't a player perform with the team of his choosing?"[104]

Football players, encouraged by Congress' disapproval of owner activities, considered filing a $4.2 million antitrust lawsuit against the NFL, but Creighton Miller advised them to retain the lawsuit as a threat to get owners to comply with their demands. Although no one was campaigning for free agency, Miller said the $4.2 million figure (in treble damages) had been based on the difference between what "the players are getting now and what they would be able to get if they were able to offer their services to an open market."[105] How Miller calculated the difference was not divulged and would have been of great interest to economists. With recent congressional scrutiny, NFL owners may have figured that acquiescence was the prudent course, so they unanimously granted all of the demands except recognition of the Players Association. Bell, though, asserted his authority. Sportswriter Joe King said Bell told the owners that they "would have to accept as a fait accomplishment his own recognition of the player organization which he had made before the Celler Committee. Bell emphasized that the topic wasn't even on the agenda; it had been consummated."[106] King believed that the owners had undermined him the previous January, leaving Miller to doubt his reliability. No wonder Bell took credit for the outcome: "I recognized the Association before Congress and the owners today approved my action."[107]

Conclusion: Indirect Pressure Alters Owner-Player Relations

The subcommittee's pressure upon NFL owners to recognize the Players Association was perhaps the most important result of the various hearings with respect to player rights. The subcommittee never recommended directly tampering with the reserve clause or the reverse-order draft. The legislators may have hoped that owner recognition of player associations or unions would provide players with sufficient leverage to adjudicate disputes regarding player rights. The subcommittee's hesitance to radically alter fundamental institutions of professional team sports may have been the best outcome owners could have realistically hoped for. The legislators did not seem willing to grant full antitrust exemptions, and efforts to coordinate partial antitrust exemptions failed repeatedly.

Baseball players and owners eventually negotiated a free agency system in the wake of Andy Messersmith's and Dave McNally's arbitration victory. Because of the collective bargaining agreement in later years and a crippling work stoppage in the late 1990s, owners and players "agreed to jointly request and cooperate in lobbying the Congress to pass a law that will clarify that Major League Baseball Players are covered under the antitrust laws."[108] The resulting legislation, the Curt Flood Act of 1998, met with initial opposition from minor league owners, until an amendment allayed their fears.[109]

Legislators failed, though, to delve into the owners' argument that the reserve clause promoted competitive balance. They would eventually begin to question the assertion. Legislators would also investigate the reverse-order draft in upcoming hearings.

5

Closing the Last Vestige of a "Free Market" in Labor *1964*

During the postwar era, baseball officials and players often mentioned free agents. Unlike the free agents of our era, however, these players were talented amateur players. Indeed, high school and college players constituted the remaining vestige of a free market for baseball labor during the postwar era. Until an amateur signed a contract in organized baseball, he could negotiate with any team, because there was no draft. Baseball owners would be better off collectively by creating "single-buyer" bidding for amateurs via a draft. However, some owners, pursuing self-interest, opposed such a draft; there was internal tension between owners within the cartel.

Exploiting the Young Ballplayer

The owners quickly discovered that this free market for labor was costly. Baseball officials and the press often exaggerated the bonuses paid to callow youths, but whatever the true figures, baseball people worried about the expenditures. Even as early as the late 1940s, some youngsters were reportedly receiving bonuses of nearly $100,000. Owners repeatedly passed legislation in hopes of curbing the spending.

The owners' attempts to curb spending on amateur players sparked allegations of cheating that led to distrust among them. Several called not for new rules but for better enforcement of the existing rules. Because effective enforcement required owners to fully divulge their finances to the commissioner's office, such calls for enforcement usually met resistance. George Weiss, of the Yankees, did not approve of the first-year rule in the mid-1950s, whereby a player given a sizable bonus had to remain on the Major League roster or else be exposed to a draft.

Weiss suggested that baseball, instead, hire a bonus administrator to monitor activity. "The first-year draft rule is a menace. It threatens baseball. It discourages the signing of many precocious young men. When you face that, you are undermining the game. . . . You are forced to rush [the bonus player] onto your major roster. This creates injustice to older players."[1]

Another problem with the rule requiring placing bonus babies on the Major League roster was the deleterious effects upon the young players. These youngsters often played sparingly in the Major League and missed the experience they would have gained in the minor leagues; bonus players were, therefore, retarded in their development. Branch Rickey made different arguments in his sermons against the demoralizing aspects of large bonuses: "The bonus is unfair to the older players, and, in general, hurts team morale. It is unearned and undeservedly by its recipient and, in many cases, corrupts the boy morally and economically."[2] Frank Lane, too, disliked the bonus system: "the bonus is a curse to too many of the young players. It destroys their incentive. With all that money in their pockets, they feel so secure that they're not keenly interested in learning how to play baseball." Baseball officials calling for the amateur draft in the hopes of curbing large bonuses were saying, in essence, "We'll exploit you and it will be good for your soul." Bing Devine, however, pointed out that the large bonuses induced youngsters to choose MLB over the other professional sports.[3]

Why did Major League teams pay so much for untested youngsters? One sportswriter thought, "it costs about $200,000 to develop a ballplayer from the time he enters a club system in the lower minors until he is ready for the majors—if he ever is. Accordingly, if a bonus player makes good his first season or two, he will have been a bargain even at $100,000."[4] Although independent minor league teams could produce players for about half as much as MLB teams using a bonus system, the owners preferred the security of controlling talented players, rather than face open bidding for an AAA star.[5]

At the December 1962 meetings, owners turned down three proposals to replace the first-year player draft. The proposals would purportedly eliminate loopholes in the current rules.[6]

Walter O'Malley weighed in with his opinion of the bonus system. He disapproved of both the unrestricted draft of minor league players and the free-agent draft: "These are good, old socialistic ideas. I don't believe such ideas have any place in baseball. The inevitable effect of all socialistic experiments is bad. . . . Those who are willing to spend their money should be permitted to do so. Those who aren't willing must accept the consequences."[7] He argued that the bonus system merely needed better enforcement and that the nation's tax structure would ensure enforcement: "Every club employs a national firm of accountants. They wouldn't run the risk of permitting any skullduggery. The clubs' books would clearly show what was paid to each player."[8]

A draft of amateur players was an obvious solution to the escalating bonuses. As early as 1959, Paul Richards, a prominent baseball manager and official, suggested an unrestricted amateur draft before a Senate hearing. Proponents urged setting minimum bonuses for boys selected in the draft, perhaps as much as $20,000 in bonus and first-year salary. Setting the level of the bonus was tricky. Too high a level and owners would not reduce their bonus payments by much; too low a level and talented youngsters might opt to play another sport or, in the case of college graduates, jobs in business. Each team would get a single pick, but there would be three drafts throughout the year; though the plan was promising, owners voted against it during their December 1959 meetings.[9]

Creating the Amateur Draft in Baseball

The amateur or free-agent draft idea would not die. By 1961, American League owners recommended that MLB institute a free-agent draft, whereby teams would pay a specified amount for players. The owners were now willing to risk any legal challenges to such a draft. Baseball's reserve clause was the chief legal issue. Pro football's policy of signing players for two years, with the second year being an option year, was essentially an informal reserve clause. However, the distinction was sufficient to raise questions about the legality of combining a draft with a reserve clause. Because baseball signed many youngsters upon high school graduation, some before they had reached majority status, there was concern about drafting high school boys. Finally, the draft would further reduce the minor leagues' incentives to discover talented youngsters. According to sportswriter Dan Daniel, twelve of the twenty teams favored a draft and four teams did not. He did not name the holdouts, although the successful Milwaukee Braves, New York Yankees, Los Angeles Dodgers, and San Francisco Giants were likely candidates. Commissioner Ford Frick supported a congressional bill making the draft legal for football, in the hope that legislators would grant baseball a similar right.[10]

Growing dissatisfaction over the first-year player rule again induced baseball owners to investigate an amateur draft as a solution to the bonus problem. The Los Angeles Angels signed Rick Reichardt for a $200,000 bonus during the summer of 1964; the bonus, if correctly reported, was enough to buy twenty-five first-year players from that draft.[11] At MLB's summer meetings, the teams split evenly on the proposed amateur draft. The dissenters wanted to toughen the existing first-year rule. A number of them were concerned over the legal ramifications of implementing an amateur draft but agreed to further discuss the proposal in

December.[12] Baseball attorney Lou Carroll suggested that, "The U.S. Supreme Court decided in the *Toolson* case that the business of baseball is not subject to federal antitrust laws. I would regard a free-agent player draft as a rule or regulation of the business of baseball."[13]

Baseball could take comfort that several of the justices who ruled on *Toolson* remained on the bench, so the result could be similar for a ruling on the amateur draft. There also did not appear to be much sympathy for any potential plaintiff: "the 17-year-old high school boy who no longer would be able to get a Pontiac convertible for each member of his family, plus a big bonus for himself, is not a particularly appealing plaintiff."[14] The owners' worries about retroactive triple-damage suits, therefore, appeared groundless.

Leslie O'Connor, longtime assistant to former commissioner Judge Kenesaw Mountain Landis, opposed the free-agent draft because he believed it denied the amateur player his constitutional right in choosing his baseball employer.[15] O'Connor gave a lengthy and, at times, eloquent argument against the draft: "If S. 2391 be enacted, its proponents ought to be congratulated or condemned, as the viewpoint may be, for an atavistic achievement. For that will be a denial of human rights, of labor's rights, and a throw-back of over six hundred years to the despotic first labor laws of England—the *Ordinance of Laborers* and the *Statute of Laborers*."[16] He continued by pointing out that the draft denied due process of law to players, allowed the owners to confiscate some of value of the player's rights to his labor, and deprived players and owners of their constitutional freedom of contract. The latter loss to the owners, of course, came as a price of the owners gaining single-buyer power over the players, so readers might not feel sympathy for the owners.[17]

Even Charles O. Finley, who was no patron saint of player rights, admitted the wrongs involved in the draft: "[Major League owners] adapted a free agent draft to eliminate the excessive bonus bidding, thereby solving its own problem at the expense of the prospective player."[18]

Bill Veeck identified a potentially explosive legal problem with signing eighteen-year-olds to contracts involving the reserve clause: "If he develops quickly enough, he is *legally entitled to disaffirm* [italics his]. When you sign an eighteen-year-old kid, you have to get his father's signature. By the nature of the baseball contract, the father is signing the boy's bargaining rights away in perpetuity." He pointed out that such a contract probably would not hold up in court, and the boy could repudiate the contract upon turning twenty-one. "Would owners conspire not to sign the theoretical free agent? No other club would sign a boy who disaffirmed? Yes, they would. Otherwise he would have them locked in a perfect conspiracy case, for he has already established, on his previous year's play, that he is more than worthy of playing in the major league. They'd sign him all right, or the baseball contract would face a court test under the worst set of circumstances that could possibly be found."[19]

Leo DeOrsey, an attorney who was once a director of the Washington Senators, also raised the "infant" question when testifying before a Senate committee in 1958; he stated that baseball understood the potential legal ramifications, but that it came up with a solution: "And you will notice that in the hearings before the House Mr. Frick testified about infants, and the gist of his testimony was that if an infant signs a contract, and when he reaches the age of 21, if he does not want to agree to continue playing with that team, entering into a new contract, he is placed on a restrictive list, which means he cannot play for anyone until he comes to terms with that club."[20] The baseball owners' solution was clearly self-serving.

Aside from legal aspects, other observers expressed doubts about the free-agent draft. Not everyone thought that a reverse-order draft would significantly reduce bonuses. Sportswriter Bill Bryson believed that the new amateur free-agent draft was not likely to reduce spending on young talent or to equalize competition; he cited ten-to-one odds against any bonus player "making good in the majors."[21] Unfortunately, he did not supply any evidence supporting his claim.

Initially, eight American League teams voted against the measure, with one club abstaining.[22] Why did some owners oppose a draft of amateur players? First, wealthier teams preferred the status quo, despite the rising bonuses. The wealthier teams could use their advantages in producing revenue to outbid their less-wealthy peers. The stronger teams were therefore against "socialism" in signing amateur players. Second, some baseball officials opposed the amateur draft because of the aforementioned legal ramifications. The football and basketball drafts dealt with college graduates, males who had reached majority.

MLB owners continued to adjust their proposed amateur draft. The revised plan called for three drafts per year. The main draft would happen in June. A second draft in the winter would cover players graduating midyear. The third draft in September would include players in American Legion baseball. Players who refused to sign with the team that drafted them would go into a special draft the following year. To forestall chicanery, the special draft would follow a random order, so a player would not know which team would get his rights on the second round. Lee MacPhail hoped that, "The big bonuses—the top 20 or so—might be cut down and the rule probably would put an end to six figure bonuses, but the average boy wouldn't be affected."[23]

Some observers hoped the new rule would whittle down the New York Yankees. As one baseball sportswriter observed, "The untold millions of CBS will not help them. Neither will the skills of the scouts gathered in the years of their glory."[24] The Yankees did, in fact, go into a decline after the 1964 season. Given that the majority of the players selected in the initial free-agent draft did not appear in the Major Leagues until the late 1960s, blaming the Yankees' slide on the draft is dubious. Researcher David Thomas pointed out that baseball's draft did not necessarily relegate good teams from having good fortune with their draft selections. The Boston Red Sox and Cincinnati Reds, despite having winning records, did quite well by the draft.[25]

When the St. Louis Cardinals began the trend toward farm systems in the 1920s, Major League teams differed greatly in their ability to introduce good players. The disparity in introducing talent dwindled in the postwar years; the amateur draft continued the trend.[26] Teams appeared more evenly matched in the competition for good young talent.

MLB owners were fortunate that although legislators questioned them regarding their proposed free-agent draft in 1964, much of the draft's purpose had been established in earlier hearings on football's and basketball's drafts.

The NFL and the Reverse-Order Draft

Baseball's efforts to get a draft coincided with legislators examining the NFL's draft. Football commissioner Bert Bell claimed that the reverse-order player drafts were necessary to ensure competitive balance, his Holy Grail. Detroit scout Bob Nussbaumer's statement, when the Lions were beginning to deteriorate, echoed Bell's argument: "It's finally catching up with us. You need good, fresh material each year—and we just haven't been getting it."[27]

Bell was proud of the player draft, because he had proposed it in 1936. At that time he owned the floundering Philadelphia Eagles. The stated purpose was to give weak franchises an opportunity to bid for top-notch collegians without being swamped by New York or Chicago dollars. Bell showed that aside from the Bears, Giants, Packers, and Redskins, other teams rarely made the championship game. He told the antitrust committee that the four top teams won 252 games and lost only fifty-nine against the other six teams between 1933 and 1946.[28] "The kids would play for less for [winning teams] than they would for us [Philadelphia]."[29] Bell convinced the owners that the reverse-order draft would promote competitive balance. He attributed passage of the proposal to the owners of wealthy teams' willingness to help their less-fortunate brethren, but economists suspect a more self-interested motive: the player draft forces collegiate players to negotiate with only one team.[30]

George Halas, as did most owners, discounted the draft-created disparity in bargaining strength between owners and players. He testified that the system was "completely fair in that it permits a team to select a player for the position it needs the most. . . . The fact that a player has been chosen for a particular position to help strengthen the team which chooses him gives him a high bargaining power for his services."[31]

Creighton Miller viewed the draft's rationale differently: The player either signed with the team that drafted him or he did not play professional football. The abrogation of a player's right to choose his employer was unique, and "It can be justified only if to depart from it would destroy the entertainer's livelihood—a possibility too remote to warrant consideration. This system is employed to equalize competition and minimize salaries." Miller, though, worried that without some sort of antitrust exemption, even if it "remove[d] one of the few legal remedies presently available to the players, it is apparent that, if this treble damage theory is misused, it can destroy professional football by bankrupting the owners."[32]

Legislators expressed concerns regarding the draft. They worried that players might be forced to play with teams they disdained. Bell and the owners testified that teams sent questionnaires to prospective players prior to the draft to ascertain a player's willingness to play for a particular team.[33] NFL owners defended their draft by claiming they would not knowingly draft a player who did not want to play for them, and also with their oft-repeated claim that theirs was a milder form of reserve clause than in baseball.

Bell cited a few cases where he persuaded owners to transfer a player to a city of his choice, given sufficient cause. He claimed, "No ballplayer is any good to a club if he is dissatisfied mentally or in any other way."[34] He also stated or bragged that, "We don't need to pay him a bonus, but when kids are just getting out of college and especially if they are married and they don't have a cent and they owe $400, $500, or $600, they usually get it." Bell said that a few players got true signing bonuses, but the players' lack of bargaining leverage undoubtedly undercut their ability to secure such bonuses.[35]

Bell opposed a system whereby players would be required to give their written consent before becoming subject to the player selection. He quoted sports columnist Lewis F. Atchison of the *Washington Evening Star* in support of his argument that written permission was unnecessary: "As for a player's freedom being abridged, that's technically correct but usually not true. . . . As [Red] Smith [New York sportswriter] pointed out, teams don't like to waste draft choices. So it's a selfish motive, but the young man doesn't get picked by a team he won't play with."[36]

After World War II, a number of the owners of stronger teams demanded an occasional crack at the top choice in the draft, so they began a draft lottery. Unlike the NBA's draft lottery where only mediocre teams participated, the NFL's version let every team have a chance at the "bonus pick," which was a choice made before the reverse-order draft. Once a team got its bonus pick, it was ineligible for another bonus choice until every other team had received one. The bonus pick revealed that the successful owners' willingness to help their less-fortunate fellows was limited.[37]

Legislators criticized the bonus pick lottery, but not because the lottery reduced any beneficial effects upon competitive balance. The legislators worried more about the lottery's randomness. Bell backpedaled quickly from the lottery and unctuously stated, "We are perfectly willing to eliminate the bonus pick." Considering only the Chicago Cardinals had not received their bonus pick, it was a convenient time to end the program. The NFL owners at first tried to revamp the bonus pick but could not devise a way to do so that it would not resemble a lottery.[38]

The owners were willing to move the draft up before the regular season ended when it suited their purposes in combatting rival leagues. Their willingness to do so belied their stated purpose of the draft for redressing competitive imbalance. A team finishing last after all of the returns were in might have ended up with a less-attractive draft position because of its partial-season record.[39]

Did the draft create more evenly matched teams? Bell admitted that the reverse-order player draft did not immediately improve competitive balance. He blamed some teams' lack of scouting collegiate players for their poor results. Craig Coenen showed that the downtrodden Steelers, Eagles, Cardinals, and Tigers won 35.2 percent of their games between 1932 and 1935, but the four teams won just 29.1 percent during the first ten seasons with the draft. Only the Washington Redskins improved much in the years after the new system.[40] After decades of predraft analysis and hype, modern fans do not realize that they probably devote more attention and effort to the draft than the owners did in February 1936.[41] To buttress his belief in the draft's later efficacy, Bert Bell testified that some teams began buying scouting information from Norman Sper, in addition to consulting Grantland Rice's All-America list. Bell further mentioned that some owners paid college coaches $200 a year to scout for them.[42]

If the draft did improve parity, it did so with a lag. *Sports Illustrated's* Tex Maule claimed that of the rookies kept on NFL rosters, "only two or three a year in the entire 12-team NFL are apt to be good enough to play first string. . . . Ordinarily, a team which must depend on more than one or two rookies in its starting lineup has little or no chance to go all the way to a title."[43] Maule's estimate of "only two or three a year" appears to be an exaggeration. If the average NFL career lasted only three or four seasons, then the turnover had to approximate 25 to 33 percent of the rosters each season.

Jay Berwanger was the first Heisman Trophy winner and the first pick in the NFL's inaugural draft. He passed up an NFL career with the hapless Philadelphia Eagles. The last-place Eagles were unable to sign any of their nine draft choices.

Owners often came up empty handed in the early drafts. Player salaries did not greatly exceed jobs in industry, so talented players did not automatically opt for a pro career. Given that the vast majority of players were college graduates, often with other attractive career choices, NFL owners faced the same problem as BAA/NBA owners of the 1940–1950s: not having enough gate receipts to be able to offer sufficiently high salaries to entice some talented scholar-athletes to play professional sports.[44]

Bell later often boasted of the draft's ability to bolster weak teams, such as the Baltimore Colts, who went from a feeble, revived club to world champions between 1953 and 1958. The Colts' ascension was led by quarterback Johnny Unitas, who the team picked up as a free agent. In an attempt to allay fears that the draft suppressed salaries, Bell also claimed player salaries jumped 300 percent during the postwar period.[45] Bell also used the Browns' decade-long dominance as evidence of why the reverse-order draft was necessary; he ignored the obvious question: If the draft was an effective leveler, how did the Browns maintain their dominance?[46]

Not all of the players applauded the draft. One player openly testified against the reverse-order draft. George Ratterman stated, "I do not believe it can definitely be determined that such [dire effects] would be the result of eliminating the player draft. Professional baseball has existed for many years without a player draft similar to that of football." He implored the committee to ensure that any antitrust exemption include safeguards for players' rights. "If the players cannot resort to the courts of this country, they must have some other body to which they can appeal."[47]

Paul Dixon pointed to an article by sportswriter Shirley Povich. Povich had interviewed a player, who requested anonymity. The player stated that he thought the draft system was unfair, because he could not seek the best offer from all of the teams. "The truths of that situation [college draft] when fully developed could be sufficient to jolt the Senators into wonderment how the pro football league has gotten away with their unconscionable draft of college boys all these years."[48]

Bell retorted that, "98 percent of the players in the National League, with the salaries they are getting, would vote in favor of the player selection question." The commissioner failed to provide any evidence of such a poll, but Dixon did not press him on the issue. Bell eventually admitted that if a player did not want to play for the NFL team that drafted him, "He can go to Canada." He also admitted under Dixon's grilling that the draft did not allow a player to market his abilities competitively. "That is right. It does not and when it does there won't be any more pro football because you go back to the days when I had a football team and there were four great teams. . . . [T]he player selection system is the greatest thing that ever happened."[49] Bell came off poorly in this aspect of his testimony.

Dixon continued to press Bell, and Bell finally claimed that without the draft, "the four top teams, financially speaking would sign each year at least 100 of the top ballplayers in the United States."[50] Given the thirty-five-player limit and the continued service of veterans, his statement could, at best, be charitably regarded as an exaggeration.

University of Oklahoma coach Bud Wilkinson also disputed Bell's claim of fabulous player salary increases, noting that unless the player made the team, he received little or no compensation.[51] Wilkinson took exception to Bell's claim that football's more liberal reserve clause mitigated any unfairness of the player draft; Wilkinson declared that young baseball players were able to sign with whichever team he wanted, offsetting baseball's more stringent reserve clause.[52]

Wilkinson was asked whether he could identify the best talent in a draft. He responded, "I would have a tremendous amount of difficulty." Wilkinson amended his statement by saying that a coach might be looking for a player to fill a particular skill or position, which might refine the search to 25 to 30 players.[53]

Another college coach, Duffy Daugherty of Michigan State University, also disliked the draft, saying, "the good Lord Jesus with all his omnipotence had one guy go astray among the disciples, and you never know when one Judas can upset the whole applecart." He further stated that he would have difficulty choosing the first draft pick out of four hundred prospective college seniors. "If Bud [Wilkinson] and Bowden [Wyatt] and I each had the opportunity now to go throughout the country, maybe Bud and Bowden can do this, but we can't and pick out the 40 or 50 best freshmen. . . . I daresay that only 10 of the 50 or maybe one-fourth of them would came [*sic*] through and play football for us." He also alluded to NFL stars who never received much glory in college.[54] Daugherty did not believe that the draft would affect competitive balance, because football depended on the morale factor. He concluded, "It would take a magician to pick the ability of certain football players."[55]

Predicting pro football stardom was difficult. Table 6 shows that having the bonus pick did not always result in a quality player. The teams had remarkably little success with their bonus picks.[56] Hornung became a superb player, but the Cleveland Browns did quite well with their pick of Jim Brown, the fifth player chosen in the first round.[57]

In touting the 1958 rookies, sportswriter Joe King applauded the reverse-order draft. He asserted that because more first-round choices were in the league than any later round, this dispelled "the charge that the draft is merely a grab-bag, with the order of picking signifying little." King, though, failed to demonstrate that the team with the first pick of each round did better than teams with later choices on every round.[58] Although the earliest rounds had the highest likelihoods of producing All-NFL players, the fact that almost half the All-Pro players went in the fifth round or later or were undrafted raises questions about the draft's ability to affect competitive balance.[59]

The availability of eventual All-NFL stars in the late rounds confirmed the difficulty in identifying such talent. A pretty solid team could have been comprised of undrafted Hall of Fame players such as Emlen Tunnell, Night Train Lane, and Big Daddy Lipscomb. These African American players may have been neglected because of their race and because they played for obscure college programs.

Teams had wildly different success in drafting players who later attained All-NFL status. The Washington Redskins and Chicago Cardinals, despite usually having early picks in the drafts, continued to wallow in mediocrity because of their inability to spot future stars.[60]

Bell expressed concern about teams, especially weaker squads, trading draft choices for immediate help. After Pittsburgh Steelers' coach Buddy Parker traded some of his picks, Bell proposed a rule forbidding "deals involving future picks after Labor Day. That date is, on the average, about four weeks before the season's opener." Bell thought his proposal would keep teams possessing an excess of talent from benefitting by "holding surplus players until the cutdown date, and would release them earlier for the benefit of teams suffering from the manpower pinch." Joe King pointed out that, "The craze [for trading draft picks] started after Jim Lee Howell of the Giants developed his world's champions of last December [1956] with the future-trading practice an important element." Howell had traded five of his 1955 picks, his first pick for 1956, and his first and fourth picks for the current season.[61]

Basketball's Draft and Provincialism

The NBA draft's explicit purpose of maintaining or improving competitive balance seemed plausible to many people. NBA fans may recall the coin flip between the Milwaukee Bucks and Phoenix Suns with Lew Alcindor—later known as Kareem Abdul-Jabbar—as first prize and Neal Walk as second prize. Milwaukee, though, eventually traded Abdul-Jabbar to the big-city Los Angeles Lakers. In contrast, the NFL's draft initially produced few dramatic moments and modest change in the league standings by 1941.

BAA owners quickly implemented a reverse-order draft of amateur players, similar to that of the NFL. The BAA created its own twist: the territorial draft. The basketball owners believed that giving teams a special right to select local college stars would boost audiences.[62]

In the NBA at the time, you almost had to possess one of three players on your team to win the championship series: George Mikan, Bill Russell, or Wilt Chamberlain. Between the 1949 and 1969 finals, just four teams won the title without one of these centers. Russell was the second pick in the 1956 draft; he was immediately traded to Boston. Rochester had the first pick in the draft, but owner Les Harrison said he could not afford to sign the player. Chamberlain was a territorial pick. The reverse-order draft was of little use in assigning these players. Mikan had been assigned to Minneapolis, after his Chicago team folded. The regular draft, therefore, was not a particularly effective instigator of competitive balance.[63]

Conclusion: Owners Win, Players Lose from the Draft

The NFL's and NBA's reverse-order draft, at best, offered only an opportunity for mediocre teams to improve, as the draft did not guarantee competitive balance. Individual owners and coaches' inattention, bad luck, and other factors transformed the draft into an uncertain process by which clever or lucky owners could maintain their team's superiority. Even had the drafts worked as predicted by contemporary wisdom, they still might not have had long-run effects upon competitive balance. If the Pittsburgh Steelers or Green Bay Packers had drafted, say, star quarterback Sid Luckman, his ability to rejuvenate a team and to attract fans could have created an arbitrage opportunity: Art Rooney or the Packers' management would have been offered lucrative offers from the Chicago Bears or New York Giants for the quarterback. Many economists believe that, at best, the reverse-order draft provides an opportunity for owners of teams in smaller cities to receive financial windfalls but creates no long-term improvement in competitive balance.

Congress did not tamper with the leagues' reverse-order draft, despite the legislators' concerns about the drafts' justice or the efficacy in promoting competitive balance. Perhaps they worried that tampering with the drafts would create irreparable harm for the sports leagues, for which the public and owners would blame them. Current players had little incentive to criticize the draft, and if the draft suppressed rookie salaries, perhaps it left more money for veteran salaries. No one really stood up for the rights of the college players.

6

Should Antitrust Apply to Sports? *1957 and 1958*

The congressional hearings frequently concentrated on a single topic, such as television blackouts or a merger, but some hearings, such as those of 1957 and 1958, were of a more general nature: should basketball, football, and hockey be given a broad antitrust exemption similar to that of baseball? This chapter examines these issues.

Legislators and sports officials recognized that the professional sports leagues' different statuses under the antitrust laws were anomalous. Legislators considered either granting basketball, football, and hockey the same antitrust exemption afforded baseball or stripping baseball of its antitrust exemption. Some legislators favored a course of granting antitrust exemptions only for specific actions, including player control, territorial rights, and commissioners' powers.

The *Radovich* case threatened to disrupt the sports leagues' unity. Early in the proceedings, commissioner Bert Bell told NFL owners that baseball commissioner Happy Chandler informed him that the baseball owners wanted the NFL to settle the case.[1] A later MLB commissioner, Ford Frick, later refused to comment on Bell's questioning of "the right of baseball to remain immune from antitrust laws after the Supreme Court had ruled professional football a 'business,' which he considered discriminatory. The baseball owners worried about the upcoming hearings and scheduled a special meeting to discuss the matter."[2]

A Stampede to Introduce Bills

The Supreme Court's ruling in *Radovich* spurred legislators to introduce bills pertaining to professional sports and antitrust. Representative Patrick J. Hillings (Calif.) was candid in explaining why he introduced his bill: it would help his constituents get Major League franchises. Another representative, Kenneth B. Keating of New York, called for a congressional investigation of abuses in pro football. The next day, Oren Harris, Democratic representative from Arkansas, introduced his bill, which would exempt all four sports from antitrust laws. His fellow Democrat, Emanuel Celler, chided Harris for taking a "step backward," before introducing his own bill.[3]

The Antitrust Subcommittee of the Committee on the Judiciary decided to hold hearings in 1957 involving the sports leagues, with Celler chairing. Keating stated the purpose of the hearings: "These bills would place the ordinary commercial activities of professional team sports under the antitrust laws, but would specifically exempt from antitrust enforcement certain practices considered essential to the successful operation of these sports." Keating and Celler opposed granting a complete exemption.[4]

The NFL's struggle with the AAFC generated publicity. Before the AAFC-NFL strife, Congress and the Department of Justice paid little attention to the NFL. Professional football's strife and ensuing prosperity came with an unanticipated cost: federal scrutiny. The committee members focused on the owners' territorial rights, reserve clause, draft, and television policies. Were these potential violations of antitrust law necessary to maintain the league?

Football, basketball, and hockey officials and owners hoped for at least a partial antitrust exemption. Their league presidents and commissioners used a Chicken Little motif: Without antitrust protection, the professional sports sky would fall. Baseball owners were sympathetic toward their fellow owners; however, they were also leery of becoming too involved.[5] The baseball owners worried that a legal challenge to their antitrust exemption might erode or negate their privileges.

The leagues took similar approaches in agitating for partial or full antitrust exemptions.

The NFL and Antitrust Legislation

The NFL, through Bert Bell, decided to seek legal protection through a partial rather than a full antitrust exemption for their practices. The owners believed they had some persuasive arguments for granting antitrust exemptions. Their business operations were similar to MLB's. The NFL owners claimed, too, to have a less stringent reserve clause than did MLB.

To develop a favorable image, the NFL sent congressional legislators "a forty-three-page brochure entitled, *The Story of Professional Football in Summary*." Although Bell was not the suave, polished master of public relations that Pete Rozelle would be, he proved pugnacious and confident in the justness of the

NFL's cause. He saw to it that the owners were depicted as viewing football as an avocation, a hobby, and that profits were incidental.[6]

Bell testified at the 1957 hearings that the NFL would be satisfied with any of the proposed bills exempting the four essentials: player draft, reserve clause, commissioner's authority, and territorial rights.[7] "If any of these should now be held by the courts to be an unreasonable restraint of trade, organized professional football, the highly competitive and colorful sport that we know today, would come to an end. It would inevitably revert to its former state when four top clubs won most of the games and the public refused to support the poor teams which were unable to acquire good players."[8]

The NFL's chief argument in an earlier television case, presided over by Judge Allan K. Grim, had been to co-opt baseball's exemption by claiming that "professional football is not a trade or commerce within the meaning of the Sherman Anti-Trust Act" and that other aspects, such as television or radio broadcasts, were incidental.[9] A second aspect of the television lawsuit that NFL owners would refer to during the later hearings was the legal costs of defending the league against antitrust charges. Bell argued that the television lawsuit had already cost the league $50,000.[10] Reporters quoted an NFL attorney who said that a government victory in the lawsuit would be the "death knell of pro football"; his statement of doom set another precedent for NFL behavior in subsequent antitrust discussions. Bell echoed the dire consequences the next day by testifying that "professional football could not survive with unlimited radio and television broadcasts of games." Although government attorneys got Bell to back down on his claim, he was persuasive enough that Judge Grim granted the league permission to blackout telecasts of live games in the home team's territory."[11]

Bell's later concern that the NFL would be besieged by lawsuits if it did not get antitrust protection possessed some credibility. The Liberty Broadcasting System, upset that the NFL did not grant it telecasting rights, filed a $2.1 million dollar lawsuit against the league, citing antitrust violations. Liberty had previously filed a lawsuit against MLB. One could consider the company's penchant for filing lawsuits as sour grapes, considering that other broadcasting companies had won the rights to telecast baseball and football games. Baseball owners settled the lawsuit for $200,000, but Bell and the owners resisted such a tactic: "we settle with no one."[12]

During the 1958 hearings, Senator Estes Kefauver questioned Bell regarding the commissioner's claim that without an antitrust exemption the NFL would be bankrupted by lawsuits. Bell used the Radovich and Liberty Broadcasting suits, as well as a threatened players association lawsuit, to buttress his claim. Senator Kefauver was not sympathetic: "Just threatening you with a suit does not cause you very much trouble, if the suit is not brought, does it?" Bell, undaunted, retorted, "No, it does not, but it causes you a lot of anxiety about what it may cost you if it is brought."[13]

To allay claims that the NFL was commerce, Bell told the 1957 committee that the NFL remained "a comparatively small operation." He testified that in 1956, the twelve teams combined had less than $13 million in gross receipts and player payrolls of $3,750,000, or rough 30 percent of receipts.[14]

During the NFL's television antitrust trial, Bell pled poverty before Judge Grim. He testified that just four clubs made "real money" during the 1952 season, while six lost money. He had advised owners to adopt cost-cutting measures such as roster reductions, decreases in food and hotel allowances, and a reduction in the visiting team's guarantee. He did not explain how the last would help the league as a whole, considering the visiting team's guarantee was simply a redistribution of revenue and not a collective expense. He said that the league considered eliminating the point after touchdown to conserve $17 footballs, which would save $6,000. The owners agreed that, if they lost the case, they would have to reduce salaries by 20 percent.[15] After Grim's favorable decision, league owners were more willing to admit, or at least not to deny, that prosperity had arrived in the NFL, and readers could now vicariously revel in the NFL's "biggest dollar profit in history."[16]

Testifying before the congressional investigation in 1957, Bell made sure that NFL owners, if not claiming insolvency, did not appear too prosperous. His *The Story of Professional Football* stated that the average team made just $50,000 in profits, or $600,000 collectively, "while the Federal government collected more than $900,000 in admission taxes—approximately 33% more than the combined net income of the 12 clubs comprising the NFL."[17]

Bell's case was later reinforced by Sam Fox, a professor of accountancy at the University of Illinois. Fox examined the data presented to Congress in 1957. He criticized the league for its poor, 2 percent rate of return on sales. "In any business, that would be a poor return on investment, and when you figure the most profitable franchise had only a 2 percent return on sales, it is indeed anything but a good business venture by any business criteria or standards." He added, "the average club owner has to virtually be a millionaire or he couldn't conceivably carry on. No businessman following principles of business policy would ever dream of investing, or should we say highly speculating on a franchise under such conditions. . . . If you haven't got millions to lose don't go into the football business."[18] His analysis was dubious, though. First, why use return on sales instead of returns on investment? NFL owners had little investment in physical capital. During this time period, few had invested more than a few hundred thousand dollars in their franchise in terms of franchise purchase prices or prior losses. Second, rising franchise values indicated that current net income or anticipated future net income were positive; the purchase provided great tax benefits; or the owner was willing to pay for the enjoyment and satisfaction of owning a professional sports team.

Most owners did not regularly pay shareholders and themselves dividends. Cleveland Browns' owner Arthur "Mickey" McBride told reporters that he had "never taken a penny out of it. Sometimes the team, as a corporation, has made a little money. Not much, just a little. But personally I've never tapped it." Most of McBride's fellow owners acted similarly. The league reported almost $2 million in net profit after taxes for the 1952–1956 seasons, but the owners distributed less than $225,000 in dividends.[19]

Some of the owners' requests were clearly anticompetitive. Bell referred the congressional committee to the NFL's policies with regard to territorial rights. International waters are just a few miles offshore in extent, but sports owners demanded and enacted protection encompassing a seventy-five-mile radius. Territorial limits applied to television broadcasts, too.[20]

The history of professional team sports, though, included exceptions to the territorial limits, even within leagues; sometimes owners would settle the disputes with cash indemnities. Bell and the owners' defense of the rule were, at times, contradictory. Bell stated that without territorial protection, other teams might encroach upon another in the same city; he indicated that this was why owners required unanimous consent for a team to move into another team's territory. He also explained how adding new franchises could cause scheduling problems; the incumbent owners also wanted to scrutinize the character and finances of prospective owners. He argued that these reasons justified the supermajorities required to sell, transfer, or add franchises.[21]

Bell admitted that two teams operated in relative harmony in the city of Chicago, well within the seventy-five-mile radius. The owners countenanced other exceptions to the territorial limits. Washington owner George Preston Marshall, somewhat less harmoniously than the Chicago teams, demanded and received an indemnity from the incoming Baltimore Colts. The league provided a letter between Marshall and the renewed Baltimore franchise detailing their agreement that consisted of four $25,000 payments made between January 3, 1953 and July 1, 1954.[22]

Some congressional committee members sought to halve the territorial limit to thirty-five miles, but Bell opposed this. He worried that reducing the territorial limits in the face of television technology could "knock that attendance off because the fellow will get in his car and drive 35, 40, or 50 miles, but the closer the picture on TV, the smaller the attendance." Bell appealed to an earlier judicial ruling: "We believe that 75 miles is fair—we went through all this with the television and radio people, in the court with Judge Grim and the Federal Government, and I think we established with Judge Grim that it was reasonable."[23]

Owners wanted an antitrust exemption for their commissioners' or presidents' authority to act on their behalf. Owners pursuing their self-interest sometimes proved detrimental to the collective. One of a league commissioner or president's duties was to resolve these dilemmas, which are essentially the famous Prisoners' Dilemma found in game theory. In a Prisoners' Dilemma situation, when all actors rationally exercised their best strategy, the net result could be that the group would be worse off. An example of the desirability of a firm hand concerned scheduling games. NFL owners perpetually fought for favorable schedules, so they opted to let Bell create the schedule.

Kenneth Harkins pinned Bell in a conundrum. He asked Bell whether any courts had ruled "the four phases of professional football activities for which you request an antitrust exemption" to be violations of the antitrust laws. Bell could only answer no. Harkins then retorted, "Is it your view that if Congress were to exempt these activities at this time, that that exemption would amount to an implication that these activities were unreasonable and unlawful before they were exempted?" Bell replied, "Well, I do not believe that if Congress enacted a law, that it should revert back." Harkins eventually induced Bell to admit that the league had changed its reserve clause in 1946 because of concerns that the original contract might not pass muster in a court.[24]

Harkins examined Article 16, Section 1 of the league's bylaws: "the minimum price for reserved tickets for any regularly scheduled championship games [regular-season games] shall be $1.50 plus tax and a minimum of $1 plus tax for all unreserved adult tickets." He asked Bell whether he was aware that price fixing was prohibited under the antitrust laws. Bell admitted that he was aware, so Harkins asked whether the NFL was asking for an exemption for price fixing. Bell replied, "I believe it is in the best interests of the player, and the best interests of the league, and in the best interests of the public." Harkins also highlighted the bylaws covering fixing prices of the "world professional football championship games" and the special arrangement between the Colts and Redskins. Baltimore could not sell tickets for less than Washington and vice versa, so the two teams had to agree on setting prices. Bell said the purpose of these bylaws was, "they want the lowest price established. They don't want to compete against each other. . . . We don't believe that two teams in the same locality, one team selling a seat for 75 cents and the other selling a seat for $4—we believe it will hurt both of them."[25]

The committee members later queried Bell about the league's compliance with the previous hearing's suggestions. Paul Dixon, the Senate counsel, asked if the league had changed its bylaws regarding minimum ticket prices. Bell took the opportunity to point out that not only did the owners change the minimum ticket price clause, but they also eliminated the lottery bonus pick in the draft. The owners also made explicit the players' right to waive their hearings in front of the commissioner and to go to court. He concluded obsequiously, "We would be happy with anything that would keep us out of the courts and spell out the things that we have to have. I understood the Celler bill approved the selection of the college players, territorial rights, and so forth. I said before, we can live with television the way we are. We have no objection. It is up to you gentlemen as to what you want to give us. We are thankful to have the hearings." Bell was humble before the congressional committee, but he boasted to owners of their lobbyist's efficacy.[26]

Vertical Integration and Player Control

Baseball and hockey owners faced an additional potential antitrust violation: their farm systems. Branch Rickey of the St. Louis Cardinals pioneered so-called farm systems. He realized that the Cardinals could not compete with wealthier teams in obtaining top talent for independent minor league teams. Rickey decided to negotiate agreements with minor leagues for first rights to promising players. Over the years, the Cardinals purchased minor league teams or subsidized other minor league teams in return for priority in signing promising players. Though Rickey's acumen and initiative gave the Cardinals an initial advantage, in the long run, wealthier teams such as the Yankees and Dodgers could not only emulate the Cardinals but would surpass them.[27] Less wealthy owners clearly could not compete with the wealthier team in setting up farm systems. The farm systems of wealthy teams actually proved self-sustaining, if not profitable, as owners sold surplus players to their fellow owners. In essence, the farm systems were a form of vertical integration, whereby a firm controls the supply of an input; an automobile producer owning a tire manufacturer is a similar concept.

Rickey's farm system idea was not universally applauded. Baseball commissioner Judge Kenesaw Mountain Landis disapproved of the institution, because not all teams commanded sufficient resources to maintain effective farm systems. When the Cardinals and Detroit Tigers violated some of the rules pertaining to minor league players, Judge Landis freed scores of players. The institution survived Landis, though, and owners without the financial wherewithal to maintain extensive farm systems found themselves at a disadvantage in building good teams. The lack of a farm system, though, was not necessarily fatal, as the Chicago White Sox rose to prominence during the 1950s without an extensive system.[28]

Player control proved a controversial issue throughout the postwar era. As some teams created large farm systems with hundreds of players under their control, critics alleged that the talent-rich teams, such as the Yankees, Dodgers, and Cardinals, signed a disproportionate share of and hoarded good prospects. The charge of player hoarding was damaging, because the weaker teams lacked good talent and the players who stagnated on the farms lost potential earnings.[29] However, the critics rarely demonstrated that many talented players actually languished an inordinate length of time in the minor leagues. The Yankees and Dodgers often sold or traded many of their promising minor league players. The charge that the Yankees controlled vast legions of potential stars, though, irritated fans and pundits alike and, worse, invited congressional attention. Other baseball officials believed that competitive parity would have been improved had MLB set stricter limits on the control of such players.[30]

The owners' control of thousands of ballplayers helped MLB thwart any upstart league. Prospective baseball leagues faced difficulties in obtaining a supply of credible talent, as college baseball was not as important a source of supply as it would become. During the 1950s, college All-America baseball players gained little publicity compared with their basketball and football brethren. MLB owners testified that they lost large sums of money with their farm systems, but they gained control over a steady supply of new talent.

MLB owners dominated "organized baseball" through interlocking agreements, whereby all minor leagues submitted themselves to the caprice of the big-league owners. An upstart league, such as the Continental League, had to seek admission to organized baseball or be labeled an "outlaw league." If the Continental League failed to become a member of organized baseball, then the league would have difficulty getting players, as players would be risking their careers in organized baseball by playing for the new, uncertain league.

During their conflict, AAFC and NFL owners considered establishing affiliations with professional teams in smaller cities. NFL owners also occasionally considered operating minor league systems similar to MLB's. Because the postwar boom in spectator sports proved ephemeral, the football owners were fortunate that they did not invest too much in such teams. The NFL owners' real purpose for considering such affiliations was that they wanted places to stash their redundant players without exposing them to teams in the opposing league. From the perspectives of team owners in the lower professional football leagues, they hoped to align themselves with the NFL and get protection and respect for their player contracts, thereby precluding costly player contract jumping and raiding.[31]

The NFL's good will toward the Pacific Coast (Football) League, Dixie League, and American Association evaporated after the AAFC's demise. These leagues suffered financial reverses as the 1940s ended, and begged the NFL for help. At the January 1948 meetings, Bell stated that, "the NFL agreements with minor league affiliates meant very little to the NFL and that the minor leagues were handling their affairs in a very unsatisfactory manner both as to finances and to the character of ownerships . . . he would agree to any request for cancellation of our agreements with our minor league affiliates." There were no objections expressed by the members.[32]

Lower-level professional football leagues continued their tenuous existence throughout the 1950s, but the NFL did not have any formal ties with them. When the congressional committee asked the NFL about vertical integration, the NFL's lack of connections or ownership of outside teams redounded to its credit. Congressional committee members, therefore, had one less reason to view the league as exploitive. Bell emphasized in 1958 that the NFL had no formal ties with any other leagues.[33] He claimed that because NFL football was not a vocation but a means to an end for its players, a major-minor setup similar to MLB's was not attractive. Playing careers were too brief. "I think if a kid can't make it in 8 weeks' tryout after he has been to college, he ought to get a job elsewhere. But that is not a criticism of baseball, because they play 10 to 12 years in baseball."[34]

The Reserve Clause and Competitive Balance

Congress questioned the Major Leagues' monopolization of players during the mid-1950s, especially in conjunction with the issues of expansion and the Continental League. Some legislators even had the temerity to question the reserve clause and its effect upon competitive balance. During the 1958 Senate hearings, Paul Dixon, counsel for the Senate, pierced the myth surrounding the reserve clause. He asked Calvin Griffith, owner of the lackluster Senators: "Does not the reserve clause, and the unlimited number of ballplayers that the other major league teams can get, make it harder for you to get good ballplayers?" Griffith replied, "Well, we are not in financial position to go out and bid $100,000 to get ballplayers."[35] Dixon was even more aggressive with commissioner Ford Frick:

> Dixon: But isn't it also true that even with this reserve clause that you have had so long in baseball, the wealthier clubs are presently outbidding the poorer clubs by the use of the bonus rule that we have talked about?
>
> Frick: The reserve clause only keeps clubs from raiding each other.
>
> Dixon: But you say you do not want anybody to legislate mediocrity. God save us from mediocrity. But hasn't baseball, by the handling of its own

> house, in effect legislated mediocrity? A good example is the comparison of the New York Yankees and the Washington Senators.[36]

Senator Joseph O'Mahoney (Wyo.) took up the inquisition: "The fact is you have the reserve clause in the American League, but you do not have the equalization of competitive strength?" Frick answered, "Senator, that is true as of the year of our Lord 1958."[37]

Owners defending the reserve clause might have emphasized the events of the late 1940s. After the war, the military services released hundreds of ballplayers, many of whom were no longer under contract with any team. In 1946, football and basketball owners signed many players as free agents. Coaches would call players and offer to sign them. Those coaches with a keen eye for talent, such as football's Paul Brown and basketball's Arnold "Red" Auerbach, could amass inordinate amounts of talent. Brown's Cleveland teams dominated the AAFC, while Auerbach's Washington Capitols set a win-loss percentage that would not be surpassed for decades.

The main impetus for disparities between teams' records, though, was the teams' different abilities to draw large crowds. Branch Rickey, who was not known as a lavish spender, proclaimed at a Brooklyn football luncheon that he would be willing to "pay $100,000 for a great passer, but not a dime for a poor one."[38] Rickey certainly did not mean he would be willing to pay $100,000 in salary for a season, but that a top quarterback who rejuvenated a mediocre team into a crowd-pleasing winner was worth a considerable amount. A winning team meant different amounts of added revenue to NFL teams. The Coase/Rottenberg theory predicts players should move to where their marginal revenue product is highest. Rickey's point was simply that a good quarterback could increase Brooklyn's revenues sufficiently to justify paying a $100,000 price for him.

Economists James Quirk and Rodney Fort analyzed competitive balance in the NBA, NFL, NHL, and MLB using the ratio of actual standard deviation to idealized standard deviation (described in chapter 2) by decades. By this measure, MLB was less balanced than the NFL. The NBA was sometimes the least balanced, but at times it approached the idealized standard deviation (see Table 7).[39]

Bell often boasted that the NFL possessed better competitive balance than did MLB. The AAFC's competitive imbalance allegedly doomed that entity; as Bell put it, "Cleveland predominated. They were hand-picked throughout the services prior to the war, and came in there with the greatest aggregation of football players ever accumulated, in my opinion, on one team."[40] The Browns' four-year .898 win-loss record in the AAFC stood in stark contrast with the three teams that fielded .250 or worse records. Sportswriter Hal Lebovitz implied that the other AAFC teams were gradually catching up to the Browns; if so, it was too little too late.[41] Even Browns' fans tired of the lack of competition. By 1949, Browns' home attendance had fallen by half since 1946. Bell repeatedly claimed that he worked to help weak teams via the schedule, the draft, and other mechanisms. His successor, Pete Rozelle, also claimed that the Philadelphia Eagles and the Green Bay Packers' rapid turnarounds from last to first in their respective divisions between the 1958 and 1960 seasons demonstrated the efficacy of the league's efforts to promote parity.[42]

An examination of NFL and AAFC teams' win-loss records demonstrates that Bell was correct on two counts. The NFL did have lower standard deviation ratios and greater churning than did the AAFC (Table 7). In later seasons, the NFL's competitive balance, as measured by the ratio of the actual standard deviation to the idealized one, was not too different from the AAFC's. The NFL's claim that it had better competitive balance than did the AAFC was not clear-cut. However, the NFL did have more churning at the top than the AAFC, as no NFL team won more than two championships in a row, unlike the AAFC's Browns' four consecutive titles. Bell was incorrect in that the NFL fielded teams that were just as inept as those in the AAFC.

The NFL's vaunted competitive balance was, therefore, exaggerated. At best the draft gave each team a chance to remain competitive year after year. The reality was that some teams floundered, while others flourished for years.

By 1950, despite the NFL's reserve clause, revenue sharing, and draft, Green Bay was in trouble financially, and pundits predicted its demise. The team's fellow owners, especially the old guard, retained a nostalgic fondness for the franchise. Years later, Rozelle liked to use Green Bay as an example of the NFL's sagacity in sharing revenue. Sportswriter Dan Parker had earlier disputed this notion: "The case of Green Bay is ridiculous, Bert Bell, and you know it. . . . It doesn't belong in the National Professional Football League any more than Kalamazoo. . . . It is not a Major League City."[43]

Aside from the Packers, who were within easy driving distance of Milwaukee, every MLB and NFL team played in a large city. The NBA still maintained teams in smaller cities such as Syracuse, Rochester, and Fort Wayne. The New York Knicks did not share the city with another NBA team, unlike the three MLB teams that shared the metro area until 1958. The disparity between the Knicks' and Fort Wayne Pistons' markets sometimes led to larger disparities in win-loss records than those in MLB or the NFL (Table 7). Smaller rosters in basketball might have meant that an individual star would have a greater effect on a team's win-loss record than in other sports, with the possible exception of quarterbacks in football.

The Minneapolis Lakers dominated the early NBA. George Mikan was the key ingredient for the team's success. Eddie Gottlieb of Philadelphia worried that the

NBA was becoming similar to the American League with regard to a dominant team that squelched interest and attendance: "The Lakers are running behind in attendance and we at the bottom are faring equally disastrously. Only two factors are keeping us in business—doubleheaders and the Harlem Globetrotters. The Trotters are really keeping the circuit going."[44]

Minneapolis' repeated success appeared to bore even Laker fans. Although information is unavailable for 1948–1951, the team's gross and home receipts declined between 1951–1952 and 1953–1954. The team's profit and loss figures, though, remained stable across the three years, although 1953–1954 was the worst year of the three. The league home receipts dropped between 1952–1953 and 1953–1954, but, again, it is difficult to interpret the trend.[45]

Of the surviving eight BAA and NBL teams, these squads experienced the usual ups and downs between 1946 and 1962. Six of the eight teams won at least one NBA championship, while the Knicks and Pistons at least reached the championship finals.

The NBA's competitive balance was affected by some unique factors: franchise upheavals that reduced the number of teams from seventeen to eight; the twenty-four-second shot clock; George Mikan's retirement; and the wave of talented, mostly African American players in the second half of the 1950s. There was another aspect to competitive balance that rarely received scrutiny. Scheduling loomed large in the competitive balance equation. NBA teams fared much better at home than did football or baseball teams. Because the NBA did not have balanced schedules, and owing to a prevalence of double-headers where four teams played two games at one venue, franchises had skewed home-road schedules. Teams in smaller cities such as Syracuse and Fort Wayne had a preponderance of home to road games, while the big-city teams of Boston, Philadelphia, and New York had the opposite preponderance. The woebegone Milwaukee/St. Louis Hawks had, by far, the most unfavorable slate of games.[46]

The NBA's system of doubleheaders may have contributed to competitive imbalance, but NFL owners considered a different route. NFL owners exhibited a ruthlessness in setting the schedule. They had to. Why? The schedule affected both the league standings and each team's attendance. Given a choice, many football owners would have chosen a lopsided set of tough opponents who drew well, rather than a group of weak teams who promised to be stepping stones toward a division title but whom the fans disdained. George Halas once testified that something had to be done, because teams wanted to schedule only attractive opponents.[47]

During the struggles with the AAFC and AFL, the NFL employed scheduling as a weapon. For instance, the New York Giants received extra home games in 1946 in hopes of stymieing the AAFC New York club, while the league boosted

Chicago's and Los Angeles' schedules to combat their AAFC rivals in those cities.[48] Years later, the NFL would explicitly design the schedule to promote parity.

Conclusion: Owners Seek, Congress Denies

NFL, NBA, and NHL owners failed to secure even partial antitrust exemptions for their reserve clause, draft, territorial rights, and commissioners' powers. The two legislative bodies never concurrently passed bills. On the other hand, the owners could feel relieved that while legislators expressed concerns about the justice or the efficacy of these institutions, lawmakers never passed any legislation banning such institutions.

The owners came close to getting what they desired on two occasions. Emanuel Celler introduced a bill in 1957 (H.R. 10378) giving professional team sports limited antitrust immunity: "All aspects of and practices of professional sports under the antitrust laws *except* those practices that the courts deemed a 'reasonably necessary' restraint of trade."[49] Such practices as player control, territorial rights, television and radio policies, and preservation of public confidence in games were issues that would have to pass the "reasonably necessary" test in court. Owners, though, were seeking a sweeping exemption similar to baseball's. Senator Kenneth Keating sponsored a bill that was similar to Celler's but provided an automatic pass for sports' institutions by deleting the "reasonably necessary" clause. The House passed Celler's bill, only after Keating added an amendment striking the "reasonably necessary" clause from the measure. The House approved the bill in 1957. The Senate launched a subcommittee, where Senator Estes Kefauver fought S. 4070 (similar to Keating's amended version of H.R. 10378). Celler testified against Keating's and Kefauver's bill, and coupled with growing concern about the reserve clause, the subcommittee decided to table the bill.[50]

Although the Celler/Keating/Kefauver bills continued to surface throughout the next few years, legislators kept tinkering with the bills in response to changes in professional sports. Senator Philip Hart's S. 950 was similar to Keating's earlier bill. The sports owners' actions, including Charles O. Finley's antics and CBS's purchase of the Yankees, made legislators wary of Hart's bill as being too lenient toward the owners. Although the Senate passed Hart's bill, the proposal reached the House too late in the legislative sessions for a vote. The bill died.[51]

Owners defended their institutions on the basis that they promoted competitive balance. Because competitive balance in terms of roughly equal outcomes was patently false in the case of the Yankees versus the Senators, the owners' arguments appeared dubious to a number of legislators and their aides. In terms of the sheer number of happy fans, a New York team winning a championship likely provided more joy than would a Kansas City team, unless, of course, ennui set in with repeated New York championships.

Unfortunately for professional team sports owners, the franchises in Washington, D.C., were inept during the 1950s. These teams' ineptitude may have contributed to the legislators' sensitivity to competitive imbalance. Marshall's Redskins lived up to their derogatory attitudes toward nonwhite races by not hiring any African American players and faring poorly on the gridiron until the 1962 season. The Griffith family's ability to compete financially with the Yankees was so futile that a contemporary hit Broadway play, *Damn Yankees,* suggested the only way the Senators could compete was to make a pact with the Devil. The Washington Capitols basketball team compiled superior regular-season records but faltered during the playoffs. In a pique of impatience, Capitols owner Mike Uline fired coach Arnold "Red" Auerbach. The team folded shortly thereafter. Congressional legislators, despite all of their power, could not transform the District of Columbia's lackluster professional sports teams.

7

We Want More Baseball and Football 1959 and 1960

The professional team sports leagues' experiences during the 1950s occurred during a period of population shifts in the United States. Cities were growing rapidly in the southern and western regions. Legislators on the committee and those who dropped by to testify sought to obtain professional sports team franchises for their constituents. If the legislators could not induce an existing team to relocate, they could try to persuade owners to expand or induce a group of prospective owners to form a new league. Incumbent owners were lukewarm about expansion and hostile towards new leagues. Legislators, therefore, keenly questioned owners and their officials regarding plans for expansions and attitudes toward new ones. The 1959 and 1960 hearings concentrated on expansion and prospective new leagues.

All of the league constitutions contained clauses pertaining to relocating or selling existing franchises and creating new franchises. Usually these clauses required a supermajority, in some cases unanimity, of owners to approve relocation or franchise sales and expansion.

Owners overstepped, though, when they claimed the authority to dictate entrance requirements to potential rival leagues. MLB professed to welcome the Continental League—if that league would meet some requirements. In a sense, having MLB stipulate what made a league "major" was akin to rival grocery store chains in a large city getting together and dictating the rules for a new chain to move in.

Methods to Create Barriers to Entry

F. M. Scherer and David Ross found that the rate of entry of new firms into an industry was higher when "pre-entry profits are ample, when demand is growing rapidly, and when barriers associated with scale economies and product differentiation are low."[1] In addition, an entrant with an innovation often enters the market. Because a cartel has better opportunities to earn economic profits than a purely competitive industry, the cartel is likely to repeatedly face envious potential entrants.

What tactics do cartels use to deter entry? Economist Robert Smiley investigated tactics used by incumbent firms to stymie entry by new competitors. By surveying managers and executives in manufacturing and service industry firms, he discovered that the majority of managers and executives employed some of the following methods occasionally: expanding capacity; advertising to maintain customer loyalty; talking tough about their response to entrants; introducing new product varieties to fill all product niches, a form of spatial preemption; and avoiding disclosing profit data.[2] With regard to spatial preemption, an incumbent league might place franchises in most, but not necessarily all, of the potentially profitable markets.

The line demarcating legal and illegal tactics in combatting a new league was not always clear. An incumbent set of owners deciding to expand to fill more of the open niches in the market might or might not be violating antitrust law. The *Harvard Law Review* suggested, "Less clear, however, is the degree to which the older league may use its established position to compete vigorously against the new entrant when the result may be his destruction." The article cited *Aluminum Co. of America v. United States* as an extreme case: "[the case] may be read as holding that Alcoa's policy of expanding as fast as the market grew was illegal; Alcoa—as a monopoly—apparently had a duty to leave part of the demand unsupplied in order to encourage competitors." The article concluded that such an extreme interpretation of the case would imply that, "an existing league would be required to refrain from expansion into new cities or from increasing TV coverage when such actions would preempt part of the market which the new league sought to enter."[3]

Smiley did not question respondents whether they had used government intervention to create barriers to entry. However, incumbent firms often enlisted political support for legislation directly benefitting them or stymieing potential entrants. Smiley's survey also did not ask about predatory pricing: setting prices so low that new firms cannot earn a profit. Although the public believes that firms frequently engage in predatory pricing, the evidence suggested that such tactics were not pervasive; indeed, incumbent owners rarely threatened to cut ticket prices in the face of a new league's encroachment.[4]

Territorial Rights as Barrier to Entry

MLB owners created a number of barriers to entry. Early baseball owners often used expanded capacity, tough talk, and keeping quiet about attendance and profits to maintain and to protect their cartel. Owners during the postwar period were similar to their modern counterparts in being unwilling to provide information regarding profits unless compelled to by Congress. At times, owners even hesitated to provide attendance figures to the public. Some of the barriers to entry arose naturally as the industry evolved, such as large concrete and steel stadiums. Owners designed other barriers specifically to deter entry, such as local political intervention on behalf of a favored franchise, the reserve clause, and league alliances. Although economist Lance Davis argued that the baseball cartel failed to maximize collective profits, the owners' attempts after 1903 to prevent entry, at least, appear astute and successful.[5] The National League operating alone proved less successful in preventing entry, facing competition from the American Association, the Union Association, the Players' League, and, finally and most enduringly, the American League. The addition of the American League and having a combined total of sixteen relatively stable franchises, however, provided sufficient strength to combat the Federal League and any other potential entrant for more than fifty years. The cartel, albeit, expanded by almost double the sixteen teams and, facing significantly altered labor rules, has now persisted for over a century.

MLB's key asset in preventing entry was its control of players. The entity's ability to draft promising players from the minor leagues also helped keep minor league teams in larger cities from aspiring to Major League status.

The Pacific Coast League aspired to Major League status after World War II. Although Los Angeles and San Francisco were obvious candidates for Major League teams, Seattle, Portland, San Diego, Oakland, and Sacramento did not yet have sufficient populations. The league attained a special category: Open. The category was above AAA and gave the league some protection against having players drafted with limited compensation by MLB teams.[6]

The leagues also discouraged entry by practicing spatial preemption; just as cereal manufacturers developed a wide range of offerings to prevent new entrants, baseball owners could place franchises in almost all of the large cities to prevent the entry of an aspiring third Major League.[7] Of course, spatial preemption touches upon the issue of whether the Major Leagues were of an optimal size and with teams in the optimal cities.[8]

After the American and National Leagues' agreement in the early 1900s, were the sixteen teams optimally located to preclude entry of a new league? The sixteen teams were in ten of the fifteen largest cities in the country. Baltimore (sixth), Buffalo (eighth), San Francisco (ninth), New Orleans (twelfth), and Milwaukee (fourteenth) were outside MLB. The Baltimore Orioles were once a National League team and later an American League team before moving to New York to become the Highlanders (later Yankees) in 1903. MLB owners thought that Buffalo was too close to New York City, while San Francisco was too far from the other MLB teams. Big-league owners disdained New Orleans both because of its distance from the Northeast and because of its citizens' relative poverty. Per-capita income in Louisiana was and remained well below the United States average throughout the twentieth century.[9]

By the 1950 census, Los Angeles had vaulted to third place in terms of the Standard Metropolitan Statistical Area (SMSA), and Detroit was fifth. Cincinnati fell to fifteenth place. Milwaukee, Kansas City, Houston, Seattle, and Portland were closing in on Cincinnati in terms of SMSA population.[10] The majority of these cities received franchises by 1962. Sixty years later, though, Buffalo and New Orleans still remain outside MLB.

Owners worried that increasing the number of teams diluted the level of playing talent; raised demand for players; diminished each team's shares of national radio and television contracts; reduced the number of games with established teams; and decreased each owner's voting power. In setting expansion fees, owners would theoretically attempt to ascertain the highest price obtainable from prospective owners. They could have implemented an explicit auction or used financial modeling to ascertain the profit-maximizing fee; unfortunately, there is not much evidence from the 1950s illuminating how the owners set the fees. They might have relied upon recent franchise sales prices. In any event, if the estimated obtainable franchise fees did not cover their losses associated with expansion, then they would not expand. Though leaving too many viable sites without franchises invited potential upstarts such as the Continental League, incumbent owners were wary of expanding.

Quirk and Fort observe that leagues often charged owners of expansion teams significantly less than what existing franchises were selling for. Although they note that expansion teams should sell for somewhat less than existing teams, the leagues sometimes charged what the authors characterize as "bargain basement prices, half or less of the going price of existing franchises." They note, too, that expansion tends to decelerate the rate of increase in existing franchise prices, giving owners another reason to hesitate granting expansion teams. They suggest that the threat of a new league often spurs expansion (NFL in 1960 and NBA in the late 1960s).[11]

The Short Life of the Continental League

There was a potentially disastrous result of the franchise movements of the 1950s. When the Dodgers and Giants vacated the New York area, they left MLB vulnerable to a new league. The National League may have made a mistake in allowing the Giants and Dodgers to vacate New York without having a replacement team ready. Indeed, the National League might have been better off if had been the

Cards, Phillies, or Braves who shifted to the West Coast in 1953 rather than the wealthier Dodgers and Giants.

Former Brooklyn general manager Branch Rickey and New York attorney William Shea saw an opportunity in 1959. They decided the time was right to launch a third major league. Rickey and Shea announced their plans on June 18, 1959. By 1960 Shea listed the eight prospective teams as being New York, Toronto, Denver, Minneapolis-St. Paul, Houston, Atlanta, Dallas-Fort Worth, and Buffalo.[12]

The league faced a formidable barrier, though: getting players. As Rickey put it, "I only know that 20 great cities cannot be permanently branded as minor league by the arbitrary and capricious methods of the controlling number of 16 clubs." Rickey understood MLB's ability to thwart any new league: "So long as the major leagues are able to maintain their existing absolute monopoly of players and territories and further continue their tactics patently employed for the purpose of defeating any organization of a third major league, we, alone, find ourselves unable to complete the formation of the Continental League."[13]

Sportswriter Herbert Simons identified other hurdles facing the Continental League: getting television contracts; providing pension benefits equivalent to MLB's plan; paying reparations for trespassing minor league territories; and getting stadiums. On the other hand, any MLB expansion team would have an advantage over teams in a brand new league, because established MLB teams would play them; Continental League teams would not have any established teams visiting them.[14]

Although the ABA and AFL could hope to gain favorable widespread publicity and credibility by signing top college players, such avenues were unavailable for potential baseball entrants. Because minor league players did not attain the national recognition of top collegiate football or basketball players, a fledgling league could not hope to get much publicity by signing even the best minor league players. In addition, such players would have been vulnerable to any reserve clause or blacklist edicts passed by the Major Leagues.[15] A *Harvard Law Review* article suggested that one way to promote the creation of new leagues would be to obtain "a holding that the practice of blacklisting players who play in new leagues violates the antitrust laws."[16]

Shea and Rickey thought that minor league realignment in the advent of eight new teams would provide a source of young talent. Teams in AAA and Open leagues possessed plenty of young players. Rickey exuberantly proclaimed, "Why there are players all over the world."[17] Rickey further believed that MLB's first-year draft rule exposing talented minor leaguers to draft by Major League teams would provide players for the Continental League, but he failed to explain why the existing teams would share these players. In addition, the owners in the new league hoped to buy players from minor league clubs. MLB commissioner Ford Frick agreed with Rickey that these avenues would be available to the nascent Continental League teams.[18] Despite Frick's cordial but dubious assurances, tension lurked.

MLB owners, recognizing congressional pressure for more major league teams, chose to issue unctuous statements claiming that a third league would be accepted if it satisfied certain conditions laid down by MLB, including indemnifying incumbent owners whose territories were violated.[19]

Frick advised the Continental League owners that they would have to meet the requirements of any potential expansion team applying to join MLB; Frick ignored the fact that there had not been an expansion team in more than fifty years. These requirements included a population base of at least 600,000; stadium capacity of 25,000; schedule of 154 games; minimum salary of $7,500; and uniform major league players' contracts. One reporter estimated that meeting these requirements might cost the new teams a combined $60,000,000, mostly in constructing new stadiums or in renovating existing minor league stadiums. By establishing these requirements, MLB owners tried to present a reasonable face to the public; what could be more equitable than to insist that the proposed league meet existing standards?[20] Surprisingly, no one protested the Major League owners' arrogance in establishing these requirements, even prospective Continental League officials and owners responded by trying to meet the requirements.

Finding large stadiums proved another barrier to potential new teams. The Major League owners' stipulation of a stadium capacity of 25,000 was probably redundant in any case; prospective Continental League owners knew they needed suitable venues in which to stage their games. The Yankees, although lukewarm about sharing New York, offered to sell their lease on Yankee Stadium to the city of New York and thereby allow the possibility of another team sharing the stadium. Rickey and Bill Shea dismissed the offer, refusing to play in such an "antique." They hoped to occupy the new stadium the city was considering building.[21] Weiss angrily blasted the Continental League's refusal to use Yankee Stadium and the proposed league's desire for a new stadium: "It's damned unfair for a stadium financed by public funds to operate against a private corporation that pays the city $200,000 a year in taxes. Anyone who says the [new] park will pay for itself is crazy. Every municipal stadium in the country is a white elephant."[22]

Other prospective cities offered to build stadiums, upon receiving a guarantee from a team to play there. The mutual contingency between city officials and team officials invoked the question, "Which came first, the team or the stadium?"

Although Shea complained about the $1 million indemnity demanded by the American Association, citing the International League's demand for only $48,000 when the Browns moved into Baltimore, he conveniently forgot about indemnities paid by the Dodgers and Giants for invading California teams' territories.[23] Walter

O'Malley and Horace Stoneham had paid the Pacific Coast League $900,000 each for their invasion of Los Angeles and San Francisco. The two teams' usurpation of the West Coast trespassed three PCL teams' territories (San Francisco, Los Angeles, and Hollywood), creating a chain reaction through the minor leagues. The league added Salt Lake City, Phoenix, and Spokane for 1958. The PCL also lost its Open status and was relegated to AAA, thereby forfeiting some privileges not accorded the two AAA leagues. Any hopes the PCL had of attaining MLB status as the third league vanished.[24]

Frick further indicated that the Continental League would have to establish a pension system similar to that operated by the Major Leagues.[25] The demand appeared reasonable, but a skeptic might observe that the pension plan was another barrier to entry.

Finally, MLB held a trump card: they could thwart the formation of a third league by expanding themselves, which they eventually did. In addition, after some hesitation, the American League approved Washington's relocation to Minneapolis–St. Paul, thereby eliminating one of the Continental League's original territories.[26]

Both MLB and the Continental League worked to garner congressional support. The Continental League hoped that Congress would force MLB to place tighter limits on the number of players who could be controlled by any one club, as suggested by former Senator Edwin Johnson. Estes Kefauver's Senate bill proposed limiting the number of players controlled to one hundred, with forty being on the parent team's roster. In addition, within two years of the bill's enactment, MLB teams would have to implement an open draft of all players not on the forty-player parent roster; any league meeting the standards of baseball—specifically the Continental League—would be allowed to participate in the open draft.[27]

Congress and baseball owners recognized the importance of this legislation. Shea claimed: "the passage of any bill validating the reserve clause without limitation on the control of players would prohibit forever the formation of any other major league—not just the Continental League—except by consent of the 16 major league club owners."[28]

Senator Phil Hart of Michigan asked Shea, "If this bill does not become law, does it mean the end of the Continental League?" Shea responded: "We could operate outside Organized Baseball, without benefit of the draft, conduct war and raids on Organized Baseball. That would not be illegal because I contend the reserve clause binding a player to a major league club is illegal anyhow. We would have to raid because there are no players anywhere else. . . . It looks like they're pushing us to it, particularly because of the time element." Senator John Carroll of Colorado asked, "Couldn't you develop your own market of players?"

"It would take years and years to get started," was Shea's reply.[29] Hart then blustered: "they [MLB] have a franchise veto coupled with a strong player control, and I think the Congress would be forced to take action to break it up."[30]

Edwin Johnson was one of those pessimistic about the Continental League's prospects without legislation: "the Continental League will be a dead duck and it isn't likely that anyone again will try to organize another major league."[31] MLB officials disputed Johnson's concerns and testified, instead, to the bill's deleterious effects upon the minors. Surprisingly, even Branch Rickey stated that the player control limit was harmful, because he believed the limit would hurt the minors. Frick asserted that the limits would "leave over 100 of the 150 Minor League clubs without Major League assistance."[32]

Senator Kenneth Keating opposed the limits for two reasons. First, he thought the limits would harm the minors because MLB would cut the subsidies. Second, "I believe that a third major league will be held up interminably if legislation is enacted which sets arbitrary Federal limits on the number of players a team may control."[33] Opponents of the limit proved persuasive enough that the legislation relating to the draft did not make it out of the subcommittee. Many observers saw the failure to get the legislation as fatal to Continental League interests. Shea admitted, "It was a severe blow, but we are not finished." Meanwhile, Frick claimed, "It was a bad piece of legislation, which would have hurt the Continental as well as the American and National Leagues."[34]

The Continental League staggered on. Although not stated publicly, the league's backers hoped that Congress would also eliminate the need to indemnify the minors for trespassing upon their territories. After their hopes of favorable legislation collapsed, the league announced that it had a plan to compensate the minors for its proposed trespass of their territories, thereby fulfilling one of the MLB's requirements. The league was willing to pay forty cents per admission as reparations in the year in which it gained Major League status.[35]

Foiling the Continental League Via Expansion

As Congress dithered over passing legislation, MLB owners acted. New York public officials quickly sought to get another National League team. By the summer of 1958, Mayor Robert Wagner and Shea offered a stadium site at Flushing Meadows to any aspiring team. Shea intimated that the city would join a third major league to get another team.[36]

Meanwhile, MLB was beginning to move on expansion. American League owners knew that the National League had preempted them in placing teams in California. The American League owners coveted California. The World Series of 1959 and the 90,000-plus attendance at each of the three games played in the Los Angeles Coliseum only heightened the realization of their blunder.[37]

Although MLB came to approve expansion on its own merit, a strong political aspect imbued the situation. Concurrent with the Dodgers and Giants' relocations, one team ran afoul of the expansion/relocation turmoil. The perennial cellar-dwelling Senators were considering shifting to Minneapolis–St. Paul. Minneapolis officials began wooing Calvin Griffith to relocate as early as 1957; these officials assured Griffith of the cities' sincerity by giving generous guarantees. As *The Sporting News* pointed out, because of Washington, D.C.'s strategic importance in placating congressmen who might raise uncomfortable questions regarding baseball's antitrust exemption, "Organized Baseball must have some countering move in Washington. Even if the Continental League does get started it may not succeed. Then O.B. must have something to offer in the way of expansion."[38]

Frick testified before Kefauver's Senate subcommittee that he opposed the transfer of the Senators; although if the team moved, he claimed the National League would expand to ten cities by planting a team there and in New York.[39] He needed to tread carefully before the Senate and House committees. Emanuel Celler warned baseball against any "irresponsible franchise shifts while Congress' back is turned in adjournment. . . . The National Pastime belongs in the National Capital and I deplore these attempts to move it without regard for fan loyalties . . . [such shifts were] more evidence of money-grabbing."[40] Senator Karl Mundt vociferously opposed the baseball-variety Senators' move from the capital and supplied some hysterics: "I simply say they do not have the right to run out of town . . . to ignore their responsibilities to the international situation, to the fight against juvenile delinquency, to the maintenance of a spirit of Americanism which reflects itself throughout baseball." He threatened Major League owners with a negative quid pro quo: "But once they decide to leave Washington, D.C., without representation in either of the two major baseball leagues, by such action, they automatically repeal the protective legislation which we pass."[41]

Griffith was sorely tempted, even in the face of legislative opposition. Minneapolis–St. Paul had offered to expand its existing baseball stadium, if baseball would guarantee a team for Minnesota's efforts. There were two potential drawbacks to the relocation. The Minneapolis Millers had been a disappointment at the gate, drawing just 135,000 for sixty-two home dates, despite finishing in second place. In addition, the remaining American Association teams were planning to demand the same $900,000 indemnities that the Pacific Coast League received for the Dodgers' and Giants' invasion of California.[42]

The Senators' situation was bleak. Griffith Stadium was cramped and located in a deteriorating neighborhood. Griffith also worried about the city's changing racial makeup: "The trend in Washington is getting to be all colored," and, indeed by 1960, the city was predominantly black. Griffith did not blame the Baltimore Orioles for his attendance woes, as he claimed that his clientele came from the District of Columbia and neighboring suburbs in Virginia. He was not even optimistic about the proposed new stadium for Washington, D.C., considering it would be built near the Maryland state line.[43] His proposed move held the attraction of hurting the fledgling Continental League by occupying one of its proposed cities, but his fellow owners' concerns about the adverse political fallout delayed the move. Griffith's proposal to move to Minnesota for the 1960 season failed without even going to vote. Yankees' owner Dan Topping was against the shift, while Chicago and Cleveland apparently also opposed it.[44]

Griffith was determined and tried again, barely receiving approval to shift his Senators to Minneapolis–St. Paul in late 1960. He received a guarantee of one million per year in attendance for the first five years and much higher radio and television revenues than he earned in Washington, D.C.[45]

By expanding, MLB would render the Continental League redundant. On August 1, 1960, Shea and Rickey agreed to stop Continental League activities, provided MLB promised to expand to ten clubs each by 1961 or 1962. Milwaukee Braves' owner Lou Perini suggested that MLB might absorb a few of the Continental League franchises, but most observers believed that the Continental League was dead as of August 1. The league's officials maintained that the organization would continue until irrevocable MLB expansion plans were finalized.[46]

Some Continental League participants fared well in the eventual outcome. Joan Payson and her group secured the New York expansion franchise in the National League, while Craig Culinan, Judge Roy Hofheinz, and K. S. (Bud) Adams were among the key owners of the new Houston franchise in the National League. Branch Rickey rejoined the St. Louis Cardinals as a "consultant on player-personnel."[47] Although the Continental League franchises were on paper only, the National League, in essence, absorbed or merged with them via the expansion process.

American League President Joe Cronin announced on August 30, 1960, that the American League would expand to ten teams, although he did not identify which cities would get teams. He also urged American League owners to finalize their plans quickly in an attempt to thwart the National League from getting the best locations; Cronin lamented the American League's earlier failure to move promptly into California. Dan Topping of the Yankees campaigned for an American League expansion team in Los Angeles by 1962.[48]

The National League once again stole a march on its rival when the league voted to expand into Houston and New York on October 17. Sportswriter Ed Prell noted that, as before, the National League preempted a lucrative territory ahead of the fumbling American League. The status of the new National League franchise in New York depended upon whether the city built a new ballpark. On October 26, the American League surprised everyone by proclaiming that it was expanding to ten teams in 1961, not 1962 as expected. The league chose Los Angeles and Washington for its new cities.[49]

After claiming that there were not enough good players to share with the Continental League, where did MLB suddenly find qualified athletes for their expansion teams? MLB supplied newcomers with players by selling the dregs of their rosters. The new American League teams would pay $75,000 for each player selected to his original franchise, for a total of $2.1 million for each expansion team. The plan had the virtue that "selling" players to the new teams generated favorable tax treatment for the new franchises relative to charging them $2.1 million as a fee. The National League offered a similar plan. One National League official said, "We think these eight men on each side will form the nucleus of a sound club for each of the new entries."[50]

The expansion teams generally boasted terrible records, although thanks to the Chicago Cubs, the Houston Colt 45s finished eighth. The New York Mets finished last and set a modern-era record for lowest win-loss percentage.

Basketball's Hesitant Expansion Policies

The NBA was still stabilizing during the late 1950s, and its owners had mixed feelings about expansion, given their tumultuous experiences. It may not have been feasible, but the NBA's forerunner—the BAA—might have required a minimum capital requirement to ensure stable franchises. Years later, Maurice Podoloff testified that only four or five of the original eleven owners were well capitalized and could absorb losses. He estimated that the remaining teams had a combined capital equal to the fourth or fifth-best capitalized team.[51]

New York's Ned Irish was ambivalent about expansion, because he was concerned that undercapitalized owners would flounder. "I estimate that a new franchise would have to be backed by $200,000 to $300,000 for the first three years, before there would be good hope to expect returns on the investment."[52] Podoloff later confirmed Irish's remarks by pointing out that while incumbent owners did not mind if a newcomer lost money for years owning an existing team, an expansion team likely cost everyone money. A new, weak team often harmed the gate of the incumbent teams. "If you want to lose your own money, that is your privilege, but you will cost the league as a whole anywhere from $50,000 to $60,000 a year in loss of gate receipts." Podoloff further added, "if [a prospective owner had $200,000 in the bank and it was unfettered], they will get a franchise so fast it will make their heads spin."[53]

The NBA played musical chairs with its franchises, with all of the surviving former National Basketball League teams relocating to larger cities by 1963–1964: Minneapolis to Los Angeles, Fort Wayne to Detroit, Syracuse to Philadelphia (after the Philadelphia Warriors moved to San Francisco), Tri-Cities/Milwaukee to St. Louis, and Rochester to Cincinnati. Interspersed with these franchise relocations and one NBA expansion team in Chicago 1961–1962 (which relocated to Baltimore after a couple of seasons) was the short-lived American Basketball League (ABL). Harlem Globetrotters owner Abe Saperstein, rebuffed in obtaining the Los Angeles NBA franchise, sought revenge by starting a new eight-team league. The league boasted teams in Chicago, Los Angeles, Hawaii, Kansas City, Pittsburgh, San Francisco, Cleveland, and Washington. The ABL completed the 1961–1962 season but folded midway through the 1962–1963 schedule.

Although sportswriter Leonard Koppett argues that "the effect of the American [Basketball] League on the NBA ranged from minuscule to nil," the league and its players had long-term repercussions.[54] ABL owners chose to sign blacklisted players such as Bill Spivey and Connie Hawkins; these players had been blacklisted despite the fact that they had never been convicted on a gambling-related crime. The league also signed top collegiate player Jerry Lucas of Ohio State University. The upstart owners inked very few NBA players. These signings led to some lawsuits and raised issues of owner fairness in dealing with players. The league also introduced later New York Yankees owner George Steinbrenner to professional sports, as well as the three-point field goal. Despite these actions, the ABL failed to seriously challenge the NBA; Koppett believes the NBA had succeeded in corralling the vast majority of top basketball talent. In addition, the NBA had public credibility, a television contract, and arenas.[55] Another challenger to the NBA, the American Basketball Association, proved a more stubborn threat and generated judicial and congressional interest a decade later.

Legislators did not seem too keen on getting more NBA teams for their constituents. The NBA proved hesitant to expand, adding only a new Chicago team in 1961, before expanding in earnest during the second half of the 1960s, coincident with the emergence of the ABA.

Football's Retaliatory Expansion Policies

Bert Bell encouraged NFL owners to expand in response to congressional pressure in 1957, but the owners resisted his efforts. Bell thought adding two teams was the prudent course, but unless the schedule was lengthened, the intraconference home-and-home series would have to be eliminated. The clubs in the NFL's Western Conference were not anxious to break up their lucrative schedule.[56]

George Preston Marshall fought Bell's plan. He admitted that some current teams might need to relocate because of small crowds and inadequate parking, and that Louisville and Buffalo were attractive sites. However, he denied Bell's claim of owner selfishness: "I don't believe there's anyone in the NFL piggish on the subject of money. They wouldn't be in it if they were." Marshall's worries about expansion revolved around television money and increased competition for players. The owners voted down both immediate expansion and removing the intraconference home-and-home schedule at the January 1958 meetings; they agreed to form a committee to investigate expansion. Bell informed owners at the January 1959 meetings that he received an offer of $650,000 for an expansion franchise. The commissioner was not calling for action; he simply wanted owners to know that quality buyers were clamoring for NFL franchises.[57]

Bell claimed before the congressional committee in 1957 that there were not sufficient good players to stock more teams. Chairman Celler asked, "Is there enough football talent to support two more teams, say, or a league?" Bell responded, "My contention is when the last 2 teams in each conference win 3 or 4 ballgames for 2 years, there is enough material—provided they get that first selection choice for 2 years—to establish two other teams. Last year was pretty close to it. I think it is inevitable that it is going to happen."[58]

During the 1959 hearings, legislators again questioned Bell regarding the possibilities of expanding the league or of a new league. Bell blurted out that there was a new league in the works. He probably figured such news would placate the legislators sufficiently to quell talk of further expansion. Bell reported that he had talked to every NFL owners and that none objected to a new league.[59]

The new league Bell touted was the brainchild of Lamar Hunt. Hunt, a wealthy Texas oilman, was disappointed in his efforts to buy an existing NFL franchise for the purpose of relocating it to Dallas. He was one of several wealthy men who had grown frustrated while pursuing an existing or an expansion team. Hunt held some unique ideas about running a league. He told the prospective owners that he wanted them to focus upon bringing professional football to their cities but not to be overly focused on making money or winning championships. Hunt also emphasized equalization of all teams.[60]

Some witnesses were not as enthusiastic as Bell with regard to a new league. Chuck Bednarik doubted that a new league would be viable because, "there wouldn't be enough good ballplayers to put on a good show for the public." He did not believe there were even enough quality players for the NFL to expand by two or three clubs.[61] Bednarik's concerns about the shortage of skilled players was a longstanding argument by entrenched owners. Sportswriters predicted that any prospective league would be hampered by its lack of credible, recognizable players. As with baseball, once the NFL approved expansion, the player shortage problem suddenly vanished.

In many ways, the AFL's challenge was, as baseball's Yogi Berra allegedly said, "déjà vu all over again." The NFL resurrected secret drafts; indulged in chicanery over stadiums; mouthed tough talk; refused to play the new teams; slung denigration; and used other tricks. But the NFL's most publicized tricks included expansion and a clumsy divide-and-conquer attempt. Bell continued to issue assurances of welcome. "There is room in this country for more pro football teams and the public demands 'em. There are plenty of good players for the teams." Bell, though, worried that the oil millionaires among the AFL owners would spend lavishly and even start raiding NFL rosters, despite their pledge not to.[62] Sportswriter Joe King, recalling the expensive bidding war during the AAFC's existence, wrote, "It is going to be fun getting out of college with an All-America football diploma this year, because there is fresh money in the pro player market. . . . An NFL source estimates that the few top prizes winding up collegiate careers this season will go for the huge sum of $30,000."[63]

The NFL announced its plans to expand shortly after Hunt and the AFL revealed their plans to start playing in 1960. Similar to MLB's co-opting several of the proposed Continental League's cities, Bell and the NFL owners told reporters of their intentions to expand into Dallas and Minneapolis–St. Paul. The latter move jeopardized the AFL's Minnesota plans, because NFL owners hoped to entice the Minnesota group of investors to switch leagues.[64]

The NFL's timing in deciding to expand to Dallas and Minneapolis–St. Paul seemed too much of a coincidence to some observers. George Halas chaired the NFL's expansion committee. He had previously said that several groups had made attractive offers throughout the late 1950s. A potential new league did have plenty of attractive cities to select from, but Bell and the NFL owners hewed to the line that no expansion would occur "until weaker current members got well."[65] The league gave no indication of being willing to expand in the foreseeable future until the AFL's formation.

Hunt found the timing of the committee's findings suspicious and he hoped legislators would investigate the NFL's tactics.[66] The potential owner's political sense failed him this time. When MLB thwarted the Continental League by announcing expansion for 1961 and 1962, legislators, even those who were advocates for the Continental League, applauded the move. Legislators simply wanted more teams, and they were not too worried about how they got them, even if the incumbents used tactics that might have sparked antitrust concerns.

Hunt felt that the NFL expansion encroached upon AFL territory, and he did not shy from confrontation. He bluntly stated the cities of Dallas and Minneapolis–St. Paul were the "private property" of the AFL, while Bell blandly replied that the NFL considered them "open" to anyone. The coincidence that Dallas was Hunt's chosen city was not lost on anyone. Hunt excoriated the NFL's overture to the Twin Cities: "The NFL is doing anything it can to prevent this league from getting off the ground, but we are in business."[67] The Continental League baseball officials simultaneously were accusing baseball's American League of chicanery in considering a move by the woebegone Senators to the Twin Cities.[68]

NFL owners succeeded in persuading the Twin Cities group to switch. The AFL initially resisted the switch but eventually accepted the inevitable and granted the Minnesota group permission to withdraw. Joe Foss, the AFL's Commissioner, repudiated Bell's 1959 testimony claiming benign intent toward the AFL.[69]

While Hunt fumed and the NFL committee set its sights to Minneapolis–St. Paul, some NFL owners continued to oppose expansion. Marshall, citing the league constitution's clause that required unanimity in approving new franchises (although owners would change the bylaws with ten votes out of twelve at the January 1960 meetings), insisted he would not grant his approval.[70]

Marshall notwithstanding, the other owners were now determined to approve expansion. Art Rooney suggested that Minneapolis and Dallas were likely expansion cities, with two more cities likely to get teams later.[71]

The NFL owners, Marshall included, voted 11–0 to approve admittance of the Dallas Rangers (Cowboys) and Minneapolis–St. Paul, with the Cardinals abstaining. Similar to the MLB setup for expansion teams, the Dallas team paid $50,000 for the franchise, but the new owners spent $550,000 buying players from the existing NFL teams' rosters.[72]

The NFL's experiences with expansion proved dismal. Although the NFL frequently boasted about its competitive balance, the incumbent owners proved ungenerous with their offerings. Dallas went 0-11-1 in its debut, while the Vikings performed a little better at 3-11. Baseball's New York Mets, by comparison, gained infamy by finishing 40-120 in their first season. The Mets spent years wallowing in futility, though, while the Vikings sported a winning record in 1964. The Cowboys won the Eastern Conference in 1966.

Showdown Between the NFL and the AFL

Although AFL owners pledged not to raid existing NFL rosters, they declared open season for college players. Both sets of owners avidly sought the top draftees, especially for their publicity value; some teams went too far in their pursuit by signing players before they had finished their college careers.[73]

To combat the AFL, the NFL again adjusted their rules limiting the number of players on a roster to suit their needs. The ostensible purpose of changing the player limits, in addition to the obvious need of adjusting to two-platoon or wartime football, was to either reduce player payrolls or to shrink the pool of players available for a rival league. The NFL owners raised the limit to thirty-eight to create a reservoir of players for the expansion Vikings, with the intent of reverting back to a thirty-five-player limit in 1961. The increased limit, though, served to deny some players to the AFL. The league changed the limit back to thirty-six in 1961.[74]

AFL owners considered various legal issues. Could they enforce a blackout of NFL games in cities where an AFL game was being played?[75] The big legal showdown, though, resulted from the NFL's threatened and eventual move into Dallas. Joe Foss told reporters, "We would not consider it a kiss of love if the NFL expanded into Dallas. It would be a clear sign they intended to continue their scorched-earth policy that caused us to surrender the Minneapolis-St. Paul territory." Foss reminded reporters of the AFL owners' policy not to tamper with NFL players as evidence of his league's benign intent.[76] AFL owners, though, were unable to get the congressional chest-thumping they hoped for when Senator Kefauver declined to schedule hearings on the NFL's move into Dallas; he did, at least, warn the NFL to treat the AFL with fairness. "I'm for expansion of football, but it is not a question of rights. It is a question of who has the better product in a city, if he produces it fairly, without monopolization and without pushing anyone around." Paul Dixon, the committee's attorney, unearthed Marshall's claim that NFL proponents of expansion were out to wreck the AFL. Marshall was opposed to expansion but voted for it when AFL owners announced their plans. As Dixon put it, "Is this a bona fide expansion or not?"[77]

Although the AFL owners threatened to seek redress from Congress or from the courts, newly minted NFL commissioner Pete Rozelle responded, "They moved into our territory in New York and in Los Angeles and in San Francisco [Oakland]. Why shouldn't we be allowed to move into Dallas?"[78] Foss eventually convinced the Department of Justice to examine the Dallas situation to see if an antitrust violation occurred. The AFL alleged that the NFL made veiled threats to players by alluding to a blacklist, and claimed the new league would "go down the drain was soon as we pull the plug." The AFL owners claimed the expansion was an attempt to destroy their league. Hunt and several of the AFL owners had been informed by NFL owners, when seeking to purchase an NFL expansion team, that "expansion is several years away." Foss told the Department of Justice that, "The NFL was very quick to react to this threat of monopoly. [The NFL] employed three main tactics—first, to entice away AFL members by promising them NFL franchises; second, when this technique did not prove entirely successful, to franchise teams in cities on top of the existing AFL teams, and third, to impede the new league in its efforts to obtain suitable players and coaches." Foss also characterized Marshall's blunt remarks as evidence.[79] A month later, Foss announced that the AFL would seek an injunction against the NFL. Foss quipped, "We couldn't sit idly by and let them cut us off at the knees."[80] NFL owners had reason to worry because, in addition to their legal wrangles, the NFL showed a decrease in per-team attendance during the 1960 season for the first time in nearly a decade.[81]

The AFL filed a $10,000,000 antitrust suit against the NFL on June 17, 1960. Their complaint repeated the accusations made earlier to the Department of Justice.[82] Meanwhile, the antitrust suit wended its way through the court system, with a rehashing of material presented in the press. The AFL petitioned the courts to order the NFL to move its Dallas franchise; to refrain from placing a team in any AFL city or AFL-designated city; to revise its constitution to allow interleague exhibition games; and to refrain from designating its championship game as a world championship game.[83] AFL owners hoped for a prohibition against interleague competition in the same city, but such an agreement would have been a clear antitrust violation, as the NFL would discover in the later Oakland Raiders suit.

The NFL's attorneys first moved to have the suit dismissed and, after that motion failed, used a defense that the NFL's actions had not damaged the AFL. An NFL attorney employed a dubious argument when he suggested that the AFL's survival implied that the NFL had not tried to kill it. NFL witnesses cited the City of Houston's denial of the NFL's application to lease its stadium as the precipitating factor for the NFL placing a franchise in the Twin Cities. Dallas Cowboys owner Clint Murchison admitted he offered to share the NFL expansion franchise with Hunt, or even to turn it over to Hunt completely. George Halas testified that the NFL's decision to expand into Dallas and Minneapolis–St. Paul was not in response to the AFL's formation but resulted from a long-considered desire to expand.[84]

Judge Roszel C. Thomsen eventually ruled against the AFL and stated that the NFL did not have a monopoly in professional football, so he acquitted the NFL of the charges leveled by the AFL. He stated the AFL failed to demonstrate that the NFL had monopoly power and that they had "undertaken some course of action to exclude competition or prevent competition." The judge further added, "Neither rough competition nor unethical business conduct is sufficient . . . the requisite intent to monopolize must be present and predominant."[85]

The judge's ruling might have destroyed many upstart leagues, but the AFL had one asset the AAFC lacked. Unfortunately for the AAFC, television was not the benefactor for professional football that it would prove in later years. Television provided little succor, if any, to the AAFC. The AFL shocked the football world in April 1960 when it announced a national television deal with the American Broadcasting Company (ABC) network. The deal was worth $2,125,000, or $125,000 per game, incumbent upon ABC being able to sell at least 60 percent of the games to advertisers and establishing the line facilities needed to create a nationwide hookup. Reporter Richard Shepard stated, "This is believed to be the first time that a major professional league has negotiated a broadcasting contract for all of its teams." The setup included blackouts in the city where a game was being played. Individual teams could, in addition, arrange any radio broadcast rights and local television rights.[86] The television deal gave the AFL credibility that it was here to stay. The league also attained Rozelle and Bell's dreams of a national television contract before the other could do so. The new league, of course, held an advantage over the NFL in that its teams had not already signed individual television contracts that might have caused teams with more lucrative contracts to balk at a national one.

Conclusion: The Incumbent Owners' Mixed Success

The incumbent owners' unwillingness to welcome new leagues is understandable, but less defensible were their anticompetitive actions. The AFL and, later, the ABA failed in their antitrust lawsuits against the NFL and NBA, as the two older leagues clearly displayed ruthlessness in attempting to thwart the insurgent leagues. MLB succeeded in stymieing the Continental League because the two leagues controlled the pool of players and because they usurped some of the Continental League's potential playing sites by expansion. MLB at least temporarily placated congressional desire for new franchises by their actions.

NFL owners failed to destroy the AFL, despite using their tried-and-formerly-true methods. Hunt proved resistant to the NFL owners' blandishments, and the league's television contract provided sufficient guaranteed funds to bolster the owners during the difficult early years. Both sets of owners tried to persuade Congress to intervene on their behalf. Because the legislators refused to become involved directly, the NFL owners could consider themselves the victors on that front. However, their victory was not sufficient to enable them to prevail in the larger war.

The NBA prevailed against the ABL without too much difficulty but failed to prevent the ABA from establishing itself. While the ABL signed collegiate stars such as Jerry Lucas and Bill Bridges, the former never played in the league. The ABA gained by signing draftees Spencer Haywood and Julius Erving and signing established NBA stars Rick Barry and Billy Cunningham.

At this point, the legislators did not seriously press the NBA to expand, and the league only did so in 1961–1962 with a lackluster Chicago team that would soon relocate to Baltimore. The league's later expansion, coincident with the debut of the ABA, provided material for a subsequent subcommittee hearing a decade later.

8

Damn Yankees and Relocations

1964 and 1965

Legislators always had something to complain about with regard to professional team sports. If they could have figured out a way to do so, they might have mandated that the Washington Senators field a respectable team. Legislators had two main concerns throughout the series of hearings: to procure teams for their constituents while avoiding losing teams via relocation.

The legislators' concerns were imbued with an element of reality, at least. Cities with multiple MLB teams usually had one team that was struggling, and legislators held a different attitude to such teams relocating than they would with regard to later relocations of prosperous teams.

Getting a Professional Sports Team

If you were interested in acquiring a big-league team, you had three options: purchase an existing team, hope for an expansion team in an established league, or enter a team into a new league, perhaps in hopes of having your team accepted into an incumbent one. If you purchased a team, you acquired rights to some players, a lease on a stadium, and the potential to relocate. The ability to relocate your team, subject to your fellow owners' approval (usually requiring a supermajority of votes for approval) could enhance the value of your franchise.

Franchise movements have proven contentious through the years. What one city gained, another city lost. Of course, from a consumer welfare perspective, if City A supported the team with 500,000 in season attendance, while City B supported the team with 1,200,000 in attendance, it would appear that overall consumer welfare was increased by the switch. Owners, too, professed concern about alienating fans by too frequent relocations, although relocation temporarily alleviated the necessity, at least for MLB, of expanding.

When the 1957 House hearings considering an antitrust exemption convened, there was a marked paucity of big-league franchises. MLB led the way with sixteen teams, while the NHL had just six (two of which were in Canada). The big leagues totaled forty-two teams, but this was a smaller number than in 1949. The number today is roughly 120. The leagues were at different stages of stability. MLB went from 1903 to 1952 without any franchise movements (the relocation of a Baltimore team to New York—the Yankees—was the final shift). MLB's stability, though, was partly an artifact of the Great Depression and World War II. The Browns' owner in 1941, Donald Barnes, had arranged for the team to move to Los Angeles. The AL owners met—on December 8, 1941—to consider the shift. Barnes was the victim of bad timing.

Even if a team stayed put, a change in ownership could trigger congressional scrutiny. Baseball's most glamorous franchise—the Yankees—were bought by television's reigning giant, CBS, and legislators expressed dismay. They did not, however, initiate any efforts to rescind the transaction.

The Economics of Franchise Relocations

Part of the property rights associated with owning a professional sports team is the right to relocate the team. Although an owners' right is constrained by the necessity, under league constitutions or bylaws, of garnering a supermajority of votes approving a proposed move, relocations are frequently approved.

Owners did not automatically get permission to relocate. Owner Bill Veeck Jr. sought permission to relocate his St. Louis Browns team to Baltimore. The other owners did not like Bill Veeck Jr.—just as they would not like Charles O. Finley or Al Davis in the future. Veeck sold out. The subsequent owners received permission to relocate to Baltimore, thereby boosting the value of their franchise.[1]

Economist Roger Noll pointed out the obvious realities behind relocations: "Teams move because they expect to make more money in the new city. They make more money because more fans will either come to the game or watch it on television. Thus, unless owners are fools, they will tend to relocate teams according to the intensities of the desires of fans for teams." In terms of consumer welfare, by Noll's logic, it is likely that most moves entail an increase in overall consumer welfare if significantly more fans are willing to attend or to watch games on television in the new city than in the original one. Noll pointed out a second fact associated with the topic: "the real monopoly power in sports is held by the teams in the big cities with the largest excess demand for sports. Generally, these teams do not even have to be good to pack in the fans—witness the recent history of most New York sports teams."[2] In a sense, then, fans in New York City might have been better off if new teams could have moved into the city. Either the new teams would have provided higher-quality performance or they would have forced incumbent teams to improve.

Owners claimed the right to approve or to prohibit franchise relocations. They had some sound reasons for doing so. Law professor Jeffrey Glick analyzed the territorial restraints exercised by sports leagues, and he cited justifications for such restraints for the purpose of avoiding "serious hardships for the other league members both in terms of travel schedules and costs . . . by balancing the interests of all teams in site selection, a legitimate restraint can promote on-field competition in locations acceptable to both participants, create a marketable product and thereby promote economic competition." He also pointed out that "League survival depends on a stable core of teams which remain in the same cities for a number of years. . . . This is where a territorial restraint is justified, for it can protect the interests of all parties by insuring stability and keeping teams in acceptable markets." Glick also identified the importance of maintaining traditional intraleague rivalries (such as baseball's Dodgers and Giants) and fan good will as justifications for owners' restrictions on franchise movement. He observed, "Although courts hesitate to accept just any argument for abandoning a *per se* analysis, the fan loyalty and support argument is fundamental to a league's existence, and its promotion is sufficient to meet the redeeming virtue requirement."[3]

Glick's argument regarding transportation costs is not definitive. Even during the 1950s, increased transportation costs were, at least for MLB, a nuisance and not a fatal flaw. The transportation expenses were much smaller than the teams' player payrolls. The Philadelphia Athletics' relocation to Kansas City raised American League traveling expenses by $50,000 per season; the Athletics faced $20,000 of that, leaving rival owners to incur perhaps $5,000 in additional transportation expenses per team.[4] The Dodgers' and Giants' owners were so confident about their franchises' prospects on the West Coast that they offered to reimburse the other owners for any increased transportation costs. The Dodgers' popularity, though, ensured that fellow National League owners more than offset any increase in transportation costs via much greater visitors' shares from gate receipts. Because the Dodgers and Giants moved in tandem, the two teams maintained their rivalry, allaying fears of damaging traditional rivalries. The relatively modest transportation expenses were, then, probably insufficient reasons to justify Glick's legal argument for strictures upon relocation during the 1950s.

The Early, Unhappy Histories of Sports Leagues

The National League's early history was easily forgotten by fans in the 1950s. Franchise turmoil was prevalent during the NL's first quarter century. Teams and new leagues entered and folded with depressing regularity. Even after the

American League's successful incursion, eight teams aspiring to big-league status went under in the wake of the Federal League.

MLB's stability was somewhat illusory. During the 1930s, some of the MLB franchises were in dire straits. The Philadelphia Phillies sold off a number of their best players to remain in business. The Boston Braves, too, struggled to stay afloat. Connie Mack, owner of the Athletics, sold or traded his entire starting lineup and starting pitching rotation in the wake of falling attendance after 1932. Mack had earlier panicked and sold his top players after the 1914 World Series, when two of his pitchers signed with the Federal League. After both fire sales, Mack's teams floundered for years.

The NFL and its predecessor, the American Professional Football Association, also endured three decades of franchise turnover. The 1920s were a particularly frenetic decade, with aspiring owners in small cities and towns across the states bordering the Great Lakes launching teams. The biblical injunction—many were called, but few were chosen—is appropriate here. After the AAFC experience and the subsequent shakeout of weak franchises, the NFL stabilized by 1953 or so, with just one more franchise relocation occurring during the next two decades, when the Chicago Cardinals moved to St. Louis.

The BAA/NBA also suffered a decade of rapid turnover in franchises. Between the National Basketball League and the Basketball Association of America, the majority of teams folded.

Baseball's Game of Musical Chairs

MLB owners worried that the movement of six of the original sixteen baseball franchises might trigger fan alienation. In addition, owners were concerned about the adverse publicity of an owner's too-opportunistic movements. Some owners relocated two or three times (Ben Kerner's basketball Hawks; baseball's Athletics). To maintain fan loyalty, the leagues created stringent rules against franchise movements. The congressional hearings sometimes had the effect of encouraging leagues to loosen the voting requirements for approving a relocation or transfer. For instance, the National League constitution required unanimity for admission to membership, but Los Angeles Dodgers' owner Walter O'Malley persuaded his peers to revise it to a $^{3}/_{4}$ majority. The American League constitution of 1910 required $^{7}/_{8}$ majority for terminating membership and unanimity for approving admission to membership. The NFL constitution presented to the 1957 hearings indicated a $^{10}/_{12}$ approval, while the NBA's 1951 constitution required a $^{2}/_{3}$ majority.[5]

Rather than let franchises transfer locations, owners sometimes helped ailing ones with cash or players. According to Ed Barrow, early in the New York Yankees' history, American League President Ban Johnson forced teams to trade some players to the Highlanders—as they were known then—on highly favorable terms. In the late 1930s, the New York Yankees and Detroit Tigers sold players to the moribund St. Louis Browns at discounted prices.[6] Such conservatism against franchise movements dissipated in the aftermath of the 1951 House subcommittee meetings that revealed the demand for baseball by the rapidly growing cities outside the northeastern quadrant of the country, as well as increasing awareness that Philadelphia, Boston, and St. Louis were unable or unwilling to support two teams.

The Braves,' Browns,' and Athletics' relocations seemed justified to most observers, as these teams struggled at the gate and on the field; the subsequent moves, however, seemed less so. In the most dramatic relocations, the Brooklyn Dodgers were quite profitable until the very end, while the New York Giants were not in as dire straits as the first wave of teams that relocated.[7] Because Emanuel Celler represented Brooklyn, he was incensed by the Dodgers' relocation; he evinced little outrage that the Giants left the city, too.

Changing transportation options affected relocation decisions. Professional team sports' reliance upon rail travel was changing during the 1950s. Commercial jet transportation was becoming reliable and competitive in price with railroads. Indeed, railroads were well into their decline as an intercity mode of transportation. Because football was played once a week, while MLB teams played most days of the week, their travel needs differed. Cross-country jaunts by rail were less convenient for baseball.[8] If transportation was undergoing a revolution, so was communication. The emergence of coaxial cable allowed telecasts of MLB and NFL games to be carried across the country, enabling Americans living on the West Coast to see big-league games. Owners began eyeing Los Angeles and San Francisco as greener pastures for ailing franchises. Although the Dodgers co-opted Los Angeles ahead of any Continental League team, clearly a Continental League team in Los Angeles was still viable. Basketball's Minneapolis Lakers headed west in 1960–1961, beating out the nascent American Basketball League's Los Angeles Jets by a year.

Owners perceived risks in relocating to California. During the postwar boom, the PCL requested an upgrade to Major League status, but the incumbent MLB owners denied the movement. Although the PCL had lobbied for Major League status for more than a decade, that league's attendance levels did not demonstrate the West Coast cities' ability to support such status. The PCL's players fell between AAA and Major League quality, but the Los Angeles Angels and Hollywood Stars rarely drew more than three thousand fans per game, hardly an encouragement for baseball moguls.[9]

How did the franchise relocations of the 1950s fare? The National League's initial franchise relocation did better than the American League's. The Braves' attendance for the last four seasons declined precipitously in Boston, and fewer than 300,000 fans showed up in 1952. The Braves were usually less popular than the Red Sox, so the team vacated the city and moved to Milwaukee in 1953. The team's success at the gate in Milwaukee—some 1.8 million fans—stunned the baseball world and got other owners dreaming of more lucrative venues; in addition, fellow National League owners shared $425,000 in increased gate-sharing revenue between 1952 and 1953 from playing the Braves in Milwaukee instead of Boston.[10]

The American League's transfers of teams were not as successful as the National League's relocations. The St. Louis Browns averaged about 300,000 fans per season during their last five years. Many of the teams in the minor leagues outdrew them. The Browns survived by selling off their best players and by receiving loans from other American League owners. During the team's last four seasons in St. Louis, the Browns sold forty-eight players for more than one million dollars and received $300,000 in loans. The Browns' management blamed fans for not attending games, even though the team supplied such amenities as a scoreboard flashing hits, errors, and updated batting and pitching records, as well as renting seat cushions. Charles DeWitt, team general manager, stated, "in cities like Detroit, New York and Washington you don't have such a privilege offered you."[11]

The situation was so dismal in St. Louis that both the Cardinals and Browns had investigated relocating. The Cardinals hoped to relocate to Detroit and share Navin Field with the Tigers; the Tigers were naturally lukewarm to the idea.[12] The Browns dreamed of relocating to Los Angeles in 1941. Browns' president Donald Barnes arranged for air transportation; negotiated a settlement with Los Angeles minor league team owner Philip Wrigley; and received guarantees from civic leaders in Los Angeles to subsidize any subpar attendance. Barnes was very thorough in negotiating the deal, even lining up a promise of $250,000 from Sam Breadon, Cardinals' owner, to reward the Browns for leaving St. Louis. Breadon was also lobbying for National League approval of the move.[13] Unfortunately for the Browns, the Japanese attacked Pearl Harbor before Barnes could secure his fellow owners' approval, and his plan collapsed. In response to Barnes's proposed trespass upon their territory, the PCL convinced MLB to pass a new amendment restricting Major League teams' ability to encroach upon the minors' territory. Baltimore proved a better location for the Browns, but the team's owners were disappointed with its reception.

Neither the Browns nor the Athletics came close to drawing as many fans as the Braves. The Orioles averaged 857,000 per season during the team's first decade in Baltimore. After a decent start with 1.3 million fans the first year, the Athletics averaged just 870,000 fans per season in the team's first decade in Kansas City.

Given the Athletics' generally mediocre records, one could argue that the franchise did pretty well at the gate. However, both teams held much higher expectations for attendance. The Athletics' radio and television revenue fell from $300,000 to $210,000 after their relocation; the Orioles, at least, got a boost in radio and television revenue from $56,000 in 1953 to $313,000 in 1954.[14]

Although Bill Veeck admitted his guilt in baseball's franchise relocation frenzy—in particular, the Braves' move—he identified a key difference between the first three relocations and the subsequent ones: "the [earlier] moves were logical and probably inevitable. The later moves were more opportunistic and detrimental to the game's image."[15]

American League owners desired the Los Angeles and San Francisco markets, but they wanted two teams to relocate to California, to minimize travel expenses. After the Orioles moved to Baltimore in 1954, the owners were less enthusiastic about relocating the Athletics to the West Coast, so the team moved to the smaller city of Kansas City. The *New York Times* commented that: "A year ago the American League might have done something since it had two weak franchises in St. Louis and Philadelphia. But the Brownies became the Baltimore Orioles. . . . That leaves that Athletics all alone. The National League, which would love to tap the rich Coast territory, is practically embarrassed to discover that it has no weak franchises."[16] The American League owners were worried about the lack of large stadiums on the West Coast. The owners were also concerned about the increased travel expense.[17]

Kansas City was not a particularly successful relocation. Fans and opposing teams complained about a series of trades between the Athletics and Yankees.[18] When owner Arnold Johnson died, Charles O. Finley purchased the team. Finley gave early indications that he would improve things for Kansas City fans. He announced: "We will have no alliances with any other club in the American League. There will be no such trades as have been made in the past. When we develop stars, we are going to keep them."[19] He claimed to have spent $400,000 on promotions and improvements to the park, but this sum would soon haunt Kansas City officials and fans.[20] His determination to keep the team in Kansas City proved illusory; he was chronically dissatisfied with the situation there. He chafed at the stadium lease with the city, especially after the new Kansas City Chiefs football team negotiated an allegedly better lease. By the middle of the 1962 season, Finley's eyes were roving, and he made little attempt to camouflage this. He began with Dallas–Fort Worth and continued with Atlanta, Louisville, and Oakland. The American League thought Dallas–Fort Worth was a good choice for relocation, but the owners hesitated to approve the move for fear of displaying "callous disregard" of the fans in Kansas City that might have jeopardized the game's image.[21]

To keep the club in town, Kansas City's mayor and city council offered lease terms that they characterized as "the most generous" in baseball. Finley snubbed these concessions and repeated his claim that he had spent $400,000 to improve the stadium. His rental agreement with the city, however, was comparable to teams in Milwaukee, Cleveland, Baltimore, and Washington, D.C.[22]

Finley's efforts in trying to move the team to Oakland angered legislators. Senator Edward Long (Mo.) supported a bill that would bring professional team sports under the federal antitrust laws, because Finley's actions demonstrated a need to protect baseball and its fans from "the abuses of renegades."[23] Long also echoed Emanuel Celler's disapproval of mixing sports with profits, as he demanded to know, "whether or not the average franchise owner makes his decisions solely on the basis of business or does he consider the fact that baseball is a sport and a game."[24] Long's Missouri colleague Stuart Symington testified: "I am just interested in the fans of Kansas City."[25] Long and Symington blustered about Finley's proposed move, but ultimately, nothing was done.

The American League issued Finley an ultimatum to settle with Kansas City or else, relying upon a clause in the league's constitution entitled "Involuntary Termination of Membership." The other owners could expel any owner whose actions threatened them or that was not in the best interests of baseball.[26] Finley finally capitulated on February 26, 1964, and signed a four-year lease. The lease's salient clauses included an annual rental of 5 percent of paid admissions and 7.5 percent of the concession income, the first $50,000 of said rent to be paid to the city and the excess to be applied against the $300,000 stadium improvement tab. If attendance did not exceed 575,000, Finley would pay no rent, except the amount on concessions.[27]

Finley was not the only restless owner. Upon setting a National League record for home attendance in the first season, Milwaukee Braves' owner Lou Perini chortled, "You are the finest fans in baseball. You have restored their pride to members of the entire Braves organization."[28] He sang a different tune a decade later.

Some observers believed part of the Braves' troubles emanated from the Senators' relocation to Minneapolis–St. Paul. The American League team reputedly siphoned off baseball fans living in the upper Midwest and western Wisconsin, thereby constraining the Braves' drawing power to eastern Wisconsin.[29] Braves' officials did not blame the Minnesota Twins for the club's poor showing in 1961. Despite his prior success in Milwaukee, Perini could not resist firing a shot at the city and its fans: "If the Braves aren't on top within two or three years, the fans can throw us out of the town. If the fans desert us, this is not a major league city."[30] The Braves looked to go south, to Atlanta.

Ironically, a Kansas City sportswriter speculated that although Atlanta's biggest asset was its potential television market, Kansas City had potentially as large a television market. Kansas City could draw from the plains states and into Colorado, including Denver, while Atlanta captured the southern states.[31]

To induce MLB to go south, the Atlanta and Fulton County Recreation Authority scrambled to get a stadium built in time for the 1964 season and to issue invitations to Major League teams to relocate. The city hoped to build a stadium for baseball seating forty-five thousand, later increased to fifty-seven thousand. Recognizing the new realities of attracting fans, the mayor touted the fact that thirty-two lanes of expressways converged upon the stadium site; these expressways ensured that most Georgians were within ninety minutes' driving time of the stadium.[32]

By the summer of 1964, even *The Sporting News*' editor, C. C. Johnson Spink, assumed the Braves' relocation was a fait accompli. Spink blamed the Minnesota Twins for siphoning some of the demand for Braves' games. He touted the benefits of moving to Atlanta: "Atlanta has a metropolitan population of 1.12 million, with no big league competition closer than Cincinnati (454 miles away by automobile). Richer radio and television receipts through a more extensive network of stations than was possible in Wisconsin also influence the decision. With the move, the N.L. again will steal a march on the A.L."[33]

Milwaukee residents, in their frustration, wrote their congressman. Representative Henry Reuss contacted Ford Frick and Warren Giles requesting them to help keep the Braves in Milwaukee, but they gave only vague assurances that "every effort" would be made to consider every angle of any proposed shift. The Milwaukee County Board eventually served the club with a restraining order, based on breach of contract, because there remained a year to go on the stadium lease. Instead of being able to pay a reasonable estimate of the expected rent and thereby satisfying the lease contract, the Braves had to stay put and play at County Stadium. This last step worked temporarily. National League owners voted to keep the Braves in Milwaukee for one last season to fulfill the lease, but they also approved the Braves' move to Atlanta in 1966 as being "in the league's best interest."[34]

The Braves' desire to move was easily understandable. The team reportedly hoped to clear $0.75 million to $1.5 million per year for five years from television revenue alone in Atlanta, instead of the $400,000 it earned in Milwaukee.[35] Wisconsin Senator William Proxmire pushed to attach an amendment requiring that all television/radio revenue be put into a common pool and shared equally among all Major League clubs. He contended that such a policy would dampen the allure of cities such as Atlanta that promised big television contracts.[36] He cited football's Green Bay Packers as an example of the beneficial effects of revenue sharing: "Television pooling has allowed the Green Bay Packers, whose home is a city with a population of 60,000, to remain in Green Bay."[37]

Surprisingly, the departure of one franchise in multi-franchise cities did not always usher in an era of prosperity for the remaining team. Sports owners claimed they needed territorial protection, as new teams entering their cities reduced demand, leading to decreased revenues and profits. Their assertion implied that gaining monopoly status should have improved the prospects of those teams remaining in their city. MLB's experiences during the 1950s cast doubt upon such assertions. The holdover teams in Boston, St. Louis, and Philadelphia did not immediately reap increases in attendance, nor did they exploit their enhanced price-setting power. The Yankees' attendance and ticket prices were largely unaffected by the transfer of the Dodgers and Giants to the West Coast.[38]

As with most leagues, many NFL franchises were formed but few survived, especially during the league's first two decades. The AAFC's debut afforded Cleveland Rams owner Dan Reeves cover to force his fellow owners to approve his move to Los Angeles. Even after peace with the AAFC, the NFL transferred the New York Yankees to Dallas for a disastrous season and resurrected the Baltimore franchise. After the NFL's early 1950s, the league contained stable franchises, although the Chicago Cardinals were finding sharing the city with the Bears difficult. The Cardinals bided their time and eventually relocated to St. Louis by 1960. Years later, broadcaster Howard Cosell would brag about how NFL teams were not "carpetbaggers" moving franchises around as did the baseball owners; Cosell's remark was accurate only if one looked at only the very recent past. Unfortunately for his prognosticating reputation, Al Davis of the Oakland Raiders would trigger an NFL version of musical chairs. Legislators wanted more NFL teams, but none seemed too distraught over the Cardinals' relocation.

Legislators were even less interested in the NBA's instability. By the late 1950s, the NBA consisted of eight hardy teams out of twenty-four franchises that fielded teams in the National Basketball League and the Basketball Association of America. Six of the eight survivors relocated in the late 1950s and early 1960s. The NBA rid itself of weak franchises and became a concentrated eight-team league, and five of its franchises relocated to larger cities. The congressional subcommittee did not spend much time investigating the wanderings of NBA teams. Perhaps the legislators realized that Rochester, Fort Wayne, Syracuse, and Tri-Cities were unsustainable venues.

Franchise relocation would attract renewed congressional attention in the 1980s.

CBS Buys a Decrepit Yankees Team

Del Webb, Dan Topping, and Larry MacPhail had purchased the New York Yankees in 1945. At the time, observers were surprised by the low price they had to pay to acquire the team, some $2.8 million. After buying out MacPhail in 1948, the two remaining owners enjoyed an unparalleled run of success: fourteen pennants in sixteen seasons. They decided to sell the team to CBS for $11.2 million in 1964.[39]

When NBC news commentator Chet Huntley announced that CBS purchased the New York Yankees, he said, "Just one more reason to hate the Yankees."[40] Huntley's remark likely resonated throughout the baseball world. Houston Colt .45s president Judge Roy Hofheinz added, "The day CBS finally purchases the Yankees will be the blackest day for baseball since the Black Sox scandal." Sports columnist Arthur Daley, though, summed it up best for the fans by pointing out that CBS had deeper pockets than most owners. He believed CBS was interested in the Yankees in order to gain access to the team's lucrative telecasts. He bemoaned the transformation of ownership from sportsmen and sportswoman, Joan Payson of the New York Mets, to corporations, before concluding, "The carpetbaggers and the quick-buck men have taken over a game that once had true sportsmen at the controls."[41]

CBS's purchase of the Yankees during the 1964 season spurred fears of an unfair alliance. A number of the owners feared the anticompetitive aspect of the deal, especially with regard to bidding for network television rights, which might renew scrutiny of the reserve clause. Senator Hart, indeed, began the Senate hearings of 1965 by stating, "it [the CBS-Yankee acquisition] killed any hopes of passage of the [Professional Sports Antitrust Bill] at the last session of Congress."[42] Much of the 1965 hearings centered upon CBS's acquisition. Adding to the fears was the fact that CBS and the NFL had a contract for the 1965 and 1966 seasons; the broadcasting company opted out of the bidding for baseball's proposed Monday night game. CBS President Dr. Frank Stanton maintained there was not any anticompetitive potential. He instead referred to that will-of-the-wisp: synergy; Stanton, however, termed it an "affinity of management skills" and drew the comparison to both industries' need to draw large audiences. He denied that the network would switch local telecasts of Yankee games to its WCBS-TV affiliate, because the television schedule had already been set.[43]

The $11.2 million price for the Yankees shocked observers, since Lou Perini had sold the Braves for $5.5 million in 1962. CBS, though, had purchased much larger businesses than the Yankees. The $11.2 million represented only 1.8 percent of the company's revenues in 1960. Indeed, the company could have bought the Yankees with the profits from its interest in the Broadway hit *My Fair Lady*.[44] CBS was not the first serious suitor for the Yankees. According to Topping, Lehman Brothers tried to buy the club in 1962; the two parties failed to resolve tax questions, so the sale fell apart a few days before the CBS purchase.[45]

The ever-suspicious Emanuel Celler immediately sensed something amiss: "I don't think CBS would be interested in the Yankees purely from an entertainment standpoint. CBS must feel there is a huge potential profit from the transaction. This deal confirms my belief that baseball is big business. I think the Department of Justice should examine this sale."[46] Others presumed that CBS hoped the purchase would allow them to successfully enter the pay-television business. CBS piously responded, "Our association with the Yankees is another step in our response to the growing public interest in sports." The network was already paying the Yankees $600,000 per year for their appearances on the "Game of the Week."[47]

The Yankees' fellow American League owners disliked the fait accompli aspect of the deal. They had received scant prior notification and felt that the Yankees just railroaded the sale.[48] Charles Finley and Art Allyn criticized the deal. They worried that because owners were not allowed to have interests in more than one club, CBS's purchase of the Yankees created potential violations of this rule. American League president Joe Cronin required owners to divulge information on whether they owned any CBS stock. Baltimore chairman J.A.W. Inglehart decided to resign as a director of CBS after disclosing that he owned 39,500 shares of the company.[49]

Senators and baseball owners also wondered whether CBS would prevent the Yankees from joining John Fetzer's Major League television plan. S. Jerry Cohen, chief counsel for the Senate subcommittee, questioned Fetzer:

> Cohen: What would be the incentive for the Yankees or for CBS to give up a $500,000 contract to participate in a $325,000 deal?
>
> Fetzer: Ultimately we can increase the price [of the national package] to the extent that all ball clubs will be receiving more money, including the Yankees.

Fetzer based his optimism on the fact that including the Yankees in the national package would increase its attractiveness to a network, and also on his continued hope for a Monday night time slot.[50]

Despite the disclaimers issued by CBS and Yankees officials, some senators remained dubious and feared that the purchase would further tilt the playing field in the Yankees' favor. Senator Hart may have voiced the fears of baseball owners and fans when he stated, "I am sure that the Yankees are not going to be weakened as a consequence of the investment by CBS." Ford Frick sidestepped questions about the competitive aspects of the deal: "I suppose the outfit that has the most money theoretically at least could have the greatest chance of getting ball players." To allay the senators' concerns, Frick emphasized the new reverse-order amateur draft as counterbalancing the Yankees' superior purchasing power.[51]

Other major league owners had ties with television, though; Gene Autry, Judge Roy Hofheinz, and John Fetzer all owned stations. Fetzer did not think the purchase negatively affected his plan for Monday night baseball, considering CBS was never interested in it anyway. The Yankees were legally committed to joining the package deal in the future.[52] CBS and the Yankees maintained that current management would remain. Team general manager Ralph Houk thought CBS would be better positioned to promote the club.[53]

The fears, indeed, proved unfounded. CBS had bought a figuratively gimpy horse. Injuries curbed Mickey Mantle's and Roger Maris's productivity, and the team sank to the bottom of the American League standings. The team would remain mediocre until George Steinbrenner bought it from CBS in 1973 for $10 million.[54] He used clever trades and some astute free agent signings to restore the Yankees' prowess.

Conclusion: No One Likes Losing a Team

The movement of franchises provoked subcommittee scrutiny on occasion. The legislators disliked losing a franchise in their district. By posturing, they could score cheap points for their reelection bids. Criticizing the Yankees sale to CBS was another opportunity for legislators to pontificate upon the ills of owner greed. There were no subcommittee hearings examining or tears shed for CBS's disastrous experience with the Yankees and later sale for a loss (in purchasing power, if not in actual dollars) a decade later.

9

Professional Sports Team Community Protection Acts *1982 and 1984–1985*

Owners sometimes sought better venues for their franchises. Usually such relocations benefit not just the individual owner but all of the owners. The Boston Braves relocation to Milwaukee proved a godsend to the struggling franchise and enriched fellow National League teams with much larger visitors' shares. In some cases, though, an owner's wandering eye might have run afoul of his/her fellow owners' interests. If the public viewed a relocation as too opportunistic (relative to the attendance and revenue gains), a public backlash could develop. Al Davis's relocation of his Raiders is a case in point. Legislators and the public began to clamor for protection against such shifts.

Charles F. Rule, acting assistant attorney general of the Antitrust Division, suggested that, "the best way to ensure optimal parity is to have a single entity control the league. That entity could allocate players, coaches, and facilities in a way that maximized on-field competition and could correct any competitive imbalance that might arise." He admitted that such an approach would likely fail, as consumers would begin to think that, "the outcome of games was predetermined, and [their] interest in games might cool."[1] He continued by stating that, "a league's franchise relocation rule should be deemed *per se* lawful, unless it adversely affects competition with other leagues or is merely a subterfuge to disguise some other egregious anticompetitive conduct." Rule said the Antitrust Division would not oppose legislation allowing an antitrust exemption for league decisions to block franchise relocations, but that the Division would not support an exemption for revenue pooling. He added that the Department of Justice also would oppose an antitrust exemption for league rules on selection and termination of owners.[2]

Two examples of Rule's proposed leagues with player allocations determined by a central office include the All-American Girls Professional Baseball League (immortalized by the motion picture *A League of Their Own*) and Major League Soccer. Although the women's baseball league's demise was more a factor of the return to normalcy in the late 1940s and early 1950s, Major League Soccer experienced serious losses early in its existence.[3]

The Hearings on Roving Franchises

In the wake of franchise relocations in the NFL and the lingering ill-will triggered by the expansion Senators' move to Texas, legislators sought ways to protect communities from losing teams and to ensure stability. Various bills labeled "Community Protection Act" emerged during the early 1980s. Al Davis's relocation of his successful Oakland Raiders to Los Angeles, where he hoped to reap financial gains from a large pay-television market, despite the NFL's disapproval, triggered a round of lawsuits and anguished fans and their politicians. Robert Irsay's literal "fly-by-night" relocation of the Baltimore Colts to Indianapolis aroused Maryland legislators to a frenzy. Legislators launched subcommittee hearings into the matter during 1984.

The rationale for such federal meddling was that many teams played in municipally owned and maintained stadiums.[4] Stadium authorities offered sports teams favorable rental terms that left local residents vulnerable to taxation to cover shortfalls in stadium revenues.

Sports teams were, in many ways, desirable renters: They played regular, fixed schedules and usually earned sufficient revenue to make timely rental payments. The teams often attracted large crowds.

Professional sports leagues drew an unfriendly chairman: Slade Gorton of Washington. Senator Gorton had been the attorney general involved in the Seattle Pilots baseball team relocation case in 1969–1970. The American League eventually agreed to replace the Pilots with another expansion team, the Mariners, in 1977. Lest the owners have any doubts, he opened the hearings by stating the committee was going to investigate "what I consider to be an inexcusable callousness by some team owners toward the cities and fans upon whom their success ultimately depends."[5] As a sign of how low the owners' esteem had sunk in the eyes of the legislators, Senator Russell Long (La.), one of the legislative architects of the success of the AFL/NFL merger bill, stated, "We have had some allegations, and I suspect there is something to it, about money made even by owners with regard to scalping tickets."[6]

At the time of the 1982 hearings, the Minnesota Twins baseball team's owners were considering relocating the franchise to Tampa. The reader can easily imagine which legislators were most vociferous in support of the proposed bills: Minnesota, Maryland, northern California, and New York City.

These community protection acts, though, revealed the latent fissures within Congress. For every set of aggrieved fans losing a team, there were joyous fans and politicians who had gained a franchise. Senator Frank Lautenberg (N.J.) pointed out that the state's residents now had a New Jersey professional sports team to celebrate—the NFL New York Jets; they no longer had to derive vicarious pleasure and pride from the antics of teams in New York City and Philadelphia. He worried whether the proposed bill, Senate Bill 2505, would force the Jets to return to New York City.[7] Norman Lent (N.Y.) put the issue starkly: "Of the eight votes in the Senate Commerce Committee against this bill, my own estimate is that approximately half of them represented the views of members who represented cities which hope somehow or other to gain a major league team."[8] While legislators and the sports leagues debated whether relocating from New York City to New Jersey should be eligible for legislative review, the Raiders' and Colts' shifts certainly constituted relocation.

The 1984 hearings concerned Senate bill 2505. The act stated that Congress, "should discourage relocation of any professional sports team which is receiving adequate support from people in the city and the region where such team plays, unless such relocation is necessary to prevent severe financial hardship." Under the bill, owners would have to notify the public that they intended to relocate, and then to meet conditions stipulated by the law, including demonstrating that the stadium had inadequacies and that the team incurred losses for three seasons.[9] They then would have to offer the team "at fair market value" to parties that would maintain the team in its original city.

Under Senate Bill 2505, if there were disagreements, an arbitration board would make a final ruling. The board would consist of one party representing the current owner; one member chosen by the governmental agency that operated the stadium in which the team currently played; and one member chosen by the Secretary of Commerce.[10] To a legislative and legal mind, these stipulations seemed eminently reasonable. To the owners, the proposed legislation appeared to be an unreasonable restraint upon their property rights. When this bill failed to pass, Senator Thomas Eagleton of Missouri proposed Senate Bill 259, which would prevent team relocations; impose revenue sharing; establish procedures and standards for the selection of owners of member clubs; and establish procedures and standards for the termination of the ownership of member clubs. The owners, naturally, disliked this bill, as they deemed it necessary to maintain control over who joined their fraternity.[11] During the hearings regarding Senate Bill 259, the Commerce Committee considered and then rejected three amendments: limiting leagues and national television contracts; mandating expansion; and prohibiting telecasts of home games unless shown on free television.[12] In the end, Eagleton's bill, too, failed to pass.

Because legislators were unable to pass any particular bill, another set of hearings occurred in 1986. Ohio Senator Howard Metzenbaum, perhaps impatient with the entire process, stated, "I say, let the leagues fight it out. Repeal the baseball exemption, require the National and American Leagues to really compete with each other. Repeal the 1966 merger legislation and let the NFL, AFL, and the USFL fight it out. Then no NFL team would dare leave a major market, for an AFL or a USFL team would quickly move in if it did." Metzenbaum, perhaps sheepishly, continued by making it clear that such a scorched earth policy was not going to happen. "I am not going to introduce any legislation, not because I do not think that it should pass, but because I am a realist."[13]

Other legislators pointed out previous favorable legislation on behalf of professional team sports, including tax breaks. Representative Fortney H. Stark (Calif.) characterized the situation thusly: "These teams are operating on the backs of the average taxpayer. They are given exclusive contracts to protect them in electronic broadcasting. They are allowed to depreciate players. Not since prior to Reconstruction have we had individuals allowed to be depreciated." Stark pointed out that taxpayers who did not enjoy professional team sports should be relieved of the burden of supporting professional sports teams; he proposed a user fee or something similar to ensure that only fans bore the burden of subsidizing a sports team.[14]

Jay Moyer, NFL counsel, denied that the NFL was given special privileges via the league's use of publicly subsidized stadiums. He argued that "the financing of facilities with tax exempt revenue bonds is available to many businesses in the United States, and professional sports are not unique in using facilities constructed with such funding." Moyer also denied that owners received special treatment under the tax code since a 1976 overhaul.[15] Whatever the reductions in tax attractiveness, the line of prospective buyers of NFL franchises did not appear to diminish significantly.

One of the key problems, though, was that any such legislation was literally "after the teams had bolted the stadium"; retroactivity was necessary. Senator Charles Mathias (Md.) had considered including a retroactivity provision in his bill, but he feared the Judiciary Committee would balk at such a clause. Senator Lautenberg opposed retroactivity; Senator Gorton tried to resolve the issue, so that the Jets did not revert back to New York City.[16]

Legislators also struggled with the reality of passing a satisfactory bill while litigation was proceeding. Moyer made this an explicit concern: "Not the least important of our objections is that the enactment of any bill such as the ones currently before you . . . would in effect ratify a $50 million plus damage judgment—damage penalty against the NFL for trying to promote the very same stability and the very same respect for community interests that these bills are designed to promote. That to us is ironic, it is bizarre, and it is perverse."[17] Moyer went on to play the doomsday card: "Because if the Raiders case antitrust reasoning survives, as the dissenting judge in the ninth circuit panel noted, sports leagues may not survive."[18]

Al Davis and the NFL's Contretemps

The Oakland Raiders were the centerpiece of the hearings. When the Los Angeles Rams decided to relocate to Anaheim, which was within their territory, the Los Angeles Coliseum was left without a major tenant. The Coliseum began seeking new tenants, including a possible NFL expansion team. The league failed to give a satisfactory answer regarding an expansion team, so the Coliseum sued "in order to obtain a declaration that the NFL's rule requiring unanimous consent before a team could be placed in another club's home territory to be an unlawful restraint of Section 1 of the Sherman Act." The court dismissed the suit, as no prospective team owner had requested to place a franchise in Los Angeles; in response, the NFL changed its rule to require just three-quarters approval.[19]

This was where Al Davis stepped into the fray. When the Oakland authorities would not accede to his requests for stadium improvements, he announced his intention to relocate his team to Los Angeles to play in the Coliseum after his lease with the Oakland Coliseum ended. He did not bother to ask for a vote of his peers. With a team seeking to play in the Coliseum, the Coliseum authorities and Davis renewed the dismissed lawsuit. After a hung jury in the first trial, the Raiders and the Coliseum won a verdict in favor of the antitrust claims, largely on the basis that the court found that the NFL "was not a 'single entity' but rather was made up of 28 separate business units exercising independent business judgments in significant areas of individual concern." A jury eventually awarded the Raiders and the Coliseum a combined $16.41 million, which was subject to statutory tripling, or more than $49 million.[20]

The NFL naturally appealed the verdict and the awarded damages, with the league clinging to its argument that its members formed a single entity, based on the fact that the vast majority of its revenues were shared and on its promotion of competitive balance. The appeals panel voted 2–1 against the single-entity argument. Although recognizing that league members cooperated on many issues, each team maintained control over key issues and retained profits/losses on an individual basis. "A relocation decision, then, in the court's view, is the result of individual actions of the league members, not the result of a unified league body." The court also noted that previous courts had, in some cases, rejected the single-entity argument.[21]

The league would use the single-entity argument again in a later lawsuit, *American Needle, Inc. v. NFL*. In that case the NFL, through its NFL Properties (NFLP), decided to solely use Reebok International Ltd. to manufacture its headwear. American Needle, Inc., which formerly held a contract to manufacture such items, then sued. The NFL argued that it acted as a single entity, which, if true, would invalidate the antitrust allegation. Two lower courts agreed with the argument, but the Supreme Court repudiated it. The Supreme Court based its decision upon the fact that, although the thirty-two NFL teams marketed their products through NFLP, the owners remained individual decision makers: "Each of the teams is a substantial, independently owned, and independently managed business." The decision to form NFLP did not sway the Court: "An ongoing Sec. 1 violation cannot evade Sec. 1 scrutiny simply by giving the ongoing violation a name and label." They continued by quoting the opinion in *Timken Roller Bearing Co. v. United States*: "Perhaps every agreement and combination in restraint of trade could be so labeled."[22]

In its ruling in the Los Angeles Coliseum lawsuit, the court suggested that the league's rule pertaining to relocation needed to specify some objective guidelines in determining approval or disapproval: "An express recognition and consideration of those objective factors espoused by the NFL as important, such as population, economic projections, facilities, regional balance, etc., would be well advised." Davis, himself, had recommended back in 1978 that the NFL enact such a set of guidelines.[23]

The dissenting judge, however, provided the NFL some hope. The jurist wrote, "a ruling that the NFL cannot enforce Rule 4.3 [pertaining to franchise relocation] is effectively ruling that it may not enforce any collective decision of its member clubs over the dissent of a club member, although this is precisely what each owner has contractually bargained for in joining the enterprise. Without power to reach collective decisions, the NFL structure becomes superfluous, and professional sports, with a cost-effective policing mechanism such as the league, will dissolve in the face of uncontrollable free-riding and loss of economies of scale."[24] This argument seemed to distort the two jurists' opinion that the NFL could collectively decide upon relocation issues but that the league simply needed to impose some objective guidelines.

The Coliseum's capacity was far greater than most NFL venues, and Los Angeles promised to be an exceptional television market, as Oakland Mayor Lionel Wilson testified before the committee.[25] These were siren calls for restless owners, even for owners of prosperous franchises such as the Raiders. Oakland lacked San Francisco's glamour, and the rough-hewn Raiders exemplified their city. The Raiders were highly successful at the turnstiles, drawing some of the best attendance marks in the league.

NFL owners likely thought that placing an expansion team in Los Angeles was the best alternative. Based upon the territory's advantages, they could charge a hefty fee to any prospective expansion team owner, which would be split among all of the others. Because Los Angeles was such a lucrative television market, the other owners could hope that an enlarged national television contract might offset most of their reduction in per-team share of the proceeds. In other words, getting 1/29th of a much large television pie might be better than 1/28th of the current pie. State Senator William Campbell provided a transcript of Pete Rozelle's testimony in the *Los Angeles Memorial Coliseum v. NFL* case. The plaintiff's attorney, Maxwell Blecher, asked Rozelle, "Is it correct in your view that the franchise here in Los Angeles is worth more money than the franchise would be in Oakland?" Rozelle answered, "I think a franchise in Los Angeles would be worth more than Oakland and—a new franchise in Oakland and a lot of other cities, yes, because of the size of the population, the fact that there are a number of people here with wealth that could afford a franchise."[26]

Before the NFL owners mulled expansion into Los Angeles, Davis struck first. The rules stipulated that an owner seeking to relocate his team into a territory already occupied by another NFL owner needed to secure approval of at least three-quarters of the voters. The Rams owner, Carroll Rosenbloom, was unlikely to accede to Davis's invasion, and the majority of the other owners undoubtedly resented Davis's usurpation of their prospective expansion fees. When the owners voted, none chose to approve Davis's move.

Davis, though, had strong allies. The Los Angeles Coliseum commission and city officials favored landing the perennially strong Raiders team instead of some weak expansion squad. The majority of Davis's peers were aghast and angered by his chutzpah, but a few of them secretly envied his boldness. Indeed, the Baltimore Colts' owner, Robert Irsay was one. A few other owners, including Leonard Tose of the Philadelphia Eagles, were also intrigued by Davis's maneuvers.

Davis's actions were carefully watched by his peers in the team sports world. Alan I. Rothenberg, president of the San Diego Clippers, presented a vitriolic statement against his fellow owners: "This pack of monopolistic thugs has an unending record of abusing their special position, and court after court has so held, whether in the area of player relations where there is a long line of record abuse . . . or the emerging history of such abuse directed against independent owners as in the Raiders case and now in the Clippers case." What was the source of his vitriol? Simply that he wanted to move his team from San Diego to Los Angeles, even though his fellow owners opposed him; naturally, he took them to court. He urged municipalities to prevent relocation by locking in their professional sports team tenants into long-term leases. Rothenberg undercut the testimony of municipal officials by pointing out that the combined gross income of every professional sports teams in the big four leagues "would barely qualify for a listing in the *Fortune 500*. So, the fact that a franchise leaves a city will not effect

[sic] the standard of living of the population. The lives of most people will be unchanged."[27]

Another factor complicating the Raiders' litigation was the venue. The case was heard in a Los Angeles court, which was a judicial home-court advantage for Davis and the L.A. Coliseum. Some observers felt that the City of Oakland's failure to move the court case out of the Los Angeles court was a primary cause for their defeat. There were allegations of blatant bias in the Los Angeles court, such as derogatory remarks about Oakland. Jay Moyer told legislators: "The venue of the trial was not neutral; it was intensely interested in the outcome. The Raiders' attorneys capitalized on the trial venue in Los Angeles—characterizing Oakland as 'the murder capital of America.'"[28] Any argument about maintaining the Raiders' traditions with Oakland was less likely to sway jurors in Los Angeles. The City of Oakland resorted to an "eminent domain" argument that had gained traction. The Raiders began to petition the state legislature to amend the state eminent domain law to retroactively stop the City of Oakland's lawsuit.[29]

Legal scholar Arthur Johnson analyzed the case and the City of Oakland's eminent domain argument. The California Supreme Court gave the city a temporary victory when it ruled that the city "does have the power under the state's eminent domain statues to acquire the intangible property rights associated with a professional sports franchise, provided a proper showing is made." The Monterey County Superior Court ruled in July 1983, however, that the city failed to prove there was a public interest involved or that the city was attempting to acquire the team for a "public use." Both the antitrust and eminent domain cases were appealed, guaranteeing that the team's ultimate location remained unclear.[30] Years later the City of Baltimore would also employ the eminent domain argument in an attempt to keep the Colts from moving to Indianapolis; the argument failed.

Cities that lost teams claimed tens of millions of dollars in economic losses, although these claims were surely inflated. For instance, Mayor Donald Fraser of Minneapolis's testimony was typical: "If we should lose our franchise. . . . The economic loss we estimate at $22 million per year based on last year's experience. . . . We estimate a loss of 1,000 jobs, the kind of jobs that we very badly need in our city. We would lose the revenue to support our new domed stadium." He finished by claiming one other potential loss: "there would be a rupturing of the bonding that goes on between the community and the team."[31] These fears were likely overstated, as other entertainment venues likely gained revenues formerly accruing to the departed professional sports teams. Stadium authorities, of course, were hit hard, as their primary tenants fled their facilities, leaving massive debts and little hope of even meeting interest payments. Cities desired teams for the cachet of being "major league," and their residents did not want to travel relatively long distances to see a game.[32]

The legislators were hostile toward opportunistic owners, but they were wary of allowing the leagues to maintain the status quo with respect to their rules pertaining to relocations. Officials strenuously defended their leagues' rights to control franchise relocation, as well as expansion and contraction. Pete Rozelle claimed, "the tools have been taken from our hands [by the court rulings]. We were able to do these things in the past."[33] He went on to boast about the NFL's stability, claiming that no franchises had changed for decades (roughly twenty years), but he neglected to mention the Chicago Cardinals' shift to St. Louis.

The NFL's Response to Rogue Owners

Rozelle told legislators, "if this Raider suit is not resolved in favor of the league, if the Raiders move without league permission, you will have a franchise free agency." He went on to bemoan the verdict: "We went through two trials lasting 5 months since 1980, and were rewarded with a $50 million antitrust judgment awarded by a jury in Los Angeles."[34] Rozelle used this verdict to justify the league's passivity in the wake of Irsay's fly-by-night transfer of the Colts. He whined, "In this case we took no action in Baltimore because of the $50 million judgment against us. [The City of] Baltimore is suing. We are involved in litigation with Baltimore over that issue. Literally, we are damned if we do and damned if we do not."[35] Rozelle would later, however, take a firm stance in the proposed Philadelphia Eagles' relocation by having the league file a lawsuit against the Eagles. As he testified before a 1985 committee hearings, "I strongly recommended to the NFL's members that they had to take a stand in spite of the severe risks and legal confusion."[36]

Rozelle and the professional sports team owners wanted an antitrust exemption covering their right to control franchise movements and relocation. A cynic might suspect the owners of using the Oakland and Baltimore situations to salvage a partial victory: to gain explicit antitrust exemptions for specified future actions. In the past, the owners had taken such antitrust exemptions and interpreted them broadly, much to the legislators' chagrin.[37] The legislators, on the other hand, were angling for a different outcome. Many of them claimed that the relocation musical chairs emanated from the leagues' hesitance or downright refusal to expand to fill all cities capable of supporting franchises.

Rozelle and the NFL wanted legislation that would stop the Baltimore transfer and retroactively rescind the Raiders' transfer and $50 million in trebled damages. He believed that a clear-cut antitrust exemption was necessary, lest piecemeal legislation leave enough loopholes for future team relocations.[38] Moyer worried that some of the bills entailed creating a federal entity with "virtually unfettered power to determine the location of all professional sports team[s]."[39]

Rozelle and various witnesses sparred over the meaning of the court's decision in the Raiders' case. Although the court did not dictate exactly what the NFL needed to do to conform its rules pertaining to relocation within antitrust law, it offered some guidance.[40]

Sportscaster Howard Cosell claimed that all the NFL needed to do to comply with the court was to "change Rule 4.3 to a simple majority vote. It could establish reasonable criteria governing franchise transfers."[41] Senator Arlen Specter (Pa.) made a similar argument. Rozelle disputed Cosell's and Specter's opinions, stating that the league's attorneys "asked the court to amend the injunction to allow the League to vote on a Raiders' move on a majority vote basis. But the Los Angeles court rejected this League proposal."[42] Specter and Moyer also debated the NFL's voting rules.

The Legislators' Push for Expansion

Because legislators wanted to deliver new franchises to please their constituents, they devoted much of the hearings to grilling sports officials as to the "artificial scarcity" of franchises. The legislators accused the team owners of purposely leaving some viable cities open, so they could gain leverage in negotiating stadium leases.[43] If Tampa or some other city had a vacant stadium, then teams negotiating lease renewals could plausibly threaten to move there. As seen earlier, Charles O. Finley was an early pioneer of pitting city against city. Legislators pressed league commissioners and presidents as to when their leagues were going to expand.[44] The league officials, of course, tread a fine line; they issued vague but promising replies.[45]

In the past, legislative pressure seemed a more potent motive for expanding than the economic motive. MLB expanded in 1961–1962 to forestall the Continental League and to placate angry legislators. The NFL expanded into Dallas and Minnesota in 1960 and 1961 for similar reasons. The league then placed a new team in New Orleans in 1966 to help gain legislative approval of their merger with the AFL.[46]

Recognizing the professional sports leagues' dilatory efforts to expand, some of the proposed bills *required* the leagues to expand by a certain date.[47] Such expansion included replacing football teams in Baltimore and Oakland. This legislative interference probably had little chance of approval, but the legislators had made their point. Some of the city officials and other legislators were lukewarm about such edicts; they wanted their own teams back, not some expansion team that would struggle for years before becoming competitive.[48]

The sports league officials denied that an artificial scarcity existed. Paul Tagliabue, counsel to and, later, commissioner of the NFL, claimed, "Scarcity is demonstrated by the ability to exact high prices." He then claimed, "Our ticket prices in 1970 were in the neighborhood of $6 a ticket on the average. In 1980, they were in the neighborhood of $4.80. In terms of real buying power, we had a drop in ticket prices. . . . That is exactly the opposite of scarcity."[49] No one disputed Tagliabue's rather startling claim.

The NFL argued that expansion was costly. Moyer claimed before the legislators: "We expand . . . not for direct financial gain. In other words, the dilution of current club revenues and resources more than overtakes the so-called franchise fee, the amount that we would ever collect. . . . So it does not take very long before the money that you collect in expansion fees is overtaken forever by the dilution in your television revenues."[50]

Economists recognize that Moyer's argument contained some validity. In addition, they have identified another aspect: too high an expansion fee may affect the new owner's viability.[51] Incumbent owners usually help the owner of an expansion franchise by putting players into an expansion draft. The new owner can purchase player contracts from this pool of aging, over-the-hill players and unpromising younger ones. The incumbents receive much of their share of the expansion fee through this sale of players, while the new owner gains a useful tax benefit by being able to depreciate the value of the individual contracts. Owners selling players could gain, too. If the price charged for players exceeded the depreciation (amortization) on the player's signing bonus or contract purchase, the owner could declare the difference as a capital gain and not ordinary income. Fans should not shed tears for any of the owners in this context.

The NFL responded to James Florio's (N.J.) question regarding court rulings on expansion. The league referred to *Mid-South Grizzlies v. NFL*, whereby the court rejected the plaintiff's claim that "it was a qualified applicant and was therefore entitled to be admitted to the NFL. The Third Circuit opinion concluded that the NFL's decision not to expand on the plaintiff's demand restrained no business competition under antitrust concepts, and therefore determined trade association and similar 'admission' cases to be inapplicable." Although the Grizzlies were a successful franchise and met all NFL criteria for membership, they were rebuffed, first by the NFL and then by the courts. The ruling against the Grizzlies meant that antitrust laws could not be used to order sports leagues to expand.[52]

Naturally, the sports leagues chafed at the possibility of coerced expansion. Rozelle argued that the NFL had been responsible in preventing the game of musical franchises up until the Oakland and Baltimore relocations. He staunchly opposed a diminution in the league's authority, suggesting that, granted an antitrust exemption concerning location, the league would continue to consider community interests when determining relocation and expansion decisions.[53] Commissioners and presidents of other leagues claimed that their leagues had been responsible regarding relocation and expansion; such team movements that had occurred were economically defensible.[54]

The various players associations disputed the need for antitrust exemptions pertaining to franchise relocation. They were, of course, more favorably inclined toward legislation requiring expansion. Expansion meant more jobs and increased demand for top-flight talent. The players' representatives joined the chorus of legislators and fans arguing that owners had maintained an artificial scarcity of franchises.[55]

Legislators' Doubts about Revenue Sharing

Revenue sharing became an associated issue. If owners were forced to share pay-television revenue, in particular, the charms of relocation would be eroded. Even free television created disparities; Seattle Mariners' owner George Argyros pointed out that superstations such as Chicago's WGN and Atlanta's TBS gave their teams a huge advantage, especially as this local television revenue did not have to be shared. Argyros argued that franchise stability depended upon reducing the disparity in local television revenues; otherwise, teams would continue to migrate in hopes of getting more lucrative television contracts.[56]

In a letter from MLB general counsel Edwin Durso to Senator Ernest Hollings, Durso stated that the clubs with ties to superstations had agreed to put some of their revenue into a common pool for all the teams to share. He mentioned, too, that "Most clubs now supplement their local television package with some package of pay telecasting." The two leagues had different plans for sharing this new source of revenue, but apparently all clubs received some of the largesse.[57]

When the Eagles threatened to relocate, Senator Specter pinpointed the NFL's equal-shares' policy with regard to a national television contract. He supposed that, in the absence of such revenue sharing, the Eagles would have earned much less from independently seeking a television contract. Rozelle had to admit, "I can tell you, based upon my experience of 25 years . . . there is no way, no way, the Philadelphia Eagles, even though they are in the fourth largest market in this country, could obtain as much as they are now from the shared NFL television contracts."[58] Because CBS was hopeful of getting a monopoly right, which would have made its telecasts more lucrative, it could afford to bid a higher price for such rights than bidding for those of individual teams. In this case, the collective value of the individual teams' rights was less than having a single, exclusive contract for all of the teams. Ira Horowitz compiled data showing that the number of professional football network telecasts fell in 1962 and 1963, before rising during the remainder of the decade. Horowitz, though, points out that some of these telecasts overlapped, so fans may not have been able to see more games than before the NFL's national television contract.[59] NFL owners, of course, were gratified that they received much larger payment for television rights.

As Moyer pointed out, legislators had long "warmly and repeatedly endorsed these [revenue sharing] practices and urged them on other leagues." In fact, Moyer was correct. Legislators had long applauded the NFL's revenue-sharing plan, so the league's perplexity at the recent criticisms and suspicions was understandable. During the 1986 hearings, Senate Bill 298 would have explicitly granted an antitrust exemption for league revenue-sharing policies.[60]

Doug Allen, executive director of the USFL Players Association, pointed out that revenue sharing harmed players by reducing the incentives of owners to bid for their services. The rules might also injure players by discouraging owners from approving expansion, because they had to share television revenue.[61] Gene Upshaw, executive director of the NFL Players Association, attributed the demise of the World Football League (WFL), in part, to revenue sharing and the NFL's antitrust exemption for the national television contract.[62]

The Department of Justice reported to Senator Mathias (Md.) and the committee holding the 1985 hearings that, "Economic theory suggests that revenue sharing by the teams in a league could reduce the incentive for owners of individual teams to put out the best product. . . . Even though a particular type or level of revenue sharing may thus reduce competition among league members, that does not mean that it reduces consumer welfare so as to violate the antitrust laws . . . the antitrust laws recognize that, as to joint ventures in general, some limitations on competition among the members may enhance consumer welfare and that in the case of sports leagues, some limitations may be necessary to ensure parity among the teams." The report also predicted, "Where only a particular category of an industry's practices is to be exempted, it is possible to analyze with some precision exactly what conduct will be exempt and thus have some certainty that an exemption will not be overbroad. An exemption for an entire industry is far more likely to be overbroad in the sense of immunizing some significantly anticompetitive conduct."[63]

The NFL Faces Another Upstart

While Raiders and Colts contretemps were occurring, the NFL faced yet another upstart professional football league: the United States Football League (USFL). The league began operation in 1983 with twelve teams, nine of which "violated" NFL territories. Initially, then, three cities gained professional football and buttressed the legislators' claims that there were several cities in the United States capable and willing of supporting professional football franchises. To avoid direct competition with the NFL, the USFL operated under a spring/summer schedule.

The driving force behind the league, David Dixon, a New Orleans businessman, recognized that direct competition with the NFL during the autumn was not propitious. The league negotiated a modest television contract with ABC. After a few relatively successful seasons, the owners, led by a young Donald Trump, decided to tackle the NFL head-on with a fall schedule, which proved disastrous to the young league.[64]

The league eventually filed an antitrust suit against the NFL. The jurors agreed with the USFL that the NFL was an illegal monopoly and that it used predatory tactics to thwart the USFL. The jurors misunderstood the instructions regarding damages and awarded only $1, which was automatically trebled. The jurors mistakenly believed that the judge could increase the amount. In making the damage award, the jurors apparently thought the USFL contributed to its own demise. In addition, a few of the jurors worried that a large verdict would compel the two leagues to merge, creating a monopoly.[65]

Doug Allen made a telling point. Legislators were clamoring to replace NFL teams in Oakland and Baltimore. Allen pointed out that the USFL currently had successful franchises in those cities. He argued, "I do not think that the USFL should be punished by a mandated expansion when the NFL had in fact abandoned those cities."[66]

The NFL used many of its old tricks to stymie the USFL. Steven E. Ehrhart, executive director of the USFL, described to legislators how NFL owners attempted to keep USFL teams from obtaining leases with municipal stadiums.[67] As with all upstart leagues, the USFL suffered from franchise instability; Ehrhart admitted the league approved a relocation of the Boston franchise to New Orleans. Some legislators, indeed, believed new leagues needed special dispensation with regard to franchise relocations.

Harry L. Usher, commissioner of the USFL, blamed the NFL and the three networks for shutting out his league from national television. Usher pointed out that during the 1961 hearings permitting the NFL to negotiate a national television contract, Rozelle denied that the NFL planned to tie up all of the networks, although he admitted a successful attempt to do so would put any other league at a "major competitive disadvantage." After the 1966 merger, when the AFL and NFL continued existing contracts with NBC and CBS, Rozelle signed up ABC for *Monday Night Football.* Usher added, "Mr. Rozelle did not go back to Congress for permission to do what he had said in 1961 he wouldn't do and, in 1969, there was no competing football league to complain to Congress or the courts about the NFL's success in tying up all three networks. . . . That sequence of events demonstrates how Congress, despite its expressed intention to the contrary, permitted the NFL to establish itself in a monopoly position with all three networks which has effectively precluded any other professional football league from fairly competing."[68] Although Usher's recollection was accurate, the legislators may not have wanted to hear how the NFL had bamboozled them.

Gene Upshaw agreed with Usher that the NFL's domination of network television contracts doomed the WFL in the mid-1970s, because that league could not secure a television contract. He feared that the USFL would meet a similar fate.[69] Pete Rozelle responded to legislators' concerns regarding the USFL's lack of a network television contract. At the time of the hearings, the NFL still had contracts with all three of the major networks. Rozelle said that television industry sources told him that previous telecasts of USFL games had drawn poor ratings and generated insufficient advertiser interest. In addition to these drawbacks, Rozelle's sources said the fact that the USFL relocated teams from such large television-market cities as Boston, Chicago, Detroit, Philadelphia, and Washington reduced the league's attractiveness to advertisers and networks.[70]

Conclusion: The Teams That Bolted

In the end, the Raiders returned to Oakland, leaving Los Angeles open, which it remains to football this day. The Colts stayed in Indianapolis and prospered under quarterback Peyton Manning. The Twins stayed in Minnesota, one domed and one open-air stadium later. The NFL, MLB, and NBA all expanded during the 1990s, but there are still cities clamoring for top-level, professional team sports.

10

Professional Sports Teams Grapple with Radio and Television

Changes in technology affected professional team sports. Baseball and football had previously adjusted to the realities of cheap newsprint, radio, and electric lights. MLB and the NFL might have needed to handle the newest kid on the technology block—television—in the early 1940s. The technology was available prior to the war, but the conflict delayed television's diffusion for several years.

Television, as with radio earlier, befuddled the owners. They wanted to be left alone to devise their own television policies. Owners discovered, however, that congressional members believed the public had an interest in when, where, and how games were televised. The legislators relied upon the fact that the airwaves were public property to assert their right to interfere.

Owners feared the effects of broadcasts and telecasts of home games upon attendance at the stadiums. Right after World War II, owners sold television rights for thousands or tens of thousands of dollars per season. Baseball's World Series' telecasting rights commanded a premium, as did all leagues' championship games, going for $800,000 in 1950. By 1961, MLB's media revenues doubled its payroll expense. The New York Yankees were earning more than one million dollars per year from broadcasts and telecasts by the early 1960s. When Pete Rozelle landed a national television contract for the fourteen NFL teams worth $300,000 per team in 1961, owners were pleasantly shocked.[1] Congress played an active role in the marriage of sports and television by passing legislation concerning national television contracts and regulating blackout rules.

Despite the legislative gains, owners claimed to feel damned if they did and damned if they did not with regard to telecasts. The subcommittee members blasted MLB for broadcasting and telecasting their games into minor league territory—suddenly, a team's territorial rights mattered—whereas NFL owners found their blackouts of telecasts of home games under fire. Legislators, too, worried about the effects of NFL telecasts on college and high school football games, although little evidence was presented regarding these effects.

This chapter examines professional team sports' history with radio and television. The next chapter covers hearings on baseball's television policies. Another covers the NFL's subsequent bid for an antitrust exemption regarding its national television contract. Two other chapters examine television blackouts and cable television.

Early History of Television and Sports

The federal government regulated television, partly through assigning stations. The Federal Communications Commission (FCC) halted the stampede for station licenses in September 1948 by imposing a moratorium upon new ones. The cessation of licensing left wide swaths of the United States without television coverage, although most of the affected regions were sparsely populated. Before the cessation, California and the northeast quadrant of the United States were blanketed with telecasts. Many of the major metropolitan areas in the South also had television.

Baseball owners had warily embraced radio broadcasts of games in the 1930s. Given the economic downturn simultaneous with the widespread broadcasting of games on radio, owners had difficulty discerning the medium's effects upon attendance and gate receipts. Several owners chose to blame radio broadcasts for their attendance doldrums, and teams in New York City prohibited broadcasts until 1939. Some owners were convinced that broadcasts of home games diminished attendance at ballparks. When radio stations and sponsors began to offer payment for broadcast rights, some owners' enthusiasm for broadcasts heightened. During a New York Yankees' board meeting, the members stated the conundrum openly: Would the proffered payments for broadcasting rights compensate for the reduced gate receipts?[2] Attendance fell during the early part of the 1930s, and some owners who had countenanced broadcasts of home games were quick to blame the technology. By 1939, however, even the Yankees broadcast home games for a fee.

Football owners, too, struggled to understand radio's effects upon home attendance. They, as with their baseball peers, hoped that radio and, later, television would create new legions of fans.

Given their wariness of radio, MLB owners performed a U-turn in their attitude toward televising games by almost unanimously scheduling telecasts of home and road contests immediately after World War II. Some owners, though, became suspicious of the effects of televising home games' upon gate attendance.

MLB attendance peaked in 1948, before there were many televisions. As televisions began to saturate American households, baseball suffered from an attendance decline that bottomed out in 1953. Thereafter, baseball attendance rebounded, albeit haphazardly, even though television ownership had become well-nigh ubiquitous. This is, of course, a cursory examination that simply raises questions about television's role in the attendance fluctuations. Disentangling fluctuations in attendance because of broadcasts and telecasts and owing to economic fluctuations or other factors required sophisticated statistical analysis, which the owners and congressional investigators did not or could not pursue.[3]

Detroit Tigers' owner John Fetzer provided an apt description of television and baseball: "baseball has been engaged in a constantly changing and developing relationship with the television industry."[4] Television was, indeed, a difficult medium to understand.

Baseball commissioner Albert "Happy" Chandler may not have understood baseball's bargaining position with respect to television networks. Bill Veeck stated, "Baseball happens to be a bargain [for television stations]. It supplies a daily 3-hour show, and provides its own location, its own actors, and its own pre-packaged audience. Television has to provide nothing except the cameras and cameramen."[5]

Professional football held a special attraction for networks. Telecasts of games created a predominantly male audience, which few types of programming could match. Scholar Donald Parente observed that, "although baseball may be as popular as football, it reaches fewer, less affluent men and therefore is less attractive to advertisers." He also noted that sports owners adjusted their games to increase their appeal to television viewers.[6]

By the mid-1950s, NBC and CBS began telecasting the baseball "Game of the Week." Of course, the networks wanted games between top teams and began dictating scheduling and even some rules. Baseball officials worried that telecasts provided a better vantage point for watching a game than many of the seats in their stadiums. Ford Frick insisted that Roone Arledge and ABC ensure that the view on television was not better than that "of the worst seat in the ball park." By 1961, MLB's radio and television broadcast revenues were sufficient to cover player payrolls twice over; such revenues amounted to 40–45 percent of total revenue.[7]

While baseball and football vied for television revenue, the sports sometimes had common ground. Frick supported Emanuel Celler's television bill that would permit the NFL and AFL to negotiate package deals with networks; baseball believed that any antitrust exemption granted football would also reinforce their sport.[8]

The NFL at first decided upon a laissez faire policy with regard to telecasts of games, similar to the one employed by MLB: the individual owner had discretion, as long as the telecast did not violate another team's territorial rights. The

New York Giants' football team arranged for NBC to televise their home games for the 1947 season. Because New York City was the epicenter of television in the late 1940s, the other teams monitored the Giants' experiences with television.[9]

Many football owners believed that televising home games would harm home gate receipts, although an optimistic few hoped that telecasts would offset any initial decrease in attendance by creating new fans, who would eventually buy tickets. Most probably would have agreed with Colonel Leland S. MacPhail, co-owner of the baseball Yankees, when he told reporters that the team had never completely sold out Yankee Stadium, not even for the World Series. He argued that television would not help achieve a sell-out, before concluding, "If the World's Series is to be sold to the television people, consideration of anything under $100,000 would be downright silly."[10]

George Halas, owner of the Chicago Bears, though, embraced television from the start, especially after the Pabst Brewing Company paid him $5,000 to telecast a season-ending game against the Cardinals. The game was sold out, but because of rain, a sparse crowd of fifteen thousand fans came to watch. Halas, while pocketing the gate receipts from the fifty thousand tickets sold, was so upset by the sight of so many empty seats that he forbade further telecasts of home games. He did, however, quickly realize that telecasting Bears' road games would be beneficial; he created a network of stations to show all of his games, though outside a seventy-five-mile radius of downtown Chicago. NFL owners followed Halas's lead and prohibited telecasts of home games within a radius of seventy-five miles from where the game was being played. They believed such a policy would protect home gate receipts. Some television executives disagreed with the league's policy, and they filed an antitrust suit with the federal government.[11]

Football attendance was difficult to disengage from television, because the number of professional football teams dropped from eighteen to twelve between 1948 and 1951. The surviving NFL teams began a steady increase in per-game attendance during the decade, an increase that mirrored the growing diffusion of televisions. The relationship between television and attendance, then, was difficult to ascertain.[12]

There was a significant difference between MLB and NFL owners' attitudes toward their sources of future players. MLB often owned, subsidized, or were allied with minor league teams. If telecasts of MLB games hurt minor league attendance, then Major League owners stood to suffer financially along with their farm teams. In the football world, while it was true that college and university football teams were the primary sources of players for the NFL, there were not any direct financial connections between the entities.

Basketball owners, too, were unsure about televising games. According to Marty Glickman, New York Knicks radio announcer, television sought out basketball and not vice versa. Glickman recounted a meeting between Knicks president Ned Irish and Burt Lee, program director for television station WHN at Toots Shor's, a famous hangout for professional athletes and officials. Lee suggested telecasting Knicks games, and Irish asked, "How much would it cost me?" Irish was apparently surprised, when Lee replied, "Not only will it cost you nothing, but we'll pay you $250 per game." Glickman said that the price eventually rose to $1,750 per game. At $250 per game and thirty home contests, the Knicks could make $7,500, enough to cover a starting player's salary. By 1948, the Knicks contracted with ABC to televise their entire 1948–1949 basketball schedule in Madison Square Garden, as well as playoff games.[13] Considering Knicks' net home game receipts fell between the two seasons from $7,943 to $6,542 per game, the overall gain, if any, in combined revenues was small.

NBA owners had cause to worry about telecasts' effects upon home attendance. These owners received only modest payments from the television stations for telecast rights, so even a small decrease in attendance would more than offset any gains from selling telecasting rights. Walter Brown, owner of the Boston Celtics, reluctantly admitted to Glickman what his team received for television rights. "It's embarrassing." Glickman pressed Brown, who admitted to $5,000. "That's pretty good," he said. Brown retorted, "For the season?"[14]

The NBA owners agreed to a deal with the Dumont Network to air thirteen games during the 1952–1953 season. League official Haskell Cohen recalled that the league received $3,000 per game, which went to the home team. "They were so anxious to get that $3,000 that they said, 'Let's try it.'" Maurice Podoloff mused that someday, "proceeds [from television] may supplement gate receipts to the point where the latter lose their importance." The owners wanted the $3,000 per game, but they remained suspicious of television. Rochester owner Les Harrison admitted to sportswriter Terry Pluto that the league failed to "sell stars." "In fact, we put our worst games on because we feared that if we broadcast the best games, no one would buy a ticket. They'd all stay home and watch it for free. So what the public saw was the worst of pro basketball."[15] Harrison's observation had some validity, at least for the 1953–1954 season, when tail-enders Milwaukee and Baltimore hosted four of the fourteen games.

Podoloff testified that a later national broadcasting contract meant that every team hosting a televised game received $7,500. The league attempted to rotate the exposures on television across the seasons. Each team had three home games televised every two seasons, so the revenue was equally shared. The equal division of revenue from the NBA's national television contract was novel, coming years before the AFL's and NFL's national contracts.[16]

Owners in all professional team sports struggled to learn how best to harmonize interest between television and their games. Players, too, had dreams for the new medium; they hoped television revenues would increase salaries, although owners resisted such possibilities. Baseball owners sought to insert a clause into the standard player contract excluding players from television profits, but their efforts failed.[17]

The owners seemed overly insecure about the attractiveness of their product. Modern fans would consider radio broadcasts of baseball or football games to be, at best, a poor substitute for witnessing the game in person. Some broadcasts did not even provide live play-by-play coverage but, instead, re-created the action. Although television was a better substitute for live attendance, early telecasts were primitive (at least from twenty-first-century perspectives). The cameras needed a great deal of light, and there were few of the enhancements today's fans take for granted: no color pictures, limited camera angles, indifferent lighting, no instant replay, and many other limitations. Most fans, though, or at least those who wrote to their editors, disputed the idea that listening to or watching a game was as good as being at a ballpark. In retrospect, the owners' fears of broadcasts and telecasts may seem overwrought.

Almost two decades after television's advent, sportswriter Dave Anderson wondered whether professional sports, and professional football specifically, would suffer from too much exposure. Pete Rozelle defined overexposure as being a situation where telecasts "drastically curtail[ed] attendance . . . and interest and therefore diminish our TV rights." He discounted any real possibility of such diminution occurring, because of the league's blackout policies and the limited number of nationally televised games.[18]

Television's Effect on Attendance

What evidence did owners have regarding the effects of televising home games upon attendance and gate receipts?

Ascertaining television's effects upon professional team sports proved difficult. When the issue assumed center stage by 1950–1951, commentators suggested several explanatory variables, including shifting economic conditions, the Korean War, suburbanization, demographic changes, and technology. How to frame the question was important. Did the woes attributable to television arise from television programming in general (entertainers such as Milton "Uncle Miltie" Berle) or from telecasts of baseball and football games specifically? Radio's revolutionary effect was to create national markets for at-home entertainment. Millions of Americans could share the same leisure-time experience of listening to Fibber McGee and Molly and many other similar programs. Radio also greatly expanded the fan base for popular musicians. Television promised to take this homogenization of at-home leisure a giant step further. By offering popular programs, television could usurp the charms of local baseball or college football teams. Consumers could choose between nationally recognized talents or the relatively obscure lads performing on the local diamond or gridiron. The NFL's 1958 championship game was hailed as a sort of coming-out event for the league, with fans and sportswriters across the country marveling about the exciting contest, won by the Colts over the Giants.

The majority of owners and their commissioners offered piecemeal evidence. Baseball executive Frank Lane's warning, "Radio aroused the curiosity of people; television satisfies it!" made sense.[19] Radio engaged only one sense; television engaged two. Being at the ballpark, of course, involved smell and taste, as well. Cleveland Indians' owner Ellis Ryan was more circumspect: "A one-year test isn't enough to justify curtailment of our television program."[20]

The Yankees were usually first in the American League standings, but they were the last in the American League to install electrical lighting for their ballpark and to allow radio broadcasts. However, they proved eager to telecast home games. By 1952 the Yankees, as with several other baseball teams, were growing suspicious of telecasting's effects. General manager George Weiss decided to not to televise a Yankees-Red Sox game in 1952; the Monday night contest drew more than fifty-one thousand, the largest crowd since 1947.[21] Weiss, though, admitted this was an experiment involving only one game.

Researcher Jerry N. Jordan attempted to disentangle the myriad effects upon attendance at baseball games. He discovered that surveys of fans at MLB games during the late 1940s revealed a higher rate of television ownership among them, and that people who owned televisions for two years or more attended ball games more frequently than others. His research suggested that television was, overall, a relatively minor factor in determining attendance and less important than such factors as team performance, personal income, and team management.[22]

Shortly after Jordan's research, MLB suffered an attendance reversal following the initial postwar boom. Attendance fell by 27.6 percent between 1947 and 1953. Owners naturally sought the cause of such a decline. The televising of home games was an obvious suspect. Because the diffusion of television ownership progressed at different rates across cities with MLB teams, statistical analysis of television ownership rates and changes in attendance was possible. Such analysis reveals that television ownership did not explain much of the drop in attendance between 1947 and 1950 or from 1947 to 1953. If anything, television revenue helped cushion the decline in real total gate revenue, making up roughly half of the shortfall.[23]

R. C. Embry, president of the Baltimore team, believed that a 25 percent decline in attendance at Colts' games owed to telecasts of the team's games, and he ordered the practice stopped, although he added that a permanent halt depended upon future attendance. The team's win-loss record was worse in the latter season, but not precipitously so.[24]

By the mid-1950s, sports officials were less worried about telecasting games. At times, Commissioner Bert Bell credited television with near-miraculous powers. He told Kenneth Harkins that, "Without radio and television and preseason games, salaries would drop to $100 a ball game, if they would play." Here, Bell's imagination faltered, as he concluded: "I don't believe . . . that the television and radio [revenue] will increase very much, for the simple reason that today the price of cables and pickups and the price of line charges and the price of time at the stations have increased so much that the sponsor . . . will not be able to pay more in rights fees than they do today."[25]

The Justice Department Files Suit

The U.S. Department of Justice eventually took notice of both baseball's and football's restrictions on telecasts and deemed them violations of antitrust statutes. After being advised of the Department of Justice's opinion regarding the ban on telecasts of MLB games into minor league territories, MLB tried to revise its rules to comply but eventually expunged the entire rule. The Justice Department filed an antitrust suit against the NFL regarding its policy of blocking telecasts of home games, with Judge Allan K. Grim presiding. A Senate subcommittee convened hearings responding to baseball's request that its rule pertaining to telecasting games be reinstated in May 1953, concurrent with the NFL antitrust action. To defend the league against the antitrust charge, NFL officials would repeatedly employ many similar arguments and tactics: hyperbole ("death knell"), facts with ambiguous interpretation (lone attendance changes without context), and the argument that the NFL was not commerce.

Bell had raised the issue of television and the government's attitude toward it by the early 1950s. George Preston Marshall observed that, "All the lawyers in America have worked on this and baseball has signed an agreement with the government. . . . The government contends that we must follow the rule on baseball. We are a monopoly because we control more than 75% of all professional football played according to them. We come under their jurisdiction the same as baseball due to radio and television." The Liberty Broadcasting System (LBS) allegedly instigated an antitrust suit against the NFL and nine of its club based on the allegation that the league created, "a system of authorizing the broadcasting of professional football game in such manner as to restrain trade unlawfully in broadcasting and to maintain a monopoly of the broadcasting" in the NFL teams' territories.[26] "Allegedly" is because the complainants were anonymous.

LBS's founder, Gordon McLendon, testified against the NFL in the television antitrust suit; indeed, Bell and the NFL owners assumed that McLendon sparked the federal investigation. LBS had declared bankruptcy before the lawsuit was filed, and readers may speculate that the company's officers were fishing for settlement money. Immediately upon serving Bell with a copy of the complaint, LBS's Dallas attorneys suggested a settlement, which the commissioner spurned.[27]

McLendon had built a network of four hundred affiliate radio stations. His network re-created professional football games for radio audiences between 1947 and 1949, prior to broadcasting live in 1950 and 1951. He had NFL permission for all these broadcasts. McLendon recalled that only two games had been sponsored, including the NFL title game in 1951, although the company broadcast thirty games that season. Judge Grim questioned him as to radio broadcasts' effects on professional sports. While admitting he could not ascertain television's effects, McLendon claimed, "speaking for radio I can say that absolutely, it has not hurt the attendance at professional football games. Radio created more interest in football and other sports." NFL defense counsel Bernard Nordlinger persuaded McLendon to admit that he had sought to purchase an interest in the now-defunct Dallas Texans NFL team (luckily for him, he failed, since the Texans hemorrhaged money), despite "his alleged objections to the league's broadcast and telecast rules and despite McLendon's pending $12,000,000 suit against MLB for alleged use of similar rules."[28]

After the usual parrying between attorneys, Judge Grim asked federal counsel W. Perry Epes, "Does it make any difference to you whether television might kill professional football?" Epes apparently understood that he might have overstated his case, but he recovered and replied, "that is not the question here Your Honor, but legally, economic justification is not a defense in an antitrust suit." "Then your answer is No," to which Epes could only nod in agreement.[29] Judge Grim's exchange with Epes provided an indication of his thinking about the case and his eventual ruling.

The government attorneys established that the "public's right to open television of football games was 'one of the fundamental problems of this case.'" The government also demonstrated that there was considerable interest in telecasts of professional football games. To buttress the argument concerning the general interest in telecasts, James. W. Seiler, director of the American Research Bureau, testified as to the size of the audience viewing various shows. Nordlinger immediately questioned Seiler's credibility, with the attorney maintaining "that a statistician couldn't possibly have the technical and other knowledge to give opinions on the feasibility of telecasting games in certain territories and on the financial benefits to sponsors of the presence or absence of restrictions."[30]

The NFL's attorneys claimed that a government victory in the antitrust suit would devastate the NFL or result in a nationwide blackout of broadcasts and telecasts. Judge Grim denied the motion to dismiss the case, as "he wished to hear the entire case before making a decision." NFL attorney Francis Myers stated that the government was forcing NFL team owners to provide "a free seat, mind you even though the granting of that free seat might empty our ball parks, bankrupt our clubs and thus eventually assure those 160 million Americans watch a Western movie rather than a football game." He disputed whether buying a television or radio entitled consumers to receive NFL games for free.[31]

NFL owners used the Los Angeles Rams' experiences with televising home games as the chief piece of evidence demonstrating television's baleful effects upon attendance. The Rams pulled in 83,501 fans for a playoff game against the Bears in the Coliseum. The game was broadcast but not telecast. Rams' officials highlighted the fact that an earlier televised game in the Coliseum attracted just 18,213 fans. Sportswriter Frank Finch immediately blamed television: "TV must take a big share of the blame for the September floperoo." The Rams had cleverly arranged their television contract with the Admiral Corporation and NBC's local video outlet, KNBH, so that if attendance fell off, these two companies would reimburse the Rams. The Rams' six regular-season home games garnered an audience of 158,845 in 1950, but this paled in comparison with the 269,327 attendees in 1949.[32] Admiral and NBC chose not to pay for telecasting rights to the team's 1951 home games.

Fortunately for the NFL, though, congressional investigators did not examine back issues of the *Los Angeles Times*. At the conclusion of the 1950 season, Reeves told a reporter, "The Rams and their sponsors feel that the experiment was a success, and we hope to work out a deal whereby we can televise again next season. Personally, I think TV did a great job of selling the Rams to the public."[33]

Bell was the NFL's primary witness. He claimed that unrestricted radio and television would diminish live audiences and eventually erode player salaries. "We would not be able to sell admission tickets in sufficient quantities to pay high salaries." Without high salaries, he worried that the quality of play would suffer, which, in turn, would lead to fans avoiding games. He claimed that fans would decide on the day of the game whether to attend or whether to watch on television, with bad weather squelching attendance. He later toned down his dire claims. Attorney Epes asked Bell whether MLB had experienced its death knell by repealing its Rule 1(d) governing broadcasts and telecasts. Bell had to admit MLB was still going strong, but he could not resist getting in the last word, "but it will."[34]

After Bell testified, an advertising executive explained how the NCAA could get $2.5 million for telecasts. With prescience, he told the court that the NCAA's deal was "exclusive and on a national basis." He continued by saying if "pro football could be telecast similarly he could see no reason why it couldn't demand the same price."[35]

The NFL presented evidence from the NCAA's experiences with telecasts. The NCAA tried to control telecasts of games, but the two cases were not the same, because the NCAA covered hundreds of college football programs whose territories overlapped. Paul B. Schetsley, a National Opinion Research Center researcher, claimed television hurt attendance at college football games; the NCAA had paid his organization to conduct the study. Paul Schissler, director of special events for the *Los Angeles Times,* operated the newspaper's annual charity game between the Redskins and Rams. He testified that the game's lowest attendance in the eight years was the one that had been televised.[36]

New York Giants president John Mara's testimony was more relevant. Mara claimed while being cross-examined that he would want "a guarantee to cover a complete sell-out for every game," as compensation for granting television rights. Government attorney Perry Epes got Mara to admit that the Giants hardly ever sold out. According to Mara, the Giants had net income of $49,000 in 1952, while receiving $50,000 for radio rights and $108,000 for television rights. Mara testified that the club stopped televising home games after 1948, when they discovered the telecasts hurt attendance. He further claimed that between 1946 and 1948, as the number of television sets in New York City increased from thirty thousand to four hundred thousand, bleacher attendance dropped from thirty-six hundred to fourteen hundred. Mara later had to admit that the fall in bleacher attendance could have resulted from the team's poor play in 1948. Bleacher sales rebounded in 1950, as the team improved. Mara wanted the seventy-five-mile blackout rule because, "We spend a lot of money building up fan interest within a 75-mile radius of New York City. . . . We want the fans to see and hear the Giants' games to arouse and keep their interest in our team. Then, too, we want to give the sponsor a break. The sponsor is entitled to an undivided audience for his advertising. We don't want any other team televising in our territory when we are at home."[37]

Mara also submitted a brief to the court demonstrating that the sales of reserved seats dropped as television sets became more prevalent, from 91.5 percent of reserved seats in 1946 down to 62.5 percent in 1950. Peterson quoted Mara as saying, "These figures do not necessarily constitute a complete indictment of television as the sole factor affecting the economics of our business. However, it had to be recognized that television was more than a straw in the wind."[38] The Giants' team deteriorated during the late 1940s, although it rebounded strongly in 1950. The interaction of attendance, television, and team record was complicated.

George Preston Marshall proved a more belligerent witness. He claimed the government was trying to *create a monopoly* rather than eliminate one. "The only complaints the Justice Department has received about our radio and television policy has been from a few men in radio and television who are not getting a piece of the pie and want to muzzle [sic] in. The people have not complained. I challenge you [government counsel] to prove that the public objects to our radio and TV policy." Federal attorney Epes told reporters that he was not allowed to identify the complainants to the Justice Department, but added that there were "many complaints, not one or two." Marshall was unique in that he bragged about not having had "a losing season financially in the last sixteen years, but that without radio and TV receipts, Washington would have been in the red in ten of those years."[39]

Two other NFL officials testified regarding broadcasts and telecasts. Nicholas Kerbawy, Detroit Lions' general manager, told the court that the team made $114,000 in profit in 1952, while receiving $113,000 from radio and television.[40] Kerbawy did recall a drop-off in ticket sales for a Rams-Lions playoff game, after a rumor arose that the game was to be televised in Detroit. Philadelphia Eagles president Frank L. McNamee claimed television had an adverse effect on attendance, but he admitted that "in 1948, when a snowstorm blanketed Shibe Park before a title game between the Eagles and the Chicago Cardinals, he stayed home and watched it on television."[41]

Unlike in the program *Dragnet,* where the narrator spoke the iconic words, "in a moment, the results of that trial," Judge Grim took several months to issue his decision. The key result of his ruling was that "the league could restrict telecasts that would interfere with gate receipts of a specific game but that it could not interfere with telecasts or radio broadcasts that would not affect attendance."[42] The NFL owners were relieved to have won the primary battle: the right to a television blackout within a seventy-five-mile radius of a home game. Judge Grim repudiated Bell's power to "approve or disapprove all contracts made by the league teams for the telecasts or broadcasts of their games." He also rejected the league's argument that it was not subject to the antitrust laws because it was not engaged in interstate commerce. Judge Grim did provide the league with a handy defense in his finding that the restriction of telecasts "was necessary for the league's existence and therefore was not an unreasonable restraint."[43] The league owners used Grim's ruling as a rationale in a later case, when they wanted an exemption to launch a national television deal. They decided not to appeal the judge's ruling, perhaps deciding that half of a favorable ruling was better than none.[44]

The NFL continued to be wary of congressional and judicial intervention. Interim commissioner Austin Gunsel partially lifted the blackout of the New York Giants-Cleveland Browns playoff game in December 1959. Because the game was played in Baltimore, Washington, D.C. would have been blacked out under normal circumstances. Gunsel, though, figured it was best to forestall any protests by permitting the game to be televised there. He told the owners, "I cannot help but believe that the decision which was made in this instance may possibly have forestalled anti-trust action on the part of the Department of Justice . . . who had received many complaints about our policy."[45]

Television Blackouts and Antitrust Issues

The NFL's blackout policy continued to draw fire from critics and politicians for years to come and would eventually invoke congressional scrutiny. Bell rejected Michigan Governor G. Mennen Williams's and Senator Charles E. Potter's requests that the NFL lift the television blackout of the Lions/Browns Championship Game in Detroit. Potter postured and demanded that the Justice Department investigate the "dictatorial and arbitrary" decision, but Bell replied: "I don't think it is honest to sell tickets to thousands of people, then afterward, when all the tickets are gone, to give the game to television."[46]

The 1959 congressional committee investigated television blackouts. *Broadcasting* worried about Senate Bill 2545, which included the seemingly innocuous phrase, "within special geographic areas." The editorial writer feared that "geographic" exemption was a potentially devastating loophole that created the possibility of "a total blackout of free TV."[47] Bell said that the NFL had satisfactorily coexisted with Grim's decision: "We assume that our regulation of broadcasting and telecasting consistently with this decision would undoubtedly be deemed 'reasonably necessary' by the FCC but we would, of course, be happy to be relieved of the necessity to go before the Federal Communications Commission and rejustifying those regulations."[48] This was Bell's final appearance before the committee, because he died later in the year. How well he would have shepherded the national television contract in a later legislative battle is difficult to say. Pete Rozelle proved adept at generating political support, and it is difficult to imagine how the outcome could have been improved.

The Allure of National Television Contracts

Owners eventually realized that selling monopoly rights to telecasting their games promised to bring in greater amounts of revenue than establishing individual contracts. Although the NBA's rather inadvertent national television contract was not particularly lucrative, it established a precedent. A stumbling block to a national television contract was the possibility that teams possessing the most lucrative individual contracts would balk at the idea of pooling the rights. How to share the monopoly pie could be a vexing problem.

The NFL did not immediately address an associated issue with television: revenue sharing. Some observers predicted that the NCAA needed to pass rules governing college football teams sharing television receipts with the visiting school.[49] MLB owners were sharply divided on the issue, with Bill Veeck Jr., then owning the penurious St. Louis Browns, arguing that because the visiting team was half the show, they were entitled to some television money. The owners with lucrative television rights refused to share, although they ran the risk of antagonizing the owners who did not have such lucrative agreements. Those owners could have retaliated by denying a team such as the Yankees the right to telecast games on the road. Kansas City owner Charlie Finley testified before the Senate committee in 1965 that MLB eventually enacted a television revenue-sharing plan. Visiting teams were to receive 25 percent of the home team's television revenue.[50]

In the histories of the NFL and football, authors have said surprisingly little about the possibility of sharing television revenue; their works focused instead on the NFL's attempt to secure a national television contract instead of sharing revenue from individual contracts, which might have leveled the disparities considerably.

The NFL owners, in fact, considered sharing television revenue at their 1951 meetings. Philadelphia and Pittsburgh officials made the motion that "The sums received by any club under a television contract for the actual live playing of a championship or non-championship contest between NFL members shall be paid 60% to the home club and 40% to the visiting club. All of this article is effective for the year 1951 only." The owners split 6–6 on the motion, and they appear to never have brought it up again.[51]

There was a danger associated with not sharing television revenue. NFL owners faced a potential Prisoners' Dilemma situation with regard to home games telecasts. If televising a home football game diminished gate receipts by $10,000 per game, but the owner received, say, $7,500 per game for telecasting rights, he would benefit from signing such a contract. The television revenue was not subject to the roughly 40 percent league and visitors' shares, which would leave a net revenue of only $6,000. If all owners exercised similar policies, they could be collectively worse off. By extending revenue-sharing rules to the television revenue, such a potentially deleterious outcome would not occur.

NFL owners debated a national radio broadcast contract in 1949. What is interesting about this was Bell's claim that "no member club would receive less for the sale of said broadcast than they were getting the previous year and that the member clubs make no commitments after 1949." The sale of monopoly rights to radio broadcasts was sufficiently lucrative for a single radio network to pay more than what the clubs collectively received via individual contracts.[52]

Detroit Tigers owner John Fetzer was arranging a national television contract for MLB that might have exceeded the NFL's contract. Fetzer envisioned a Monday night "Game of the Week" that presaged the famous ABC/NFL Monday night game. Fetzer planned to roll all national games, including CBS and NBC's "Game(s) of the Week," into one large contract. Although the Yankees' co-owner Dan Topping and Dodgers' owner Walter O'Malley had the largest individual television deals, they gave support to the concept of the commissioner's office negotiating national television pacts with greater, if not equal, revenue sharing.[53]

Sportswriter Shirley Povich observed: "It has been to the profit of the Yankees that they stay out of the previously projected package deals in which all revenues were to be pooled and divided among all the clubs. The Yankees commanded rights fees that ran to $1,500,000 a year because they owned the best show in the majors, and it would not profit them to share the loot in a common pool."[54] Fetzer's plan ultimately failed.

National television contracts would become the focus of the 1961 hearings.

The Future Is Nigh

The technological capability to limit telecasts to only those who paid a fee loomed large. Owners considered the potentially lucrative pay-per-view option, but so did legislators.

As Fetzer and Frick were trying to close collective agreements with the networks, Walter O'Malley, owner of baseball's Dodgers, sought even more lucrative television deals. He planned to launch a pay-television deal, with Brooklyn fans paying fifty cents to watch a game. "I've no idea what a fair price for a subscriber would be, but I'm hoping it wouldn't be more than the lowest-priced seat in the ball park. I like to think of our bleachers as 50-cent seats, the cheapest in town, although the city tax adds to it."[55] After leaving Brooklyn for Los Angeles, he planned to televise Dodger games for a price similar to the cheapest seat in his new stadium (roughly $1.50). O'Malley's dreams required FCC approval. The FCC delayed making a decision.[56] O'Malley persuaded Giants' owner Horace Stoneham to pursue a similar pay-television contract. The two of them had previously just telecast road games from each other's stadiums to pique California's appetite for televised baseball.[57]

The two owners, as well as other proponents of pay television, faced implacable foes in Congress. Emanuel Celler testified in 1958 that owners could eventually replace free telecasts with pay television: "I defy anyone to tell me that these covetous owners would not, if they could, force all of us to pay a dollar or more to see a game by way of a closed circuit. You should have listened to the testimony of Mr. Walter O'Malley before our committee. He was brash enough to ask why he shouldn't have a closed circuit as far as the Dodgers were concerned. Why shouldn't he blanket out anybody that wants to see the game for nothing."[58] O'Malley repeatedly said that he hoped the All-Star Game and World Series would never be on pay television.[59] For various reasons, O'Malley's bold attempt failed owing to lack of viewers, a California citizens' petition, and general disapproval of requiring people to pay for the national pastime on television.[60]

Although Los Angeles and San Francisco football owners were interested in their baseball counterparts' pay-television endeavors, Bell, too, piously proclaimed before a committee in 1957, "I think the kids of this country deserve to see every sporting event they can without paying for it."[61] Bell further stated that he opposed closed-circuit or pay television, particularly if it resulted in boxing or other sporting events being held in a studio and staged solely for television audiences. "I hope I am not in sports if that day ever arrives."[62] In the aftermath of the Giants-Colts 1958 Championship Game, the anointed "Greatest Game Ever Played," reporters again questioned Bell whether the league was planning to implement pay television, as some suggested the sport was "a ready-made feature for pay-tv." Bell never wavered from his long-held opposition: "A great part of our success came about because through TV we were able to show the public the kind of game we play, and we can maintain our fan support best by continuing to send out our sponsored pictures."[63]

The possibility of pay television had induced Ford Frick to declare before the Senate Antitrust Subcommittee, "Unless we handle the problem of free TV now, within 10 years there will be no TV problem . . . there will be no baseball."[64] If the reader can ascertain Frick's logic, then he or she is very astute. The commissioners were wise to proclaim that their championship games would not be telecast via pay television. Prefacing the 1958 congressional committee investigation, Celler told reporters that professional team sports owners were asking for antitrust exemptions for their television policies, including anticipated pay television schemes: "The real reason behind the House-passed bill, is that they [club owners] want to be free to continue to be unreasonable in the way they manage baseball's business."[65] Celler may have singled out baseball, but the other sports knew he was aiming at all of them. With the NFL boasting about its success and prosperity, Celler became doubly suspicious about the league's activities.[66]

Celler had reason to wonder to what extent football owners intended to pursue pay television, as the issue would not disappear. The owners later submitted minutes from the "Joint Committee Meeting" of July 21, 1966. "Mr. [Ralph] Wilson (Buffalo owner) pointed out that carrying the [championship] game only on closed circuit television could mean 25–30 million dollars in revenue. . . . Commissioner Rozelle suggested that it might be possible to try closed circuit television on an experimental basis in Los Angeles if the game were held in the Rose Bowl."[67] Cleveland Browns owner Art Modell wanted to pool pay television and closed-circuit income. AFL owners, too, had wrestled with pay television; in their amendments to their constitution, they included a section detailing sharing of theater and pay television income.[68]

Celler summed up the issue in 1966: "we can conclude that if we approve the merger in the form that you indicate . . . we could by saying that an agreement among the clubs for pay television would be exempt from antitrust laws." Rozelle retorted, "No, Mr. Chairman, we specifically exclude that in our request for this legislation. Any practice of a single league as we have stressed, including pay television, could be challenged if this legislation were passed."[69] A few years later, legislators would recall this exchange.

Conclusion: Pro Sports Learn to Live With Television

Pro team sports owners grappled with how to use television. Their decisions sometimes raised the ire of Congress. Far from being altruistic, baseball and football owners initially kept all of the revenue from telecasts of their home games and only reluctantly shared any with the visiting team. The NBA owners, with their relatively trivial television revenues, did not come under much congressional scrutiny on the topic.

Owners enviously eyed the potential jackpot from pay television, but they understood the potential political fallout of charging viewers to watch their premiere events. Legislators did not seem perturbed that tickets to such events were priced much higher than regular-season games, but they wanted their constituents to be able to watch all games for free on television.

11

Baseball and Broadcasting

1953

Intertwined with baseball owners' fears of adverse effects upon their gate receipts from broadcasting and televising MLB games was their concern over their supply of minor league players. The NFL was not too concerned about the effects of their telecasts upon college football, although they professed as much. NFL owners relied on collegiate football to generate well-known, gifted players, but baseball owners did not depend on this source.

By owning or controlling minor league teams, big-league owners practiced a form of "vertical integration" similar to an automobile manufacturer who purchased a tire manufacturer. Congressional investigators were interested in MLB's control over thousands of players. They did not seem to make the connection during the hearings examining if a MLB team telecast its games into the territory of a minor league team it owned, then the damages to the minor league team would be internalized. Such owners would have to weigh the benefit of the telecasting rights versus the decline in its farm team's gate receipts. Of course, if the big-league team telecast its games into the home territories of minor league teams in which it had no financial interests, then this internalization would not occur.

The issue was complicated by the variety of broadcasts into minor league territories: telecasts, live radio broadcasts, and radio broadcasts of re-created games. Although television was a stronger substitute for attendance at the ballpark, given that it engaged sight and sound, baseball officials frequently blamed live radio broadcasts and broadcasts of re-created games for the minor leagues' attendance doldrums. There was another factor to consider: many of the new minor league teams were independent of MLB support and were located in very small towns.[1]

Baseball Feeding Upon Itself?

Baseball and hockey differed from football and basketball in the 1950s and 1960s in having minor league teams that were affiliated with big-league teams. Many accounts of postwar baseball document the rise and fall of the minor leagues. Americans flocked to baseball games at all levels of competition immediately after World War II, emboldening many entrepreneurs to launch new minor league teams. When enthusiasm and demand for minor league baseball faltered by 1949–1950, teams in small towns proved vulnerable. Many of the historians blamed television for the minor leagues' demise, and the new medium was a handy scapegoat. Some of the focus on television arose from New York City writers, who noticed that telecasts of Yankees, Dodgers, and Giants games essentially killed minor league teams in New Jersey. New York City was, of course, the epicenter of television for at least the first decade after the war.

Baseball historians, officials, pundits, and legislators alike agreed that telecasts of MLB games "killed" minor league baseball. Was the "Television Killed the Minors" account true? If not, was there an ulterior motive for using it? MLB owners used the story to justify their antitrust exemption. Owners frequently and proudly proclaimed that they successfully self-regulated their industry, and that their treatment of their minor league little brothers was a case in point. Benjamin Fiery, counsel for the American League, applauded rule 1(d) that kept Major League teams from trespassing into minor league territories.[2] Organized baseball's position might be stated as: the minor leagues and organized baseball were doing just fine; had the Department of Justice not opened the floodgates to network radio broadcasts and telecasts of Major League games, then more of the minor leagues would have survived.

The prima facie evidence appears, at first glance, irrefutable. There had been 316 minor league teams in 1946 but the number mushroomed to 448 in 1949. The boom quickly burst and, by 1953, there were only 292 teams left. Attendance at minor league games followed a similar pattern. The boom's termination, though, should have been no great surprise, as even by 1948 many minor league teams were losing money.[3]

During the 1951 hearings, baseball officials resorted to a variety of reasons as to why the minor leagues were suffering. Radio broadcasts of MLB games, the Korean War and the loss of players to military service, an economic slowdown, widespread automobile ownership, demographic factors, and television were among the causes cited.[4] Because the Department of Justice overturned MLB's prohibition on broadcasting its games into towns hosting minor league baseball in 1949, big-league owners scrambled to earn revenue from broadcasting their games. In later years, baseball officials became more convinced that telecasting MLB games into minor league towns was the culprit for the leagues' woes. Ford Frick warily attributed the minors' doldrums to television, but he also cited other factors.[5]

Other baseball officials suggested different reasons for the minors' woes. Senators owner Clark Griffith blamed the farm system, as well as the removal of the fifty-mile territorial rights to broadcasting, for causing the minors' troubles. He believed that owners of independent teams faced a difficult struggle with outfits affiliated with Major League teams, and he advocated prohibiting such affiliations. Griffith lacked the resources for an extensive farm system, so his testimony was self-serving. During the 1958 Senate hearings, Paul Dixon, counsel for the Senate, stated: "I have been told by minor league managers and owners directly, that the minor league ball clubs started downward and practically disappeared when this unlimited control of ballplayers [via the farm system] began to come into major league ball."[6]

Senator Edwin Johnson proposed an amendment to a sports antitrust exemption bill that required MLB to share their television revenue with minor league clubs, but Frick was lukewarm about the idea. He feared Department of Justice strictures against such arrangements and downplayed television's role: "television is not the sole rascal in this picture."[7] By either owning or affiliating with minor league teams and paying them subsidies, MLB teams were indirectly paying, perhaps, for damages done. Though not explicitly making this connection, Frick did cite the millions of dollars of subsidies paid by MLB to their minor league subsidiaries.[8] Indeed, such a vertical integration approach to internalize the external costs between Major and minor league teams could have been an effective resolution.

The minor leagues' woes were persistent. Frick testified before Congress in 1957 that "The minors are being wrecked." At this time, he was more vociferous about television's role. "The one thing I want to do is to be able to control, within reason, major league telecasts in minor league territory."[9] He still hesitated, though, to blame television for all of the minor leagues' woes; he even used a nonsensical figure, "60 percent," to apportion blame.[10]

Because the FCC froze the assignment of channels to broadcasting companies between September 30, 1948 and April 11, 1952, there were roughly one hundred operating stations in the country. The mountain and southern states were slow in getting television stations, affording an experiment of sorts in gauging television's effects upon attendance at minor league games. Teams playing in smaller towns had a higher probability of folding than those in larger cities. Almost half of the teams that folded were in states with very low rates of television ownership.[11] Television's role in hurting attendance was more plausible in the northeast quadrant of the country. However, even here, statistical analysis suggests that television's negative effect upon minor league attendance was modest.[12]

Broadcasting and Televising Baseball Games

MLB enacted rule 1(d) in 1946 that gave owners the right to broadcast or telecast all of their games, except when such broadcasts or telecasts (including rebroadcast or network broadcast) "made from a station outside its home territory and within the 'home territory' of any other baseball club, major or minor, without the consent of such other baseball club." In 1949, the Justice Department informed the owners that the rule was a violation of antitrust laws.[13]

The Department of Justice released a statement to the press on October 27, 1949 stating that, "Complainants had also asserted that the contract between the commissioner of baseball, the Mutual Broadcasting System, and the sponsor of the world series [sic] games denied many people the opportunity to hear these games because no Mutual station happened to be located in their particular areas."[14]

The issue was more complicated than it appeared. MLB teams could have chosen not to sell rights to broadcast or to telecast their games. The Justice Department surely was not demanding an active response in selling such rights. Any professed concern for the welfare of minor league teams was trampled in the owners' rush to acquire broadcasting revenue. At the time, roughly half of the minor league teams were independents. An interesting question the committee should have asked was whether MLB discriminated between selling rights that might injure minor league teams affiliated with Major League teams or those clubs that were independent.

To investigate the effects of broadcasts and telecasts on minor league baseball, a Senate committee convened in 1953. Senator Charles W. Tobey (N.H.) opened the hearings to "authorize the adoption of certain rules with respect to the broadcasting or telecasting of professional exhibitions in interstate commerce, and for other purposes" on May 6. Senate Bill 1396 intended to restore, at baseball's discretion, rule 1(d).[15]

Fortuitously for baseball, Senator Johnson sat on the committee. Johnson had been president of the Western League. He was the first witness and introduced his bill to, "protect the weak and helpless elements of America's national game of baseball from a cruel and ruthless monopoly which, strangely enough was forced upon organized baseball by the Antitrust Division of our own Justice Department." Baseball officials could hardly have better stated their case. He continued by saying that baseball was doing quite well, thank you, before the Justice Department's interference with rule 1(d). Johnson claimed that many, if not most, owners of minor league teams were civic-minded and not profit-maximizers, citing the losses a majority of them earned in 1950. He maintained, "I assert most emphatically that territorial limits are necessary to the preservation of minor league baseball."[16]

As with several other senators in other hearings, Johnson lauded baseball. His reflections were eerily similar to the pundits on Ken Burns's documentary, *Baseball* (you can almost hear the dramatic music playing in the background):

> Baseball is democracy in action. On the diamond, no questions are asked about which side of the railroad tracks a player came from, or who his parents might have been. Questions as to ability to play the game with spirit and skill are the only questions. That is all the managers and the fans want to know about any player. Here men of all colors, races, national origins, and religions meet on a common ground, to engage on even terms in a great contest of skill and strategy and wits. Baseball teaches youth fair play, sportsmanship, clean living, respect for those in authority, and obedience to its laws and rules. On the diamond, rivalry is keen and tempers fly, but men are taught to control their emotions as the supreme requirement of the game.[17]

Johnson believed that of rule 1(d) had been a "wise rule" that allowed Major and minor league teams to exist in economy harmony until the Justice Department rescinded it: "The minor leagues find themselves in the anomalous and ridiculous circumstance and situation of being destroyed by major-league monopoly under the antitrust laws of the United States enacted primarily to eliminate monopoly."[18]

Johnson indicated that his bill was not a regulation of baseball but primarily a statement that rule 1(d) was not illegal. He said baseball owners could decide whether to reinstate it. The senator emphasized the bill would not affect MLB's All-Star Game or the World Series. He realized that some owners did not desire a return to rule 1(d), preferring to reap revenue from radio and television rights for games sent into minor league teams' territories, but he felt most owners recognized the desirability and necessity of protecting the minor leagues. Johnson identified radio broadcasts along with telecasts as being harmful. After the rescinding of rule 1(d), several MLB teams had quickly established networks of radio stations to broadcast their games. Because of the limited number of television stations, such networks were not yet as feasible for television.[19]

Frick was the next witness. He began by emphasizing baseball's "peculiar position" in which competition and cooperation mixed. He, too, testified that unless rule 1(d) was reinstated, the collapse of minor league baseball would lead to the demise of the Major League, "which goes into the sandlots, into the lives of our young people." Frick and Johnson's rhapsodies about baseball may have served a second purpose; by identifying baseball as a near-sacred American institution, these officials were issuing a subtle warning to legislators: tamper with baseball at your own risk. Frick presented baseball's amended rule 1(d), which stated that "a major league club shall not broadcast in minor league territory during the hours that the minor league club is playing a ball game" in contrast to the original rule completely prohibiting such broadcasts, regardless of any actual conflicts. The reader should note that Frick used the term "broadcast" instead of "telecast" or a combination.[20]

Senator John W. Bricker (Ohio) began delving into the details. He asked Frick whether there was any evidence regarding television's effects upon attendance at baseball games.[21] Frick admitted there was little evidence available, although George Trautman, president of the National Association of Baseball Leagues, later informed the committee that baseball had hired an engineering firm to do a study on the effects.[22] Trautman admitted, "I am not here to say that it is radio and television exclusively. But I do think the saturation in minor league territory is not helpful." Senator Bricker asked whether the minor league owners had raised their admission prices. He also inquired about the admission tax's effects upon attendance. Trautman said he did not have an answer to the first question, but said that of 139 clubs reporting their finances, the average local admission taxes paid was $25,000 per. Senator Andrew Schoeppel (Kan.) and Trautman agreed that this amount could have been the difference between profit and loss for many teams.[23]

Trautman pointed out that while minor league owners could sell rights to radio broadcasts of their games, they were often undercut by other entities offering broadcasts and telecasts of MLB games. The re-broadcasts often featured re-creations of games, and the radio broadcasters were frequently accused of sensationalizing the contests. Senator Schoeppel quoted "sponsors of broadcasting," who told him they could not envision sponsoring local ball clubs when outside teams could divert the local audience.[24]

Senator Johnson pointed out that the federal government's antitrust suit against the NFL for its television policies discouraged baseball owners from challenging the Justice Department's edict.[25] National League president Warren C. Giles told the committee that MLB owners were afraid to help the minor leagues. "We are afraid of the harassment. We are afraid to move. It is keeping us broke now. We can't pay our lawyer bills. It is a terrific strain on the thinking of the major leagues." Giles further mentioned that as early as January 1949, the FBI was investigating MLB clubs with regard to broadcasting and telecasting games.[26]

Frank Shaughnessy, president of the International League, at least provided a comparison in attendance figures. His minor league had three Canadian teams. While overall attendance fell by 25 percent between 1949 and 1950 before stabilizing, the three Canadian teams maintained their attendance throughout.[27]

Senator Bricker asked Ford Frick a germane question: "If this bill were passed, the dollar return to the major-league clubs would not offset the advantage gained by protecting the minor-league clubs?" Frick replied, "It doesn't make any difference how many dollars you make this year, if you are going to kill the game next year."[28] Bricker responded that he wanted Frick to state that for the record. Warren Giles claimed that MLB owners would accept less money for rights to broadcast their games if they could prohibit broadcasts into minor league territories. Frick pointed out that MLB clubs earned $3.3 million from radio and television in 1950. Clubs charged nominal $7.50 per game fees for broadcasts of their games into minor league towns and cities, which crowded out broadcasts of the local teams. Frick repeatedly suggested that teams were afraid not to allow these broadcasts for fear of being sued by the Justice Department.[29]

NFL team owner George Preston Marshall testified before the committee. Marshall began by declaring that MLB and the NFL were not monopolies. "We are not a scarce commodity. We do not control anything of that sort. . . . The only thing that has happened is that this present baseball structure and this present football structure have been the only two that have been able to economically exist. But if you could get together a group of men that could financially do it, there is nothing to prevent anybody from having a baseball league or football league."[30]

Marshall was just warming up. Senator Schoeppel bemoaned the concentration of broadcasting and telecasting into the hands of a few and MLB's broadcasts' ill effects upon local teams. Marshall immediately took the cue. "The reason I would never agree to a part of our constitution enabling the commissioner of our league to sell our league as a package is because I always demanded that the Washington football team give its first interest to the fans of Washington."[31] True to his word, Marshall consistently asserted the interests of his team against the collective interest.

Marshall excoriated the Department of Justice and accused them of hypocrisy. "What they are trying to do is create a monopoly, and the only argument I had with them was that I said the Federal Communications Act is far more monopolistic than the NFL. 'You license people,' I said, 'and now to turn around to give them the license, right, and title, and have some fellow then who cannot sell time on his radio or television station come down here and complain—' that is how the entire action came about." He went on to quote the federal attorney's admission that he did not care whether the Justice Department's antitrust case would "put these fellows out of business." He spilled the latest news: "Even as late as yesterday, Westinghouse was in Philadelphia trying to make a deal for taking over all the National League football [sic] activities or discussing it. And we have never done that, and the baseball people have never done that."[32]

Marshall blasted the parties he identified as inspiring the Justice Department's lawsuit: "Yes; listening to a screwball from Texas, a complete idiot who has gone broke three times now. He threatened everybody on this gosh darn thing and he started this thing and then somebody else picked it up." Marshall then made his key point: "All we want to do is have the right to run our own business without legal interference from anybody. That is why I am for this Johnson bill. I am against any law of any type, as you know, personally." Senator Johnson quickly seconded Marshall's sentiments: "Baseball has proven through many, many years that it can make its own rules and do a splendid job of it. It can govern itself, and I have always been opposed to laws on that." After this pleasant exchange, Marshall disputed the idea that the NFL was commerce: "Baseball, football, or anything else, in any sense of the word, is not a commercial enterprise. I do not think that there has ever been a worry that the thing would get too monopolistic unless somebody gets too many good hitters on his team. That is the monopoly. You cannot legislate against that because you cannot legislate against stupidity in management."[33]

At times, Marshall seemed to be a "straight man" for the legislators' questions. Senator Johnson began by pointing out that the Redskins and other teams "are operating a part of a joint venture." Marshall agreed, whereupon Johnson continued by asking leading questions. "And when you have a joint venture of this kind, you have to have meetings?" and "You have to talk with these other people. You have to set up rules to govern the league?" Marshall could only agree. Johnson continued. "And does it not seem ridiculous to you when you set up a rule, that you are charged with conspiracy when, as a matter of fact, the league has to have conferences and has to have rules?" Marshall kept repeating, "That is right," to Johnson's remarks. "No league is any stronger than its teams; is that right?" Johnson wound up this line of "questioning" by stating, "And it seems to me that is where the Justice Department is completely erroneous, when they step in and try to view this thing as an individual operation when, as a matter of fact, a league is a joint operation and a joint venture and has to be by its very nature." For the seventh time, Marshall answered, "That is right."[34]

Former Senator Francis J. Myers (Pa.) was the NFL's legal counsel involved with the Justice Department's lawsuit against the football league regarding its television policies. Of course he disagreed with the Justice Department's rulings and tied baseball's and football's television policies together. He stated his opinion that the NFL's article X and baseball's rule 1(d) were almost identical. Myers believed the NFL's rule permitting home game blackouts was crucial. "Without the rule, I have no doubt, there would be no NFL in existence today." He also expressed concern about baseball's experiences with television and radio, using such now-familiar terms as "death knell" and the "domino effect" in his predictions that the death of the minors meant the death of baseball, "reverently referred to as our national pastime."[35] At the conclusion of Myers's remarks, Senator Johnson gushed, "Senator, that was a very splendid presentation of the case."[36]

In subsequent questioning, Myers explained why the NFL was concerned about the pending baseball legislation. He believed that baseball's restraint, being similar to football's restraint, was reasonable and therefore not a violation of antitrust laws. He also scorned the government's position that a television owner had a right to free games instead of paying admission; he insisted television owners had no such right. He did make the interesting point, though, that the view on television was superior to that of being in the stands, and weather was not a factor in one's living room.[37]

Harold E. Fellows, representing the National Association of Radio and Television Broadcasters, opposed the proposed bills, citing the general public and association members' interest in preserving their rights to purchase program rights in an unrestricted market. By doing so, the broadcasting industry provided useful services for the public and also for creating interest in baseball. He claimed that rule 1(d) denied much of the country the opportunity of hearing games on the radio and forced minor league clubs to allow such broadcasts or face public enmity. The local stations were injured by importations of these broadcasts by the antitrust complainants. Here Fellows employed his own domino theory: "if this law is passed it will initiate a parade of seekers of special treatment."[38]

Ralph L. Atlass, president of radio station WIND (out of Chicago), rebutted Fellows. WIND had broadcast Major League games for twenty years and had been feeding broadcasts to a network comprised of stations throughout the middle west. He testified that he found the regulations reasonable and easy to comply with. Atlass indicated that he expected to pay for the rights, just as he would for any entertainment event.[39]

The committee was then treated to an oratory, courtesy of baseball legend Branch Rickey. Rickey waxed eloquent: "I have never been present in a legislative meeting of any league . . . where the primary and governing motive in all baseball has not been the projection of good health of the game, realizing that public goodwill is our greatest asset, even to the point, and I will point it out, oh, in so many places . . . that all of our so-called legislative decisions point out their desire to protect the players and the consideration of the players." After that lengthy sentence, he continued, "Baseball as an organization has to hold a close fidelity to its public and it realizes that." Rickey presumptuously claimed that, "Baseball is a better friend of Mr. [Harold] Fellows than he is of himself in this proposed legislation."[40]

Senator Johnson and Rickey continued their mutual-admiration conversation throughout Rickey's testimony. Johnson cited cases where local radio stations threatened the Pueblo and Denver teams with broadcasts of re-created MLB games. These re-created games were a longstanding feature of radio broadcasts. The two agreed that live minor league action could not compare with the re-created games, because the broadcasters felt free to dramatize and sometimes to fabricate action on the diamond. They also disliked the minimal fees paid by the radio stations for such games. The broadcasters using re-created games had argued that once a game had been played, the events were in the public domain.[41]

The real fireworks began when Gordon McLendon, a thirty-one-year-old radio station owner and likely instigator of the Justice Department's investigation (and Marshall's "screwball"), testified. McLendon was currently involved with the Trinity Broadcasting Co. of Dallas, Texas, but he had been a minority shareholder in the now-defunct Liberty Broadcasting System (LBS). As McLendon described it, LBS ran afoul of baseball's rules on broadcasting as early as 1947, when it wanted to broadcast games into Dallas. Frick and then-commissioner A. B. "Happy" Chandler told the company that it would have to get permission from all minor league teams within fifty miles of Dallas. When such consent was not forthcoming, McLendon told the committee, "Liberty had no other alternative but to set up its own news service and do the games by re-creation." He described how the company hired someone in New York to listen to the games over the radio or watch them on television. This person then teletyped the play-by-play to Dallas, "where they were re-created and dramatized with sound effect." Even though the Justice Department convinced baseball to rescind Rule 1(d), McLendon claimed, "The repeal of that rule was a sham and of face value, only."[42]

McLendon made some good points about the changing nature of entertainment venues. He cited the introduction of drive-in theaters as a potential substitute for minor league baseball. Additionally, he challenged baseball to produce evidence that broadcasts or telecasts hurt attendance at minor league games.[43] Senator Johnson clearly found McLendon's remarks offensive. Johnson commented that McLendon and the radio stations were "getting this property that belongs to somebody else, which was created by somebody else. You are getting their property, and you are surreptitiously getting it, and then you are rebroadcasting it, for your own personal profit and your own personal benefit and not for the benefit of any baseball player, for whom your heart bleeds." When McLendon remonstrated that, "I am working for a living. I am hired to do that, and besides the courts say it is all right," Johnson retorted, "Your heart is bleeding—I don't know, but there ought to be a pool of blood down there."[44]

Johnson later accused McLendon's ally, attorney William Burrow, of filibustering (apparently, in a legislator's lexicon, this was the worst epithet). He repeatedly made snide remarks about McLendon: "your arguments are farfetched" and "This is such a provocative witness, that I can hardly restrain myself from going into all the ramifications of his very peculiar and extremely selfish viewpoint." Johnson criticized McLendon for bringing up the reserve clause in conjunction with his argument that MLB was a monopoly. He later accused McLendon of base motives: "I do not think that he is so concerned about the liberty of the people as he is the liberty that is in the name of the company that he operates. And the reason I say that is because all of his testimony clearly indicates that what he is mad about is that he cannot share in the property of the other people."[45]

McLendon raised a point that attacked baseball's proclaimed fears about the loss of minor league teams threatening MLB. He introduced a United Press clipping quoting Dick Seibert, former Major League player and now college coach, who said, "colleges will step in to develop baseball talent."[46] What is odd is that, given the NFL's and NBA's player drafts of college stars, no one else in the hearings raised this possibility. Why did big-league baseball have to rely on minor league talent? The answer to this question may be reflected by the fact that even top college players often required a season or two of seasoning in the minor leagues, but no one investigated this question.

Nathan R. Kobey was an attorney from Denver and a former owner of minor league teams. He favored the bill and took a swipe at Gordon McLendon: "It [the bill approving rule 1(d)] is reasonable to every man, sir, except him who would steal the game." Kobey went on to provide a thesis that baseball was not big business: "All of baseball does not have the gross income of one of the larger department stores, any one of them, in New York City."[47] He then highlighted the fact that although baseball was not big business, it loomed large in the public's estimation, as witness its prevalence in even the most august newspaper, the *New York Times,* where six pages were devoted to sports and only a page-and-a-half to financial news that morning.

Kobey made an interesting revisionist interpretation about baseball history, claiming that the National League's formation in 1876 and its attendant rules, "were not passed to exclude anybody." Even more provocative was his assertion that the selective system draft was not enacted to protect club owners. "That is pure hogwash. . . . The draft was to protect the ballplayer so that if a ballplayer were unable to play in a higher classification, the degree of avarice, the absolute sheer stubbornness of a baseball club owner could not keep him in a status quo." He lauded baseball: "what other profession pays it recruits for learning their lessons? Just the profession of organized baseball."[48] Kobey also described the owners' willingness to consider advancing the Pacific Coast League from "Open" status to "Major League" status, if the PCL would only accede to a set of rules promulgated by MLB. Kobey saw nothing untoward about one set of owners establishing entrance requirements for another set of owners. For his efforts, Kobey was awarded with Senator Johnson's compliment: "I want to express great appreciation for the very scholarly and learned statement that you have made . . . your statement ranks pretty high in analyzing the whole situation that is confronting this committee."[49]

The next witness, former baseball commissioner Chandler, quickly established baseball's animus toward the re-created games. "What right has some other fellow to come into the ball park and take that [right to a baseball game], without paying a cent for it, and re-create it?"[50] This was certainly a legitimate point, and Senator Johnson embraced Chandler, in a verbal sense: "Senator, I hope you succeed, because I know your motive is pure. I know that your heart is pure." Johnson took this opportunity to again reiterate his vision of baseball as a sport and not a business: "If you sell it as a business, it will not succeed, because the American people have always thought it belonged to them, and they always thought of it as a sport. They are not always interested in the business part of it. Of course, you have to make enough money to keep the parks open and pay the salaries."[51] Rather than press Chandler for relevant information, Johnson and the committee gave him a free pass. Presumably Chandler was privy to the owners' discussion of Rule 1(d) and their response to the Justice Department's edicts, so the legislators' failure to question him thoroughly was lamentable.

Louis F. Carroll, National League counsel, at least provided some germane testimony. He focused on baseball's hostility toward radio stations that re-created MLB games without permission. He cited an FCC decision of 1936 prohibiting deceptive re-creations, before providing examples from Dallas radio station KLIF, whose re-creations were inaccurate.[52]

Paul A. Porter, the committee's counsel, introduced MLB financial data prepared by Arthur Anderson Co. These data, which were condensed versions of those presented during the 1951 hearings, suggested that the Major League owners lost money on their farm systems. Porter used these dismal figures to conclude, "It follows that this committee is not faced with issues of antitrust enforcement in respect of a business of economic importance in American trade or commerce."[53]

The Minor Leagues' "Demise" Revisited

After all this testimony, much of it inane or irrelevant, what really happened to the minor leagues? Minor league baseball experienced a boom and bust cycle between 1946, when there were 316 teams, and 1953, when the number went from 316 to 448 to 292 teams. The number shrank to 136 by 1960. The pent-up demand for entertainment encouraged entrepreneurs in small towns across America to launch new teams and leagues. Many of these new teams were in absurdly small towns. In 1946, minor league teams played in towns with an average population of ninety thousand. The average population of the cities for the 150 teams created between 1946 and 1949 was less than thirty-seven thousand. An additional thirty-five teams debuted between 1949 and 1953, with an average population less than thirty thousand.[54]

Just as striking as the small population bases of new teams was their lack of affiliation with MLB teams. In 1946, 61.1 percent of minor league teams were affiliated, but four years later, that figure fell below 50 percent. As the minor leagues diminished, the vast majority of surviving teams had affiliations. The majority of the teams that perished, then, played in small towns and lacked connections with MLB. Minor league teams in the lower classifications were losing money as early as the 1948 season, although such losses escalated in later years. The minor leagues were hurting well before the rescinding of Rule 1(d). All of this information could have been compiled and presented to the 1953 committee.[55]

During the 1950 season, the Mutual and Liberty Broadcasting systems broadcast a *Game of the Day* over six hundred stations. Using regression analysis, the *Game of the Day* broadcast was not statistically significant in explaining minor league attendance between 1947 and 1953. Television, too, had, at most, an ambiguous effect upon minor league attendance. Because the FCC suspended issuing licenses for new television stations between 1948 and 1952, much of the country lacked television coverage. Minor league teams in these regions experienced falling attendance, too.[56]

Those few witnesses testifying before the hearings who argued that MLB was more concerned about control than about the welfare of the minor leagues may have been astute. The already-teetering minor leagues boasted too many teams in small towns incapable of sustaining them. MLB probably did not lament the demise of independent minor league teams. If those minor league teams owned by MLB suffered from radio broadcasts of MLB games, the big-league owners could have weighed the gains in broadcast revenues versus the losses sustained by their farm systems.

Conclusion: Television Proves an Unruly Element

All of the hand wringing about the minors' travails seems misplaced. The likelihood of MLB collapsing if the minors collapsed was refuted by the eventuality: MLB did quite nicely with fewer than 150 minor league teams by 1961 or so. What MLB really wanted was control over their supply of players. Baseball official Leslie O'Connor explained the owners' animus toward a free market for rookie players: "It would leave too much to chance, and good businessmen like Walter O'Malley of the Dodgers, Lou Perini of the Braves and Del Webb of the Yankees are not going to buy very much of that."[57] Therefore, a complete elimination of the minors was unlikely in any event. The winnowing process of the 1950s left very few independent minor league teams. MLB owners exerted greater control of the minor leagues and the player supply pipeline.

If anything, the coincidental timing of the rescinding of Rule 1(d) and the minors' woes gave MLB an opportunity to justify their antitrust exemption: baseball was doing just fine in regulating itself, thank you, before the Justice Department intervened, and now look at the fine mess the federal government has created. Legislators did not restore rule 1(d), but baseball survived.

Senator Edwin Johnson submitted S. 1396, which would have let baseball revert back to rule 1(d) prohibiting broadcasts into another club's territory without the permission of the home team. The *New York Times* reported that although the bill passed the Senate committee in June, Johnson was still considering bringing the bill to a vote in December 1953: "The Colorado Democrat has not yet decided whether to press for enactment of the so-called baseball bill. . . . Johnson said the decision on the baseball bill will depend on what action the major leagues take on a minor league request for protection from major league radio and television." The committee approved the bill but the Senate did not pass it.[58]

12

The NFL'S Big Television Score

1961

The NFL did not pioneer national television contracts. The NBA and then the AFL already had such deals, before the NFL negotiated its contract with CBS. Uncomfortably for the NFL, it was the sole league called before a congressional subcommittee on antitrust to defend its national television contract.

Although the hearings pertaining to "Telecasting of Professional Sports Contests" occurred at the behest of the NFL, the bills, H.R. 8757 and S. 2427, covered the four major professional team sports. The Senate bill contained a proviso protecting college and high school games. The bills only applied to telecasts and not to pay television (including cable). NFL commissioner Pete Rozelle was the main witness in the brief hearing, which lasted just one day. NBA and NHL officials did not testify, even though these leagues had hopes of gaining a similar antitrust exemption for national television contracts as the NFL. MLB commissioner Ford Frick did testify, and he hoped to gain an explicit exemption for this practice, too, instead of relying upon an agreement with the Department of Justice.[1]

Because the NFL, as the only national professional football league, currently had market power that harmed consumers and competitors, its national television contract threatened to enhance its market power. The AFL did not yet have market power when it signed its national television contract. In the case of the NBA, its contract provided much smaller amounts of revenue for owners just beginning to reap prosperity. Allowing the AFL and NBA to have national television contracts could foster competition and benefit consumers by helping the AFL survive its birth pangs while keeping NBA owners from going out of business.

The NFL and Television Prior to 1961

Table 8 demonstrates that NFL teams' television revenues were growing steadily, although their broadcast revenues continued to pale beside MLB's. Adjusted for the relatively mild inflation during the 1950s, the increases in broadcast revenues during the period would be reduced by roughly one-sixth. In 1960, the ratio between baseball and football's per-team broadcast revenues peaked at 4.14:1, the highest ratio since 1952. Although observers believed that the NFL handled television better than did MLB, the revenue figures up to 1960 lend scant support for the belief. In the years after Pete Rozelle became commissioner, the gap narrowed, and with its second big national television contract, the NFL finally surpassed MLB on a per-team basis.

AFL owners sold their collective national television rights to ABC. ABC was the weakest of the three major networks, but its president, Roone Arledge, and others recognized professional football's potential to lift a struggling network to prominence. ABC and the AFL proved a mutually beneficial partnership. Before awarding the contract, AFL commissioner Joe Foss speculated that bids of "up to $2,500,000," or $312,500 for each of the eight teams, would be made. Harry Wismer, president of the New York Titans AFL franchise, bragged that he had rejected a $1.5 million television offer because it required the Titans to play home games on Saturday afternoons. Wismer had earlier advised that television would provide a major advantage for the AFL that the AAFC lacked.[2] Foss told reporters in 1961 that "they were doing business in 1961 solely by virtue of their television money." ABC was not only supplying necessary revenue but badly needed publicity.[3]

The AFL's national television contract undoubtedly frustrated NFL owners.

The NFL's Lucrative New Television World

Pete Rozelle was worried. Concurrent with increasing disparities in television revenue between teams, CBS's Bill MacPhail advised Rozelle that the NFL's current reliance upon individual team television contracts was unsustainable. NFL television games overlapped, which diluted audiences; the networks found several individual markets unattractive. Worst of all, even though most teams used CBS, a few used NBC or regional networks. MacPhail told the owners that CBS was willing to pay $3 million for exclusive rights to NFL telecasts, and the league could divide the sum as it saw fit.[4]

At the March 11, 1960 league meeting, Rozelle reviewed the league's television situation. He informed the owners that CBS was willing to pay $3.5 million per season for a monopoly on national telecasts of the league's games. He advised signing a three-year contract but thought CBS might agree to a five-year agreement. To handle the existing television-revenue disparities, he proposed a variation from the eventual equal shares policy: "One plan for distributing the package TV income that seems to meet with the greatest accord is having clubs keep their TV base for 1959, add to this a flat $150,000 for Dallas as a new club and $75,000 for the League office, subtracting these amounts from the total of $3,500,000 and distributing the balance equally among the twelve clubs."[5]

Eleven of the teams already had signed contracts with CBS. Baltimore and Pittsburgh had a joint contract with NBC, while Cleveland maintained its own regional network. Had one team, perhaps Baltimore or New York, rejected the national television contract, the other owners might have outvoted them, or if unanimity was required, offered a side payment. It also helped that CBS's $250,000 per-team offer was commensurate with the amount the team with the most lucrative contract was currently receiving.[6]

The owners considered potential antitrust implications from a national television contract. The NFL was planning to sell monopoly rights to CBS, which was a major incentive for the network's willingness to pay such a large amount.[7]

On January 27, 1961, Rozelle won a crucial vote authorizing him to negotiate a television contract, subject to retaining the home blackout policy and telecasting road games back to home markets. As New York's Wellington Mara stated, "We should all share, I guess. Or we're going to lose some of the smaller teams down the line, and we've all stuck together." Mara's line reflects the attitude that Michael MacCambridge believes was ingrained in the NFL to a greater extent than in the other professional leagues: "a sense in which the interior world of pro football—with its draft, salary cap, revenue sharing, stacked scheduling, and 'equity rule' was a reflection of the best impulses of American egalitarianism."[8] The owners' attitudes to sharing television revenue, though, belied MacCambridge's rosy portrayal of NFL as one big, happy family. The owners had considered and rejected sharing television revenue in the past, as shown in chapter 10 of this work.

The actual contract proved even more lucrative than anticipated. Rozelle signed a two-year deal with CBS for $9.3 million. Each of the fourteen teams was to receive $320,000 per year, more than enough, in most cases, to cover each team's player payroll. Rozelle said that the Baltimore Colts were the only team getting less television revenue than in the previous year. Articles in *Broadcasting* and *The Sporting News,* however, stated that the Giants were the sole team not getting an increase in television revenue as a result of the deal. As a comparison, the NCAA got $10.2 million for two years from CBS for college football telecasts.[9] Continuing the NFL's television bonanza, Rozelle announced two months later that NBC won the rights to the league's 1961 and 1962 championship games, with a "record sum of $615,000 for television and radio rights." *New York Times* reporter Val Adams believed that the payment was triple what the league had received under the previous NBC contract, and that the $615,000 was more than twice the highest amount paid for a single sporting events—a boxing match between Rocky Marciano and Joe Walcott in 1953.[10]

Judge Grim squelched the NFL's euphoria by ruling that the deal violated antitrust laws. He wrote, "By this agreement, the member clubs . . . have eliminated competition among themselves in the sale of television rights to their games. Clearly, this restricts the individual clubs from determining from which areas the telecasts of their games may be made, since defendants (the NFL) have by their contract given to CBS the power to determine which games shall be telecast and where."[11] Considering that Bell and the owners had not anticipated they would be looking at a national television deal during the earlier antitrust action, they never sought an exemption for such a possibility. Grim's earlier ruling primarily covered blackouts. His current ruling threatened to cost the NFL owners more than $2,000,000 in lost television revenues. The NFL petitioned Grim to delay enforcing his ruling, but he declined.[12]

Commentators wondered whether Grim's ruling would affect existing exclusive contracts between ABC and the AFL. Had the ruling invalidated the AFL contract, the NFL might have been poorer in television dollars but more likely to see the AFL competition fatally weakened. The antitrust case threatened to leave the issue in limbo for too long a period, so Rozelle gambled on gaining legislation granting an antitrust exemption.

Rozelle had foreseen that a national television contract might trigger a Justice Department investigation. When the contract was halted, Rozelle quickly canvassed Washington, D.C. He garnered the support of Wisconsin representative John W. Byrnes, representing Green Bay, who wrote to the committee stating his concerns.[13]

Mostly, though, Rozelle capably sold himself and the NFL to the legislators. His prepared statement highlighted growing costs for independent television stations, precluding their competition in televising NFL games and, as always, the NFL's "weakest link" theory. "Only by grouping the weaker and stronger clubs and the clubs with more and less favored geographic locations can the league hope to achieve any control over the manner in which its games are telecast. This is the only way the league can maintain sponsorship interest in telecasts of NFL games, restore order and stability to league television arrangements, equalize television income among the clubs, secure realistic values for television rights, and assure all member clubs of the league of continued access to television facilities and television income."[14]

Rozelle mentioned the unique aspect of professional sports leagues, in that "the members of a sports league are engaged in a joint venture where their business interests are closely intertwined and each club is jointly in business with every other club in its league." He also emphasized that even successful teams such as Baltimore needed television revenue to remain profitable, while Green Bay's survival was predicated on getting a proportional share of the television pie. Rozelle also claimed, "the NFL, alone among existing sports leagues, is singled out for prohibitions on joint television contracts."[15]

Rozelle's proposal was also strengthened by the AFL's national television pact with ABC. As Craig Coenen put it, "CBS claimed that only good teams in large markets had profitable telecasts. Soon thereafter, NFL officials made an appeal for a re-hearing. Rozelle thought they had a good argument because Grim's ruling gave the AFL a competitive advantage. Furthermore, Grim's judgment was not in the public interest because CBS's unwillingness to televise games in half of the league's markets meant millions of Americans would not get to watch pro football."[16]

The Hearings Go Down Smoothly

Emanuel Celler stated at the opening of the hearings, "The sole purpose of [H.R. 8757] is to enable the member teams of a league to pool their separate television rights and to sell the resulting package of pooled rights to a customer, such as a television network. It is stated that such arrangements are needed to enable a league to assure a significant share of television revenue to its weaker teams, whose economic survival is essential to the continued operation of the league itself."[17]

Herbert Maletz, chief counsel for the Antitrust Subcommittee, demonstrated that Judge Grim's earlier ruling in 1953 was predicated on "the theory that the telecasting of football games, resulted in a diminution of gate receipts and, therefore, if attractive games were to be allowed to be shown in another team's territory on the day that team was playing in that territory, a serious financial loss would inure to the home team."[18] Maletz's remarks clearly gave the NFL an opening; by focusing on Green Bay's ability to survive, the league provided the cover the legislators needed to endorse the exemption.

Maletz indicated that "Not until it was prohibited from entering into a package network contract, the NFL has been operating satisfactorily, has it not, within the framework of Judge Grim's 1953 decision?" Rozelle could only agree. Maletz then proceeded to quote Bert Bell's testimony from the 1958 hearings: "the NFL operates satisfactorily within the framework of the 1953 football radio and television decision of Federal Judge Grim. . . . Indeed, the NFL would be glad to have Judge Grim's decision written into this bill if that would be satisfactory to baseball, basketball, and hockey."[19]

The committee examined revenue figures for Radio-TV rights published in *Broadcasting* for 1960 and 1961. In 1960, the combined rights varied from Green Bay's $105,000 to New York's $340,000; in 1961, the combined Radio-TV rights ranged from Green Bay's $120,000 to New York's $370,000. Rozelle subsequently sent Celler a letter maintaining that the true (television only) revenues for 1960 were between $117,000 and $445,000, with all clubs totaling $2,577,000. Rozelle's figures did not identify individual clubs.[20] Presumably, the greater disparities revealed in Rozelle's data lent support to the league's weakest-link theory.

Rozelle was compelled to explain why he had only negotiated with CBS, without allowing the other networks opportunities to bid. Rozelle admitted he received a telegram from NBC objecting to their exclusion from bidding. He defended his decision: "Realizing the importance of the single network-type contract for some time, we explored how we might bring this about. As of the 1961 season, one network, CBS, had contractual ties on, I believe 9 or 10 of our clubs. CBS was the only network that had firm ties on our clubs for 1961 and beyond. Their tie was a 1961—a 1961 contract, firm, with 1962 and 1963 first refusal options. So, in effect, they had 9 or 10 of our clubs legally tied for a period of 3 years: 1961, 1962, and 1963. They were the only network that had such ties on any of our clubs." Rozelle further stated that the league's Championship Game was awarded via open bidding.[21]

The NFL's deal with CBS held the potential to injure other parties interested in telecasting games. These parties, of course, testified as to the detrimental aspects of the proposed legislation. Vincent T. Wasilewski of the National Association of Broadcasters asserted that CBS's monopolization of games would mean many areas would no longer get two or three NFL games to choose from, only what CBS offered. Wasilewski also made a valid point, which was not explored, that if the NFL was worried about television revenue disparity, the teams could put their current television revenues into a common pool without needing an exclusive national television contract with one telecaster.[22]

Lee Loevinger, assistant attorney general, Antitrust Division, notified the committee by telegram. He expressed the Justice Department's concerns about the legislation:

> The bill would place in the hands of a few private persons tremendous power over a popular and lucrative sport. . . . The CBS vice president in charge of sports telecasting testified that CBS paid about $1,500,000 to televise 80 percent of the NFL regular season games in 1960. Under the contract declared illegal it proposed to pay $4,650,000 for the television rights to 100 percent of the NFL regular season games in 1961. Thus, to acquire the remaining 20 percent of the games and hold exclusive telecasting rights to the games of all teams, CBS was willing to pay 200 percent of the price it paid for 80 percent of the games. This, to us, is a striking example of the evils of monopoly.[23]

Herbert Maletz speculated upon whether the NFL could tie up all three major networks and prevent a rival, such as the AFL, from getting any television money.

> Maletz: Under the bill one football league could enter into TV package contracts with all three networks whereby each network could carry games of certain member clubs; is that not right?
>
> Rozelle: Except that would not be a package contract. That would be doing basically what we are doing now, using more than one network, which we are attempting to get away from.
>
> Maletz: Under the bill, the National Football League could tie up all the three networks; could it not?
>
> Rozelle: We could do it today. I assume we could under the bill.
>
> Maletz: Now, if all the networks were tied up by one football league, by the National Football League, for example, would not the other league, the American Football League, possibly be at a major competitive disadvantage?
>
> Rozelle: I should certainly think so. . . . If I might say, there is no intention on our part of using more than one network, if this legislation is passed. That is just what we are attempting to get away from and have been for 18 months.[24]

When Celler questioned Foss whether the AFL could tie up all three networks, the latter replied that his league could only negotiate with ABC, because CBS and NBC were already committed to the NFL. The legislators also pressed Rozelle on future technologies and how the bill would affect these options. Maletz reminded Rozelle that the bill covered "only the free telecasting of professional sports contests, and does not cover pay TV?" Rozelle concurred.[25] This idea of a league monopolizing all three networks would assume relevance a decade later.

Conclusion: Rozelle's End Run Scores a Bonanza

Sportswriter Jack Walsh reported that NFL lobbyist Clinton Hester seemed optimistic about the bill's passage, citing the passage of the 1957 bill by the House but failure in the Senate. Hester believed Senator Estes Kefauver and Celler were sympathetic to the antitrust problems of professional football. An anonymous reporter in the *New York Times* characterized the NFL's actions as an "end run" around the Justice Department.[26]

Celler, of all people, sponsored the House bill to approve the NFL national television contract. His stance owed in part to existing NBA and AFL national television contracts; he worried that if Congress did not approve the NFL contract, these other leagues would go out of business.[27] If this interpretation is accurate,

Celler's actions were ironic, indeed—NFL success was predicated, in part, upon the AFL's earlier contract.

After President Kennedy signed the sports televising bill on October 10, 1961, the Green Bay Packers appeared in the NFL Championship Game. Sportswriter Joe King marveled at the small town hosting the first "million-dollar game in pro football history" in combined gate receipts and NBC television rights.[28] The NFL must have savored the symbolism of the smallest town in all of professional team sports having the honor of hosting such a game.

Rozelle would testify before Congress on subsequent occasions, but the 1961 hearings could be considered a highlight of his lengthy stint as commissioner.[29]

13

Television Blackout Hearings *1972–1977*

With their 1961 antitrust exemption (Public Law 87-331) granted for negotiating a national television contract, NFL owners continued to blackout telecasts of local games within the home team's territory. In practice, NFL owners chose to blackout telecasts from stations outside the stipulated seventy-five-mile radius if their telecasts penetrated the radius, so stations more than one hundred miles away could telecast home games.

Some stations attempted to mitigate the blackout by reducing their transmitting power during telecasts to avoid penetrating the seventy-five-mile radius, while still allowing fans just outside the zone to enjoy the game. The FCC took a dim view of this and issued a pronouncement prohibiting such measures.[1]

In Judge Grim's 1953 ruling, the rationale for allowing the NFL to blackout games was to preserve the home gate receipts, especially because the NFL convinced the judge of potentially grievous losses to the home gate that could injure the league. Pundits, though, believed that by 1961, NFL teams' attendance was so strong that the blackout of local games was no longer necessary (see Table 1).

As the 1960s wore on, football fans began to chafe at the blackouts of home games. Many NFL fans could only watch their home team play when the team was on the road, because tickets to home games were scarce. Fans especially resented the inability to watch their team play locally, even when the game was sold out. They reasoned that if the game was sold out, what was the harm of telecasting the game to those unfortunate fans who could not obtain tickets? Legislators were keenly aware that the Redskins had sold out their games for years and maintained a long list of prospective season-ticket buyers. Despite the team's popularity, its owners refused to telecast its home games.

The 1971 Super Bowl was a decisive moment, considering the game was sold out in Miami but local fans could not watch their Dolphins play on television. As always, fans contacted their local television stations, newspaper editors, and friendly neighborhood politicians. Even President Richard Nixon became involved, favoring an end to the blackout. An interesting question arises: Why should politicians be so worried about blackouts when they had much more pressing issues? During the hearings, Senators excused themselves to vote on the Strategic Arms Limitation Treaty. Chairman Senator John Pastore tacitly admitted as much when he told FCC chair Dean Burch, "In other words, an inference was made that there was political sensationalism behind these hearings. . . . [W]e did not pull this problem out of thin air. This is a result of complaints being made by the public."[2] Senators pointed out that the previous antitrust exemptions had enriched the owners, so now it was time to benefit the public.

Economic and Legal Aspects of the Bills

Not all observers were enchanted with the proposed antiblackout law. Scholar Ira Horowitz examined property rights to telecasts of professional teams. Although team owners sometimes forgot, both the home and visiting teams held telecasting and broadcasting rights. A visiting team could refuse to allow the home team to telecast its game and vice versa. Horowitz pointed out that teams usually set up reciprocal agreements regarding telecasting rights. The related issue of payment for such rights was less clear cut. Fred Saigh Jr., of the St. Louis Cardinals, and a couple of other baseball owners believed that the home team should share part of its television revenue, because teams were needed to produce a telecast. In MLB, the home team kept all of the local telecasting revenue until well into the 1960s.[3]

Horowitz observed that fans did not have an implicit right to sports telecasts and broadcasts, which should have been obvious, considering that no one was agitating for fans' rights to attend a sporting event in person for free. He argued, "the seemingly well-intentioned sporadic attempts to legislate the telecasting of various sports events represent rather presumptuous efforts on the part of legislators to interfere with the free-market system through state interventions that would be unthinkable in any other industry in our capitalistic society."[4] He also pointed out that the clubs did not have a right to "restrict the broadcasting activities of *other* clubs playing in other locations, that the clubs can compete amongst themselves in order to eliminate all broadcast competition and create broadcast monopolies, or that by assigning their broadcast rights to the league the member clubs can form a combination 'in restraint of trade' that will have the ability to raise the broadcast revenue of all members of the ensuing cartel. . . .

Sports broadcasting has become a profitable and vexing issue because Congress has either failed to recognize or has chosen to ignore these two simple facts."[5]

Horowitz scorned the legislators' attempt to force an antiblackout law by using Public Law 87-331 as a belated quid pro quo. "The fact is that this law compels the home club to give away a property right." He recognized the weakness of Rozelle's "no-shows" and "no-buys" argument: "It is unlikely that even Commissioner Rozelle believes the argument, but rather that he feels compelled to so argue in order to establish the first line of defense against Congressional action that would compel the local telecasting of *all* home games that are being telecast anywhere."[6] The antiblackout law would work to the benefit of the television networks, which would get a boost to their ratings without, initially, paying for the property right; the NFL would, presumably, demand greater payment for the enhanced telecasting rights in the next round of negotiations.

The networks stood to gain a second benefit from the antiblackout rule. By forcing the NFL to telecast sold-out home games, the antiblackout laws would simultaneously provide more games for the national networks, while moving these games out of reach of cable and pay-television companies owing to the FCC's antisiphoning rules governing which sporting events cable and pay-television companies could telecast. The FCC favored network television over the upstarts. Horowitz concluded, "Thus the FCC's anti-siphoning rules complete the process started by the Congress in 1961, whereby ABC, CBS, and NBC are assured that the professional team-sports programming that they offer will face minimal, generally no competition from comparable events, and that in the initial bidding process the networks will only have to compete among themselves for the broadcast rights to those events."[7]

Football fans were the putative winners from the antiblackout law. They could now watch the sold-out home games of their local heroes. Horowitz suggested that the outcome was not without costs: "Insofar as consumers ultimately pay some or all of a television sponsor's advertising costs through higher prices than would otherwise obtain, conventional telecasts of sports events are by no means 'free' to the public." He did not explicitly state the proposition that non-football fans might be losers, as a result of the higher advertising costs and the crowding out of other television shows that would have aired in lieu of NFL games. Still, he raised the possibility that football fans could be better off under freer competition for rights to telecast sporting events that might result in "a greater quantity and variety of choice of sports telecasts."[8] Thomas Kauper, assistant attorney general for the Antitrust Division, expressed a similar opinion regarding free television. He also pointed out, "it may also be appropriate to consider than in some of our cities, professional sports teams play in stadia built by governmental authorities, using public credit and tax revenue. To this degree, the citizen may have supported a team even when he does not buy a ticket [or is even a fan]."[9]

Kauper referred to certain nuances of the previous antitrust issues. He suggested that while it was permissible for individual owners to determine policies toward telecasting their home games, "the present blackout arrangement is not simply a matter of individual judgment by each member club as to when or whether a home game is telecast. It is in the collective nature of the league judgment that the anti-trust issue arises. No member team is free to implement its own decision. Neither, for that matter is the network." He continued by pointing out that antitrust laws typically encouraged independent business judgments as to what, when, and where products would be marketed. He also noted, that "any amendment of Public Law 87-331, whether by S. 4010 or S. 4007, will affect home game blackouts only where such blackouts are part and parcel of the type of arrangement covered by the present statute, i.e. blackouts imposed by joint agreement among the clubs by which the league transfers television rights to the networks."[10] Kauper later discussed Judge Grim's 1961 finding that the CBS national contract violated antitrust laws. "The court held that since the pooling arrangement gave CBS the power to determine which game would be televised and where they would be televised, it necessarily restricted member clubs from determining the areas in which their games would be televised."[11]

Kauper also identified another issue in a later hearing. If any bills were passed as an amendment of the Communications Act of 1934, then there would be enforcement difficulties, because "The Federal Communications Commission would appear to have no enforcement power over professional sports clubs." The amendment originally pertained to communications media. Kauper warned the committee members that any such legislation ran the risks of litigation and a potential repudiation by the courts. Representative Torbert Macdonald downplayed any such possibility.[12]

Lend Me a (Favorable) Tenor

The Senate held hearings on a policy to lift the blackout, with the first set taking place in 1972; the House held similar hearings in 1973. The hearings resulted in a temporary experiment in lifting the blackouts under specified circumstances. After the law lapsed in 1975, attempts to renew it on a permanent basis failed. Although all professional team sports had some sort of policy regarding blackouts, professional football was the primary subject of the hearings.

Chairman John Pastore (R.I.) set the tenor of the 1972 hearings. Though he claimed the committee was not "going to prejudge anything," he made his position clear: "What we are concerned with here is the fact that the airwaves belong to all the people, and we have made certain allowances for professional sports . . . in granting them an exemption from the antitrust law in 1961."[13]

Lest the owners were unclear of the legislators' sentiment, Senator Vance Hartke (Ind.) reiterated Pastore's opening remarks: "I don't understand how you can in good conscience come and say that it is the obligation of Congress to protect your gate receipts and proprietary interests with the public airwaves which are a privilege."[14] Probably the cheapest shot came from Michigan representative William Brodhead in an acrimonious exchange with Pete Rozelle: "To deny senior citizens a chance to see football games on television for these reasons is one of the most arrogant things I have heard of in my entire life." To which Rozelle responded, "Would you like to see Broadway shows in your living room on television, too?" Brodhead retorted, "If Broadway gets an antitrust exemption, if Broadway gets the benefit of using the air waves to advertise their product as football has, yes." The entire exchange was silly; senior citizens could watch telecasts of the local team when it played an away game.[15]

The policy of requiring NFL home teams to lift the television blackout when a game was sold out seemed a political windfall for legislators.[16] There were millions of frustrated football fans clamoring for free telecasts of their team's home games. The legislators reasoned that because the game had to be sold out, owners would not lose much, if any, revenues. They hoped, with some reason, that the rule had a self-equilibrium: If attendance began to fall off as more games were televised, then there would be fewer sellouts and fans would be induced to return to the stadiums. Macdonald reiterated precisely this point in 1975 when he sought a renewal of the two-year experiment on an antiblackout bill. In addition, he referred to the law as, "almost a perfect law . . . I mean the law itself is self-correcting."[17] League officials sometimes ignored this potential counterbalance in their testimony.

Some legislators even implied that the antiblackout policy would improve NFL teams' bottom lines. For instance, Senator Pastore claimed that for the Redskins, a focal point of the debate, "It would mean more money [from selling enhanced telecasting rights] than they would realize from a few seats that were empty. I mean, there is a profit even in our suggestion to the clubs."[18] No one was impolitic enough to ask that if this was so, why NFL owners did not voluntarily adopt the policy.

The NFL's Defense of Blackouts

The NFL owners through Rozelle expressed disapproval of the proposed policy. Rozelle began by claiming "it is not a blackout issue at all. . . . [This proposal] is an effort to prescribe by statute which NFL game must be telecast in what area on what occasion. . . . I am not aware that Congress has proposed this for any other form of public entertainment."[19] He pointed out that the NFL had voluntarily lifted its blackout in the sense that it now allowed telecasts of other teams' games into a home team's territory, even when it was playing at home. Rozelle ignored the likelihood that lifting the blackout of the home team's game would have created a stronger substitute for home attendance than importing games from other stadiums. The commissioner also did not mention that the league had voluntarily lifted its blackout in response to AFL telecasts that invaded NFL teams' territories. He recalled that Cleveland owner Art Modell moaned, "This is going to kill my attendance." Rozelle continued by saying, "Frankly, this has hurt us some, and frankly that is one of the reasons we have for the 'no-shows' now." He did not, however, supply any figures from 1966 to prove his assertion.[20] Rozelle was, however, alluding to a key issue: control of NFL telecasts. The owners may well have disliked the rule more for its taking away some of their control than for any manifestations from it.

Rozelle claimed that "Local telecast of local games have never at any time been an issue in any league antitrust litigation."[21] His statement seemed a misrepresentation of the 1953 case. In any event, the NFL, as with its peers in basketball and hockey, may have hoped that the league's relatively small combined income might lend credence to the argument that professional football was not commerce.

Rozelle prepared several lines of defense in his testimony. Some of his arguments were speculative.[22]

The first line was that fans would speculate on whether the game would be telecast or not, thereby dampening demand for tickets. Rozelle made the bizarre argument, "This proposal could create some of the strangest Friday morning ticket lines in the history of public entertainment—with everyone jockeying to remain at the end of the line." Senator Pastore disputed Rozelle's statement: "You don't really believe that. . . . I think you undersell your own product. I think the excitement of being there, nothing compares with it."[23]

When Senators pointed out their skepticism regarding this process, Rozelle retreated to the next line of defense. Even if a particular game was sold out, the telecast would encourage fans with tickets to stay at home, especially in inclement weather. The NFL disliked no-shows. As with all sports promoters, the spectacle of blocs of empty seats was poor publicity. But no-shows had existed prior to the lifting of blackouts and also had existed for games that were not sold out; the question was how many additional no-shows would occur because of the television policy. Rozelle highlighted one game where there were forty-eight thousand no-shows. He reminded the committee that the "roar of the crowd" was part of the home-field advantage and excitement.[24]

In addition, no-shows did not pay for parking and concessions. These supplemental sources of revenues were not trivial.[25] Senator Pastore appeared willing to discount this aspect when he asked Rozelle, "Well, do you think the profit from selling hot dogs is commensurate with the joy and the satisfaction and the enthusiasm of thousands and thousands of people who watch that game on television?"[26] He continued to excoriate Rozelle's concerns regarding no-shows: "That argument didn't impress me much. They already have the money for the ticket. They gave the razzmatazz that an empty seat doesn't buy a hotdog. We are not talking about that."[27]

Rozelle tried to turn on its head the argument that teams playing in publicly owned stadiums owed the public: no-shows injured the taxpayers, as less money was retained by stadium authorities to defray the cost of the stadiums. He asserted that the number of no-shows increased when home games were televised. Senator Pastore tried to rebut Rozelle's assertion by reminding the commissioner that the blackout would only be lifted if the game was sold out. In this context, Pastore's comment missed the mark, as there could still be more no-shows than before.[28]

Even if the number of no-shows did not appreciably increase in the wake of the lifting of blackouts, Rozelle had another line of defense: eventually the antiblackout policy would erode season ticket sales and increase no-shows. At his most hysterical, Rozelle implied that eventually NFL games would be played before empty stadiums.

Rozelle also pointed out that telecasts of home games would reduce the attraction of radio broadcasts of such games and, in fact, NFL teams had to rebate some of their radio rights in the wake of the lifting of blackouts. He claimed that NFL teams had collectively lost $500,000 per season for the previous two owing to the rebates.[29] George H. Duncan, president of Metromedia Radio Division, expressed the radio industry's opposition to lifting the television blackout of local home games. He predictably described how the proposed law would injure radio ratings and revenues.[30] Many listeners of radio broadcasts of NFL games were driving in their cars or trucks, or were listening when there was no access to television. Gerald S. Blum, general manager of two Atlanta radio stations, posed the key conundrum: "If a radio station presents its best efforts in promoting the home team, as most NFL contracts require, and succeeds in helping sell out the stadium, the station is then penalized by having that particular home game televised locally."[31]

Rozelle also appealed to an ethical aspect of lifting the blackouts. The commissioner's belief that lifting a blackout broke a covenant with purchasers of tickets had some validity. Fans purchasing tickets for a game that they thought would not be telecast and then finding the blackout would be lifted could feel aggrieved, even defrauded. In the long run, of course, once it was common practice to lift blackouts for sold-out games, then fans could factor that into their calculation of whether to purchase tickets or gamble that enough other people would purchase tickets to ensure a sellout and lifting of the blackout. The latter calculation, of course, hearkened to Rozelle's earlier point about fans jockeying to be last in line.[32]

Rozelle claimed that the forty-eight-hour advance lifting of a blackout would prove inconvenient for the television stations, creating technical problems. Television network officials, though, opposed the blackouts. They anticipated higher ratings from telecasting home games, and presumably they would be willing to pay more for rights to telecast such games, thereby offsetting, to some degree, the reduction in gate, concessions, and parking receipts. The network officials claimed that it was a simple process to insert a previously blacked-out game into their schedule. Of course, networks recognized that telecasts of home team's home games would reduce the ratings for the imported NFL games.

Rozelle's final defense consisted of speculation concerning oversaturation of televised NFL football. "Public Law 93-107 has taken from the league's hands a tested and experienced television policy which developed this volume of NFL television and introduced a wholly new set of factors. There are serious risks of local team over-saturation in the process. The premium value of ticket ownership has been seriously discounted . . . the distinction between attendance and nonattendance at home games is becoming increasingly blurred." He finished this argument by stating that attendance at NFL preseason games was declining, thanks to oversaturation.[33] Rozelle also reminded legislators of boxing's unhappy fate by claiming, "The sport simply ate itself with overexposure."[34] No one bothered to point out that boxing had other problems, such as ties with organized crime and rigged outcomes. Rozelle suggested that the antiblackout bills were inducing owners to reconsider their overall television strategy: "Were it not for the fact that the NFL is currently locked into long-term television arrangements, the league would now, because of the pendency of these bills, be giving serious consideration to adopting the television practices of other professional sports."[35]

In an exchange with representative John Murphy (N.Y.), Rozelle insinuated that the NFL's tentative four-team expansion might be put on hold: "if this [blackout] legislation passes . . . the 26 owners of the NFL will have to vote on the expansion and psychologically would be most reluctant to do so until we have had an opportunity to observe whether this affects our sports adversely as we now believe it will."[36] This was a nifty veiled threat.

If Rozelle's arguments sounded tenuous, he probably had some long-term goal in mind. Sportswriter Stanley Frank speculated that, "Pete has a shrewd sense of public relations and he knows blackouts are doomed. I think he'll drop them voluntarily in two years, even if Congress doesn't knock them out. Why two years? His contracts with the three networks expire then and he'll use the move as a wedge for money. . . . Most clubs have such long waiting lists for season tickets that the end of blackouts will have no serious effect of attendance."[37]

And Now for Some Evidence

When it came to empirical evidence regarding lifting the blackouts, both sides debated the data's meaning. Both saw what they wanted from the same data.

During the 1975 hearings, Rozelle proclaimed that the drop in season ticket sales was a result of the antiblackout rules: "93 percent of that decline came from clubs whose games have been all, or for the most part, televised locally. Now, it just seems like too much of a coincidence."[38] Louis Frey Jr. (Fla.) tried to force Rozelle to admit that the season was still the third or fourth best ever for the NFL in terms of paid attendance, but Rozelle slipped out of the question by saying, "Well, based upon percentage of profit as against gross, it was the lowest in 15 years."[39] He did not supply any supporting financial figures. Frey also took Rozelle to task on the no-show issue. Games where the blackout had been lifted had 6,413 no-shows on average, whereas games where the blackout was maintained averaged 4,965. Rozelle eventually resorted to claiming that no-shows almost doubled in 1973, after the imposition of the law, compared with 1972, but Frey pointed out that the no-shows figures for 1972 were incomplete and possibly inaccurate because the league had had no reason to compile accurate figures prior to 1973. Rozelle would later dismiss the 1973 figures, because season ticket sales were completed prior to the enactment of the law.[40]

When Torbert Macdonald pinned Rozelle down on supplying financial figures, the commissioner said the league would be willing to submit audited figures but on an average, per-team basis instead of team-by-team. When the data arrived, the per-team averages were grouped in terms of "Top 8," "Middle 10," and "Bottom 8."[41] Macdonald waxed sarcastic when he said, "I hope it is not the same kind of bookkeeping that the Redskins did last year, when on paper they lost money, where they actually made $1.5 million." Rozelle rebutted by saying the data were operating figures, without any interest or depreciation taken. During the same hearing, Macdonald also implied that Rozelle used misleading arithmetic. He believed Rozelle included only the attendance drop associated with fewer season tickets sold, but that the commissioner neglected, intentionally or not, to add up gains in single-game ticket sales. Torbert emphasized this aspect because he thought this implied more people got to see at least one NFL home game.[42]

Later in the same hearing, Rozelle testified that gross ticket sales had fallen by 6 percent between 1973 and 1974, which he claimed demonstrated the financial fallout from the antiblackout law. Some of the committee members suggested that the World Football League (WFL) and the NFL players' strike may have curbed demand. The argument then shifted to the Miami Dolphins, a team that had lost three key players to the WFL and suffered attendance and no-show woes.

Rozelle also bemoaned the reduction in season ticket sales, which he claimed went down for the first time in NFL experience in 1974 and continued to dwindle in 1975. "Of the total decrease [of 150,674 between 1973 and 1975] 55 percent comes from teams who had regularly televised their home games during the 1973 and 1974 seasons. . . . The net result is that fully 93 percent of the decrease in season ticket sales comes from those member clubs who were required to televise some or all of their home games locally during the 1973 and 1974 seasons."[43] Before the legislators broke out their kerchiefs to wipe away their tears, they should have asked how many teams were involved in these 55 and 93 figures. Rozelle simply failed to supply much context for the isolated numbers.

Cable Television Sparks Fears

Legislators feared the new cable television industry. They worried that NFL owners might allow cable and pay television to swoop in and telecast games after the blackout was lifted. Members queried Rozelle on the topic, and he proved adept at not saying, "No." As Lionel Van Deerlin (Ga.) pointed out: "Your statement seems to indicate that this [selling rights to NFL games to pay television or wired cable] is not so, but you do throw in the caveat of 'no present intention.'" He pressed Rozelle on whether the owners had discussed such possibilities. Rozelle again parried the question: "We said we have no immediate plans, but we do not like to be prohibited by contract from the time that may arrive when everyone is doing it [showing their programs on cable television], and where we would be prevented by contract from making the political and business judgment as to whether we wanted to extend the box office risk of 'no shows' and all the other ramifications of going into cable." He added that CBS was adamant that it wanted an NFL guarantee that the league would not get into cable telecasts, but that the other two networks were not as agitated by the possibility.[44] Perhaps the hallmark of Rozelle's genius was his ability to parry criticism and scrutiny without committing to anything.

Owners of local television stations also wanted cable banned. They, too, suggested inserting a clause stipulating that the pending antitrust exemption prohibit cable television from the exemption.[45]

Other Leagues' Responses to the Bills

The proposed legislation would apply to all four team sports. Other professional team sports offered alternatives to the NFL's policies. MLB did not blackout All-

Star and World Series games, although it did blackout League Championship games. The NBA and NHL commissioners rarely sold out their playoff games, so the blackout issue was largely irrelevant. The NFL differed from these other leagues in that its playoffs were single-game elimination, while the other leagues had multigame playoff series. World Series games were rarely sellouts.

Bowie Kuhn (MLB commissioner), Walter Kennedy (NBA commissioner), Don Ruck (NHL vice president), and some of their subordinates testified. They admitted that the antiblackout law would have, at most, modest effects, but they remained lukewarm about the bills. The men expressed concerns about the long-term effects of the bill upon no-shows and future ticket sales; they disliked losing the ability to decide when and where to telecast their games. The officials also suggested that the leagues were in the best position to decide when and where to televise games. Kennedy pointed out, "The supporters of the legislation should not assume that they know better what is good for the professional sports business than do the owners whose investment is at stake."[46]

The sports officials also worried about the mechanics of implementing an antiblackout rule, which entailed changing television schedules. They also echoed some of Rozelle's arguments, while noting differences between the sports—football teams played once per week, while teams in the other sports played multiple times per week. At most they were willing to consider a trial period for the law.[47] The officials may well have feared that what legislators would do for the most prosperous of leagues, they might also do to the less prosperous ones.

Television Officials Weigh In

Network television officials, of course, came out in favor of the antiblackout bills, with some suggested revisions pertaining to banning cable and pay television from access to the blackout-lifted telecasts.[48] They realized they could get higher ratings and possibly greater advertising revenue by telecasting popular home games to local audiences, although rival televised games would suffer lower ratings. The networks would end up with more viewers, but just how many more was speculative.[49] The network officials, though, were coy in estimating how much these new rights were worth. Roone Arledge, ABC Sports president, stated, "It is hard to put a dollar value on what it would mean. It obviously would enhance the attraction of the overall television packages that the leagues sell to the networks."[50] The unanswered question was, why had the NFL and the networks not already negotiated an agreement for these property rights, if they were so valuable?

John Schneider, CBS president, attempted to characterize the negotiations as dealing with monopolies (while not self-identifying the three networks as oligopolists—a group of large firms that dominate an industry). "They [the owners], in effect, set down the rules under which they, and we, must play. If they so desire, they can remove games from free television and millions of homes to pay cable and a smaller audience." He buttressed his expressed fears by testifying, "The NFL insisted for the first time, on a nonnegotiable basis, that it must be given the right to take the blacked-out games to pay cable."[51] When Macdonald raised questions about Rozelle's willingness to sign a four-year contract instead of a one-year agreement in the face of changing network and cable television capabilities, Schneider replied, "His intent is that within the 4 years, he can experiment. He has his cake and eats it, too. He gets the income from the league contract with CBS and reserves for himself the right to experiment with cable to test the water."[52]

Schneider returned to testify in 1975. He told the committee that ratings for the telecasts of local home games reached 31 percent of the households, compared with 19 percent watching telecasts of games with nonlocal teams. Surprisingly, perhaps, the general trend was not replicated in New York City, but he attributed this to the fact the "fans were dissatisfied with the performance of the team." Schneider's figures were confirmed by a report from ARB, a local television ratings firm. This firm discovered that ratings of local home game telecasts were slightly higher than the ratings for telecasts of games where the local team was on the road—32.1 versus 29.7.[53]

Carl Lindemann Jr. of NBC expressed fears about cable television: "Pay cable could reach a point where it might outbid free television for sports rights. For example, if cable television obtains from only 30 percent of its present subscribers an extra $2 for each . . . game, it would have a fund greater than what the trade press has reported that all three networks paid in total for the 1973 season."[54]

The network television executives also assured Congress that they would have no difficulty working with the forty-eight- or seventy-two-hour notice of a team lifting a blackout. Schneider reminded Congress that his crews were already in the stadiums televising games to the nation, aside from the home locality, "so that there is no technical problem. . . . It is a matter of plugging another station in [instantaneously]."[55] Vincent Wasilewski said television stations "would be very, very pleased and happy to have the opportunity to carry that sold out home game."[56]

The FCC had already tilted the competitive scales in favor of the television networks by its rules on siphoning. The rules stipulated that cable television could not telecast sporting events that had been previously telecast on network television until two years elapsed without such network telecasts. In other words, if the NFL wanted to switch its national television contract to cable or pay television, if would have to cease telecasting via the networks for two years—a hefty price to pay.[57] The cable companies would eventually fight these antisiphoning laws in court and prevail.

Cable television executives, of course, sang a different tune in their testimony than the network television officials. The reader may note that the blackout situation was a game played by two sets of monopolists—the NFL and the network television companies; a set of fledgling entrepreneurs—cable and pay-television companies—that may or may not have harbored dreams of monopoly power; and consumers. The cable executives stated they were attempting to benefit consumers by enlarging the selection of programs available. Older readers may recall the good old days when most cities, outside of the largest, had three network television stations, perhaps an independent station, and a public station. The plethora of choices was still largely an entrepreneur's dream. David Foster, president of the National Cable Television Association (NCTA), pointed out that the FCC had delayed the diffusion of cable with a "virtual freeze" on cable growth in the largest markets. The FCC's decision kept a majority of the country's television owners without access to cable service, but it had recently been lifted. Foster continued by pointing out that the FCC constricted CATV's access to programming.[58]

Foster had the temerity to raise the issue of who had property rights to telecast the newly available home games. The network television executives assumed they had the right to these rights under their contract with the NFL, as they were already televising the game to viewers outside the proscribed radius. "Must the NFC sell that black out area to CBS who would transfer it to its affiliate? Or, to put it differently, can the game be retained by the league in the home city for sale to someone other than CBS, that is, an independent television station or the local cable system, and not be branded a blackout?" Senator Pastore immediately repudiated Foster's suggestion: "This would be a terrible thing to do. I mean . . . it isn't a question of depriving CATV from taking that signal and bringing it in if they can. . . . What we want to do is open that screen. . . . I mean, you can't take it away from the free television viewer and sell it to the fellow who can afford to pay a subscription fee."[59]

Amos B. Hostetter Jr., NCTA chair, disputed assertions that cable television could outbid the networks and thereby poach telecasts of NFL games. He quoted a trade journal article that reported the vast disparity between the profits accruing to the television networks and to the cable industry—nearly $100 million. Hostetter also pointed out that the cable industry remained very diffuse, with three thousand separate systems, "which for the most part have no means of interconnecting and therefore cannot provide national or even regional network capability."[60]

Rozelle labored to allay the legislators' fears that the NFL had some long-term plan to switch to cable and pay television, but he failed. Van Deerlin told his fellow committee members, "I think one of the most poorly kept secrets in this whole question is the desire of professional football to get onto wired television for pay as fast as possible."[61]

Van Deerlin pressed Dean Burch, FCC chair, on his attitudes toward cable and pay television. Burch replied, "it is a supplemental source of information, and obviously I have no desire to pay for the Super Bowl if I can watch it on NBC, CBS, or ABC; but if I cannot see the home games of the Washington Redskins because of a public law and an antitrust exemption but pay a dollar and see it on cable, I want to do that. . . . I think they are entitled to carry that which otherwise can't be seen." Burch's answer was not good enough for Macdonald: "Can't you see if that happens pretty soon, there will be no sports on TV?" Macdonald went on to predict that cable and pay television would outbid the networks for popular sporting events. Though his prediction did not prove entirely accurate, it was a pretty good prediction of the future.[62]

Burch had already raised the hackles of a number of the legislators. After describing the four bills currently pending, he admitted there was some merit in the quid pro quo aspect of the legislation: lifting the blackouts as return for the antitrust exemption for network contracts. He, however, made clear that his sentiments were against if "the Congress or the Commission should tell a private entrepreneur how to package and market his product. . . . I must question the wisdom of thus interfering with marketplace realities and thus diminishing the rights to the disposition of private property."[63]

Hard Analysis of the Data

Unlike most of the hearings and laws passed, the television blackout law triggered a series of reports on the effects of the law. The FCC issued five annual reports. When FCC chairman Richard E. Wiley testified in 1975, he relied upon these reports.

The initial *Report of the FCC,* issued in 1974, was in a sense premature, considering that the law took effect after most of the 1973 season tickets had been sold. Paid attendance increased in 1973 compared with 1972. The report noted that televising home games boosted local television ratings, compared with the ratings from televised games involving nonlocal teams. It pointed out that a few of the NFL teams had inadequate data pertaining to no-shows in 1972, making a comparison between 1972 and 1973 less definitive. There were 182 regular season games, of which 109 sold out sufficiently in advance to be shown locally on television. In 1972, obviously, there were no such games shown on television. The prevalence of no-shows increased slightly for games that were televised locally compared to games that were not televised locally. The report concluded optimistically, "At least in the first season, there is little evidence to support the NFL claim that the anti-blackout law will result in football becoming a television, or studio, sport as a result of increasing no shows." Rozelle responded by mail to Wiley: "Our position that 'no shows' will eventually be transformed into non-ticket-buyers has not been changed."[64] Given the limitations of the data, his response was understandable.

Although the number of games that sold out far enough in advance shrank in the next season, the season ticket sales and no-shows provided some justification for Rozelle's and the NFL owners' pessimism. The *Third Annual Report of the FCC* reported a diminution in the number of season ticket sales.[65] The NFL quickly seized upon this fact as proof of their predictions. As noted, during the 1974 and 1975 seasons, though, Americans struggled through the remnants of a serious recession; the WFL may have siphoned some patrons; and some of the NFL teams, such as the Miami Dolphins, suffered serious personnel losses to the WFL that may have dampened fans' enthusiasm.

The *Third Annual Report,* though, included a sophisticated statistical analysis of the data (which did not include gate receipts) provided by the NFL. The regression analysis—a form of analysis that isolates the effects upon, say, attendance from different variables such as weather, ticket prices, home team's quality, visiting team's quality, and whether the game was televised locally or not—demonstrated that "the average number of season tickets sold by NFL teams increased when the number of home games locally televised during the preceding season also increased as a result of Public Law 93-107." The researchers stressed that there was not necessarily a causal relationship between season tickets sold and the number of home games locally televised, but they wrote, "it is reasonable to conclude that the NFL's total ticket sales have not been seriously affect by the Sports Anti-Blackout Law."[66] The report did state that a few individual teams, such as Miami, had significantly more no-shows when their games were televised locally. The report also indicated that revenues from sales of concessions and the NFL's *Pro* magazine dropped off, but the losses did not appear substantial.[67]

The annual reports made much of the fact that season ticket sales as a percentage of available seats went down. The reports attributed this partly to the owners enlarging the number of seats available during this time period. In addition to this fine point, the *Third Annual Report* indicated, "In 1974 the NFL experienced its first decline in annual ticket sales since 1968." The decline continued into 1975, albeit at a slower rate of decrease. Season ticket sales had fallen by 5.3 percent, but some of this reduction was offset by greater numbers of tickets to individual games.[68]

The *Third Annual Report* also dismissed the NFL owners' worries concerning "oversaturation" of professional football on television. It stated, "If this were a problem, it should be reflected in a decline in average audience ratings particularly for those teams which have locally televised all or nearly all of their home games . . . teams which have televised most of their games tend to achieve higher than normal audience ratings."[69]

The FCC reports were confirmed by a pair of independent economists, John Siegfried and C. Elton Hinshaw. They concluded, "The NFL's contention that televising home games causes no-shows to increase is not supported by the evidence. . . . [Regarding the 1973, 1974, and 1975 seasons] we discovered that the televising of football games, by itself, has little to do with the frequency of no-shows." They continued by reporting, "When we examined the interactions between weather and the availability of the game on television, we discovered that bad weather, *in the presence of a televised home game* [italics theirs], did lead to more no-shows than would have occurred if a game were not televised. But even under adverse weather conditions, televising the game reduced live attendance by *at most* one percent of the tickets distributed." These economists also pointed out that, "Even the NFL would be hard put to argue that the demise of one sporting activity is necessarily harmful to social welfare since such a position would imply that current football fans would be happier if boxing had survived and football had not diverted their attention." They also dismissed the claim that increased no-shows hurt parking revenues and radio revenues by stating, "There is such a parking shortage at most stadiums that lots will continue to fill up even if there are substantial numbers of no-shows" and "Radio rights may lose their value, but we have confidence that the NFL will remind the television networks of their additional advertising revenue resulting from the televising of home games at the next renegotiation of their contract."[70]

By the FCC's *Fourth Annual Report,* however, the tenor changed. "[T]he results indicate that season ticket sales fell significantly following the 1973 season. This is precisely what one would expect assuming the NFL is correct in asserting that locally televised games would have diminished demand for season tickets. . . . Given that season ticket sales declined significantly in 1974 and 1975, it would appear that the legislation is at least partially responsible for recent reductions in sales. . . . Local telecasts would seem to afford the only feasible explanation of why sales have fallen off during the past three seasons."[71] The report cautioned, though, that "teams which sell out and broadcast a large number of home games have experienced relatively fewer no shows than teams which have lifted the blackout on a smaller number of home games." They attributed this to the fact that teams that sold out most of their games were more likely to be successful on the field, so their appeal lingered into the next season.[72]

The researchers found that, "local telecasts of home games appear to exacerbate the adverse impact of the club's performance on its season ticket sales for the subsequent year [and the reverse was true]. . . . Based on available information, it is estimated that season ticket sales since 1974 have remained approximately 10 percent below those levels which probably would have been realized had no home games been locally televised. . . . Public Law 93-107, since 1974, appears to have cost the NFL approximately $1 million a year in terms of lower gate receipts, or less than 1 percent of the league's total revenue."[73] Although losing 1 percent of one's revenues may not seem dire, the effect on profits would be magnified because profits are the *differences* between revenues and costs.[74] The researchers continued to dismiss the NFL's argument that televising sold-out home games would lead to oversaturation, as ratings for televised homes games remained high.[75]

The *Fifth Annual Report of the FCC* was the most pessimistic in terms of finding negative effects upon the NFL. "The new lower level represents lost revenue of about $4.6 million per year as compared to the 1973 level. This represents approximately 2.4 percent of the $192.4 million total league revenue reported in 1975. . . . Subsequent analysis suggests that a substantial proportion of this lost revenue may be due to locally televised home games." The report suggested that the problem of no-shows had stabilized, considering the league average was relatively constant over the last few seasons, albeit at a higher level—8.5 versus 6.1 percent—compared with 1972. The rates of no shows, however, were higher both for televised local home games and for nontelevised home games. Offsetting these losses were increased fan satisfaction emanating from the home games televised and the NFL's large increase in national television revenues from $2.442 million to $5.775 million per team per annum starting in 1978. Of course, the researchers were unable to discern how much of this per-team increase owed to the availability of televised home games.[76]

The *Fifth Annual Report* admitted that the antiblackout policy may have contributed to the decline in season ticket sales, which were down 14 percent since 1973. Since stadium capacity had increased, the report suggested that more tickets were available on a game-by-game basis, which potentially meant that a greater number of fans could attend games. After the fifth season with the antiblackout policy, the report pointed out that the finding that "the greater the number of televised home games in one season, the higher the season ticket sales in the following season" still held.[77]

Conclusion: The NFL Accepts Tolerable Damage

The antiblackout rule adversely affected NFL gate attendance, no-shows, and revenues, as the NFL officials and owners predicted. Against these losses were increased consumer welfare. Whatever the effects of lifting the blackouts, increases in the league's national television contracts during the 1970s swamped any losses from the antiblackout rules. The NFL emerged from five years under the rules, mandatorily or voluntarily, in fine fettle.

When the initial bill expired, legislators were unable to get a bill extending the antiblackout law passed. The NFL, though, agreed to abide by the initial law through the 1977 season, affording a longer trial. The Senate committee requested the FCC to continue to study the situation after the initial bill expired.[78] The NFL apparently decided the antiblackout rules were not so onerous; they voluntarily continued to adhere to the policies for years to come.

The FCC remains involved in regulating blackouts, although the NFL remains the only league employing them. In 2012, a group of petitioners urged the FCC to "eliminate the Commission's rules regarding sports blackouts, which prohibit MVPDs [multichannel video programming distributors] from carrying a sporting event if the event is blacked out on local broadcast television stations . . . because the rules prevent consumers' access to local sports events, particularly with ticket prices and unemployment at their current high levels."[79]

Blackouts rarely occur anymore, with only two during the 2013 season. With the extremely cold weather in early January 2014, fears of possible blackouts of NFL playoff games in Cincinnati, Green Bay, and Indianapolis arose. Team sponsors purchased enough tickets to ensure sellouts and to allow the games to be televised locally.[80]

14

The Future Arrives Via Cable Television *1989*

Long anticipated and feared, cable television began to realize its promise during the 1980s, as it became available throughout the country. Similar to television's diffusion, cable did not spread uniformly, and many parts of the country would not receive service for years to come.[1]

Because the technology evolved so rapidly, congressional and FCC attempts to regulate the industry often proved clumsy. NFL commissioner Paul Tagliabue, who had recently replaced the retired Pete Rozelle, told a Senate subcommittee investigating cable television, "it is impossible to predict with certainty what television patterns will be like 10 or 20 years from now. Technology is evolving and consumer preferences are constantly changing."[2]

The battle between the younger technologies of cable and satellite television versus the older, over-the-air television, though, demonstrated the role Congress played in choosing winners and losers. For many years, Congress aided and abetted over-the-air television's dominance via antisiphoning regulations that retarded cable's and satellite's growth by restricting cable and pay-television access to many sporting events that were being telecast over-the-air for free. The intent of the regulations was to prevent programs from switching from free over-the-air to pay-television delivery. While the regulations presumably protected citizens, they also freed network and other free television stations from competition with cable for desirable sporting and entertainment events.

People were willing to pay for cable, because the system gave them many more choices than the traditional television setup. Cable television also offered better reception in some cases and often fewer, if any, advertisements. In the case of better reception, Preston R. Padden, president of the Association of Independent Television Stations, recalled that cable had been viewed as "an antenna service to improve the reception of broadcast signals," and that such a rationale was encapsulated in the Copyright Act of 1976.[3] By the late 1980s, cable's services were far more varied. Padden's recollection revealed the difficulty lawmakers had in devising sensible, enduring laws covering a rapidly changing technology.

Home Box Office (HBO) filed suit over the antisiphoning rules and eventually won in court, thereby ending the antisiphoning regulation. The courts found that there was no evidence to suggest that cable television companies were going to usurp free television. Antitrust law expert Stephen Ross points out that in *Home Box Office v. FCC*, "the Court of Appeals struck down the regulation as arbitrary. This decision was correct—the regulation was both overbroad and underinclusive. Under the regulation, a significant number of games would remain untelevised, even if fans willingly would pay to view those games on cable."[4]

With these changes, cable television was ready to compete with the networks and independent television stations. These companies still hoped that Congress would act to stuff the cable genie back into the bottle.

The 1989 Hearings Get Underway

As Senate subcommittee chair Howard Metzenbaum (Ohio) characterized the change, "The 1980s was the decade in which fans could pay to watch more sports, but the 1990s may become the decade in which fans must pay to watch any sports."[5] He pointed out that cable penetration of the country was 56 percent, with the industry hoping to reach 70 percent of the nation's homes by the end of the century. Metzenbaum warned, "Once cable penetration gets that high, watch out. The lure of big bucks may well prompt sports leagues and teams to completely bypass free TV, writing off those people who can't afford cable or can't get it." Cable television attained a 70 percent market penetration by 1998 but lost market share to alternative delivery systems, including satellites, during the next decade.[6]

Previous committees had discussed cable television, but the industry had not yet achieved sufficient diffusion to threaten free television. In previous hearings, league commissioners and presidents stated that owners had no definite plans to switch from free television to cable or pay television.

One event incited legislators and became a focal point during the 1989 hearings: The New York Yankees' deal with the Madison Square Garden Network (MSGN) to show all the team's games on the cable channel, thereby depriving millions of New Yorkers free access to Yankees' games on television. Senator Metzenbaum criticized this contract and hoped that baseball commissioner Fay Vincent would void the contract or at least force a revision to allow free television to telecast most of the games simultaneously with MSGN.[7] Concurrent with the Yankees' agreement, the NFL signed a contract with the Entertainment and Sports Programming Network (better known as ESPN) for a package of thirteen Sunday and Thursday night games. MLB also dallied with ESPN; the contract included a Wednesday night exclusivity clause, whereby no other games would be telecast anywhere during the ESPN telecast.[8] MLB had already reduced its nationally televised games on the traditional networks.

Charles Schumer (N.Y.) introduced legislation, "The Baseball Viewers Protection Act of 1989," to "guarantee that all fans can watch baseball games on television, and not only those fans lucky enough to have cable." The bill required baseball teams signing cable contracts to stipulate that at least 50 percent of the games broadcast would be shown on free television. The penalty for violating the proposed law was for the team to lose its antitrust exemption for two years.[9] Although Schumer focused on baseball, presumably in response to the Yankees' cable deal, other legislators wanted to extend any prospective bill to the NFL; they rarely mentioned NBA and NHL games. Senator Arlen Specter (Pa.) made the connection between the exemption and Congress' desires: "in a system which was entirely free enterprise, a strong argument could be made that that is the right of the Yankee ownership to negotiate any way that the Yankee ownership chooses. But baseball enjoys an antitrust exemption."[10]

The legislators and free television executives saw cable as a supplemental source of sports telecasting. They did not want games currently shown for free to migrate to cable television, which many legislators lumped with pay television. They pressed sports officials to demonstrate that cable contracts were not diminishing the number of games shown on free television.[11] Tagliabue emphasized that the suggestion that, "the NFL's contract with ESPN has caused fans not subscribing to cable television to be without NFL games on broadcast television," was inaccurate. Because the league maintained contracts with two of the networks for Sunday afternoon games, there was no diminution in the number of games telecast nationally.[12] The legislators were especially worried that the Super Bowl and World Series would migrate to cable or pay-per-view television; league officials had to reassure the legislators, without firmly committing to free telecasts in perpetuity.[13]

Tagliabue and former commissioner Pete Rozelle testified that the mid-1980s witnessed a reversal of the NFL's popularity on television. Ratings and advertising were "softer" than in the past. ABC hesitated in renewing its Monday Night Football telecasts, while the other two networks barely increased their per-season payment for rights to NFL games. Rozelle told the committee that the league offered the thirteen-game package eventually sold to ESPN to NBC and CBS, but these networks were not enthusiastic. In negotiating with ESPN, Rozelle stipulated that the ESPN telecasts be shown for free in the two cities whose teams were playing, so the NFL shielded itself from much of the animosity that arose in the Yankees/MSGN deal.[14]

Roger L. Werner Jr., president of ESPN, described the company as a "nationally distributed sports programming service" with 20,500 affiliates reaching almost 60 percent of American television households. He emphasized that ESPN was not a pay sports channel, in the sense of pay-per-view boxing matches. ESPN stipulated that it be carried on the basic cable service package and not on the premium service. "We intend to do everything we can to keep ESPN on basic cable and available to the maximum number of subscribers."[15] He told legislators that ESPN and other national cable programmers were providing new competition for television rights to sporting events, which resulted in more sports programming, although he claimed, "we have viewed our role as supplemental . . . bringing the American public access to sports events, news and information and lifestyle programs that we believe would not have been available elsewhere."[16]

The committee heard from free television industry officials. These officials whined about the unfair competition they now faced from cable television. One executive, Edward Fritts, president and CEO of the National Association of Broadcasters, claimed, "Cable starts with the advantages of vertical and horizontal integration and the compulsory license. In addition, they bid on sports programming with a triple—not dual, a triple—revenue stream. First, they pass the increased costs to their subscribers. Second, they can charge pay-per-view and, third, they can sell advertising. The net effect is that cable has an unfair advantage when it comes to bidding for sports."[17]

The free television executives attributed cable's growth to the court's disavowal of the antisiphoning rules and to the compulsory license regulation, whereby cable stations could retransmit telecasts from free television stations without permission and without pay. The original intent of the compulsory license regulation had been to enable early cable television companies to gain a foothold in the marketplace.[18]

The networks wanted Congress to reinstate the antisiphoning rules; to require that teams make their games available on free television and not exclusively on cable; and to force cable companies to compensate broadcasters for the programs they retransmitted.[19] The executives' plaints were certainly self-serving and hypocritical, considering that the antisiphoning rules had been used for years to thwart cable television.

Padden believed that a narrower antisiphoning rule could pass legal muster. His legal advisors informed him that the court ruled in the *Home Box Office v. FCC* case that there was "no evidence of a threat to Free TV events." He pointed out that a sports-only antisiphoning rule was feasible, and he thought that some of the senators on the committee agreed with this legal reasoning.[20]

Some Legal and Economic Theorizing

Law professor Stephen F. Ross testified that he had formulated a simple rule of thumb in determining whether cable telecasts of sporting events ran afoul of the antitrust law. He suggested that the Cable Communication Policy Act of 1984 should be reconsidered, because it allowed local cable franchisees to operate as unregulated monopolies, leading to increased prices for cable services and curbing the public's access to sports telecasts. Ross suggested that for a government or private plaintiff disputing the validity of "a cable contract under the antitrust laws to show that, were the cable contract held invalid, the sports team or league would select another alternative that would result in greater viewership by fans. . . . This test promotes the sound public policy of encouraging cable networks to contract to show games that would otherwise not be shown on television at all." Ross's rule smacks of the old antisiphoning law, except it was narrower in applicability. He cited as support for his interpretation the court's ruling in the *HBO v. FCC* case: "As the court observed, those with pay cable also receive over-the-air television and would retain access to these telecasts, while those without cable would be no worse off than at present." Ross admitted that such a rule might force club owners to forego some profits, but concluded, "there is no right to monopoly profits simply because the monopolist is engaging in speech."[21]

Later in the hearings, Senator Metzenbaum asked Ross to apply his interpretation to the two situations inciting the cable television controversy. Ross thought the NFL/ESPN deal would comply with antitrust law because it was not displacing telecasts formerly shown on network television, while the Yankees/MSGN deal would not satisfy antitrust law. He was not as certain regarding whether baseball commissioner Fay Vincent had the authority to force the Yankees and MSGN to void or to alter their agreement. He added that the Supreme Court's ruling in the NCAA college football case, whereby the court ruled the NCAA's exclusive negotiations for telecasts was unlawful, established a rule of reason: "That agreement has potential for helping consumers, and therefore is evaluated under the antitrust rule of reason."[22]

Ross suggested in a scholarly article that the government should consider removing baseball's and football's antitrust exemptions. He touted free competition as providing many benefits for taxpayers, players, and fans. Owners would compete against each other to place franchises in all cities capable of supporting professional team sports, and they would compete for stadium leases and thereby alleviate taxpayer subsidization. Owners would hesitate to put games on cable or pay television, lest their rivals remain on free television and generate higher ratings. They would have to compete for players, forcing them to pay players fair-market value. Ross pointed out that the antitrust exemptions protecting MLB and the NFL from competition let the owners constrict the supply of franchises, although he described the NFL's adroit use of potential expansion teams as a political lever.[23]

Ross discussed a common objection to his idea of splitting up MLB and the NFL: the natural monopoly argument. He dismissed the argument on economic terms, because there was no evidence that one league of sixteen teams produced baseball games more cheaply than two leagues of eight teams would have. He pointed out that, unlike railroads and utility companies, where average costs shrank as output increased, largely owing to large fixed costs, sports team owners incurred relatively small fixed costs.[24] The natural monopoly argument is applicable to producing a national champion. Although rival leagues have to cooperate to produce such a champion, the leagues do not have to form a cartel to gain this result. The first World Series in 1903 was between the champions of two separate leagues.

Conclusion: Predicting the Future at Your Own Risk

Cable television and pay television had been on the horizon for decades, since Walter O'Malley dreamed of charging fans to watch their beloved Dodgers during the 1950s.[25] His vision was not shared by legislators. They worried, of course, that if sports telecasts switched from the free, public airwaves to cable or pay television, where there was an explicit charge for watching, their constituents would grow angry and maybe even blame their legislators.

As with many technological advances, many people feared that there would be "haves" and "have-nots." The rapid diffusion of television, though, should have allayed any fears that vast numbers of American citizens would be unable to afford cable. Television might have been a greater investment for families in the 1950s than cable service would be in the 1980s. Purchasing a television would, of course, provide entertainment for years, but the comparison is apt. Cable would not long remain the province of the wealthy.

The legislators were resisting the tide of technology. ESPN has proved to be a major player in the sports world. Specialty cable channels allow sports fans to customize their viewing. The internet, too, has allowed fans unimagined access to sports. Fortunately, even though Metzenbaum proved prescient with regard to the migration of premium sporting events from over-the-air television to the newer television delivery systems, the legislators of 1989 were not able to stymie the tide.

15

Can't We All Get Along?
1966

NFL owners had successfully resisted the All-America Football Conference in the late 1940s, although the established league absorbed three AAFC teams into its ranks. The NFL monopolized professional football for the next decade. With the changing patterns of population growth in the United States, cities outside the northeast quadrant of the country lobbied for teams. The dual Texas cities of Dallas and Houston, especially, loomed large in talk of expansion. The NFL owners, however, were sufficiently attuned to the political desires of legislators throughout the country, whose constituents wanted NFL or similar football. NFL owners had endured antitrust lawsuits throughout the 1950s and understood that their actions would be closely watched.

When Texas oilman Lamar Hunt was repeatedly rebuffed in his efforts to secure a team, he decided to contact other frustrated entrepreneurs seeking teams. Because Hunt was a legitimate prospective buyer, some NFL owners had opened their books to him. He had a facility with financial information and quickly grasped the basics of professional football finance. Within a few months, Hunt and other like-minded businessmen announced the formation of the AFL in mid-1959. These owners faced the hurdles of obtaining stadium leases and skilled players. Unlike the AAFC, though, the AFL quickly gained a valuable asset: a national television contract. The contract guaranteed hundreds of thousands of dollars per team per season and promised to offset potential shortfalls at the gate.[1]

NFL owners were no more willing to share the professional football market in 1959 than they had been in 1946–1949, and they resisted the interlopers. These men hoped to divide and conquer the AFL owners by enticing the AFL's Minnesota group to switch leagues. The NFL also made offers to Hunt and a couple of other AFL owners to buy into existing NFL teams. Hunt proved stalwart to his

AFL peers, so the NFL's attempt failed. The NFL owners quickly responded by deciding to expand by two teams. Unlike MLB's success with expansion, the NFL's half-hearted plan failed to squelch the upstart league. The two leagues fought for several years, with owners claiming ruinous losses. None of the teams folded, though. Players and fans benefited: players because they faced competition for their services, and fans because there was more professional football. While the AFL undoubtedly sported inferior teams for a few years, the new league eventually began to catch up in terms of talent. Fans and sportswriters clamored for an accord that would allow for a championship game.

The AFL filed an antitrust lawsuit against the NFL, but the court ruled in favor of the NFL. Steven R. Rivkin, a legal scholar, pointed out that, "the Court found that the 'relevant market' for major league football combination was a national one, not local or regional, so that the NFL did not have the requisite degree of market power to exclude from competition."[2]

Football owners realized that neither league was going to capitulate. They began to seek an agreement. The owners recognized that any such agreement would have to pass muster with antitrust authorities or via a congressional bill granting special dispensation. Football owners understood that gaining a full-fledged antitrust exemption was not likely, so they concentrated on getting a merger agreement approved by Congress.

A Bumpy Ride at the Hearings

Given the obvious antitrust implications of rival leagues asking for permission to create "one out of two," the House committee might have required detailed financial information from the owners. The committee's staff could have subjected such financial information to critical scrutiny, as was done for the 1951 hearings. Even without such financial data, congressional staffers could easily examine trends in competitive balance—a perusal of season standings in the *New York Times* or *Sporting News* required little effort. In the case of baseball, the New York Yankees' dominance of the American League between 1949 and 1964 was apparent even to a casual observer, while Paul Brown's Cleveland club's football fortunes contrasted sharply with the Chicago Cardinals' experiences. During the 1960s, the Boston Celtics dominated the NBA. Considering that Congress had given professional teams sports an exemption for negotiating national television contracts, the committee members might have examined the effects of this exemption. At least the House committee held hearings; the relevant Senate committee did not. The Senate's actions were a lesson in the bizarre manner of passing legislation.

On October 6, 1966, Emanuel Celler presided over yet another investigation of sports leagues. Senate Bill 3817 would "authorize the merger of two or more professional football leagues and to protect football contests between secondary schools from professional telecast." The Senate had approved the bill on September 26, 1966. As Celler recognized, S. 3817 was not the only bill pertaining to the proposed merger, as twenty-five similar ones were circulating. The Senate bill, as with most of the House variants, countenanced the pro football merger, only if high school and college football games were protected from professional competition.[3]

Celler explained that the subcommittee needed to consider whether an antitrust exemption should be granted or a governmental regulatory body established. He wondered, too, whether the NFL commissioner was able to protect the interests of not just the owners but the players and fans. Celler recalled that football officials wanted an antitrust exemption back in 1957, claiming their sport was in dire straits. In the intervening years, though, the league prospered and was now a sport with a national following. "Football is now one of the most important spectator sports in the United States. The Antitrust Subcommittee must be very careful that this outstanding growth in professional football is not arrested by precipitous legislation."[4]

After Celler concluded, a parade of representatives presented their amendments, including future president of the United States Gerald Ford. At the height of the Vietnam War, legislators clamored over each other to weigh in on professional football.[5]

The legislators then began delving into the merger's intricacies. Some of the committee members were wary that the football owners were attempting an end run, via a vague stipulation: "And the provisions of which are directly relevant thereto." Unlike in earlier years, league officials stated they were not seeking a full antitrust exemption, just a narrow exemption covering the act of merger. Incidentally, this would have been challenged and likely overturned by the players association, television networks (seeking to prevent combining television rights into one league), or the antitrust division. The NFL's attorney, Hamilton Carothers, explained: "That language was . . . to insure that the limited objective which we urged upon that committee would be achieved. If we go ahead with this transaction, we carry a double burden. We carry a burden of not only being vulnerable to the extent that any single sports league is vulnerable under the antitrust laws, but we would carry with us the historical fact that every practice that we engaged in as a single league could be attributable to an agreement date June 8, 1966. Our sole request . . . is to permit us to begin operations as a single league." Celler pointed out that if the Senate bill were interpreted solely and simply to mean an approval of the merger but was not extended to league practices, such as the player draft, then "it would give you an empty right; it would be just as worthless as a wine cellar without a corkscrew. You would get nothing out of it; it would mean nothing." Carothers responded, "But the exemption would only extend to those acts as acts of bringing the two leagues together. It would not extend to the practices of the league as a single league. . . . We do not know whether that draft system is vulnerable under the antitrust laws." Celler expressed his opinion that the draft was vulnerable to antitrust laws. After football officials and Celler debated the meaning of the statement in the bill—"Would not extend to the combined league any greater antitrust immunity than that now existing for the existing professional football leagues"—the discussion continued.[6]

Pete Rozelle's Stellar Testimony

Pete Rozelle was a star witness. He explained that the merger would occur over three or four seasons, as the two leagues had separate television contracts to fulfill. He then launched into his public relations effort by acknowledging public support. He described the fans' desire for a championship game between the leagues and a curtailment of the bonuses paid untried college seniors. Some of the fans, too, bemoaned the competitive imbalance, although Green Bay Packers fans of the mid-1960s undoubtedly were satisfied with the current balance. Rozelle's remarks were notable for his attempt to portray the players, who would be among the losers from such a merger, as somehow receiving undeserved remuneration. He later stressed a "minimum salary" for those newly drafted, as well as enhanced benefits for AFL players.[7]

Rozelle finessed the point that there would no longer be competitive bidding for drafted players by blandly stating, "The later player selection meeting will eliminate interference with the college football program and improve the relationship between amateur and professional athletes." He argued, too, that football's merger would differ from, say, a merger between two automobile producers: "Our plan does not involve a merger in any traditional business or antitrust sense. All clubs of both leagues remain under their present ownership and there are no exchanges of stock or business assets. What it is, in essence, is an agreement between the member clubs of the two leagues to play games with one another and to conduct their affairs in the manner in which professional sports leagues operate."[8] Rozelle contradicted his other statements that the league was a single entity; the NFL claimed it was a single entity or a joint venture, whichever was advantageous at the time.

His main selling point, though, seemed to be the merger's effect upon competitive balance. Rozelle claimed the merger would improve competitive balance, because all AFL and NFL teams would be operating by the same rules, on and off the playing field. In his words, "football competition rather than ability to withstand [financial] losses can [again] be made the dominant element of the game," instead of dominance by teams in the largest cities.[9] At this point in time, 1965–1966, though, teams in New York, Los Angeles, and Chicago were struggling to win half of their games.

Rozelle then argued that implementing the merger was complicated, with many contracts and a myriad of other details. The owners needed legislative assurance that making these arrangements would not trigger litigation; the Department of Justice had indicated some misgivings about the merger. Rozelle then played the NFL-in-Peril card: "It is conceivable that the sum total of financial risks resulting from legal action could easily be larger than the total value and net assets of all the existing franchises. This is what led me to emphasize at the outset that I would have no responsible alternative, but to recommend that we not proceed." If this was not sufficiently lugubrious, Rozelle continued by painting a bleak picture for the millionaires owning franchises: ever-escalating player costs, internal deterioration of both leagues, increasing imbalance on the field, and, "the development of conditions where the ability to field representative football teams will depend solely on the franchise's willingness and ability to stand increasing losses." He reiterated, "These are not simply self-serving speculations. The familiar process is already well underway."[10]

Sportswriters' reactions to the proposed merger were predominantly favorable. Arthur Daley, *New York Times* columnist, concluded that almost everyone—fans, team owners, television networks, coaches, and even players—would benefit from the merger. In his words, "The only losers will be those unfortunate football-playing college seniors who just witnessed the slaying of the golden goose. Because a common draft will eliminate the payment of ridiculous bonuses by competing leagues, the more gifted of the campus heroes will miss out on instant wealth." He did not think many would mourn the college seniors' lost leverage in bargaining. He concluded, "And this warfare showed signs of escalating into a cruel and ruthless battle to the death. The end came just in time."[11]

Lest the reader think Daley was merely an envious observer, some players echoed his remarks. Rather than cheer the collegians for benefiting from the competitive bidding, these players criticized the payments. Several cited morale problems emanating from bonus payments to rookies, although a number of veteran players had been drafted during a time of competition between leagues and may well have benefited from such competition. They hewed the owners' line that the bidding for college players was threatening to drive the sport into bankruptcy.[12]

Daley made two interesting points, though. First, he thought the two league champions should play a game in Miami or New Orleans, where the January weather would be better. He realized that fans wanted the league championship game played in one of the two contenders' home stadium, but he felt the merger and the accompanying championship game could break this precedent. He also alluded to competitive balance. Daley was prescient, if a year off, in predicting, considering the Jets won the Super Bowl on January 12, 1969: "When it takes final form in 1970 the A.F.L. undoubtedly will gained full talent parity with the N.F.L." He believed that the common draft would make it more difficult for teams to rebound as quickly, before saying, "But the merger will bring stability into pro ball to the mutual benefit of all concerned."[13]

Kenneth Harkins pressed Rozelle to identify the primary objective of the legislation. Harkins led the witness by saying, "Would you agree that the primary objective of the negotiations was peace between the leagues and a necessity of avoiding an all-out war?"[14] Rozelle cited three reasons to justify the merger: the fear that some teams might fold owing to financial exigencies; the demoralization arising from constant litigation and controversy; and the demoralization stemming from "excessive bonuses and payments to players." He depicted owners as being in the sport as an avocation. "Some people of means collect stamps, others might have boats, others would like a football team."[15] Once again Rozelle, and presumably the owners, were painting the players as receiving unwarranted windfalls, "excessive bonuses and payments," while long-suffering and altruistic owners struggled to provide the games despite losses, controversy, and, heaven forbid, litigation.

Rozelle appeared candid when he responded to Byron Rogers's (Colo.) question, "is this [competition for players] one of the objectives of this proposal that we are now considering?" Rozelle stated, "It is one of the main objectives, Mr. Rogers." He continued by describing how the Denver Broncos (fortuitously located in Rogers's district) had been unable or unwilling to sign any of its first- or second-round draft choices for six years. The Broncos' failure negated the ostensible purpose of the draft in fostering competitive balance and forced some teams to draft lesser but easier to sign collegians.[16]

The legislators did not ask Rozelle to submit any evidence that disparities between teams' win-loss records increased between 1960 and 1965. Tables 7 and 9 show that Rozelle's claims were dubious at best; though Green Bay had experienced a renaissance, this owed to coach Vince Lombardi's genius. The 1962 and 1963 ratios of actual to idealized standard deviations were higher than usual, but most of the seasons since the AFL's debut fell well within the usual range.

Some legislators stood this concern regarding collegiate players on its head, claiming reduced competition for college players would redound to the established players' benefit. John D. Dingell (Ohio) testified, "I am generally opposed to the granting of exemptions from the antitrust laws, I find certain extenuating circumstances in the professional football situation." He continued by claiming, "this savings [from reduced bonuses paid to players drafted out of college] will enable the professional football teams to raise minimum salaries and adjust certain inequities which have been adversely affecting the morale of established professional football players."[17] Thomas G. Morris (Calif.) was more explicit in stating the reduction of bonuses and salaries paid to rookies would benefit veterans, perhaps even increase the league's minimum salaries.[18] Few suggested that the owners would simply pocket the savings without raising salaries.

Legislators also raised questions regarding the AFL paying an indemnity to NFL owners. The indemnities amounted to $18 million over twenty years. Legislators had difficulty figuring out why teams that were merging with the NFL were required to pay indemnities. Rozelle responded, "the plan for equal division of television, which is part of this, would help the present AFL clubs; that more established teams would be playing AFL teams." His explanation made sense, if one assumed that having the Chicago Bears or New York Giants play your local AFL franchise boosted its attendance. In the mid-1960s, most observers still believed that NFL teams had better personnel than their AFL rivals. Celler appeared to accept this reasoning: "the American League is probably the weaker and therefore it will enjoy greater privileges and greater strength by joining in this league and therefore they must pay $20 million to the NFL, which accords them or makes possible this advantage; is that what it means?"[19]

Legislators also wondered about clauses in the NFL-AFL agreement pertaining to the New York Giants and Jets, the San Francisco 49ers, and the Oakland Raiders. These sets of teams violated each other's territorial rights, and they were still trying to work out scheduling and televising details in ways that created the least amount of conflict.[20]

After discussing the New York City and Bay Area situations, legislators returned to the intent of the proposed bill. They wanted definitive answers to what NFL owners expected to gain from the bill's passage. Rozelle and Carothers repeatedly emphasized that the league viewed the legislation as strictly limited to exempting the merger itself from antitrust litigation. The league's other activities were still vulnerable to challenge.[21] Celler again expressed the opinion that such a strict limitation on the extent of the bill meant that it was "of no value or use to you." Carothers responded, "In the present context, we would for the indefinite future be bearing the burden of not only defending our practices as a single league under the antitrust laws, but the fact that the single league was created by this transaction. We would carry a double burden. We would be defending ourselves not in the sense that basketball may have to defend itself or hockey may have to defend itself."[22]

Celler switched to another line of questioning, perhaps a more salient one. "Now, if you have these two leagues merged, you could not have competition for the acquisition of players. That is what you are trying to prevent, prevent these players asking what in your estimation are exorbitant salaries or wages and you want to be sure that you can cut them down." Carothers answered in the affirmative, but made an interesting counterargument: "May I say that among the purposes of the antitrust laws, I would include an ultimate interest in consumers and in this instance, the ultimate consumer favors this transaction. Another purpose of the antitrust law is to prevent very large businesses and dominant businesses from driving smaller businesses out of existence and that is precisely the results which will be achieved if this transaction does not go through."[23] Carothers's argument, if taken at face value, implied that exploitation of labor was justified, if the consumers liked the end result.

Legislators expressed concerns for high school and college football. They pressed Rozelle to guarantee protection of these entities by agreeing not to televise NFL/AFL games on Friday nights and during Saturdays. Harkins asked Rozelle to recount why there were still NFL games and telecasts on these two days of the week. Rozelle answered that because of MLB games, some NFL teams could not play on some Sundays during the season. He indicated that there had been five Friday night games during the previous eleven seasons.[24]

A Louisiana Legislator's Interest

Hale Boggs (La.) was not on the subcommittee, but he wielded considerable power. Boggs sought an NFL franchise for New Orleans. He stated, "New Orleans is the prime candidate for a franchise in the merger plans." The House majority leader cited the public's support for the merger before concluding, "We are seeking peace with this merger and I believe we should do all we can to accommodate that peace. We must also consider the other cities that will get teams in the expansion plans. We must spread this game to as many of our citizens as we can."[25]

Boggs also submitted a memorandum rebutting an argument that, "granting of such an exemption would lay the precedent for other industries to seek similar exemptions." The memorandum detailed how the House of Representatives passed H.R. 9096 in 1961. "The justification of this legislation by its sponsors was to permit joint negotiation of television contracts would serve to strengthen the weakest members of the league."[26] These attorneys prepared a second memorandum detailing baseball's adventures in antitrust land, citing the *Federal Baseball Club, Gardella, Toolson,* and the recent *State of Wisconsin v. Milwaukee Braves, Inc.* cases. The attorneys also mentioned the *Radovich* case, citing that, "the volume of interstate business in organized professional football places it within the provisions of the Sherman Act, the Court concluded that the orderly way to eliminate error or discrimination in favor of baseball is by 'legislation and not by court decision.'" The memorandum concluded, "that any investment in a professional football league franchise at this time will be seriously jeopardized by possible treble-damage losses in antitrust litigation stemming from the merger of the two leagues. The legislation contemplated by the *Radovich* decision, at least to the extent of the mergers, is now pending in the Congress. Until such time as this legislation becomes effective, the risks of liability are great."[27]

The NFL Makes Its Case

The committee examined copies of the proposals the NFL had submitted to the Senate in August. The NFL claimed its proposal was in the public interest because it would create more not fewer professional football teams; the reduction in player bonuses would stabilize weak franchises; and the attendant prosperity would admit new members to the league. NFL owners advanced the idea that the merger "calls for a substantial increase in the player salary minimum now in effect in the NFL, the creation of a player salary minimum for AFL players at the same level, and increased pension plan benefits to all present AFL players." Nor were these the only benefits touted for the players. NFL officials used the canard that veterans would get the money formerly paid college draftees. There would also be more jobs, as owners would create more expansion teams.[28]

The owners argued that they were succumbing to "capacity to withstand losses," along with pride, tax privileges, and civic allegiances instead of good business sense because of the interleague competition. They also claimed that professional football was a "natural monopoly." Owing to professional football's peculiarities, "there is room for only one league seeking to operate at major league levels of competition."[29] Some legal scholars, though, were unsure: "The history of the AFL-NFL competition leaves unresolved the question of whether 'major leagueness' is indivisible; whether over a long period there can be only one major league commanding nationwide fan interest. But it is clear that competition creates sufficient instability to make a 'merger' extremely attractive to the owners' economic interests and at least plausibly justified in sports teams."[30]

After identifying the unique nature of professional sports leagues—the mixture of cooperation and competition—the proposal claimed that playing talent needed to be equalized across clubs to ensure the survival of a league. "This follows because the economic relationship between member clubs of a league is like no other relationship found on the American scene. . . . A 'sick' franchise is almost as much a problem for the other clubs of its league as it is for the club itself. Indeed, it has on occasion been necessary for the remaining clubs of a league to contribute financially to one club simply to insure the league's continued operation."[31]

The proposal acknowledged that all professional sports leagues shared the "partnership-joint venture" aspect, but it claimed football differed because, "It is given primary play in professional football operations where game opportunities are necessarily limited in number, economic success requires near capacity crowds, and inequalities in team play and franchise strength have an immediate and pronounced effect on the gate receipts of all clubs in the league. By its nature, football is a game of climax where close contests and league balance are essential to the maintenance of fan interest."[32] Given the prevalence of season tickets in football at the time, the proposal's argument may have been dubious, at least in the short run; only a minority of tickets sold were for a particular game. In MLB, woebegone teams such as the Browns and Athletics had been detrimental to other teams' home gate receipts.

The proposal claimed that in the NFL, the principle of joint success was carried further than in any professional sports league. Clubs faced uniform squad limits and player pension plan. "Television income is equally divided among all member clubs of the League, regardless of the relative size of their individual television audiences. Game receipts are divided 60%–40% to the home and visiting team, a more equal division than any other professional sport." Not only did owners share revenues equally, they faced equal opportunities in acquiring top talent because of the draft and an equal opportunity to "field a winning team and to insure regular rotation of the League championship. Even the NFL ownership policy is directed at preserving a balanced league—no corporate ownership, no public ownership, and majority ownership by one individual who is not primarily motivated by tax loss objectives. All of these rules are directed at maintaining fan interest and insuring the league's survival."[33] Here the NFL put on its "game face." Although not asserting that its owners were altruistic, the football owners wanted to bask in the aura of stressing "more equal" than their counterparts in baseball and basketball. No one was impolite enough to ask whether all of the equal sharing curbed some owners' incentives to field strong teams and instead to bank the shared revenue.

The proposal further emphasized the equalization aspects of the league's policies, citing the gate-sharing rules. It warned that allowing unrestricted competition would generate increasing inequalities between teams and actual destruction of the weaker franchises. The stronger teams would eventually find themselves in dire straits, and the league would collapse. All of these ill effects were avoided, though, by the league's equalization measures.

The owners' assertions of the effectiveness of their equalization aspects largely went unexamined. Did the reverse-order draft have much effect on team strengths during the 1950s, when the NFL operated as a monopoly? The owners claimed that whatever effectiveness the reverse-order draft offered in maintaining competitive balance had been negated by having two teams bid for a given player, with stronger teams likely driving weaker teams in both leagues out of business. "Ultimately the survival of one league or the other depends on its ability to carry its less successful franchises and to withstand over-all deterioration of league play."[34] The proposal predicted that without the merger, the have-nots would soon be begging for support of the haves.[35] An accompanying endnote stated an interesting twist: survival now depended upon depreciation of player contracts and government subsidies, because the AFL owners had rarely, if ever, made a profit. The teams would have gone out of business without these benefits.[36]

The proposal compared professional football with a "single newspaper" town, citing legal cases, including *United States v. Harte-Hanks Newspapers, Inc.,* where the court ruled:

> In *Union Leader Corp. v. Newspapers of New England, Inc.,* 180 F. Su 125 (D. Mass. 1960): If this were a city in which at least two newspapers could economically survive, the offer to purchase would be an attempt to monopolize (Cf. *United States v. Aluminum Corp. of America*). It would not be a victory won by skill, foresight, and industry. But the situation is different where a city can accommodate only one successful newspaper, and two roughly equally able companies are competing for the single prize that is available. Skill, foresight, and industry by themselves will not give either company the victory.

The opinion concluded that in cases where outcome between two competitors depended upon one outlasting the other by absorbing continued losses, then it would be permissible for one newspaper to buy out the other to stanch the losses incurred in shortening the time that competition would persist.[37]

The owners and their officials emphasized that their plan for a single league was not a typical merger, where ownership changed hands. Instead, the merger plan "more nearly preserves football competition, in the sense that consumers and local interests desire it, than impedes it. The plan has merely 'shortened' the time within which competition could continue between the two present leagues. *Union Leader, supra.*" In case legislators did not get the point, the NFL stressed the necessity of acting now when ensuring all twenty-four franchises' survival was still possible.[38]

The proposal concluded, "The fact is, however, as a Federal court has noted, that American cities, with the exception of New York and possibly one or two others, are natural monopoly markets for professional football purposes."[39] According to an article in the *Harvard Law Review,* "Although the superiority of the NFL was not sufficient to enable it to exclude a national competitor, it was sufficient to exclude the competitor from certain local markets. The court indicated that had the exclusion of the AFL from these cities been fatal to the new league, a different market definition would have been appropriate." The article pointed out that the NFL's move into Dallas and Minnesota was not unlawful, because the NFL had a preexisting plan to expand into those cities. "There is no economic gain from wasteful competition of this character and neither league has had any realistic interest in accentuating the already suicidal levels of present competition."[40]

The owners brazenly stated, "There is no realistic television competition between the two leagues. Each of the three networks is tied to a specific television contract with one of the three football organizations; the colleges have a contract with ABC, the AFL has a contract with NBC, and the NFL has a contract with CBS. These contracts have no organized pattern of termination dates and rarely afford the opportunity for competition in rights placement. Indeed, the NFL has recently been required to undertake a program for a self-created network simply to re-establish competition in the market for its rights."[41]

If the merger was approved, the proposal claimed that competition for players would be under more rational conditions affording all teams an opportunity to improve themselves. It repeated the owners' assertions about overspending on college talent.[42]

Baseball officials nervously watched the NFL/AFL merger hearings. William D. Eckert, baseball's commissioner, telegraphed Paul Porter, the sport's legal counsel, "organized baseball will make no attempt to alter or modify any legislative proposal," in the hopes that Celler and his committee "should not alter, affect, or seek to alter or affect baseball's existing legal status."[43]

Conclusion: Football Owners Cry "Wolf," Get Merger

By now the reader may recognize many of the dubious arguments employed in attempting to gain approval for a merger: the existence of competitive imbalance; horrendous losses (but no fatalities among teams); unwarranted salaries for rookie players; and fan desires. These arguments were not infallible. The NFL won with them; the NBA would lose with them. As in previous hearings, hard evidence regarding competitive balance was lacking. Because owners refused to supply relevant financial data, their piteous claims were unsubstantiated, much to the frustration of the committee members.

Pro football got its merger. Celler tried to delay the merger bill, but Senators Russell Long (La.) and Everett Dirksen (Ill.) attached a merger bill as a rider to a popular Investment Tax Credit bill. The merger sailed through the Senate. Rozelle almost stumbled just as approval appeared certain. Before the House vote, Representative Boggs congratulated Rozelle and said, "Just for the record,

I assume we can say the franchise for New Orleans is firm?" Rozelle replied by saying things looked favorable for awarding the expansion franchise, but added, "I can't make any promises on my own." In a show of legislative power, Boggs said, "Well, Pete, why don't you just go back and check with the owners. I'll hold things up here until you get back." Rozelle quickly backtracked and said, "You can count on their [the owners'] approval."[44] With Rozelle's backpedaling, Boggs shepherded the bill through the House, and professional football had its merger.

As previously noted, owners had reason for hesitating to expand. The threat of a new league gave an added impetus to expansion. Legislators, undoubtedly pleased that the late 1960s witnessed a sharp rise in the number of teams, worried that an AFL-NFL merger would deter further expansion. Rozelle and the NFL promised expansion (Atlanta in 1966 and New Orleans in 1967), and the AFL expanded in 1966 and 1968 to Miami and Cincinnati. No more growth occurred until 1976. One casualty of expansion was a proposed AFL team for Washington, D.C., which would have entered Redskins and Colts territory. The ownership group of the proposed Washington team sued professional football, claiming that a restrictive covenant in the stadium lease prohibiting any pro football team other than the Washington Redskins using RFK Stadium violated the "prohibition of contracts in restraint of trade.[45] The defendants won a summary judgment, which was later reversed by the D.C. Circuit Court. The defendants then prevailed in a jury trial, but this was reversed because the jury instructions misstated the law. The parties settled before a retrial. The ruling centered upon: "the leasing of the stadium was pursuant to the mandate of the [Sherman] Act and was governmental action. As such it was . . . exempt from the antitrust laws. . . . No violation of the Act can be made out even where there is a restraint upon trade or monopolization if it resulted from valid governmental action."[46] The merger would have unintended fallout for professional basketball, as a separate group of owners would find to their dismay a few years later.[47]

16

The Proposed NBA/ABA Merger *1971–1972*

A merger between the only two firms in an industry would typically be considered an antitrust violation. When owners wanted to merge two sports leagues, they should have borne the burden of proof in satisfying antitrust authorities.

The ABA sought to merge with the NBA. The upstart league began play in 1967–1968 and was comprised of a colorful if volatile collection of teams and players. The league introduced the three-point shot and used a tri-colored ball. Yale Law School lawyers analyzed the proposed merger, comparing it with the professional football merger: "the concerted action produces efficiencies which arguably outweigh whatever restraints on competition are involved." They suggested thinking of leagues as being similar to "law partnerships, a 'firm.' A merger of these 'firms' is hard to justify, however, for there is less reason to think that competition for players between leagues is consistent with evenly matched contests within them or that there will not be a sufficient number of good players in each league." They cited another interested party with regard to the merger. "Fan interest may be stimulated whether or not individual leagues are joined in financial wedlock. If that is the case, the impact of a merger would be anti-competitive and antitrust principles would seem to bar it."[1] NBA Players Association general counsel Larry Fleisher also argued similarly. Much of the gains to the fans from a championship game between the leagues' best teams or interleague games did not require a formal merger.[2]

Unlike mergers in other industries, legal scholar Steven R. Rivkin characterized the public's sentiment toward professional sports as "activities that sometimes approach national mania: to the extent organized athletics maintains the respect of the public, there is little to force professional sports to conform to arbitrary and irrelevant norms of behavior drawn from other realms of economic activity."[3] Even with this public sentiment, the basketball owners picked the wrong time to petition Congress for a partial antitrust exemption for the merger. Legislators were in a cranky mood. The second incarnation of the Washington Senators had recently left the city, while football owners flaunted their limited antitrust exemption, especially with regard to television blackouts.

The Owners Receive Unwelcoming Greetings

The two sets of owners sought congressional approval for their proposed merger. The House and Senate held hearings during 1971 and 1972. Senators John Tunney (Calif.) and Roman Hruska (Neb.) introduced a bill giving merged leagues limited exemption from antitrust laws; Representative Jack Brooks of Texas sponsored a similar bill in the House. The ABA owners unanimously backed the merger, but five out of seventeen NBA teams opposed the plan (Atlanta Hawks, Golden State Warriors, Milwaukee Bucks, Philadelphia 76ers, and Phoenix Suns), partly because they recognized the potential antitrust implications.[4] The owners in favor of this merger based their hope of approval upon the 1966 AFL/NFL one, but, to paraphrase the investment warning: past hearings are not indicative of future hearings.

There was another, quirky factor: Senator Philip Hart (Mich.) chose not to chair the hearings—he recused himself, because his wife's family were owners of the Detroit Tigers. He designated Senator Sam Ervin Jr. (N.C.)—soon to be of Watergate fame—to chair the committee. Sportswriter Shirley Povich wrote, "For the owners, their luck in that draw was all bad. For their purposes, a more forbidding figure than chairman Ervin could not be found."[5] Another journalist, Arlen J. Large, confirmed Povich's opinion by quoting Ervin's statement, "Their bill [favoring the merger] proposes to rob every man in America who possess skill in basketball of the right to sell his skill to the highest bidder on a free market."[6]

Ervin quickly made clear his displeasure at the professional football merger: "I deeply hope that Congress will not follow the precedent it set in its handling of the pro football merger question."[7] He said, "the callous abuse of unwarranted privilege by the professional team owners has steadily victimized the legitimate interests of fans and severely restricted the legal rights of players."[8] Ervin was still upset about pro football's tactics, stating "the owners scored on a quarterback sneak. The Senate committee with jurisdiction on the bill didn't hold hearings and the measure passed the Senate without any floor debate, without any record vote and without the opposition being notified. The House did have a committee hearing but it too failed to look into the issues."[9]

In the House, Emanuel Celler also complained, "Yet, the owners have come to us petitioning for a grant of monopoly status as the only means of preserving their industry. . . . Before we can help impoverished and allegedly poor owners of poor teams, we ought to know something about the financial condition of these teams."[10]

The basketball owners were also unfortunate in that the general climate for sports owners was unfavorable. Star basketball player Oscar Robertson filed a lawsuit against the owners pertaining to free agency. The lawsuit, filed in 1970, was not settled until 1976. The pending litigation helped stymie the two leagues' merger attempts for years. Curt Flood had filed a lawsuit against MLB with respect to the reserve clause. Basketball player Spencer Haywood was involved in two lawsuits.[11]

As the hearings were occurring, Robertson's lawsuit against the NBA was wending its way through the legal system. Judge Charles Tenney issued a preliminary injunction that players' attorney Ira Millstein believed indicated the proposed merger discussions violated existing law, as the two leagues were "enjoined from effectuating a merger."[12]

In addition, jurists were beginning to criticize pro sports. Robert B. Smith Jr., chief counsel for the Senate Judiciary Subcommittee, told the National Association of Attorneys General in December 1971, "The professional sport monopolies are assisted in every possible way by the Federal government, and there is no question that no other segment of our economy is so heavily subsidized by the Federal government."[13]

Under this disputatious atmosphere, Representative Jack Brooks (Tex.) asserted his bill was similar to the one passed in 1966 to enable the NFL and AFL to merge: "I believe it is in the best interest of the players, the clubs, and the American public to retain professional basketball as a sport and to preserve as many of the teams as possible."[14]

The Basketball Owners Plead Their Case

Basketball owners maintained that a merger was needed to prevent several teams from folding. They claimed significant losses, emanating from increased player salaries, especially for rookies. Owners asserted that the merger would reduce player salaries and enable their teams to survive. The survival aspect was a crucial argument: A number of the legislators were hesitant to be deemed responsible for any casualties among the franchises, and their bills reflected a desire that all of the teams survive a merger.

The owners did provide some detailed information regarding their finances to economists Robert Nathan, Roger Noll, and Benjamin Okner. Although Nathan seemed satisfied that the information he received was sufficient to draw conclusions, Noll and Okner couched their findings under the caution that the information was insufficient to draw definite conclusions; they deemed it plausible that several ABA teams were "on the verge of financial collapse."[15]

The owners refused to divulge sufficient financial information for legislators to even determine whether all, most, or a minority of teams were truly losing money. The information the owners supplied pertained to "book losses," an elastic term that allowed them to claim lots of expenses. Other expenses, such as arena rentals, might have been paid to a parent company or to the same owner (if the owner owned both an arena and a team). How owners expensed deferred salaries and whether they placed themselves on the payrolls also affected a team's profitability.

The depreciation of player contracts proved particularly controversial. Depreciation allowances are designed to enable businesses to translate an investment in a long-lived capital asset, such as a professional sports franchise, into annualized costs over the useful life of the asset. Because many capital assets deteriorate in value and usefulness over time, owners can expense depreciation. In cases of tangible assets, such as a machine, there are accepted rules for depreciation. A professional sports franchise usually (but certainly not always) appreciates in value, thereby jeopardizing the rationale for a depreciation allowance. This committee heard in much greater detail than previous committees had about how these player contract depreciation allowances operated; Congress later revised the tax laws and limited the allowance.

To better gauge the owners' losses, Ervin and Celler sought to review the owners' personal income tax records. The owners, though, were unwilling to provide audited personal tax returns, not even to Thomas Kuchel, former United States senator and attorney representing them before Congress. Kuchel claimed the individual tax returns were not relevant to the situation. The owners were indignant that Ervin even made the request, claiming it impugned their honesty. They argued that Congress only requested income tax returns of racketeers, an argument Ervin dismissed.[16]

In addition to the ambiguity surrounding owners' depreciation write-offs and other deductions, there was limited information pertaining to player salaries. The owners, as always, blamed increasing player costs for their losses. Many of them were willing to pay extraordinary salaries and signing bonuses to graduating college seniors. Owners claimed that the race to sign top-flight collegiate talent meant that veteran players were paid less.

Economists Noll and Okner provided another interpretation of the spiraling sums ABA owners paid to collegiate players. They viewed such actions as the ABA's attempt to demonstrate their seriousness about and ability to remain in the market. The NBA owners retaliated by bidding up salaries to raise costs for the ABA owners to cause their league to fold or at least to absorb large losses. Noll compared this to a predatory price cut.[17] Noll and Okner stated that, "even if player costs fell to zero, the weakest ABA franchises will continue to be unprofitable, while player salaries would have to be cut in half to bring the middling ABA and weakest NBA teams to the break-even point." They pointed out that, "Player compensation in professional football has fallen since the merger, but not by half." [18]

Nathan took Noll and Okner to task for their conspiracy theory regarding bidding for rookie players. He thought the rapid escalation in rookie salaries "reflected desperate bidding for talent which might turn losses into profits rather than a do-or-die type of economic-suicide-or-merger policy."[19]

Basketball owners argued, similarly to football owners, that the merger would end the big salaries and bonuses paid to rookies and leave more for the veterans. Ed Garvey, executive director of the NFL Players Association, testified that the AFL/NFL merger did not create benefits for veterans. Garvey claimed that the football veterans received scant increases in average salary in the wake of the merger.[20]

In the discussions about increases in player salaries, no one mentioned that changes in the overall price level were beginning to accelerate. Between 1968 and 1971, the Consumer Price Index increased by more than 16 percent.[21] As in the case of the postwar strife between the NFL and AAFC, some of the rise in player salaries simply restored players to their same level of purchasing power.

Noll and Okner suggested that player salaries alone did not explain the rising expenses incurred by owners of ABA teams: "Player costs account for less than half of the costs increases these [ABA] teams have experienced during the period of interleague competition." In fact, the increase in "other costs" per team—all costs other than player costs—was $783,000, while ABA player costs went up $339,000 between 1970 and 1971.[22] If the complaint that competition was driving up player salaries was old, the owners' failure to tell legislators that their other costs were rising as fast, if not faster, than player salaries was also repetitious.

One NBA owner, the Baltimore Bullets' Abe Pollin, discussed his team's finances. He stated that even though his team participated in the NBA Finals, he still lost $213,000. Pollin maintained that he was only able to claim $33,000 in depreciation of player contracts and $30,000 nondeductible amortization of the franchise. He further added that players' compensation consumed 85 percent of total net gate receipts.[23]

Pollin raised a crucial point. Much of the debate between the three economists revolved around the most applicable measure of profitability, with Nathan relying more on the book profits reported by the owners although conceding some of the points made by Noll and Okner. The economists debated the extent of the use of depreciation of player contracts and whether owners paid themselves or their family members salaries for serving as officers of the team.[24]

There was an element of irony in this argument. Unless an owner recently purchased a team or paid for an expansion franchise, he had very few player contracts to deduct. The original ABA owners initially paid a nominal amount ($25,000) to help fund the league office, but they had little value in player contracts. Subsequent owners of ABA teams often paid relatively small amounts for them—some had even forfeited their franchises, again leaving little value for a subsequent owner to depreciate. Most ABA owners, therefore, received little succor from this tax rule. Longtime franchise owners in the NBA also lacked the ability to depreciate much in player contracts or expansion fees.[25] On the other hand, some costs were not made explicit under generally accepted accounting rules. ABA Kentucky Colonels owner Wendell Cherry pointed out that owning a professional sports team incurred an implicit opportunity cost: the foregone interest on the investment.[26]

In the argument concerning profitability, another factor emerged. Original owners of ABA teams did not own the arenas that their teams played in, so they paid rent to another party. Some NBA owners owned their arenas; by charging a large rental to their team, they could make their team's profits shrink or their losses grow.

Because several ABA teams eventually folded, the ABA owners' claims of losses had credibility. Most professional sports leagues began in a pool of red ink as teams faced start-up costs and the challenge of attracting fans. Many of the nascent franchises relocated. As Noll and Okner pointed out, several ABA teams' losses resulted primarily from their inability to draw even a paucity of fans, a fate shared by many BAA and NBA teams in the late 1940s and 1950s. James J. Kirst, former owner of the ABA Los Angeles Stars, testified that his team's home gate receipts for the year 1969 (spanning parts of two seasons) were $94,492, of which he shared $10,094 with visiting teams. The team's publicity expenses alone were 39 percent more than the gate receipts, while the combined players' and coaches' salaries were three times as much as the gate receipts.[27]

Noll and Okner painted a dismal picture of several ABA teams: these suffered from a lack of gate receipts and inadequate-sized arenas. "If a team has an arena seating less than 10,000 fans, it can never break even no matter what happens to player costs, and several ABA teams are in that situation."[28] The two economists admitted that they previously erred in estimating ABA gate receipts: "In fact, the major error in our earlier testimony was that we vastly overestimated the average ticket price for the weak ABA teams. Based on gate receipts reported, it would appear that these teams are discounting their list prices—the prices we collected from their season ticket brochures by 50 to 75 percent."[29]

Wendell Cherry stated that although his team drew an average of nine thousand fans per game—in contrast to three thousand per game in 1970—he was still losing money, more than $400,000 per season. Cherry provided figures showing that the Colonels overall player/coaches expenses rose by just more than $100,000 between the 1969–1970 and 1971–1972 seasons; other expenses rose by $200,000 over this period. The Colonels' ticket receipts, however, zoomed from $323,000 to $701,000.[30]

After examining the information the owners supplied them, economists Noll and Okner estimated that the combined book losses reported by teams in both leagues amounted to $13.6 million, but after adjusting for "potential tax reductions," the losses might have aggregated to $4.4 million.[31] The two economists also revealed another conundrum: the most recent seven NBA franchises "are more profitable on the average than the rest of the league by all measures except book profit. The book profit figure is very low for these teams, but only because they account for most of the depreciation of player contracts in the league."[32]

Committee counsel Daniel L. Cohen had performed some research into the owners and their commissioners' prior statements regarding losses. He produced a *New York Times* article quoting past ABA commissioner Jack Dolph saying, "As a result of the meeting [where two ABA teams were folded], the ABA will now be strong enough to compete with the NBA. We are now going with our varsity and can compete against the other league." Cohen asked Dolph if the quote was correct, and whether it implied the ABA was strong enough to survive without a merger. Dolph essentially retorted that he was exaggerating for public consumption: "We have to sell tickets the best way we can, and that is the reason we are in business. When I make a statement to the press, we are going to be a stronger league, because we are a smaller league, it is making a silk purse out of a sow's ear, if I may say so. It is cheerleading. We have to sell tickets, and that is one of the jobs of the commissioner." He went on to say, "There is no possibility we can be as strong as the NBA next year. We will compete the best we can for survival."[33]

In the end, Celler and Ervin remained skeptical about the owners' claims of losses. Ervin excoriated their main expert: "I charge that the owners are not only trying to fool Congress, but they fooled Mr. Bob Nathan. Because, Mr. Bob Nathan testified under my examination that they didn't allow him to see the individual income tax returns, where they could take off their alleged losses that they sustained on the club. They even concealed it from their expert accountant."[34]

Two Economists Wheel Out the Big Guns

Noll and Okner employed regression analysis to the data made available by the owner and found some surprising results. One was that a variable for ABA teams was statistically insignificant. The differences in attendance between teams in the two leagues were attributable to other factors and not to being in one league or the other. From this result, they concluded that a merger was not likely to increase ABA attendance. They also concluded that if the ABA teams were inferior to NBA teams, then a merger could erode attendance at ABA games.[35]

Noll and Okner deduced that, "A team needs around 325,000 regular season fans, plus perhaps 50,000 more in the playoffs, to be in the black, with the exact figure depending on ticket prices, the costs of players, and arena rents." Based on this rough break-even point, they identified several teams that likely lost substantial amounts of money. ABA teams had lower player payrolls, with the average player making about half the amount players in the NBA earned. From this, they deduced that ABA teams averaged $300,000 less in operating costs. They concluded that ABA teams needed 300,000 regular-season attendees to break even. None of the teams came close to this level, so ABA teams were, indeed, losing money.[36]

Other Evidence Pertaining to Losses

If legislators were dubious about the owners' claim of losses, there were other pieces of evidence to consider. NBA franchises tended to appreciate in value, whether through explicit sales or as demonstrated by rising expansion fees. Although most sales of NBA franchises in the 1950s were limited to hundreds of thousands of dollars, by the mid-1960s, stellar franchises such as the Los Angeles Lakers and Boston Celtics were selling for millions of dollars.[37] ABA teams, though, experienced little if any appreciation and, indeed, a number of the teams proved so unprofitable that not only were there no prospective owners, the current owners abandoned them.

Some owners, though, belied their wails of losses by seeking NHL franchises, even though hockey was also going through a "war" with the World Hockey Association (someday, some impish set of league owners will name their league the *Universe* League). Daniel Cohen pointed out that some basketball owners had purchased hockey teams, even though hockey was experiencing league warfare.[38] The basketball owners claimed they did so to have a second tenant for their arenas. Abe Pollin claimed that it was easier to get a new arena financed if two professional teams would be tenants, hence his interest in obtaining a hockey team.[39]

Senators Tunney's and Hruska's concerns about there being a diminution in the number of teams in professional basketball in the aftermath of a merger seem misplaced. A team that failed to attract sufficient fans probably should have relocated or folded, as the fewer the fans, the smaller the social cost from the team's demise. Larry Fleisher made an additional point. The ABA was a start-up concern, and it could be expected that not all of the franchises would prove successful. At the same time, the NBA expanded by from nine to seventeen teams between the 1965–1966 and 1970–1971 seasons. Fleisher scornfully characterized the owners' complaints as, "We should be guaranteed a right to make a profit because we just opened up a new business."[40] Noll and Okner also suggested that having all teams survive was not necessarily a favorable outcome: "fans in the cities with poorer teams are, and will continue to be, faced with unattractive alternatives of having no team at all or having a highly priced poor team. Fans in large cities also face high prices, and they can watch good teams—but they must watch their good teams play a large number of games against unnecessarily weak opposition because the very high profits of their own teams are not shared."[41]

Celler then raised an issue he had long espoused: Why not redress professional team sports leagues' woes by more generous revenue sharing? Celler cited the differences in stadium capacities to again tout revenue sharing as a cure for professional sports' ills. Wendell Cherry disagreed with Celler regarding the desirability of revenue sharing. Cherry thought revenue sharing futile, when all of the teams were losing money. The ABA owners rescinded their 15 percent gate share rule and went to a 6 percent assessment to fund the operation of the league.[42] If the league failed to spend all of the assessment, the remainder was divided equally between all of the teams, providing modest succor to financially weak teams.

NBA commissioner Walter Kennedy admitted that the league had no gate-sharing rule, although 6 percent of each team's gate receipts went to the league office. Kennedy argued that the league's paucity of gate sharing was offset by its equal sharing of national television money.[43]

A number of ABA teams were not viable without significant inflows of money from revenue sharing. Presumably other owners, though, would not willingly countenance subsidizing teams that were incapable of drawing sufficient fans. Whether such sharing would have been effective in transferring large sums from teams in larger cities to teams in smaller cities depended upon the revenue sharing rules and the patterns of attendance.

During the early 1970s, the Knicks were popular both at home and on the road; the team's popularity on the road offset the revenues shared from games in Madison Square Garden, the team's home court. The Knicks' popularity would have muted the amounts transferred to teams in smaller cities, whether a proportional or a flat-rate revenue-sharing plan was used. A check of the *New York Times* box scores of Knicks' games demonstrates both points. The Knicks sold out many of their games, but even in those games that were not, the team sold 18,500 or more of the 19,588 capacity. All visiting teams, therefore, played before large crowds, who had paid higher-than-average ticket prices for the pleasure. When the Knicks went on the road, newspaper accounts frequently mentioned that fans filled the home arena to capacity. The key, of course, was that most every other team played in arenas with much smaller capacities than Madison Square Garden. The Portland Trailblazers' arena, for instance, had a capacity of less than eleven thousand. Although the Knicks were good draws on the road, the host teams' stadium capacities kept them from reaping the fullest advantage of the New York team's attractiveness.

Sportswriter Leonard Koppett pointed out that in a twenty-eight-team league, the weak teams would receive little succor from the wealthier teams because they would not get enough dates at Madison Square Garden or Los Angeles to raise revenues. Even if the twenty-eight teams were split into conferences or division, few would get to play the Knicks more than two or three times in New York. Koppett suggested that professional basketball would benefit from winnowing the weak teams: "with 16 to 20 teams, there would be a better chance, since only the 'weak' ones would have gone out of existence and the proportion of 'strong' teams left would be much greater."[44] Fans in the smaller cities might dispute Koppett's analysis; after all, he lived in New York, so neither of his local teams would disappear. To forestall the ABA owners from forming a coalition with their NBA counterparts in smaller cities, the NBA owners stipulated that the ABA owners could not vote on any gate-sharing proposals for five years; when legislators raised questions about this stipulation, the NBA owners quickly changed it to three years.[45]

Owner Wendell Cherry claimed that one of the reasons the ABA ended its 15 percent revenue-sharing plan was the difficulty of administering it. Because the plan was based on gate receipts and not attendance, monitoring became an issue. Leagues using gate attendance as the basis for revenue sharing typically had turnstiles, which made checking the figures straightforward. Cherry also pointed out the futility of implementing a revenue-sharing plan, when all of the teams were losing money.[46]

The legislators' faith in revenue sharing as an effective palliative required careful analysis that was not forthcoming. Revenue sharing's effectiveness, then, remained an opening question.

Player Rights and the Proposed Merger

Legislators were troubled by the one-sidedness of the reserve clause or option year. Basketball owners claimed that they were offering the most liberal player rights package in professional sports. Kuchel mentioned that the average NBA salary exceeded $60,000. He also claimed, in a Richard Nixonesque phrase, "I wish to make it abundantly clear that there is no reserve clause in professional basketball. . . . [T]he position of professional basketball is that any option clause is restricted to a 1-year single option, and not a repeated option, year after year."

Kuchel's statement failed to impress Celler, who asked, "you don't call it a reserve clause; you call it an option clause. What is the difference?" Kuchel cited the opinion of a deputy attorney general who had appeared in an earlier hearing; this legal authority defined a reserve clause as "a series of options."[47]

After playing out his option year, a player could opt for free agency, but his original team had the right to match the top offer; if the player left for a new team, a three-person arbitration board awarded compensation to his old team. Although the arbitration policy clearly stipulated that the compensation would not be so large as to discourage free agent movements, legislators were dubious. The uncertainty surrounding the compensation would act as a brake against signing free agents, or so legislators believed.[48] Baseball owners eventually and temporarily adopted a compensation plan based upon draft choices in the amateur draft. Basketball owners might have done so, too, using a second-round choice, perhaps, to avoid impeding free-agent movement.

Walter Kennedy candidly admitted the proposal might deter some free-agent signings: "But I submit that such a restraint would be entirely reasonable and not excessive in the light of the peculiar problems that are faced by professional sports and by basketball." Kennedy then made the novel argument that there were restraints on the movement of amateur players from the little leagues through college.[49] Though his observation was true, it was not particularly relevant.

Noll and Okner disputed the need for compensation on another basis. They suggested that any indemnity should represent the "difference between the value of the player to the old team and the actual salary he was paid. If this difference is significant, then the player was being seriously underpaid." If the original team was underpaying a player, then it should not let the player go as a free agent without attempting to sign him for a higher salary. Any indemnity would reflect "the full extent it underpaid him should the player sign with a new team." They pointed out that "a team persistently paying players less than their contribution to team revenues faces no economic penalty, while teams willing to pay a salary closer to the value of the player must pay a fine—with the fine increasing the greater the extent to which the player was underpaid by his former team."[50]

The owners claimed that unrestricted free agency would result in a basketball version of "chaos theory," with players going hither and yon, alienating fans. Bill Bradley, Knicks' player and later U.S. senator, punctured this argument by demonstrating that team rosters experienced considerable turnover even with the reserve clause.[51]

John Mackey, president of the NFL Players Association, depicted another troubling aspect of the owners' control of players: "hundreds of players have sat on the bench, and many have never made it in the NFL simply cause of the team they were with. Had they been able to move to another team, many would have been good and possibly great football players. Many others would not have made it. But that is a risk every American should have the right to take."[52]

The idea that the reserve clause and reverse-order draft promoted competitive balance was dubious, at best. Some senators, however, chose to believe in the reverse-order draft's efficacy in promoting competitive balance, with Senator Hruska citing baseball's implementation of a draft of amateur players that coincided with the Yankees' descent into mediocrity.[53] Considering the Yankees often had good draft picks in the late 1960s, Hruska's argument seems dubious. Hruska also pointed to professional basketball's upheavals of the late 1940s, when the NBL and the BAA competed for players. To a large extent, however, the attrition of teams resulted from deficient gate receipts and too inadequate bases.[54]

Wendell Cherry predicted doom, if the reverse-order draft was not retained. "I am saying that in the interest—in the public interest of the country, that if there is not some reasonable restraint based on where the man plays . . . you will destroy the sport and there will be no professional basketball sooner or later. Probably sooner." Senator Ervin pounced on this claim, "And notwithstanding that fact, you and your associates invested in that club knew this condition existed?" Cherry responded, "We did. There was no question that there was risk. I told you before. I make no apologies for it. We took the risk. We are not complaining."[55]

The ABA's existence, though, gave NBA owners an opportunity to bemoan the diluted effects of the reverse-order draft. A weak team possessing the top pick in the NBA draft had less of an asset, because it now had to compete with an ABA team for a top prospect. The ABA owners were willing to shift rights to collegiate players between teams when they thought it would improve the league's chances of landing a top collegiate star.

The ABA was also willing to employ undergraduates such as Spencer Haywood and blacklisted players such as Connie Hawkins. Senator Ervin saw ulterior motives in the league's signing of such young players: "[The ABA's] idea is that all college coaches will bring pressure to bear on Congress to allow the leagues to merge."[56]

Haywood was involved in two legal actions. He was blacklisted by the NBA when the ABA's Denver Rockets signed him. Shortly thereafter, he jumped to the Seattle Supersonics. The Supersonics' fellow owners were aghast that an NBA team would sign a player before his college class had graduated. This was the gist of lawsuit one. The second lawsuit was between the Rockets and Supersonics. Haywood's actions resulted in a court ruling that struck down the NBA's rules pertaining to the player draft: "[Haywood] does not desire to, or may not be eligible to, attend college and even though he does not desire to, and is ineligible to, participate in collegiate athletics. . . . It is clear from the constitution and by-laws of the NBA that there is no provision for even the most rudimentary hearings before the four-year college rule is applied to exclude an individual player." The court concluded that "the rules in question are absolute and prohibit the signing of not only college basketball players but also those who lack the mental and financial ability to do so. As such they are overly broad and thus improper under *Silver* [a previous case]."[57]

Ervin was not against signing underclassmen; in fact, he was one of the few who approved of professional teams signing high school graduates, as well as college underclassmen: "every human being [should] be allowed to do with his own life and athletic skills what he desires to do as long as he does not unlawfully injure any other persons."[58] Meanwhile, NCAA executive director Walter Byers was distraught over the ABA's tactics of signing youngsters before their class graduated: "I submit that this country could well survive—it would be painful—the loss of professional sports, but I hold the personal view . . . that this country might not survive the deterioration and eventual elimination of interscholastic and intercollegiate athletics."[59]

ABA owners were also willing to raid NBA rosters of established stars such as Rick Barry, Zelmo Beaty, and Billy Cunningham. The league also developed its own stars in Artis Gilmore, Julius Erving, George Gervin, and George McGinnis, among others. The overall depth of ABA rosters may have been inferior to those of the NBA, but the ABA developed a core of loyal fans. The league's embracing of innovations such as the three-point shot and tri-colored basketball also helped.

Indemnities and Other Oddities

The committee members noticed some anomalies in the basketball owners' proposed merger. First, the NBA owners were charging an indemnity to join the league. Second, the ABA had recently sued the NBA for antitrust violations.

The committee made much of the $1,250,000 indemnity each ABA team would have to pay to join the new league. The senators were nonplussed that weak, struggling ABA teams were required to pay this indemnity, as well as receiving no television revenues from the NBA national television contract for a few years. The indemnity, while seemingly large, was payable over ten years; given the accelerating changes in the Consumer Price Index, the actual purchasing power of the $1,250,000 would be significantly reduced. In addition, ABA owners may have thought the indemnity a minor payment for joining the NBA without going through the usual expansion process—paying millions of dollars for a roster full of NBA castoffs. True, owners of expansion teams could assign a large percentage of the expansion fee to "player contracts" and gain the depreciation allowance, but all told, the $1,250,000 was not exorbitant (although ABA owners probably would have considered their previous losses as part of their "expansion fees").

Owners of NBA expansion teams would understand and applaud the indemnities.[60]

Wendell Cherry did not seem perturbed at the $1.25 million indemnity. He suggested that the ABA owners would eventually recoup this money, especially because it was payable over ten years, from their enlarged share of national television money to come. Noll pointed out, "the price that ABA teams are paying is a lower price than you would pay for an expansion team in the NBA. . . . But I agree that the payment is strange . . . It is strange that the poorest teams in the sport whom the merger is supposed to save financially, must pay heavily for it."[61]

Both Celler and Ervin marveled at the ABA owners' turnabout regarding its lawsuit charging monopoly practice against the NBA, which the ABA owners never explained. Ervin put it this way: "it is just an absurd proposal on the face of it, that the owners of professional sports should be given a legal right to do things that would be crimes if they had been done by anyone else. That is what this proposition comes down to."[62] Ervin excoriated the ABA owners for their hypocrisy and was amazed that "the ABA would ask 300 million dollars in damages from the NBA because of alleged monopolistic practices and then come in here to Congress and ask us to legalize these monopolistic practices on their behalf by approving the merger bill."[63] The two senior legislators should not have been surprised by the ABA owners' actions; after all, the AFL owners had done the same thing a few years earlier.

The ABA and NBA submitted copies of their lawsuit complaints. In the ABA's complaint, their attorneys listed a series of "Offenses Charged." Many of these, of course, were similar to those charged by the AFL in its lawsuit against the NFL.[64] The NBA responded with their answer and counterclaim. Their attorneys cited the Rick Barry breach of contract and ABA threats to induce other players to switch leagues, among other "Offenses Charged."[65]

The Economists' Recommendations, with Caveats

The three economists endorsed the proposed merger, but only with stipulations providing for revenue sharing, a true free agency, reduction of the indemnities, and elimination of the territorial restrictions. These stipulations, while accepted by Congress, proved anathema to the owners. Noll and Okner worried about the owners' continued price-setting power over ticket prices, as witnessed by their artificially high levels. They estimated that the cost of an additional fan was less than $3 and possibly closer to $2.50. Because the average seat price exceeded $4.50 (and most arenas had no seats below $2.50), the economists concluded that owners were exercising their price-setting power. They did note, however, that "such pricing still does not prevent widespread financial losses within the sport because the monopoly profits are retained by a small group of rich franchises."[66]

Another economist, Michael Canes, wrote a scholarly article analyzing the effects of establishing a common draft, gate- and television-revenue sharing, a reserve system, and the playing schedule. He purported to show "that such common arrangement reduce the private returns to team quality such that the private returns are approximately equal to the social value of the quality. Because of this, a merger would result in a higher level of social welfare and would be in the public interest."[67] Basically, Canes's insight was that individual owners, acting in their self-interest, would invest in too much quality for their team while ignoring the deleterious effect upon the other teams. Yankees' owner Jacob Ruppert once exemplified this by stating, "I want to win the pennant every year, if that is possible."[68] Although Yankees fans should cheer such an attitude, left unchecked, the Yankees' financial advantages could lead to monotony and ennui among fans. Canes pointed out that the owners could devise rules to curb an individual owner's appetite for talent. The real question, though, was whether revenue sharing, reverse-order drafts, and reserve clauses improved competitive balance.

The committees, therefore, received mixed signals from the economists. The reader may ask, "So what else is new?" Compared with previous hearings, though, the economists' input was a major change.

Congress Acts and Owners Are Disappointed

The Senate committee reflected their line of thinking during the hearings in their final report, *Authorizing the Merger of Two or More Professional Basketball Leagues*. "The Committee has concluded that a merger of the two professional basketball leagues is in the public interest, but only if certain restrictions are placed upon the operating rules of the merged entity. It is clear that merger should do more than simply create lucrative monopoly rights beyond the reach of the antitrust laws or public regulation." This preamble should have warned the basketball owners that something was amiss. The report continued, "an essential element in this planned merger seeking Congressional sanction and upon which it is conditioned, is that the merger does not result in decreasing the number of professional basketball clubs operating in the United States."[69]

The committees' concerns over abuses of player rights and the ability of weak teams to survive caused them to revise the original Senate bill (2373). The revised bill required the leagues to implement several policies: gate sharing; ensuring at least a 30 percent share (this despite no evidence of whether this would truly help financially weak teams); dividing television revenues equally; eliminating either a reserve or option clause in player contracts after his original contract expired, unless agreed upon by the player; and prohibiting compensation for free agents. Rookies could not sign for more than a one-year contract with one option year. The committee also recommended that the indemnity payment be payable only out of "television revenues accrued to each team as a result of the merger agreement. The Committee had received testimony that such television revenues would be substantially larger than those received prior to a merger."[70] Ervin disagreed with the prohibition on signing collegiate players before their class graduated, viewing it as an unnecessary abridgement of the player's freedom to contract.

Professional basketball owners were disappointed with the committee's report and decided to continue their separate existences.

Conclusion: Basketball Owners Drink from a Poisoned Well

The basketball owners were not as adroit as their football peers. They were unable to find a sympathetic legislator who was willing to get a merger bill approved by subtle, even devious, means. Nor did they dangle new franchises in front of legislators. The committee's revised bill included an amendment stipulating that the basketball league implement several polices that proved unpalatable to the owners. The owners declined to accept such a revised merger plan. The ABA staggered on for a few more seasons, unable to get a merger with the Robertson lawsuit pending. The NBA absorbed four ABA teams into the league in 1976. The St. Louis team did not join the NBA but was granted a share of the national television money.[71]

Tied to the basketball owners' efforts to obtain a merger was the shifting situation with respect to labor. The players' collective bargaining units transformed the arguments concerning the reserve clause and reverse-order draft. As the two Yale lawyers, Michael S. Jacobs and Ralph K. Winter Jr., argued, players collectively held the bargaining strength to negotiate changes to these restrictive rules. The antitrust laws were rendered somewhat less relevant in the world of sports. Owners and players were free to create their brave new world.[72]

That their football peers had boasted about and exaggerated the extent of their favorable legislation in 1966 was to the basketball owners' misfortune. In 1971 and 1972, several legislators proved skeptical regarding the basketball owners' claims of near penury and doom. Sam Ervin Jr. and Emanuel Celler were determined not to let the owners spin spurious tales in their attempt to gain approval of their merger. Unfortunately for the basketball owners, their football peers had poisoned the legislative well of goodwill.

CONCLUSION

A Look Back at The Hearings

On the whole, professional team sports owners did rather well in the aftermath of the hearings. Legislators rarely granted explicit antitrust protections (the NFL's national television contract and merger agreement being the outstanding gains), as the committees proved relatively conservative. They did not repudiate the reserve clause, the reverse-order draft, or territorial protection, despite their qualms regarding these institutions. Legislators' refusal to radically reshape professional team sports proved beneficial for the owners. During the hearings covered in this book, the owners' general prerogatives survived essentially intact, although free agency of some sort was imminent in all sports by 1976.

Owners found the task of convincing legislators to grant special favors that converted "dollar bills from fifty-cent pieces," to use Senator Karl Mundt's pithy remark, to be a volatile process. When the merits of their arguments failed to persuade a majority of committee members, team owners, especially the NFL ones, could hope that helpful legislators, on and off the committee, might circumvent an antitrust subcommittee altogether. An example of such hopes fulfilled was Hale Boggs' ramming the professional football merger through Congress.

Congress hesitated to tamper with the reserve clause, perhaps recognizing there would be hell to pay if the pros collapsed after any such tampering. Though some legislators began to realize that the reserve clause and reverse-order draft did not foster competitive balance, they rarely enlisted their aides to gather any relevant facts, such as scrutinizing league standings for a number of years or the draft's effects on teams' performances. The legislators and their aides also missed some opportunities to subject the team financial data from the 1950s to analysis. In-depth analysis could have shed light on such questions as the effects of revenue sharing. Millions of potentially outraged fans made the legislative calculus simple: better to throw the players overboard. Fans were not very sympathetic regarding the players' exploitation by owners, if they indeed even recognized that such exploitation existed. More likely, most fans probably believed players were overpaid, given their above-average incomes. Players, too, sometimes accepted the necessity of the reserve clause.

The legislators may have also decided that since the players had formed associations or unions, they could fend for themselves. Such an attitude reflected an actual benefit to the players from the hearings: not-so-subtle congressional pressure induced the owners to recognize the players' associations (or else the reader can believe that Bert Bell's recognition of the NFL Players Association during one of the hearings was simply an amazing coincidence).

Some fans gained when their hometown landed an expansion or existing franchise. Other fans lost when legislators did not prevent relocation. Fans of established teams that remained stationary may have been worse off because of the diluted talent remaining on their teams after expansion drafts. More fans might have benefited had the legislators overturned the territorial rights and player controls helping foster new leagues. With more leagues, fans, especially those in the biggest cities, might have had more teams to choose from.

Congress has held several hearings in the intervening decades since 1989. The leagues have evolved since then, too.

Technology, also, has altered the landscape. Further congressional investigations of professional team sports appear inevitable, as owners, players, and legislators grapple with new possibilities inherent in the evolving technology. Future legislators, if they have learned from their predecessors, are likely to be wary of owner claims. These lawmakers, though, are likely to be as self-interested as Hale Boggs and committee members from the past. It is a virtual certainty that professional team sports owners will return to Washington, D.C.

APPENDIX

Tables

Table 1. MLB, NFL, and NBA Season Attendance, 1946–64 (000s)

Year	MLB (AL)		MLB (NL)		NFL		NBA	
	#	Atten.	#	Atten.	#	Atten.	#	Atten.
1946	8	9,621	8	8,902	10	1,852		
1947	8	9,486	8	10,388	10	1,880	11	800
1948	8	11,150	8	9,771	10	1,614	8	610
1949	8	10,731	8	9,485	10	1,602	12	n/a
1950	8	9,142	8	8,321	13	2,092	17	n/a
1951	8	8,883	8	7,244	12	1,987	11	1,140
1952	8	8,294	8	6,339	12	2,187	10	n/a
1953	8	6,964	8	7,420	12	2,360	10	1,127
1954	8	7,922	8	8,014	12	2,378	9	982
1955	8	8,943	8	7,674	12	2,680	8	900
1956	8	7,894	8	8,650	12	2,750	8	1,102
1957	8	8,196	8	8,820	12	3,030	8	1,199
1958	8	7,296	8	10,165	12	3,183	8	1,167
1959	8	9,149	8	9,995	12	3,292	8	1,249
1960	8	9,227	8	10,685	13	3,370	8	1,297
1961	10	10,163	8	8,732	14	4,209	8	1,456
1962	10	10,015	10	11,360	14	4,226	9	1,434
1963	10	9,095	10	11,382	14	4,433	9	1,658
1964	10	9,235	10	12,045	14	4,808	9	1,796

#: Number of teams in league.
Atten.: Total league attendance (000s).
NBA 1946–47 season shown as 1947, 1947–48 season shown as 1948, and so on.
Games played per season varied over time: the American League schedule went from 154 to 162 games in 1961; the National League schedule went from 154 to 162 games in 1962; the NFL schedule went from 11 to 12 games in 1947 and from 12 games to 14 games in 1961; the NBA schedule went from 60 games in 1946–1947 to 48 games in 1947–1948, then 66–69 games in 1949–1950, 72 games in 1953–1954, 79 games in 1960–1961, and 80 games in 1961–1962.
Sources: Thorn, Palmer, and Gershman, *Total Baseball,* 76–77; Maher and Gill, *Pro Football Encyclopedia,* 117–20; JMOHRC, Professional Men, National Basketball Association, loose page (January 1947–May 1947) for 1946–1947; "Bulletins (January 1948–June 1948)," "BAA Bulletins #50," April 26, 1948; "NBA Bulletin #187B," (April 1951–July 1951 folder), June 19, 1951; "Attendance" Folder, loose page for 1952–1964.

Table 2. MLB Financial Information (Per Team), 1952–1956 ($000s)

	1952	1953	1954	1955	1956	Total
Income Sources:						
Games at Home	1,059	1,099	1,314	1,444	1,461	6,377
Games Away	239	233	281	294	292	1,339
Concessions	195	211	234	256	260	1,156
Radio/TV Rights	260	296	347	383	450	1,736
Gross Operating Income	1,955	2,039	2,383	2,619	2,677	11,673
Expense Sources:						
Administrative Salaries	85	84	87	88	91	436
Other Expenses	1,233	1,284	1,383	1,560	1,601	7,061
Player Payroll	417	429	444	463	464	2,217
Gross Operating Expenses	1,836	1,903	2,015	2,251	2,292	10,297
Net Income before Taxes	−77	−53	93	91	119	173
Salary/Gross Operating Income	.213	.211	.186	.177	.173	.190

Notes: Income sources do not add up to Gross Operating Income, as some sources are not shown. Expense sources do not add up to Gross Operating Expense, as some sources are not shown. Totals may not add up due to rounding.
Net Income before Taxes figures do not include net income (loss) from farm clubs.
Source: U.S. Congress, House, 1957, *Organized Professional Team Sports*, 353–58, 2,034–44, and 2,048–52.

Table 3. NFL Financial Information (Per Team), 1952–1956 ($000s)

	1952	1953	1954	1955	1956	Total
Income Sources:						
Games at Home	360	358	393	455	472	4,189
Games Away	164	168	186	216	225	962
Radio/TV Rights	70	103	147	114	143	581
Gross Operating Income	757	793	896	955	1,031	4,442
Expense Sources:						
Administrative Salaries	76	81	95	105	119	478
Other Expenses	376	396	414	455	483	2,127
Player Payroll	251	253	275	299	315	1,396
Gross Operating Expenses	713	756	798	866	934	4,076
Net Income before Taxes	44	36	98	88	97	367
Salary/Gross Operating Income	.332	.319	.307	.313	.305	.314

Notes: Income sources do not add up to Gross Operating Income, as some sources are not shown. Expense sources do not add up to Gross Operating Expense, as some sources are not shown. Totals may not add up due to rounding.
Source: U.S. Congress, House, 1957, *Organized Professional Team Sports,* 2,562–65 and 2,567.

Table 4. NBA Financial Information (Per Team), 1951–1957 ($000s)

	1951–52	1952–53	1953–54	1954–55	1955–56	1956–57	Total
Income Sources:							
Games at Home	180	172	151	154	198	247	1,026
Games Away	0	0	0	0	0	0	0
Radio/TV Rights	20	18	22	26	27	28	140
Gross Receipts	219	210	202	209	241	254	1,329
Expense Sources:							
Administrative Salaries	n/a	n/a	n/a	n/a	n/a	n/a	n/a
Other Expenses	108	114	102	99	120	128	660
Player Payroll	76	79	91	92	103	99	540
Gross Operating Expenses	233	216	215	208	238	248	1,351
Net Income before Taxes	−14	−7	−13	0	15	7	−10
Salary/Gross Receipts	.346	.376	.448	.443	.428	.390	.406

Notes: Income sources do not sum to Gross Operating Income, as some sources are not shown. Expense sources do not sum to Gross Operating Expense, as some sources are not shown. Totals may not add up due to rounding.

Some teams did not list administrative salaries in their data, other teams showed "none," and a few teams showed amounts.

Source: U.S. Congress, House, 1957, *Organized Professional Team Sports,* 2,928–35.

Table 5. Top:Bottom Distribution Ratios of Financial Information, 1952–1956

	1952	1953	1954	1955	1956	1957	Total
Receipts from Home Games							
MLB	7.09	6.18	7.31	4.78	4.62	n/a	4.08
NFL	4.81	3.49	3.14	3.66	3.98	n/a	3.53
NBA	3.22	3.62	4.56	4.41	3.69	4.21	3.20
Receipts from Away Games							
MLB	3.99	2.92	2.76	2.87	2.72	n/a	2.74
NFL	1.91	1.73	1.97	2.01	1.94	n/a	1.60
NBA*	—	—	—	—	—	—	—
Radio/Television Receipts							
MLB	64.94	11.25	5.62	7.16	8.43	n/a	5.50
NFL	10.53	3.00	2.09	6.18	2.12	n/a	2.76
NBA	n/a	n/a	17.7	32.1	6.13	4.04	8.15
Gross Operating Income							
MLB	4.28	5.53	3.75	3.54	3.55	n/a	3.21
NFL	2.64	2.30	2.43	2.35	2.40	n/a	2.36
NBA**	3.17	3.23	3.53	3.19	2.12	3.28	2.34
Player Salaries							
MLB	1.80	2.10	2.07	1.80	2.15	n/a	1.80
NFL	1.41	1.35	1.48	1.48	1.33	n/a	1.30
NBA	1.99	1.69	1.84	1.55	1.72	1.71	1.45
Other Expenses							
MLB	3.20	3.21	4.09	3.85	3.48	n/a	3.58
NFL	3.34	3.41	2.97	3.16	2.97	n/a	3.05
NBA	2.07	2.03	2.14	2.25	1.83	3.28	2.14
Gross Operating Expenses							
MLB	2.76	2.85	2.98	3.12	3.14	n/a	2.98
NFL	2.13	2.03	1.94	2.33	2.22	n/a	2.01
NBA	2.98	2.76	2.99	1.85	1.57	1.92	1.77

Top:Bottom distribution ratio: Team with greatest amount / Team with least amount of the financial category listed, e.g. "Receipts from Home Games" ratio represents the amount the team with the most Receipts from Home Games received, divided by the amount the team with the least Receipts from Home Games received.

*No "Away Games" revenues listed for the NBA because home teams did not share gate with visiting teams.

**Gross Receipts listed instead of Gross Operating Income.

Source: U.S. Congress, House, 1957, *Organized Professional Team Sports*, 354–58, 2,048–52, 2,562–65, and 2,930–35.

Table 6. NFL Bonus Picks, 1947–1958

Year	Player	Team	Pos.	Prev. W-L	All-NFL	Games Played
1947	Bob Fenimore	Chi. Bears	Back	.773	0	10
1948	Harry Gilmer	Washington	Back	.333	0	71
1949	Chuck Bednarik	Philadelphia	Center	.792	9	169
1950	Leon Hart	Detroit	End	.333	1	92
1951	Kyle Rote	NY Giants	Back	.833	0	115
1952	Bill Wade	Los Angeles	QB	.667	0	128
1953	Harry Babcock	San Francisco	End	.583	0	30
1954	Bobby Garrett	Cleveland	QB	.917	0	9
1955	George Shaw	Baltimore	QB	.250	0	71
1956	Gary Glick	Pittsburgh	QB	.333	0	76
1957	Paul Hornung	Green Bay	QB	.333	2	104
1958	King Hill	Chi. Cardinals	QB	.250	0	127

Prev. W-L: Drafting team's record the season before the bonus pick.
All-NFL: Number of times player was named to All-NFL team.
Games Played: Number of regular-season games played during career.
Sources: Carroll, Gershman, Neft, and Thorn, *Total Football,* 1,481–1,506 for bonus pick information. Maher and Gill, *Pro Football Encyclopedia,* 35–39 for all other data.

Table 7. Competitive Balance in Professional Sports (as Measured by the Ratio of Standard Deviation to Idealized Standard Deviation), 1946–1965

	BAA/NBA	NFL	AAFC	AFL	MLB (NL)	MLB (AL)
1946	—	1.33	1.84	—	2.25	2.75
1947	2.55	1.30	2.28	—	1.98	1.97
1948	2.25	1.89	2.36	—	1.74	3.00
1949	2.60	1.78	1.86	—	2.21	3.06
1950	2.77	1.70	—	—	2.03	3.13
1951	1.88	1.63	—	—	2.11	2.53
1952	2.10	1.35	—	—	2.90	2.36
1953	3.20	1.87	—	—	2.78	2.82
1954	2.62	1.46	—	—	2.40	3.65
1955	1.48	1.21	—	—	1.86	2.75
1956	1.04	1.18	—	—	2.13	2.49
1957	0.92	1.17	—	—	1.92	2.30
1958	2.05	1.62	—	—	1.26	1.40
1959	2.55	1.56	—	—	1.24	1.68
1960	3.25	1.48	—	1.15	2.16	2.11
1961	2.57	1.53	—	1.88	2.42	2.57
1962	2.98	1.87	—	1.89	3.16	1.60
1963	2.88	1.33	—	1.43	2.20	2.15
1964	2.98	1.41	—	1.71	2.07	2.29
1965	2.91	1.39	—	1.46	2.31	2.30

Idealized Standard Deviation is $.5/\sqrt{N}$, where N = the number of games per team in a season.
The ratio of standard deviation to idealized standard deviation would be close to one if the league was akin to a coin-tossing league. A greater ratio indicates a greater competitive imbalance. Comparisons of the ratios across sports should be done with caution, given the sports' differing number of players and prevalence of injuries.
For the BAA (1946–1949) and the NBA (1949–65), the 1946–47 season is shown as 1947, the 1947–48 season is shown as 1948, and so on.
For the NFL, AAFC, and AFL, ties count as one-half of a win.
Sources: *Sporting News Official NBA Guide, 2002–2003 edition,* 648–742; Maher and Gill, *Pro Football Encyclopedia,* 256–74; Thorn, Palmer, and Gershman, *Total Baseball,* 2,176–2,215.

Table 8. MLB and NFL Broadcast Revenues, 1952–1964 ($000s)

	Major League Baseball				National Football League			
Year	Local	League	Total	Team	Local	League	Total	Team
1952	4,165	n.a.	5,400	338	769	n.a.	769	70
1953	4,741	n.a.	5,952	372	1,239	n.a.	1,239	103
1954	5,556	n.a.	6,741	421	1,764	n.a.	1,764	147
1955	6,123	n.a.	7,308	457	1,364	n.a.	1,364	114
1956	7,206	n.a.	8,366	523	1,720	n.a.	1,720	143
1957	5,290	1,750	10,290	643	1,958	n.a.	1,958	163
1958	5,950	2,475	11,475	717	2,296	n.a.	2,296	191
1959	6,315	3,225	12,790	799	2,634	n.a.	2,634	220
1960	9,355	3,174	15,779	986	3,100	n.a.	3,100	238
1961	10,780	2,666	16,696	928	3,510	n.a.	4,200	300
1962	12,775	2,000	18,525	926	563	4,650	5,903	422
1963	13,000	2,225	18,775	939	710	4,650	6,486	463
1964	14,325	1,700	19,775	989	748	14,100	16,943	1,210

Local: Total local broadcast revenues for league.
Total: May includes other broadcast revenues not shown.
Team: Average of all broadcast revenues per team.
n.a.: Not available or no national contract.
MLB total includes World Series and All-Star Games; NFL total includes all playoff games and Championship Game, except where noted.
Source: U.S. Congress, House, 1977, *Inquiry Into Professional Sports,* 668.

Table 9. NFL Franchise Records Before and After the AFL, 1954–1965

Team	1954–59 W-L Pct.	1960–65 W-L Pct.	1960–65 W-L Pct.*
Baltimore	.528	.622	.592
Chicago Bears	.639	.573	.565
Chi./St. Louis Cardinals	.278	.488	.443
Cleveland	.667	.659	.629
Dallas	—	.305	—
Detroit	.500	.537	.514
Green Bay	.347	.744	.710
Los Angeles	.472	.280	.271
Minnesota	—	.357	—
New York Giants	.653	.585	.623
Philadelphia	.375	.439	.406
Pittsburgh	.458	.415	.377
San Francisco	.514	.402	.377
Washington	.403	.268	.239
Standard Deviation	.124	.149	.150
Ratio St. Dev : Ideal. St. Dev.	2.11	2.69	2.50

*Win-loss records against only established (non-expansion) teams; games with Dallas and Minnesota not included. The two expansion teams presumably would skew the ratio of actual standard deviation to idealized standard deviation.

Ratio St. Dev : Ideal. St. Dev. is Actual standard deviation / Idealized standard deviation.

Source: Maher and Gill, *Pro Football Encyclopedia,* 122–28 and 264–74.

Notes

Abbreviations

AFL LM	*AFL League Minutes*
BSE	*Blackout of Sporting Events*
BTBG	*Broadcasting and Televising Baseball Games*
FARF	*Fifth Annual Report of the FCC*
IPSR	*Inquiry into Professional Sports, Report*
NFL LM	*NFL League Minutes*
NYT	*New York Times*
OB	*Organized Baseball*
OPTS	*Organized Professional Team Sports*
PB1	*Professional Basketball, Part 1*
PB2	*Professional Basketball, Part 2*
PFHOFAIC	Pro Football Hall of Fame Archives and Information Center
PFLM	*Professional Football League Merger*
PMABA/NBA	*Proposed Merger of the ABA/NBA*
PSAB-1964	*Professional Sports Antitrust Bill-1964*
PSAB-1965	*Professional Sports Antitrust Bill-1965*
PSAI	*Professional Sports Antitrust Immunity*
PSB	*Professional Sports Blackouts*
PSCPA of 1985	*Professional Sports Community Protection Act of 1985*
PSTCPA	*Professional Sports Team Community Protection Act*
SBA75	*Sports Broadcasting Act of 1975*
SPCT	*Sports Programming and Cable Television*
TARF	*Third Annual Report of the FCC*
TPSC	*Telecasting of Professional Sports Contests*
TSN	*The Sporting News*

Introduction

1. U.S. Congress, Senate, 1959, *OPTS*, 222, cites *Washington Post*, August 7, 1959.
2. Scherer and Ross, *Industrial Market Structure*, 174–75.
3. Truman, *Governmental Process*, 372.
4. Lowe, *Kid on the Sandlot*, 131–33.
5. See www.opensecrets.org/bigpicture/reelect.php, viewed September 16, 2011, for instance; www.bioguide.congress.gov/scripts/biodisplay.pl?index=c000264, viewed October 17, 2011.
6. U.S. Congress, House, 1957, *OPTS*, 2,965 and 3,148–49.
7. Fort, *Sports Economics*, 437–40.

Chapter 1. A Brief History of Professional Team Sports

1. Good histories of professional baseball include Harold Seymour, *Baseball: The Early Years* and *Baseball: The Golden Years* and David Voigt, *American Baseball*, three volumes; the Congressional hearings of 1951 produced much historical information about baseball's early years, U.S. Congress, House, 1952, *OB: Report*.
2. Lewis Meacham, "The Professional Base Ball Association—what it must do to be saved," *Chicago Tribune*, October 24, 1875.
3. Pietrusza, *Major Leagues*, 29.
4. Seymour, *Baseball: The Early Years*, 88; U.S. Congress, House, 1952, *OB: Report*, 20.
5. See Burk, *Never Just a Game* and *Much More Than a Game* for a detailed history of the relationship between baseball owners and players.
6. U.S. Congress, House, 1952, *OB: Report*, 22–24.
7. Seymour, *Baseball: The Early Years*, 146.
8. Legal scholar Stephen Ross points out that with truly competitive leagues, unlike those leagues bound by the National Agreement, "Courts can be more tolerant of restraints on players in a world of competing leagues. Such leagues are less likely to adopt rules that are not truly justified by some legitimate competitive goal, such as promotion of competitive balance or more exciting games. . . . Thus, if vigorous inter-league competition actually existed for players, an intra-league restraint that one league independently adopted would not usually constitute an unreasonable restraint of trade" (Ross, "Monopoly Sports Leagues," 736)."
9. U.S. Congress, House, 1952, *OB: Report*, 36–38.
10. Glick, "Professional Sports Franchise Movements," 67.
11. National League and American Association, *Annual Meeting*, 92 and 104.
12. U.S. Congress, House, 1952, *OB: Report*, 40.
13. Seymour, *Baseball: The Early Years*, 323.
14. Miller, *Whole Different Ball Game*, 167–68.
15. U.S. Congress, House, 1952, *OB: Report*, 56–57; Quirk and Fort *Pay Dirt*, 318–19.
16. U.S. Congress, House, 1952, *OB: Report*, 54.
17. U.S. Congress, House, 1952, *OB: Report*, 197–98.
18. Nathanson, "The Sovereign Nation of Baseball," 75. In an earlier case involving star player Napoleon Lajoie who switched from the National League Philadelphia team to the

American League Philadelphia team in 1901, Judge Robert Ralston ruled that the reserve clause lacked mutuality; a later Pennsylvania Supreme Court judge, Justice Potter [no first name] . . . characterized baseball as different from typical businesses, being a "'game,' a 'sport, that was deserving of special consideration'" (Duquette, *Regulating the National Pastime,* 8).

19. Wolohan, "Curt Flood Act of 1998," 351.

20. U.S. Congress, House, 1977, *IPSR,* 54; Poggi, *Theater in America,* 17; U.S. Congress, Senate, 1972, *PB1,* 1,207.

21. Coenen provides an excellent history of the NFL's rise, (*Sandlots to the Super Bowl*).

22. See Nelson, *National Basketball League* for a good overview.

23. See Koppett, *24 Seconds to Shoot,* and Surdam, *Rise of the National Basketball Association,* for accounts of the NBA's early days.

24. Burk, *Much More than a Game,* 106 for quote; A. Van Pelt, "Demand for O.B. Files Withdrawn in Gardella Case," *TSN,* August 31, 1949, 13; Hy Turkin, "Gardella's Counsel to Seek More Data from Chandler," *TSN,* September 28, 1949, 2. Wolohan notes that, "the sale of broadcasting rights for radio and television distinguished the case from *Federal Baseball,* the Sixth Circuit found the broadcasting rights to be essential in the same manner as the telegraph rights that were examined in *Federal Baseball*" (Wolohan, "Curt Flood Act of 1998," 356).

25. U.S. Congress, Senate, 1972, *PB1,* 1,207.

26. Bob Broeg, "'Games Need Reserve Clause'—Lanier," *TSN,* September 28, 1949, 1–2; Dan Daniel, "Gardella Drops His Suit, Will Sign with Cardinals," *TSN,* October 19, 1949, 2; Miller, *Whole Different Ball Game,* 177 and 179.

27. Steven R. Rivkin provides a good overview of these cases; his article was reprinted in U.S. Congress, Senate, 1972, *PB1,* 1,205–1,215.

28. H. G. Salsinger, "Contrast in Skill Snag Player Unions," *TSN,* April 25, 1946, 3.

29. Burk, *Much More Than a Game,* 123–24; Miller, *Whole Different Ball Game,* 6–8.

30. Myron Cope, "Big Z and His Misfiring Piston," *Sports Illustrated,* December 18, 1967, 27; Davis, *Papa Bear,* 139–40.

31. *NYT,* "Pros Weigh Labor Tie," December 27, 1956, 31; *NYT,* "Football Players Form Pro Bargaining Group," November 29, 1956, 45.

32. *NYT,* "NBA Players Threaten Strike in Dispute Over Pension Plan," January 15, 1964.

33. Burk, *Much More than a Game,* 157–58.

34. Burk, *Much More than a Game,* 164–65.

35. An article in the *Maine Law Review* described the NFL Players Association's astute tactics in organizing and presenting their proposals (*Maine Law Review,* "The Balance of Power in Professional Sports," 475).

36. U.S. Congress, Senate, 1973, *Federal Sports Act of 1972,* 198; "N.F.L. Rejects Expansion and Players' Association," *NYT,* February 3, 1957, 159 and 2, probably 1 and 2; "Pro Players List 304 as Members," *NYT,* February 6, 1957, 31.

37. Miller, *Whole Different Ball Game,* 195.

38. Burk, *Much More than a Game,* 179.

39. Pitcher Jim Bouton joked with the owners, asking whether they'd accept terminating the reserve clause when a player reached age sixty-five. The owners said they would

not, because "next time you'll want it reduced to age fifty-five" (Miller, *Whole Different Ball Game,* 193).

40. Jacobs and Winter, "Antitrust Principles and Collective Bargaining"; see also *Maine Law Review,* "The Balance of Power."

41. U.S. Congress, House, 1972, *PMABA/NBA,* 199 and 202; reprinted from Jacobs and Winter, "Antitrust Principles."

42. U.S. Congress, House, 1972, *PMABA/NBA,* 204–5.

43. Koppett, Leonard, "High Court Hears Baseball Back Antitrust Exemption," *NYT,* March 21, 1972.

44. Koppett, Leonard, "Baseball's Exempt Status Upheld by Supreme Court," *NYT,* June 20, 1972."

45. Koppett, "Baseball's Exempt Status Upheld by Supreme Court."

46. Miller, *Whole Different Ball Game,* 194.

47. Red Smith, "The Buck Passes," *NYT*, June 21, 1972.

48. *NYT,* "Harrelson (.273) Is Released For Remarks About A's Owner," August 22, 1967; Leonard Koppett, "Eckert Takes Up A's-Finley Case," *NYT,* September 12, 1967.

49. Miller, *Whole Different Ball Game,* 238–44.

50. Miller, *Whole Different Ball Game,* 247–50.

51. Miller, *Whole Different Ball Game,* 266–67.

52. U.S. Congress, House, 1977, *IPSR,* 31–32.

53. U.S. Congress, House, 1977, *IPSR,* 230–31.

54. U.S. Congress, House, 1977, *IPSR,* 19–21.

55. U.S. Congress, House, 1977, *IPSR,* 33.

56. U.S. Congress, House, 1977, *IPSR,* 32.

57. Even if an owner got a Babe Ruth for free, the owner would likely raise ticket prices because he was putting a higher-quality product on the field.

58. Curt Flood Act of 1998, *Public Law 105-297,* October 27, 1998.

Chapter 2. Economics of Antitrust

1. archive.org/stream/Shermanantitrust024534mbp/shermanantitrust024534mbp_djvu.text, viewed July 22, 2013.

2. Scherer and Ross, *Industrial Market Structure,* 450–52.

3. Scherer and Ross, *Industrial Market Structure,* 317.

4. *NYT*, "Blunt Talk on the Phone," February 24, 1983, D4.

5. Scherer and Ross, *Industrial Market Structure,* 323.

6. Ross, "Monopoly Sports Leagues," 748, see n. 468.

7. Neale, "The Peculiar Economics of Professional Sports," quote on 6, see also 4.

8. Roberts, "Antitrust Status of Sports Leagues Revisited," 229–30.

9. Roberts, "Antitrust Status," 119–20 and 127.

10. Http://supreme.justia.com/cases/federal/US/467/752/, viewed July 22, 2013.

11. An article in the *Harvard Law Review* pointed out, "Usually when the structure of an industry justifies anticompetitive cooperation through a trade association, the courts require at least that the organization be open equally to all reasonably qualified persons

or firms who seek membership so that the market rather than the self-interest of those already in the business will determine the number of firms in the industry" (*Harvard Law Review,* "Super Bowl and the Sherman Act," 426). The article did suggest that leagues could impose some reasonable requirements, since adding new teams creates scheduling and team strength difficulties.

12. *Harvard Law Review,* "Super Bowl," 429. The courts allow a league to impose exclusive territorial monopolies, if doing so creates efficiency gains that outweigh the higher prices and profits of individual teams. Sports teams, though, often create the exclusive territories instead of the leagues creating such, thereby leaving teams and leagues vulnerable to antitrust attacks as agreements not to compete.

13. Ross, "Monopoly Sports Leagues," 698.

14. U.S. Congress, House, 1952, *OB: Report,* 20.

15. Readers should note that, as a general rule, free markets, similar to mass transit, are good for the "other guy."

16. Legal scholar Stephen Ross analyzed the idea of ruinous competition, presumably where teams overspent on player talent in the hopes that they would drive rival owners out of business. The idea had more credibility if the owners had the hopes of retaining or creating monopoly power by driving others out, as the victorious owners could recoup their overpayments through charging monopoly prices. The new entrants, however, presumably accepted the expectations of incurring losses early in the game, so the incumbents might not succeed with predatory spending (Ross, "Monopoly Sports Leagues," 728 and 731).

17. *Harvard Law Review,* "Super Bowl," 424; see also Ross, "Monopoly Sports Leagues," 677. Ross argues that economists, lawyers, and owners are missing a key point: "monopoly sports leagues under the present scheme employ inefficient player allocation systems that harm fans" (Ross, "Monopoly Sports Leagues," 669).

18. Ross, "Monopoly Sports Leagues," 673, see also 671–72 and 685.

19. U.S. Congress, House, 1952, *OB: Hearings,* 1,516–17. There are some built-in checks to the data supplied by the owners, such as revenue-sharing rules based upon attendance or revenues.

20. U.S. Congress, House, 1957, *OPTS,* 2,896.

21. Surdam, "What Brings Fans to the Ball Parks," 41.

22. Quirk and Fort, *Pay Dirt,* 244–46.

23. U.S. Congress, Senate, 1972, *Professional Basketball, Part 1,* 388; U.S. Congress, House, 1972, *Proposed Merger of the ABA/NBA,* 61.

24. U.S. Dept. of Justice, FTC, *Horizontal Merger Guidelines,* 7.

25. Vrooman, "General Theory of Sports Leagues," 971–90.

26. Coase, "Theory of Social Cost," 1–44; Rottenberg, "Baseball Players Labor Market," 242–58.

27. U.S. Congress, House, 1952, *OB: Report,* 20.

28. There are numerous articles on revenue sharing. Some of the more prominent include Canes, "The Social Benefits of Restrictions on Team Quality;" Fort and Quirk, "Cross-Subsidization, Incentives, and Outcomes"; Kesenne, "Revenue Sharing and Com-

petitive Balance"; Szymanski and Kesenne, "Competitive Balance and Gate Revenue Sharing"; Vrooman, "General Theory of Sports Leagues."

29. Levin, et al., *Report of the Blue Ribbon Panel,* 29.

30. Pluto, *Tall Tales,* 216.

31. Surdam, "Tale of Two Gate-Sharing Plans," 934. An article in the *Harvard Law Review* pointed out that fans often benefited when an ailing team moved to a new city (*Harvard Law Review,* "Super Bowl," 429).

32. Ross, "Monopoly Sports Leagues," 684. The American League's expansion in 1961 resulted in greater attendance in 1960, but not on a per-team basis; fans in the original eight cities reduced their attendance.

33. Ross, "Monopoly Sports Leagues," 707; Demmert, *Economics of Professional Team Sports,* 88–89. Pushing this example to an extreme, a true entrepreneur could reduce his player costs to negative amounts, by selling spots on his team to celebrities and other wealthy people who want to experience playing in the big leagues.

34. *Harvard Law Review,* "Super Bowl," 428.

Chapter 3. An Overview of the Hearings

1. Lowe, *Kid on the Sandlot,* 15–16.

2. Lowe, *Kid on the Sandlot,* 18.

3. *NYT,* "Warning Sounded on House Inquiry," August 3, 1951, 15; Lowe, *Kid on the Sandlot,* 23.

4. U.S. Congress, Senate, 1958, *OPTS,* 313; see also Robert Elias, *The Empire Strikes Out.*

5. U.S. Congress, Senate, 1958, *OPTS,* 315.

6. U.S. Congress, Senate, 1960, *OPTS,* 30.

7. U.S. Congress, House, 1952, *OB: Report,* 199.

8. U.S. Congress, House, 1952, *OB: Report,* 201–2. Celler caught Frick in a contradiction. Celler cited the league's minutes describing the PCL's attempt to attain Major League status in 1947. The incumbent owners merely stonewalled and suggested adding a couple of clubs (U.S. Congress, House, 1952, *OB: Report,* 200 and 201).

9. U.S. Congress, House, 1952, *OB: Report,* 88 and 91.

10. Surdam, *Postwar Yankees,* 60–61 and 317–19.

11. The baseball and football information generally conformed to the leagues' rules on revenue sharing and payments to the league offices. For a discussion of the accuracy of the data, see Surdam, *Postwar Yankees,* 59–60.

12. Quirk and Fort, *Pay Dirt,* 49–67, 407–34, and 446–59.

13. Surdam, *Run to Glory,* 330; Al Silverman, "Will Pro Football Have Union Trouble This Year?" *Sport,* September 1957, 24–27 and 96–98.

14. For a look at the costs of clothing a player, see John Geyer, "Snappy Togs for Squad Cost $5,586 Plus $1,960," *TSN,* November 3, 1948, 11.

15. Levin, Mitchell, Volcker, and Will, *Blue Ribbon Panel,* 61–77.

16. Surdam, *Postwar Yankees,* 67 and 72; U.S. Congress, House, 1957, *OPTS,* 2,048–52.

17. U.S. Congress, House, 1952, *OB: Report,* 230–32; U.S. Congress, House, 1977, *IPSR,* 38–39.

18. U.S. Congress, House, 1977, *IPSR,* 40.
19. U.S. Congress, Senate, 1973, *Federal Sports Act of 1972,* 1–3 and 139–40.
20. U.S. Congress, House, 1977, *IPSR,* 3.
21. U.S. Congress, House, 1977, *IPSR,* 4, 5, and 158.
22. U.S. Congress, House, 1977, *IPSR,* 40–41.
23. U.S. Congress, House, 1977, *IPSR,* 4.
24. U.S. Congress, House, 1977, *IPSR,* 54.
25. U.S. Congress, House, 1977, *IPSR,* 54.
26. U.S. Congress, House, 1977, *IPSR,* 59.
27. U.S. Congress, House, 1977, *IPSR,* 102–3.
28. U.S. Congress, House, 1977, *IPSR,* 94–96. Congress and the IRS also eliminated "whipsawing," whereby an owner used both the player depreciation allowance and a capital gain.

Chapter 4. Player Rights

1. The professional sports owners have succeeded in glamorizing outright exploitation, as the weeks leading up to and including the draft itself become high drama, replete with endless analysis.
2. U.S. Congress, House, 1952, *OB: Report,* 213 and 218–19.
3. U.S. Congress, House, 1952, *OB: Report,* 183. The subcommittee also cited, "that baseball should have rules to equalize the strength of teams and to minimize the power of money-making clubs . . . where the player limits are raised to a point where a club can purchase many players to the disadvantage of other clubs, playing strength is not equalized (U.S. Congress, House, 1952, *OB: Report,* 184)." Bowie Kuhn later made the argument that free agency would prevent owners from recouping their investment in player development. Ross disputed this rationale, "Such expenses are ordinary costs of doing business and . . . are not peculiar to professional sports leagues" (Ross, "Monopoly Sports Leagues," 692).
4. Natie Brown and Tom Davis, "How Wrestling Looks From the Inside," *Sport,* November 1954, 22–23 and 91–93; Jeane Hoffman, "Lady Wrestlers Strike It Rich," *Sport,* June 1951, 36–38.
5. U.S. Department of Commerce 1952, *Statistical Abstract,* 189, 252, 263. Because the Northeast region tended to have higher incomes, earning $6,000 would rank somewhat lower for players performing for Boston, New York, and Philadelphia.
6. U.S. Congress, House, 1957, *OPTS,* 2,873.
7. Basketball Association of America, "League Minutes," June 6, 1946.
8. U.S. Congress, House, 1957, *OPTS,* 2,594 and 2,677 has Norm Van Brocklin's recognition of this lack of bargaining leverage.
9. *Time,* "'It's Wonderful,'" December 19, 1949, 53; Coenen, *Sandlots to the Super Bowl,* 136.
10. *NYT,* "Proposed Pro Football League Plans to Beat N.F.L. on Salaries," August 24, 1959, 25; Al Hirshberg, "Sound Off! Joe Foss Diagnoses the Pro Football War," *Sport,* November 1962, 46–49 and 95.

11. Jeremiah Tax, "The Man Who Must Be Different," *Sports Illustrated,* February 3, 1958, 32.

12. Bob Broeg, "Unwieldy Basket Loop Sags at Gate," *TSN,* Sec. 2, 1.

13. Pluto, *Tall Tales,* 147; Lowell Reidenbaugh, "Cool Clyde Helping Hawks Set Hot Pace," *TSN,* December 17, 1958, Sec. 2, 6.

14. Gordon Cobbledick, "'Free' Players Would Wreck Game," *Baseball Digest,* July 1946, 15.

15. Salzberg, *Set Shot to Slam Dunk,* 93–94.

16. Leonard Shecter, "Rational Rebel," *Sports Illustrated,* May 13, 1963, 81–82.

17. U.S. Congress, House, 1957, *OPTS,* 2,676.

18. PFHOFAIC, *NFL LM,* July 22, 1939, 14 and 17; August 12, 1940, 3.

19. U.S. Congress, House, 1957, *OPTS,* 2,699.

20. Dan Parker, "Baseball's Bombshell," *Sport,* April 1949, 12–13, 80, and 82–83.

21. *NYT,* "Sues to Break Contract," December 13, 1946, 32; *NYT,* "Mikan Sued by Gears," January 18, 1947, 17; Schumacher, *Mr. Basketball,* 76–77; *NYT,* "Mikan Returns to Gears," January 29, 1947, 33; *NYT,* "Mikan Suit Called Test Case for Pros," January 21, 1947, 19.

22. *NYT,* "Pro Football Suit in Federal Court," December 20, 1949, 40; *NYT,* "Ruthstrom Loses Suit Against Redskins in Test of Football Reserve Clause," December 21, 1949, 43.

23. *NYT,* "Giants Sue Weinmeister," May 19, 1954, 40; *NYT,* "Ruling for Weinmeister," May 22, 1954, 22.

24. *NYT,* "U.S. Supreme Court Agrees to Hear Suit Charging Monopoly in Pro Football," October 9, 1956, 57; *NYT,* "U.S. Urges Trial of Football Suit," January 18, 1957, 34.

25. *NYT,* "U.S. Supreme Court Agrees to Hear Suit Charging Monopoly in Pro Football," October 9, 1956, 57; *NYT,* "U.S. Urges Trial of Football Suit," January 18, 1957, 34.

26. *NYT,* "Texts of the Court's Majority Opinion and Dissents," February 2, 1957, 36. Three justices dissented, but the majority cited previous desegregation cases: "a unanimous court had no difficulty in demolishing the 'rule of stare decisis' when it overturned the entrenched holding of the court that statutes enforcing racial segregation in the public schools are constitutional" (Arthur Krock, "In the Nation: Now Congress Has the Ball—Foot, Base and Basket," *NYT,* February 28, 1957, 26).

27. *NYT,* "Ex-Lineman Says He's 'Vindicated,'" February 26, 1957, 36; Luther Huston, "'Pro' Football Placed Under Antitrust Law," *NYT,* February 26, 1957, 1 and 36; Howard Tuckner, "Bell, National League Commissioner, Hits Court Ruling as Discriminatory," *NYT,* February 26, 1957, 36; *NYT,* "Supreme Court Rebuffs N.F.L. on Antitrust Plea," April 9, 1957, 55.

28. Allen Drury, "Pro Football Hits Antitrust Curbs," *NYT,* July 25, 1957, 13; U.S. Congress, House, 1957, *OPTS,* 2,504.

29. U.S. Congress, House, 1957, *OPTS,* 2,503–4.

30. U.S. Congress, House, 1957, *OPTS,* 2,583 and 2,588.

31. U.S. Congress, House, 1957, *OPTS,* 2,649.

32. U.S. Congress, House, 1957, *OPTS,* 2,609, quote on contract on 2,611 and 2,612; Davis, *Papa Bear,* 220–21.

33. U.S. Congress, Senate, 1958, *OPTS*, 24–73.

34. Dave Brady, "Player Rep Friend Raps Proposal That Athletes Form Labor Union," *TSN*, August 3, 1963, 1 and 4.

35. U.S. Congress, Senate, 1964, *Professional Sports Antitrust Bill-1964*, 42.

36. U.S. Congress, Senate, 1965, *Professional Sports Antitrust Bill-1965*, 144.

37. U.S. Congress, House, 1957, *OPTS*, 2,662.

38. U.S. Congress, House, 1957, *OPTS*, 2,653.

39. U.S. Congress, House, 1957, *OPTS*, 2,644–45.

40. U.S. Congress, House, 1957, *OPTS*, 2,589.

41. Rottenberg, "Baseball Players Labor Market," 242–58.

42. PFHOFAIC, *NFL LM*, April 29, 1946, 6 and 8 and April 30, 1946, 10.

43. Allison Danzig, "Pro Loop Changes Player Contract," *NYT*, May 1, 1946, 43.

44. U.S. Congress, Senate, 1958, *OPTS*, 396.

45. U.S. Congress, Senate, 1958, *OPTS*, 401–2. Even Celler apparently was lulled into believing this charade. He lauded Bell's presentation of the reserve clause NFL-style as, "a refreshing statement to hear" (*Sports Illustrated*, "Family Man," August 5, 1957, 21).

46. *NYT*, "Players Defend Football Draft," July 26, 1957, 38. MLB owners employed similar tactics during the 1958 hearings, resulting in one of the few moments of mirth. After New York Yankees manager Casey Stengel mesmerized the committee with his inimitable brand of double-speak, Mickey Mantle followed him. When questioned as to his views of the applicability of the antitrust laws to baseball, Mantle replied, "My views are just about the same as Casey's" (U.S. Congress, Senate, 1958, *OPTS*, 24).

47. U.S. Congress, Senate, 1958, *OPTS*, 396

48. U.S. Congress, Senate, 1958, *OPTS*, 404; U.S. Congress, House, 1957, *OPTS*, 2,494, 2,728, 2,750; Joe King, "New York Rattles the Rafters for Ratterman," *TSN*, November 8, 1950, Sec. 2, 5. Ratterman refused to sign a contract with a reserve or option clause; Jim Breuil of Buffalo gave him a one-year non-holdover deal, but Ratterman played for the New York Yanks the next season.

49. U.S. Congress, House, 1957, *OPTS*, 2,659.

50. U.S. Congress, House, 1957, *OPTS*, 2,590.

51. U.S. Congress, House, 1957, *OPTS*, 2,660.

52. U.S. Congress, House, 1957, *OPTS*, 2,837–47.

53. U.S. Congress, House, 1957, *OPTS*, 2,683–85.

54. U.S. Congress, House, 1957, *OPTS*, 2,707. If this had been a situation comedy, the laugh track would have been cued at "just a son-in-law" and "trying to save a buck."

55. Dick Schapp, "Why Pro Football Players Revolt," *Sport*, January 1964, 6–8 and 73–74. Although Rozelle, himself, initially determined the compensation, owners eventually decided to use draft picks as compensation (Ross, "Monopoly Sports Leagues," 668).

56. U.S. Congress, House, 1957, *OPTS*, 2,664 and 2,734.

57. Sandy Grady, "Resurgence in Cincinnati," *Sport*, March 1961, 18–19 and 67–70; Barry Gottehrer, "Will Oscar Robertson Play in the NBA?" *Sport*, June 1960, 47; Jeremiah Tax, "Bunyan Strides Again," *Sports Illustrated*, April 6, 1959, 18.

58. U.S. Congress, Senate, 1958, *OPTS,* 398.

59. U.S. Congress, House, 1957, *OPTS,* 2,628–29; *Time,* "Fantastic Situation?" January 3, 1949, 31.

60. U.S. Congress, House, 1957, *OPTS,* 2,630.

61. Frank Finch, "Rams, Bears, Browns, Redskins Place Seven Apiece in Pro Bowl," *TSN,* December 21, 1955, Sec. 2, 7.

62. U.S. Congress, Senate, 1959, *OPTS,* 33–34.

63. U.S. Congress, Senate, 1959, *OPTS,* 35 and 37.

64. U.S. Congress, Senate, 1959, *OPTS,* 36.

65. U.S. Congress, House, 1957, *OPTS,* 2,578.

66. U.S. Congress, House, 1957, *OPTS,* anonymous quote on 2,586. The players' letter-writing campaign backfired, as wary legislators raised questions about who had orchestrated the effort.

67. U.S. Congress, House, 1957, *OPTS,* 2,682.

68. Joe King, "NFL to Let Draftee Switch Clubs If He Offers Valid Reason," *TSN*, January 15, 1958, Sec. 2, 10.

69. U.S. Congress, House, 1957, *OPTS,* 2,615. George Halas, owner of the Bears was a staunch foe of player associations, so it should be no surprise that his henchman, Connor, would toe the antiunion line.

70. H. G. Salsinger, "Contrast in Skill Snag Player Unions," *TSN,* April 25, 1946, 3.

71. Dan Daniel, "Television Clause Snags Player Contract," *TSN,* September 25, 1946, 1–2; Dan Daniel, "Executive Council Votes to Hike Players' Minimum Pay to $7,000," *TSN,* October 9, 1957, 7; Dan Daniel, "Game's Prestige Growing with Pension Plan," *TSN,* July 25, 1962, 73; Dan Daniel, "Scott Sets Record Straight on Player Pension Demands," *TSN,* August 16, 1961, 9.

72. *NYT,* "Football Players Form Pro Bargaining Group," November 29, 1956, 45.

73. *TSN,* "NFL Players Organize, Pick Voice," December 12, 1956, Sec. 2, 1 and 2.

74. U.S. Congress, House, 1957, *OPTS,* 2,817.

75. *NYT,* "Players' Unit in Talks," January 29, 1957, 37.

76. *NYT,* "N.F.L. Rejects Expansion and Players' Association," February 3, 1957, 159 and 160; *NYT,* "Pro Players List 304 as Members," February 6, 1957, 31. Some players were receiving $6 per day for meal money, but would get $9 in 1957 (U.S. Congress, House, 1957, *OPTS,* 2,643).

77. U.S. Congress, House, 1957, *OPTS,* 2,647–48.

78. U.S. Congress, House, 1957, *OPTS,* 2,822.

79. U.S. Congress, House, 1957, *OPTS,* 2,823–30; PFHOFAIC, *NFL LM,* January 24, 1947, 11.

80. U.S. Congress, House, 1957, *OPTS,* 2,689.

81. Joe King, "NFL Considers Player Pension Plan for $100 a Month at 65," *TSN,* January 28, 1959, Sec. 2, 6; *NYT,* "Football Players Open Pension Talks," January 28, 1958, 33.

82. *NYT,* "Bell Alters View on Pension Plan," January 23, 1959, 28; PFHOFAIC, *NFL LM,* April 23, 1959, 2 and January 22, 1959, 1–3 and 5–9; *NYT,* "Football League to Pay Pensions," April 4, 1959, 32; *NYT,* "Football Players Get Pension Terms," May 25, 1962, 39.

83. U.S. Congress, House, 1957, *OPTS*, 2,635–36.

84. U.S. Congress, House, 1957, *OPTS*, 2,509–11.

85. U.S. Congress, House, 1957, *OPTS*, 2,688.

86. U.S. Congress, House, 1957, *OPTS*, 2,711.

87. *NYT*, "Court Players Organized," January 19, 1955, 32; Hy Hurwitz, "Cousy Seeks to Form Cage Players' Group," *TSN*, January 19, 1955, Sec. 2, 9; Bob Cousy, "Pro Basketball Needs a Bill of Rights," *Sport*, April 1956, 12–13 and 68–69.

88. Ben Gould, "NBA Rigs Zone Defense Against Union," *TSN*, February 2, 1955, Sec. 2, 1–2.

89. *TSN*, "NBA Players File Demands: Seek a Limit on Exhibitions," February 1, 1956, Sec. 2, 7.

90. *NYT*, "Podoloff's Plea Heads Off Union," January 16, 1957, 37; *NYT*, "Pros Weigh Labor Tie," December 27, 1956, 31.

91. Jack Barry, "Cousy Will Quit as Player Prexy—If," *TSN*, January 15, 1958, Sec. 2, 1.

92. U.S. Congress, House, 1957, *OPTS*, 2,897–99, and 2,904.

93. U.S. Congress, House, 1957, *OPTS*, 2,877.

94. U.S. Congress, House, 1957, *OPTS*, 2,899.

95. Clif Keane, "Tip-Off Tidbits," TSN, December 25, 1957, Sec. 2, 10; Surdam, *Postwar Yankees*, 220 and 229; Lowell Reidenbaugh, "NBA Shuns Coast Expansion, Eyes Entry in Chicago," *TSN*, February 4, 1959, Sec. 2, 2; U.S. Congress, House, 1998, *Pension Fairness for NBA Pioneers*.

96. Arthur Daley, "Sports of *The Times*: Mutiny on the Bounty," *NYT*, January 23, 1964, 40.

97. *NYT*, "NBA Players Threaten Strike in Dispute Over Pension Plan," January 15, 1964, 34; Koppett, *Essence of the Game*, 236.

98. U.S. Congress, House, 1957, *OPTS*, 2,890.

99. In the words of Dana Carvey's "Church Lady" on *Saturday Night Live*: "How con-*veen*-ient."

100. U.S. Congress, House, 1957, *OPTS*, 2,691 and 2,832–36.

101. Allen Drury, "Bell Recognizes Football Union," *NYT*, August 2, 1957, 7; *NYT*, "Pro Football Union Weights N.L.R.B. Plea," August 1, 1957, 20; U.S. Congress, House, 1957, *OPTS*, 2,502.

102. *NYT*, "Bell Will See Lawyers on Written Union Pact," August 11, 1957, 154.

103. U.S. Congress, Senate, 1958, *OPTS*, 417. The owners had approved some palliatives in February 1957 before the hearings, but made the major changes in December (PFHOFAIC, *NFL LM*, February 2, 1957, 10–11 and December 2, 1957, 2).

104. U.S. Congress, Senate, 1958, *OPTS*, 711, also quoted on 406.

105. *NYT*, "Players' Group Plans $4,200,000 Suit Against National Football League," November 22, 1957, 39.

106. Joe King, "NFL Magnates Back Bell on Player Demands," *TSN*, December 11, 1957, Sec. 2, 5.

107. *NYT*, "National Football League Accedes to Demands of Players," December 3, 1957, 58; see also Al Silverman, "Will Pro Football Have Union Trouble This Year?" *Sport*, September 1957, 24–27 and 96–98. The players wanted 5 percent of the net receipts of the

league championship game to be designated for a player welfare fund (*NYT,* "Players Seek Aid Fund," December 5, 1957, 61).

108. Wolohan, "The Curt Flood Act of 1998 and Major League Baseball's Federal Antitrust Exemption," 348.

109. Murray Chass, "Deal Struck on Antitrust Bill," *NYT,* July 30, 1998, C3.

Chapter 5. Closing the Last Vestige of a "Free Market" in Labor

1. Dan Daniel, "Rickey Still Satisfied by Revised Bill—O.B. Maps Fight," *TSN*, June 15, 1960, 7 and 20.

2. U.S. Congress, Senate, 1960, *OPTS,* 69.

3. Both Lane's and Devine's quotes in J. Roy Stockton, "'Bonus Here to Stay'—Bing; 'Destroys Incentive'—Lane," *TSN,* March 22, 1961, 19–20.

4. Robert Coughlan, "Baseball's Happy Serf," *Sports Illustrated,* March 5, 1956, 38.

5. Roy Terrell, "Doom Around the Corner," *Sports Illustrated,* December 16, 1957, 36.

6. Clifford Kachline, "Minors Block Bids to Kill First-Year Draft," *TSN,* December 8, 1962, 5–6.

7. Clifford Kachline, "'Socialism Threatens Game'—O'Malley, *TSN,* December 22, 1962, 1." O'Malley's remarks conjured the surreal image of socialists conducting a draft—"The Politburo is pleased to select Fidel Castro as its number one pick."

8. Kachline, "'Socialism Threatens Game'—O'Malley, 1–2.

9. Dave Brady, "Richards Suggests 'Free Agent Draft' at Senate Hearings," *TSN,* August 5, 1959, 17 and 25; Bob Burnes, Tyros Tap Major Jackpot for Record $1,200,000 Haul," *TSN,* July 15, 1959, 2.

10. J. G. Taylor Spink, "Uneasy Majors Eye Free-Agent Draft," *TSN,* June 28, 1961, 1–2; Dan Daniel, "NL Execs Okay Grab-Bag Plan in Marathon Huddle," *TSN,* July 5, 1961, 5–6; Dave Brady, "Senate Bill-Backers to Huddle with Frick," *TSN,* July 5, 1961, 5.

11. Edwin Shrake, "Richest Bonus Baby Ever," *Sports Illustrated,* July 6, 1964, 16–21.

12. Oscar Kahan, "Majors Run Up $572,000 Tab," *TSN,* December 12, 1964, 5–6; Clifford Kachline, "Free-Agent Draft in Works; Brass Gives 'Go-Ahead,'" *TSN,* January 25, 1964, 4; Jerome Holtzman, "Majors Split on Free Agent Draft, Table Plan," *TSN,* August 22, 1964, 22.

13. Russell Schneider, "'Dodger Brass Plots against Free-Agent Draft,' Paul Claims," *TSN,* December 5, 1964, 2 and 40.

14. C. C. Johnson Spink, "'Free-Agent Draft Legal'—Antitrust Expert," *TSN,* December 12, 1964, 4.

15. Edgar Munzel, "O'Connor No. 1 Foe of Free-Agent Draft," *TSN,* April 11, 1964, 24.

16. U.S. Congress, Senate, 1964, *PSAB-1964,* 358.

17. U.S. Congress, Senate, 1964, *PSAB-1964,* 370.

18. U.S. Congress, Senate, 1965, *PSAB-1965,* 117.

19. Veeck, *Veeck as in Wreck,* 274.

20. U.S. Congress, Senate, 1958, *OPTS,* 462–63.

21. Bill Bryson, "It's 10–1 Against Draft as Equalizer," *Baseball Digest,* April 1965, 5–9.

22. Jerome Holtzman, "Majors Split on Free Agent Draft, Table Plan," *TSN,* August 22, 1964, 22.

23. Clifford Kachline, "Path Cleared for Draft of Free Agents," *TSN,* November 21, 1964, 4 and 30.

24. Charles Dexter, "The Old Scout's a Bookkeeper Now," *Baseball Digest,* August 1967, 67–71.

25. Thomas, "Baseball's Amateur Draft," 92–96.

26. Surdam, "Coase Theorem and Player Movement," 201–21.

27. *Sports Illustrated,* "The Rookies Are Stealing the Football Show," November 21, 1955, 23.

28. U.S. Congress, House, 1957, *OPTS,* 2,522.

29. U.S. Congress, House, 1957, *OPTS,* 2,515. The AFL used both a reverse-order draft and ad hoc methods to help out weaker teams (U.S. Congress, Senate, 1964, *PSAB,* 92).

30. The minutes of the 1936 League Meetings simply stated that Bell proposed the draft. The minutes did not record any discussion, unlike some other proposals (PFHOFAIC, *NFL LM,* May 19, 1935, 3).

31. U.S. Congress, House, 1957, *OPTS,* 2,696.

32. U.S. Congress, House, 1957, *OPTS,* 2,660.

33. U.S. Congress, House, 1957, *OPTS,* 2,604.

34. U.S. Congress, House, 1957, *OPTS,* quote on 2,514 and 2,728. Bell said he convinced teams to trade dissatisfied players such as Mike Jarmoluk, Tom Finnin, Andy Robustelli, and Herb Rich to teams more to their liking (U.S. Congress, House, 1957, *OPTS,* 2,730).

35. U.S. Congress, Senate, 1959, *OPTS,* 40.

36. U.S. Congress, House, 1957, *OPTS,* quote on 2,728 and Bell's remark on 2,738; U.S. Congress, Senate, 1959, *OPTS,* 38.

37. U.S. Congress, House, 1957, *OPTS,* 2,513.

38. U.S. Congress, House, 1957, *OPTS,* 2,513–14; *NYT,* "National Football League Drops Bonus Choice in Players' Draft," January 30, 1958, 28; Joe King, "NFL Scraps Bonus Picks, Okays Study of Player Pensions," *TSN,* February 5, 1958, Sec. 2, 4.

39. *NYT,* "Glick Goes First in Football Draw," November 29, 1955, 35; Tommy Devine, "QBs To Be Prize Plums in Pro Grid Draft," *TSN,* November 21, 1956, Sec. 2, 1 and 8.

40. U.S. Congress, House, 1957, *OPTS,* 2,727; Coenen, *Sandlots to the Super Bowl,* 89–90.

41. ESPN had a stroke of programming genius in figuring out that people would actually *watch* the draft on television—Bert Bell would have been amazed.

42. U.S. Congress, House, 1957, OPTS, 2,746.

43. Tex Maule, "Survivors of the Turk," *Sports Illustrated,* November 2, 1959, 48, 50, and 52.

44. Surdam, *Run to Glory,* 324.

45. U.S. Congress, House, 1957, *OPTS,* 2,539.

46. U.S. Congress, House, 1957, *OPTS,* 2,726.

47. U.S. Congress, House, 1957, *OPTS,* 2,680.

48. U.S. Congress, Senate, 1958, *OPTS,* 710.

49. U.S. Congress, Senate, 1958, *OPTS,* 406–8.

50. U.S. Congress, Senate, 1958, *OPTS,* 409.

51. U.S. Congress, Senate, 1958, *OPTS,* 438.

52. U.S. Congress, Senate, 1958, *OPTS,* 428.

53. U.S. Congress, Senate, 1958, *OPTS*, 429.

54. U.S. Congress, Senate, 1958, *OPTS*, 443.

55. U.S. Congress, Senate, 1958, *OPTS*, 451, 453–54.

56. Hugh Brown, "Hornung Top Plum Among 49 Plucked in Pro Grid Draft," *TSN*, December 5, 1956, Sec. 2, 6; *NYT*, "Green Bay Selects Hornung in Draft," November 27, 1956, 59.

57. Joe King, "Rising Pro Standards Reduce QB Field," *TSN*, November 19, 1958, Sec. 2, 1 and 2.

58. Joe King, "NFL Harvesting Bumper Crop of Brilliant Rookies," *TSN*, October 15, 1958, 1 and Sec. 2, 2.

59. Surdam, *Run to Glory*, 325.

60. Surdam, *Run to Glory*, 326.

61. Joe King, "Bell Seeks to Curb Draft Pick Deals," *TSN*, November 6, 1957, Sec. 2, 1 and 2.

62. Salzberg, *Set Shot to Slam Dunk*, 36; Barry, "Pro Basketball's Future Promising," 9; see U.S. Congress, House, 1957, *OPTS*, 2,857.

63. Surdam, *Rise of the NBA*, 147.

Chapter 6. Should Antitrust Apply to Sports?

1. PFHOFAIC, *NFL LM*, November 7, 1949, 5.

2. Bell's question found in *NYT*, "Baseball Names a Defense Group," March 23, 1957, 22; *NYT*, "Bell Meets With Leaders in Congress to Defend Pro Football Reserve Clause," March 21, 1957, 38.

3. *NYT*, "House Gets Proposal to Place Baseball Under Antitrust Laws," February 27, 1957, 43; *NYT*, "Immunity Sought for Four Sports," February 28, 1957, 34.

4. U.S. Congress, House, 1957, *OPTS*, 2,495.

5. *NYT*, "Baseball Names a Defense Group," March 23, 1957, 22.

6. *NYT*, "Football 'Story' Goes to Congress," May 7, 1957, 45.

7. U.S. Congress, House, 1957, *OPTS*, 2,734.

8. U.S. Congress, House, 1957, *OPTS*, 2,497.

9. *NYT*, "Pro Football Loop Files Brief in Anti-Trust Suit," December 23, 1951, S6; *NYT*, "Football League Denies Sherman Act Violations," February 24, 1952, S6.

10. *NYT*, "Pro Football Suit Is Resumed by U.S.," February 3, 1953, 29.

11. *NYT*, "'Death Knell' of N.F.L. Predicted If Government Wins Court Action," February 25, 1953, 30; *NYT*, "Bell Tells Court N.F.L. Needs Curbs," February 26, 1953, 35; *NYT*, "Bell Hedges on TV Destroying N.F.L.," February 27, 1953, 29.

12. *NYT*, "Bell Loop Faces Anti-Trust Suit," September 28, 1954, 36; *NYT*, "Football League Hits Court Action," January 25, 1955, 12.

13. U.S. Congress, Senate, 1958, *OPTS*, 393.

14. U.S. Congress, House, 1957, *OPTS*, 2,733.

15. *Chicago Tribune*, "Pro Football Structure Ripe for Revamping," January 4, 1953, Sec. 2, 3; Edward Prell, "Football Pros Speed Player Draft," *Chicago Tribune*, January 21, 1953,

Sec. 3, 1; Coenen, *Sandlots to the Super Bowl,* 158; *TSN,* "Only 4 Pro Clubs to Dodge Red Ink—Bell," October 28, 1953, Sec. 2, 3.

16. *NYT,* "1953 Pro Football Best Financially," December 23, 1953, 29.

17. U.S. Congress, House, 1957, *OPTS,* 2,765. Although Bell thought $900,000 was an impressive amount, he might have been advised to recall the quote attributed to Everett Dirksen, Illinois senator: "A billion here, a billion there, and pretty soon you're talking about real money" (www.brainyquote.com/quotes/authors/e/everett_dirksen.hmtl, viewed December 19, 2010.)

18. U.S. Congress, House, 1957, *OPTS,* 2,821.

19. Franklin Lewis, "Start Browns All Over Again? No—Not for McBride," *TSN,* November 19, 1952, Sec. 2, 8; U.S. Congress, House, 1957, *OPTS,* 2,733.

20. U.S. Congress, House, 1957, *OPTS,* 2,580l-2,580m; PFHOFAIC, *NFL LM,* January 24, 1947, 15.

21. U.S. Congress, House, 1957, *OPTS,* 2580l; PFHOFAIC, *NFL LM,* January 11, 1946, 3; U.S. Congress, House, 1957, *OPTS,* 2,733; U.S. Congress, Senate, 1958, *OPTS,* 399–400; for an early newspaper description of the rule, see *NYT,* "Dudley, Steelers, Offered for Sale," January 26, 1947, S1 and S4.

22. U.S. Congress, House, 1957, *OPTS,* 2,569, see also 2,531 and 2,568; U.S. Congress, Senate, 1958, *OPTS,* 400, discusses the Chicago teams and Baltimore and Washington. Bell stated: "If they get together, they can operate. Mr. Marshall and the Baltimore Colts got together and they operate within 45 miles, and the Cardinals and the Bears have been there . . . 36 years" (*NYT,* "Colts Must Pay $150,000," January 25, 1950, 42).

23. U.S. Congress, Senate, 1959, *OPTS,* 49.

24. U.S. Congress, House, 1957, *OPTS,* 2,499.

25. U.S. Congress, House, 1957, *OPTS,* 2,533–34. Owners had voted on whether to raise the minimum ticket price to $2 at the January 1951 meetings, but they did not pass the measure (*NYT,* "Player Limit Raised to 33 Men For National Football Loop Teams," January 21, 1951, 135).

26. Bell's quote in U.S. Congress, Senate, 1958, *OPTS,* 414–15; PFHOFAIC, *NFL LM,* January 21, 1959, 5.

27. Surdam, *Wins, Losses, and Empty Seats,* 96–98.

28. Surdam, *Postwar Yankees,* 39–40 and 157–59.

29. U.S. Congress, Senate, 1964, *PSAB-1964,* 33; Herbert Simons, "Farm Foe O'Connor Grabs a Plow," *Baseball Digest,* March 1946, 17–18.

30. U.S. Congress, Senate, 1960, *OPTS,* 149.

31. *NYT,* "All-America Group Shelves Plan to Use Association's Ball Park," May 21, 1946, 27; Roscoe McGowen, "Cleveland Rams Transfer Eleven to Los Angeles," *NYT,* January 13, 1946, S7 and S9.

32. PFHOFAIC, *NFL LM,* January 13, 1946, 8; April 29, 1946, 5–6; January 23, 1947, 6; July 20, 1947, 3; January 17, 1948, 8; Edward Prell, "N.F.L. Gets Coast Hint of Break," *Chicago Tribune,* January 22, 1948, Sec. 3, 1.

33. U.S. Congress, Senate, 1958, *OPTS,* 396.

34. U.S. Congress, House, 1957, *OPTS,* 2,529.

35. U.S. Congress, Senate, 1958, *OPTS,* 101.

36. U.S. Congress, Senate, 1958, *OPTS,* 183.

37. U.S. Congress, Senate, 1958, *OPTS,* 188.

38. Harold Burr, "Grid Dodgers Eye New Look," *TSN,* February 18, 1948, Sec. 2, 8.

39. Quirk and Fort, *Pay Dirt,* 244–46; Surdam, *Rise of the NBA,* 181.

40. U.S. Congress, House, 1957, *OPTS,* 2,526; MacCambridge, *America's Game,* 51; see also Herman Goldstein, "Unbeaten Browns Sweep to Third Title in Row," *TSN,* December 29, 1948, Sec. 2, 6; Joe Williams, "$25,000 to Sign, Pal? Lush Days Are Over," *TSN,* December 21, 1949, Sec. 2, 8.

41. Hal Lebovitz, "Eagles and Browns Loom as Pro Repeaters: NFL Titlists Show Power; All AAC Teams Toughies. Forty-Niners Again Appear to Be Chief Rival for Conference Champions," *TSN,* September 28, 1949, Sec. 2, 7.

42. U.S. Congress, Senate, 1964, *PSAB-1964,* 113.

43. Dan Parker quote found in Coenen, *Sandlots to the Super Bowl,* 147–48; Jack Sher, "Of Green Bay: The Story of a Great Town and a Great Team," *Sport,* December 1946, 58–68, 64 and 66; Harris, *The League,* 154.

44. Stan Baumgarter, "Talent Pileup at Top May Topple NBA," *TSN,* December 24, 1952, Sec. 2, 1.

45. U.S. Congress, House, 1957, *OPTS,* 2,928–35.

46. Surdam, *Rise of the NBA,* 99–100.

47. Surdam, *Run to Glory and Profits,* 161; Fort, *Sports Economics,* 135.

48. Maher and Gill, *Football Encyclopedia,* 113; Coenen, *Sandlots to the Super Bowl,* 123.

49. Lowe, *Kid on the Sandlot,* 30; Freedman, *Professional Sports and Anti-Trust,* 4.

50. Lowe, *Kid on the Sand Lot,* 33–36; *NYT,* "Antitrust Bill Tabled," August 2, 1958, 12.

51. Lowe, *Kid on the Sandlot,* 48–51; *NYT,* "Antitrust Exemption Voted For 4 Key Sports by Senate," September 1, 1965, 45.

Chapter 7. We Want More Baseball and Football

1. Scherer and Ross, *Industrial Market Structure,* 392.

2. Smiley, "Empirical Evidence on Strategic Entry," 167–80.

3. *Harvard Law Review,* "Super Bowl and the Sherman Act," 430.

4. Areeda and Turner, "Predatory Pricing," 697–733; Koller, "Myth of Predatory Pricing," 105–23.

5. Davis, "Self-Regulation in Baseball." Quirk also wrote, "Moves which have the effect of more evenly balancing revenue potential among league members have the long-run effect of more evenly balancing playing strengths in the league, and hence increase public interest and total league revenues. Thus, it is to be expected that such moves would be approved routinely by the league" (Quirk, "Economic Analysis of Team Movements," 47).

6. Bob Stevens, "$900,000 Poultice Soothes Coast Loop," *TSN,* December 11, 1957, 13.

7. U.S. Congress, House, 1952, *OB: Report,* 76 and 196; Topkis, "Monopoly in Professional Sports," 701; J. G. Taylor Spink, "Full Story of Browns' Near-Shift in '41," *TSN,* August 31, 1949, 3–4, 10, and 17; White, *Creating the National Pastime,* 321. On page 196 of the *Report,* Mr. Hillings questioned Will Harridge as to the American League's occasional

subsidization of the St. Louis Browns. Harridge replied that despite the subsidies, "there was no pressure put on the St. Louis Club by the American League to sell its franchise or transfer its franchise to another city."

8. Palmer, "Consolidation: A League Official's Views," for consolidation movement in 1880s; Levine, *A.G. Spalding,* 55–56; Seymour, *Baseball: The Golden Age,* 230, for thoughts about expanding and incorporating some Federal League clubs.

9. U.S. Department of Commerce 1975, *Historical Statistics,* Vol. 1, 244; Dodd, *Historical Abstract,* Vol. 1, 243–45.

10. U.S. Department of Commerce 1952, *Statistical Abstract,* Vol. I, 16–17.

11. Quirk and Fort, *Pay Dirt,* 65.

12. Dan Daniel, "3rd Loop Faces 'Name' Player Hurdle," *TSN,* July 1, 1959, 1-2 and 10; Dan Daniel, "Third Leaguers Putting Majors on Spot," *TSN,* August 5, 1959, 7–8; Dan Daniel, "11 Other Prospective Cities for New Circuit," *TSN,* August 5, 1959, 7–8; U.S. Congress, Senate, 1960, *OPTS,* 14.

13. Oscar Kahan, "Mahatma Dares Majors to Attempt Expansion," *TSN,* December 16, 1959, 9 and 12.

14. Herbert Simons, "Continental—or Just Plain CON?" *Baseball Digest,* October/November 1959, 67–70; see also Gordon Cobbledick, "Accent's Still on the 'Con,'" *Baseball Digest,* August 1960, 83–84; Furman Bisher, "Not a Case for Charity," *Baseball Digest,* August 1960, 85–86.

15. Topkis, "Monopoly in Professional Sports," 702.

16. *Harvard Law Review,* "Super Bowl and the Sherman Act," 430.

17. U.S. Congress, Senate, 1959, *OPTS,* 161; see also Dan Daniel, "Shea Says Third League Will Recruit Young Talent," *TSN,* July 29, 1959, 7; Dick Young, "Talent No Problem, 'It Will come from the World,'" *TSN,* July 1, 1959, 10.

18. U.S. Congress, Senate, 1959, *OPTS,* 73 and 78; U.S. Congress, Senate, 1960, *OPTS,* 124.

19. Dan Daniel, "Majors Flash Green Light to Third League," *TSN,* August 26, 1959, 2.

20. U.S. Congress, Senate, 1959, *OPTS,* 76; Dan Daniel, "Majors Flash Green Light to Third League," *TSN,* August 26, 1959, 2 and 8; Dan Daniel, "Gigantic Headache Looms as Promoters Begin Uphill Climb," *TSN,* September 2, 1959, 15-17; Shirley Povich, "Continental Sure to Collapse, Says Top Observers," *TSN,* December 16, 1959, 10 and 16.

21. Dan Daniel, "Angry Weiss Puts Up His Dukes for Hot Fight with CL," *TSN,* February 24, 1960, 9; Dan Daniel, "Hot Reactions to NL Bomb on Expansion," *TSN,* July 27, 1960, 2 and 8.

22. Stanley Frank, "Boss of the Yankees," *Saturday Evening Post,* April 16, 1960, 113.

23. U.S. Congress, Senate, 1960, *OPTS,* 18.

24. Johnson and Wolff, *Encyclopedia of Minor League Baseball,* 435–54.

25. U.S. Congress, Senate, 1960, *OPTS,* 102.

26. J. G. Taylor Spink, "Nats Will Shift to Minneapolis," *TSN,* October 7, 1959.

27. U.S. Congress, Senate, 1958, *OPTS,* 239; U.S. Congress, Senate, 1959, *OPTS,* 125–29; U.S. Congress, Senate, 1960, *OPTS,* 51 and 69.

28. U.S. Congress, Senate, 1960, *OPTS,* 15.

29. Dave Brady, "Frick Clears Sacks Testifying against Kefauver Sports Bill," *TSN*, May 25, 1960, 9 and 14; Dave Brady, "Rickey, Trautman, Frick Will Testify on Kefauver's Bill," *TSN*, May 18, 1960, 7. Shea's disavowal of the reserve clause may have not been too credible; would he really have countenanced a league without the clause?

30. U.S. Congress, Senate, 1959, *OPTS*, 80.

31. U.S. Congress, Senate, 1960, *OPTS*, 52.

32. U.S. Congress, Senate, 1959, *OPTS*, 58–61 and 161.

33. U.S. Congress, Senate, 1959, *OPTS*, 12; see also 8.

34. Dave Brady, "C.L. Hopes Fade after Sport Bill's Failure in Senate," *TSN*, July 6, 1960, 8.

35. Dan Daniel, "Frick Warns CL It Must Act in Hurry," *TSN*, July 6, 1960, 2 and 7–8.

36. Frederick Lieb, "NL Weighing Expansion to 10 Clubs," *TSN*, July 16, 1958, 1; Dan Daniel, "Yanks Ridicule New York's Third Major Idea," *TSN*, November 26, 1958, 5.

37. Dan Daniel, "AL Lays Expansion Groundwork, Will Study Twin-Cities' Request," *TSN*, October 28, 1959, 5-6; Dan Daniel, "Al Sets Goal—10-Club Loop for '61—Expansion Out for '60," *TSN*, November 4, 1959, 7.

38. *TSN*, "First-Year Draft Looks Like the Answer," June 1, 1960, 10; for a representative Senatorial response, see Senator Joseph O'Mahoney's remarks during the 1958 hearings in U.S. Congress, Senate, 1958, *OPTS*, 169 and 171.

39. U.S. Congress, Senate, 1958, *OPTS*, 171 and 466; Dan Daniel, "Frick Questioned on Shifts to West and Nat Situation," *TSN*, July 30, 1958, 8.

40. Jack Walsh, "Celler Warns against Washington Exit," *TSN*, September 3, 1958, 5.

41. U.S. Congress, Senate, 1958, *OPTS*, 315 and 317.

42. Halsey Hall, "Minneapolis Winds Up for Big League Pitch," *TSN*, September 3, 1958, 5; Halsey Hall, "Minneapolis Clears Snag on Majors Bid," *TSN*, September 10, 1958, 9; Jack Walsh, "Celler Warns against Washington Exit," *TSN*, September 3, 1958, 6.

43. *Sports Illustrated*, "Baseball Candor via Air Vent," September 22, 1958, 20.

44. Shirley Povich, "Sound Reasons for Rejecting Nat Shift Bid," *TSN*, October 28, 1959, 5-6, 10, and 12.

45. Bob Addie, "Nats Barely Made It—Transfer Backed by Minimum of Six Votes," *TSN*, November 2, 1960, 7 and 10.

46. Jerome Holtzman, "Big Timers Clearing Decks for Expansion," *TSN*, August 10, 1960, 3–4; Joe King, "Topping's Pitch for AL Club on Coast May Touch Off Row," *TSN*, August 17, 1960, 7.

47. *NYT*, "Rickey Rejoins Cards After 20-Year Span," October 30, 1962, 55; Louis Effrat, "National League Admits New York, Houston for 1962," *NYT*, October 18, 1960, 1.

48. Dan Daniel, "AL Moguls Okay Ten-Club League—Keep Eye on LA," *TSN*, September 7, 1960, 4 and 9; Dan Daniel, "Cronin Backed Topping, Webb in Coast Drive," *TSN*, November 9, 1960, 11 and 24; Dan Daniel, "Webb and Rickey See Peaceful Expansion before '62 Season," *TSN*, September 14, 1960, 9.

49. Ed Prell, "Senior Circuit Grabs New York, Houston," *TSN*, October 26, 1960, 2; Joe King, "Topping's Pitch for NL," *TSN*, August 17, 1960, 7; Joe King, "AL Speeds Expansion," *TSN*, November 2, 1960, 3–4; Joe King, "'No More Expansion Surprises,' Says Frick," *TSN*, November 9, 1960, 1 and 4.

50. Bob Burnes, "NL Plans Roster Cuts to Stock New Teams," *TSN,* January 18, 1961, 2.

51. U.S. Congress, House, 1957, *OPTS,* 2,854.

52. Joe King, "'NBA Needs Territorial Draft,'—Irish," *TSN,* January 30, 1957, Sec. 2, 1.

53. U.S. Congress, House, 1957, *OPTS,* 2,867–68.

54. Koppett, *24 Seconds to Shoot,* 14.

55. Koppett, *24 Seconds to Shoot,* 146–49; Surdam, *Rise of the NBA,* 59.

56. Joe King, "Bell Urges Two-Club Expansion in NFL," *TSN,* November 13, 1957, Sec. 2, 1 and 2.

57. PFHOFAIC, *NFL LM,* February 1, 1957, 4 and January 21, 1959, 3; Jack Walsh, "Marshall Raps Bell's 14-Team Plan," *TSN,* November 20, 1957, Sec. 2, 1 and 2; *NYT,* "Owners Vote to Investigate Feasibility of Expanding National Football League," January 31, 1958, 15.

58. U.S. Congress, House, 1957, *OPTS,* 2,527.

59. U.S. Congress, Senate, 1959, *OPTS,* 48. Bell apparently called Davey O'Brien of the AFL, to ask permission to mention the new league. Hunt was initially pleased that Bell was mentioning the AFL. As historian Michael MacCambridge points out, Bell was a good salesman. He may have, though, distorted the NFL's position: "The more football there is and the more advertisement of pro football, the better off we are. We are in favor of the new league." While Senator Hart was skeptical that Bell accurately depicted NFL owners' view, the commissioner persuaded the committee to not tamper with NFL practices (MacCambridge, *America's Game,* 123).

60. PFHOFAIC, *AFL LM,* September 12, 1959, 2.

61. U.S. Congress, House, 1957, *OPTS,* 2,592; college coach Bud Wilkinson thought there were sufficient players (U.S. Congress, Senate, 1958, *OPTS,* 431).

62. Joe King, "Grid Loops Will Trigger Bidding Binge," *TSN,* November 11, 1959, Sec. 2, 1 and 2; MacCambridge, *America's Game,* 125.

63. Joe King, "Grid Loops Will Trigger Bidding Binge," *TSN,* November 11, 1959, Sec. 2, 1 and 2.

64. *NYT,* "Minneapolis-St. Paul Accept 1960 Franchise in National Football League," November 23, 1959, 43; *NYT,* "Boston Gets Spot in Football Loop," November 20, 1959, 39; *NYT,* "American Football League's Draft Sets Stage for Bidding War With N.F.L.," November 24, 1959, 48.

65. Joe King, "NFL Brushing Off Rival—Loop Rumors—'Just Let 'Em Try,'" *TSN,* February 4, 1959, Sec. 2, 5.

66. *NYT,* "Halas Bids N.F.L. Add Texas Cities," August 30, 1959, S1 and 6.

67. *Sports Illustrated,* "Competition in Texas," September 14, 1959, 37; Joe King, "New League Hurls Challenge at NFL—Drafts 'Name' Stars," *TSN,* December 2, 1959, Sec. 2, 6; *NYT,* "N.F.L. Disputes New League on Texas," August 31, 1959, 27.

68. Howard Tuckner, "Expansion Move Attacked as Plot," *NYT,* October 23, 1959, 32.

69. *NYT,* "Twin Cities Drop New League Plan," January 4, 1960, 40; PFHOFAIC, *AFL LM,* November 22–23, 1959, various pages and January 27, 1960, 6; Howard Tuckner, "Foss Threatens Plea to Congress," *NYT,* January 8, 1960, 28.

70. Jack Walsh, "'Easy on Expansion,' Says Marshall, Citing Campus Grid Effect," *TSN,* November 19, 1959, Sec. 2, 2; *NYT,* "New Group Seeks N.F.L. Franchise," December 21, 1959, 35; PFHOFAIC, *NFL LM,* January 22, 1960, 13.

71. David Condon, "600 Gs Likely Tab for New NFL Franchise," *TSN,* December 16, 1959, Sec. 2, 8.

72. Louis Effrat, "National Football League Admits Dallas for '60 and Twin Cities for '61," *NYT,* January 29, 1960, 18; MacCambridge, *America's Game,* 117–18; PFHOFAIC, *NFL LM*, January 17, 1960, 2; January 18, 1960, 3–4; and January 28, 1960, 21–27.

73. *NYT,* "Rymkus to Coach Houston Eleven," January 3, 1960, S1 and S3; William Briordy, "Giants Ask A.F.L. Head for Help," *NYT,* January 14, 1960, 41; *NYT,* "Flowers Is Freed form Giant Pact," June 24, 1960, 21.

74. Louis Effrat, "2 Changes Voted by N.F.L. Owners," *NYT,* January 24, 1960, S1 and S2; *NYT,* "Giants and Lions Meet Sunday In Benefit Game at Yale Bowl," September 9, 1960, 22; Joe King, "Packers Picked to Pocket NFL Pennant," *TSN,* September 13, 1961, Sec. 2, 1.

75. Joe King, "Briefcase Battle Brewing—Pros Call in Lawyers," *TSN,* January 27, 1960, Sec. 2, 1 and 6.

76. Howard Tuckner, "American Football League Tells N.F.L. to Stay Clear of Dallas," *NYT,* January 28, 1960, 37; *TSN,* "AFL May Seek Court Action To Stop NFL's Dallas Move," February 3, 1960, Sec. 2, 2; see also *NYT,* "Rozelle Reveals Parley with Foss," February 9, 1960, 37 about a meeting between Foss and Rozelle whereby the two leagues agreed not to raid each other.

77. *NYT,* "Kefauver Says Football Quarrel Over Dallas Is a Private Battle," January 30, 1960, 15.

78. Tex Maule, "Pro Football: The infighting was vicious," *Sports Illustrated,* February 8, 1960, 50–52.

79. *NYT,* "N.F.L. Is Accused by Rival League," March 10, 1960, 42.

80. *NYT,* "U.S. View Awaited in Football Feud," April 6, 1960, 52.

81. Joe King, "Rival Loop No. 1 on NFL's List of Its Big Headaches," *TSN,* January 11, 1961, Sec. 2, 1 and 8.

82. *NYT,* "New Football Group Sues Rival League," June 18, 1960, 1 and 17; *NYT,* "Football League Is Sued by Rival," October 15, 1960, 20.

83. *NYT,* "National Football Loop Accused of Obstruction," February 27, 1962, 42; *NYT,* "Hunt Says N.F.L. Fought New Loop," February 28, 1962, 54; *NYT,* "N.F.L. Asks Data on Damage Claim," March 2, 1962, 35; *NYT,* "Lawyer Testifies in Football Suit," March 13, 1962, 43.

84. *NYT,* "Dismissal Asked in Football Case," March 14, 1962, 49; *NYT,* "National Football League Fails to Get Dismissal of Rival's Suit," March 16, 1962, 36.

85. *NYT,* "Court Rules National League Is Not a Monopoly in Pro Football," May 22, 1962, 41.

86. Richard Shepard, "A.B.C.-TV May Sign Football League," *NYT,* April 23, 1960, 47.

Chapter 8. Damn Yankees and Relocations

1. Edgar Williams, "Lowdown on Baltimore," *Baseball Digest,* May 1954, 57–62.

2. U.S. Congress, Senate, 1985, *PSCPA of 1985*, 167–68. At the time Noll wrote, the Yankees had missed the World Series for a few years, while the Knicks were contenders for

the Patrick Ewing lottery pick, which they won. The Jets have not been in the Super Bowl since Joe Namath led them there.

3. Glick, "Professional Sports Franchise Movements," first quote on 80; second quote on 81; third quote on 68, see also 82 and 84. Glick cited *San Francisco [69] Seals, Ltd. V. National Hockey League* as a case where the district court "found that the enforcement of the franchise location restraint section of the NHL constitution did not restrain trade. The Court in *San Francisco Seals*, however, viewed the league as a single economic unit" (Glick, "Professional Sports Franchise Movements," 68).

4. Edgar Munzel, "1955 Chart Adds $52,360 to Traveling Costs in AL," *TSN*, January 19, 1955, 19; Dan Daniel, "Majors Study 'Dry Run' 10-Club Chart, *TSN*, February 2, 1955, 1–2; and Voigt, *American Baseball: From the Commissioners*, 129 [1970] 1983, 129.

5. U.S. Congress, House, 1957, *OPTS*, 1388–92, 1404, 1421–22, 2580l, and 2938; Surdam, *Postwar Yankees*, 246.

6. Barrow, *My Fifty Years in Baseball*, 56; Surdam, *Wins, Losses, and Empty Seats*, 148.

7. U.S. Congress, Senate, 1959, *OPTS*, 180.

8. Carl Lundquist, "Fare Hike to Speed Majors Shift to Air," *TSN*, August 29, 1956, 1–2.

9. U.S. Congress, House, 1952, *OB: Hearings*, 1,620–24; Henderson, "Los Angeles," 262; Al Wolf, "P.C.L. Jittery," *Baseball Digest*, November 1951, 11–12.

10. Surdam, *Postwar Yankees*, 197.

11. Lyall Smith, "What Did the Browns Expect?" *Baseball Digest*, September 1948, 51; U.S. Congress, House, 1952, *OB: Report*, 85, 95, 194, and 197.

12. H. G. Salsinger, "No Chance for N.L. in Detroit," *Baseball Digest*, April 1953, 23.

13. J. G. Taylor Spink, "Full Story of Browns' Near-Shift in '41," *TSN*, August 31, 1949, 3–4, 10 and 17; Ray Gillespie, "Coast Missed Major Ball by Day in '41," *TSN*, December 4, 1957, 5–6; U.S. Congress, House, 1952, *OB: Report*, 76, 107, and 196.

14. Thorn, Palmer, and Gershman, *Total Baseball*, 76–77; Surdam, *Postwar Yankees*, 194–95; U.S. Congress, House, 1957, *OPTS*, 1957, 2,048–52.

15. Veeck, *Hustler's Handbook*, 303–4 and 308.

16. *NYT*, "League to Discuss Athletics' Plight," October 12, 1954, pt. 3, 32.

17. *NYT*, "Cash Bid Decisive Factor in Authorization of Athletics' Shift to Kansas City," October 14, 1954, 39; Harry Simmons, "Dodger-Giant Shift Boosts NL Travel 90 Pct," *TSN*, September 4, 1957, 1 and 6.

18. Surdam, *Postwar Yankees*, 44–54.

19. Ernest Mehl, "'A's Will Develop Stars and Keep Them'—Finley," *TSN*, December 28, 1960, 7 and 14.

20. Ernest Mehl, "Big Spender Finley Offers New Comfort for A's Fans," *TSN*, March 15, 1961, 5.

21. Edgar Munzel, "Majors Guarantee to Back 100 Minor Clubs," *TSN*, June 2, 1962, 13.

22. Joe McGuff, "A's Cancellation Clause, Based on Attendance, to Be Challenged," *TSN*, June 22, 1963, 19.

23. U.S. Congress, Senate, 1964, *PSAB-1964*, 5; see also 6, 20, 137–38.

24. U.S. Congress, Senate, 1964, *PSAB-1964*, 22.

25. U.S. Congress, Senate, 1964, *PSAB-1964*, 25.

26. Clifford Kachline, "AL Ready to Bid Finley Farewell," *TSN*, January 18, 1964, 1-2 and 4; Joe King, "'Ink Kaycee Pact or Lose AL Franchise,' Owners Tell Finley," *TSN*, January 25, 1964, 4.

27. Joe McGuff, "Finley Sets Lease Terms for A's Park," *TSN*, January 4, 1964, 18; Ernest Mehl, "White Flag Hoisted by Finley—Can Kaycee Rebuild Fan Faith?" *TSN*, March 7, 1964, 8.

28. *NYT*, "Braves Set National League Attendance Mark," September 21, 1953, 29; Edgar Munzel, "Braves' Bonanza to Start Trend to Rich Rural Area, Says Giles," *TSN*, September 30, 1953, 37.

29. Bob Broeg, "Braves' Doorbell Rings—It's Atlanta," *TSN*, August 3, 1963, 7.

30. Bob Wolf, "Will Braves Stay in Milwaukee? 'It's Up to Fans,' Perini Declares," *TSN*, September 22, 1962, 11; for a description of the economics of the Braves' sale, see Veeck, *Hustler's Handbook*, 330–39.

31. Ernest Mehl, "K.C. Ranked Right behind Atlanta as Lush Video Market," *TSN*, October 24, 1964, 4; Bob Broeg, "Braves' Doorbell Rings—It's Atlanta," *TSN*, August 3, 1963, 7; Clifford Kachline, "Atlanta Whiffs, Renews Bid for Big-Time Clubs," *TSN*, July 20, 1963, 3 and 6.

32. John Logue, "Atlanta's Stadium Zooms Off Ground, Heads for Reality," *TSN*, June 22, 1963, 4.

33. C. C. Johnson Spink, "Braves' Shift Needs Only Okay by NL," *TSN*, July 11, 1964, 1.

34. Bob Wolf, "Milwaukee Solon Wants TV Pool, Expansion; Frick Vetoes Idea," *TSN*, August 1, 1964, 11; Bob Wolf, "Legal Red Tape Snarls Braves' Moving Plan," *TSN*, November 7, 1964, 7; Veeck, *Hustler's Handbook*, 323–24.

35. Bob Wolf, "'Unpack,' NL Tells Itchy-Footed Braves," *TSN*, November 21, 1964, 7-8.

36. U.S. Congress, Senate, 1965, *PSAB-1965*, quote on 103; see also 44 and 106.

37. U.S. Congress, Senate, 1965, *PSAB-1965*, 105.

38. Surdam, *Postwar Yankees*, 199–200; Quinn and Surdam, "Case of the Missing Fans."

39. Quirk and Fort, *Pay Dirt*, 405–6.

40. Val Adams, "Big Pitch at Networks Still in Nielsen Curve," *NYT*, August 15, 1964, 14.

41. Arthur Daley, "A Strange Union," *NYT*, August 16, 1964, Sec. 5, 2.

42. U.S. Congress, Senate, 1965, *PSAB-1965*, 2.

43. Stanton's quote in U.S. Congress, Senate, 1965, *PSAB-1965*, 8 and *Broadcasting*, 22 February 1965, 64–65.

44. Richard Rutter, "Big-League Deal Is Minor to CBS," *NYT*, August 15, 1964, 14; Lester Smith, "CBS Deal Pinpoints Soaring Price Tag on Big-Time Clubs, *TSN*, November 28, 1964, 11.

45. Jack Gould, "Yank Deal's TV Rating," *NYT*, August 15, 1964, 14; U.S. Congress, Senate, 1965, *PSAB-1965*, 34; William Furlong, "A Sad Day for Baseball," *Sports Illustrated*, September 21, 1964, 26.

46. Ralph Ray, "Bomber Sale Stirs Bees' Nest of Boos," *TSN*, August 29, 1964, 1–2 and 6

47. Joseph Durso, "All Eyes in Sports Seek the Why for New Gleam in CBS's Eye," *NYT*, August 16, 1964, Sec. 5, 2.

48. William Wallace, "CBS Buys 80% of Stock in Yankee Baseball Team," *NYT,* August 14, 1964, 1 and 18.

49. C. C. Johnson Spink, "Finley, Allyn Carry Fight against Yankee Sale to Justice Department," *TSN,* October 10, 1964, 6; Lester Smith, "All AL Owners Asked to Reveal Holdings in CBS," *TSN,* December 5, 1964, 26.

50. U.S. Congress, Senate, 1965, *PSAB-1965,* 64.

51. U.S. Congress, Senate, 1965, *PSAB-1965,* 36 and 61. Senator Hart's wife, Jane, was the daughter of Walter Briggs, owner of baseball's Detroit Tigers.

52. Ralph Ray, "Bomber Sale Stirs Bees' Nest of Boos," *TSN,* August 29, 1964, 1–2 and 6.

53. U.S. Congress, Senate, 1965, *PSAB-1965,* 34; Til Ferdenzi, "Topping and Webb to Remain in Posts as Bomber Execs," *TSN,* August 29, 1964, 2.

54. Quirk and Fort, *Pay Dirt,* 406.

Chapter 9. Professional Sports Team Community Protection Acts

1. U.S. Congress, Senate, 1986, *PSAI,* 384.

2. U.S. Congress, Senate, 1986, *PSAI,* 390; see also 377 for a detailed discussion of the Antitrust Division's opinion regarding relocating franchises.

3. En.wikipedia.org/wiki/Major_League_Soccer, viewed July 4, 2013; www.aagbl.org/index.cfm/pages/league/12/league-history, viewed July 4, 2013.

4. Apparently legislators did not worry about the public interest when a team that owned its stadium relocated (U.S. Congress, Senate, 1986, *PSAI,* 8).

5. U.S. Congress, Senate, 1984, *PSTCPA,* 2.

6. U.S. Congress, Senate, 1984, *PSTCPA,* 51. Senator Long opposed free market operation in the NFL, because he feared the teams in Los Angeles and New York would dominate and, "we [the New Orleans Saints] would just get stomped from now till kingdom come. I would not live long enough to see us have a winning football team in New Orleans." As prescience goes, Long was close to the mark, as he died in 2003 and never witnessed the Saints in the Super Bowl (U.S. Congress, Senate, 1985, *PSCPA of 1985,* 88).

7. U.S. Congress, Senate, 1984, *PSTCPA,* 3 and 53; U.S. Congress, House, 1984, *PSTCPA,* 53.

8. U.S. Congress, House, 1984, *PSTCPA,* 56.

9. Robert Brown, American League President, pointed out that the stipulation of losses for three years might create perverse incentives: "Instituting a financial test alone will merely encourage relocation rather than prevent it." A Charles O. Finley might purposely lose small amounts of money to justify relocating his team (U.S. Congress, Senate, 1984, *PSTCPA,* 125).

10. U.S. Congress, House, 1984, *PSTCPA,* 12. There were several alternative bills; most were sponsored by legislators whose constituents had lost or gained a professional sports team (U.S. Congress, House, 1984, *PSTCPA,* 4).

11. U.S. Congress, Senate, 1985, *PSCPA of 1985,* 47.

12. U.S. Congress, Senate, 1986, *PSAI,* 207–8.

13. U.S. Congress, Senate, 1986, *PSAI,* 32; for a description of the various bills being considered in 1986, see page 323 of the same hearing. Metzenbaum's rant was reminiscent

of Peter Finch's portrayal of newsman Howard Beale in the 1976 movie, *Network,* who exhorted people to yell, "I'm mad as hell, and I'm not going to take this anymore!"

14. U.S. Congress, Senate, 1984, *PSTCPA,* 29. A former NFL player, Bernard Parrish, had earlier gone much further than Stark. Parrish suggested that the franchises should be owned by municipal or public service entities and that any profits would go to improve the inner cities, "Pro football could do a great deal more for the cities than to milk them for a while and then move to the suburbs" (U.S. Congress, Senate, 1972, *Professional Basketball, Part 2,* 918). Parrish's suggestion was, at best, quixotic.

15. U.S. Congress, Senate, 1986, *PSAI,* 91.

16. U.S. Congress, House, 1984, *PSTCPA,* 23 and 58.

17. U.S. Congress, House, 1984, *PSTCPA,* 59.

18. U.S. Congress, House, 1984, *PSTCPA,* 63.

19. U.S. Congress, Senate, 1986, *PSAI,* 289.

20. U.S. Congress, Senate, 1986, *PSAI,* 290–91. Gary Roberts believes the court erred in its opinion: "Logic compels the conclusion that if league members agree to schedule one club's home games in one city rather than another in which a second member is located, the impact on intraleague 'competition' is the same regardless of whether the rejected city is one *to which* or *from which* the club would have moved. If disallowing the Raiders' move to Los Angeles diminished intra-NFL 'competition between the Raiders and the Los Angeles Rams, then allowing the Raiders to move from Oakland diminished just as much intra—NFL 'competition' between the Raiders and the San Francisco 49ers." He concludes, "the Raiders holding coupled with the Grizzlies dictum effectively bars a league from preventing relocation to an area where another member club is already based, or from declining to grant a new franchise to any applicant seeking one in an area where another member club is based; doing so in either case would expose the league to enormous antitrust risks" (Roberts, "Sports Leagues and the Sherman Act," 17–18).

21. U.S. Congress, Senate, 1986, *PSAI,* 292.

22. Supreme Court of the United States, *American Needle, Inc. v. National Football League et al.,* 12–13.

23. U.S. Congress, Senate, 1986, *PSAI,* 295.

24. U.S. Congress, Senate, 1986, *PSAI,* 297.

25. U.S. Congress, Senate, 1984, *PSTCPA,* 45.

26. U.S. Congress, Senate, 1986, *PSAI,* 352, see also page 343.

27. U.S. Congress, Senate, 1986, *PSAI,* 409 and 412. Presumably Senator Arlen Specter of Pennsylvania would have disagreed with Rothenberg. In his statement to the 1986 committee, he wrote, "I respond to that [why Congress should be interested in the owners' actions] by pointing out the enormous economic influence of professional football in our country, the tremendous number of jobs which professional sports provides and are related to in terms of tourism and hotels and restaurants" (U.S. Congress, Senate, 1986, *PSAI,* 12).

28. U.S. Congress, House, 1984, *PSTCPA,* 67.

29. U.S. Congress, Senate, 1984, *PSTCPA,* 61. Representative Fortney H. "Pete" Stark recalled that the 1966 merger bill stipulated that there would be two teams in the Bay Area:

one in San Francisco and the other in Oakland (U.S. Congress, House, 1984, *PSTCPA*, 51; see U.S. Congress, Senate, 1985, *PSCPA of 1985*, 141).

30. U.S. Congress, Senate, 1984, *PSTCPA*, 160.

31. U.S. Congress, House, 1984, *PSTCPA*, 47, also 32; U.S. Congress, Senate, 1985, *PSCPA of 1985*, 121. For a collection of articles discussing aspects of professional sports and stadiums, see Noll and Zimbalist, editors, *Sports, Jobs, and Taxes*.

32. U.S. Congress, Senate, 1985, *PSCPA of 1985*, 162.

33. U.S. Congress, Senate 1984, *PSTCPA*, 55.

34. U.S. Congress, Senate, 1984, *PSTCPA*, 55.

35. U.S. Congress, Senate, 1984, *PSTCPA*, 56.

36. U.S. Congress, Senate, 1985, *PSCPA of 1985*, 66.

37. U.S. Congress, Senate, 1985, *PSCPA of 1985*, 103.

38. U.S. Congress, Senate, 1984, *PSTCPA*, 62.

39. U.S. Congress, House, 1984, *PSTCPA*, 84.

40. George VuKasin, Oakland Coliseum Board of Commissioners president, marveled at the court's criticism of the three-quarters/unanimity rule: "not one NFL owner voted to allow the Raiders to move. When reasonable logic is applied to this fact, I fail to see the validity of the court's argument or the jury's decision" (U.S. Congress, Senate, 1985, *PSCPA of 1985*, 157). A year later, Jay Moyer made a similar argument (U.S. Congress, Senate, 1986, *PSAI*, 94). In both cases, though, they neglected to mention that the vote was 22–0, with five members abstaining (U.S. Congress, Senate, 1986, *PSAI*, 290).

41. U.S. Congress, Senate, 1986, *PSAI*, 40.

42. U.S. Congress, Senate, 1986, *PSAI*, 15, 21, and 63, see 59 for MLB rules.

43. Pete Rozelle claimed that in the Raiders' case, the "majority of the Ninth Circuit panel thus noted that the Raiders' move from Oakland to Los Angeles produced 'competition between the L.A. Coliseum and the Oakland Coliseum for the tenancy for the Raiders, and its ruling affirmed the jury's apparent conclusion that bidding by cities and stadiums for NFL tenants was warranted'" (U.S. Congress, Senate, 1986, *PSAI*, 26; see also page 235 for Senator Al Gore's reiteration of the artificial scarcity argument).

44. U.S. Congress, Senate, 1984, *PSTCPA*, 77.

45. U.S. Congress, Senate, 1985, *PSCPA of 1985*, 153.

46. Harry Hughes, governor of Maryland, was one of several witnesses who made this point (U.S. Congress, Senate, 1985, *PSCPA of 1985*, 129). Hughes may have overstated his case, since the AFL's birth lent an impetus for the NFL's expansion into Dallas and Minnesota.

47. U.S. Congress, House, 1984, *PSTCPA*, 50.

48. U.S. Congress, House, 1984, *PSTCPA*, 51.

49. U.S. Congress, House, 1984, *PSTCPA*, 91. From his phrasing, it appears Tagliabue meant inflation-adjusted ticket prices, not the face value. NFL ticket price information is difficult to obtain. The league used to publicize them in *The Sporting News*, while individual teams listed ticket prices in their programs. With the advent of a uniform league publication, *Pro*, ticket price information disappeared. Pete Rozelle testified that, "between 1970 and 1980, NFL ticket prices, in constant dollar terms, actually declined from $6.06

in 1970 to the equivalent of $5.05 in 1980" (U.S. Congress, Senate, 1985, *PSCPA of 1985,* 75). Given the Nixon-era imposition of a freeze on wages and prices, this might have been true for the first half of the 1970s. Edward Bennett Williams testified in 1973 that he had to petition the Price Board to raise the Redskins' ticket prices (U.S. Congress, House, 1973, *Professional Sports Blackouts,* 227–28).

50. U.S. Congress, House, 1984, *PSTCPA,* 89.

51. Fort, *Sports Economics,* 143–45.

52. U.S. Congress, House, 1984, *PSTCPA,* 95.

53. U.S. Congress, House, 1984, *PSTCPA,* 96.

54. U.S. Congress, Senate, 1984, *PSTCPA,* 153, 155; U.S. Congress, Senate, 1985, *PSCPA of 1985,* 54–56. In the case of the NBA, that league fought a four-year legal battle with the State of Louisiana and the agency in charge of the New Orleans Superdome over the relocation of the moribund New Orleans Jazz to Utah. The league also fought a relocation of the San Diego team to Los Angeles (U.S. Congress, Senate, 1984, *PSTCPA,* 153).

55. U.S. Congress, Senate, 1984, *PSTCPA,* 98–99 and 104; U.S. Congress, Senate, 1985, *PSCPA of 1985,* 105.

56. U.S. Congress, Senate, 1985, *PSCPA of 1985,* 137 and 146.

57. U.S. Congress, Senate, 1985, *PSCPA of 1985,* 59.

58. U.S. Congress, Senate, 1986, *PSAI,* 141. Wisconsin legislators frequently echoed the NFL's boast that revenue sharing allowed Green Bay to stay in the league; they wanted to ensure that revenue sharing continued (U.S. Congress, Senate, 1985, *PSCPA of 1985,* 7). No one was so impolite as to suggest that Green Bay fans were watching a heavily subsidized team, thanks to fans in other cities.

59. Horowitz, "Sports Broadcasting," 307–8.

60. U.S. Congress, Senate, 1986, *PSAI,* 74.

61. U.S. Congress, Senate, 1985, *PSCPA of 1985,* 105; Gene Upshaw had just previously made a similar argument, see page 98–99. Allen made an interesting observation regarding Green Bay. The team was a community-owned, nonprofit entity with some restrictions on relocating the team. Allen thought this aspect was more responsible for the team's survival and stability than the revenue-sharing policies, which he disliked (U.S. Congress, Senate, 1985, *PSCPA of 1985,* 105).

62. U.S. Congress, Senate, 1985, *PSCPA of 1985,* 102.

63. U.S. Congress, Senate, 1986, *PSAI,* 403 and 405.

64. MacCambridge, *America's Game,* 358.

65. Robert McG. Thomas Jr. "One Argued for Major Award," *NYT,* July 30, 1986; Michael Janofsky was the *New York Times* reporter covering the trial. See his "N.F.L. Found Liable on Only One Charge—Confusion on Award," *NYT,* July 30, 1986, A1 and "Final Stages Near in U.S.F.L. Trial," *NYT,* July 21, 1986, C11.

66. U.S. Congress, Senate, 1985, *PSCPA of 1985,* 95.

67. U.S. Congress, Senate, 1984, *PSTCPA,* 69; U.S. Congress, Senate, 1986, *PSAI,* 106.

68. U.S. Congress, Senate, 1986, *PSAI,* 174.

69. U.S. Congress, Senate, 1985, *PSCPA of 1985,* 102.

70. U.S. Congress, Senate, 1986, *PSAI,* 138.

Chapter 10. Professional Team Sports Grapples with Radio and Television

1. Surdam, *Postwar Yankees,* 128–31; Surdam, *Run to Glory,* 248.

2. New York Yankee Base Ball Club, *Yankee Baseball Collection,* "Minutes of a Special Meeting of the Board of Directors, October 24, 1939," and "Minutes of February 20, 1941 Meeting;" Surdam, *Wins, Losses, and Empty Seats,* 198–99.

3. Surdam, *Postwar Yankees,* 336.

4. U.S. Congress, Senate, 1965, *Professional Sports Antitrust Bill-1965,* 50.

5. Veeck, *Hustler's Handbook,* 303.

6. Parente, "Interdependence of Sports and Television," 130–31.

7. *NYT,* "Frick Appoints Six to Study Radio-TV," December 31, 1952, 18; Harold Rosenthal, "TV to Demand Top Games," *TSN,* March 14, 1964, 5; Roone Arledge and Gilbert Rogin, "It's Sports," *Sports Illustrated,* April 25, 1966, 100; Dave Brady, "Cost of Aircasting Majors' Tilts Soar to $75 Million," *TSN,* March 15, 1961, 15; Oscar Kahan, "Sponsors of TV Games to Shell Out $39 Million," *TSN,* March 24, 1962, 24.

8. U.S. Congress, House, 1961, *Telecasting of Professional Sports Contests,* 64–66; Dave Brady, "Frick with Eye to Future, Backs Celler's TV Bill," *TSN,* September 6, 1961, 27.

9. PFHOFAIC, *NFL LM,* January 24, 1947, 12; January 17, 1948; January 20, 1949, 5; and June 2, 1950, 10; *NYT,* "The News of Radio," July 19, 1947, 24; Coenen, *Sandlots to the Super Bowl,* 153; for the Chicago Bears' early experiences with television, see Peterson, *Pigskin,* 196.

10. *TSN,* Col. MacPhail and Television," September 3, 1947, 12.

11. Davis, *Papa Bear,* 269–70. Sports historian Jeff Davis credits Halas for convincing Bert Bell that the league needed to enforce a seventy-five-mile radius blackout of telecasts of home games.

12. Surdam, *Run to Glory,* 339.

13. Quote in Isaacs, *Vintage NBA,* 109; *NYT,* "The News of Radio," May 19, 1948, 54; *New York Knickerbockers program,* "Knicks' 18 Garden League Games This Season Will be Televised," October 28, 1950, 11.

14. Isaacs, *Vintage NBA,* 114.

15. First quote in Peterson, *Cages to Jump Shots,* 173–74; second quote in Pluto, *Tall Tales,* 23; National Basketball Association, James M. O'Brien Historical Research Center, Professional Men, NBA, "NBA Bulletin #33a," October 21, 1949.

16. U.S. Congress, House, 1957, *OPTS,* 2,883–84. Because NBA owners divided home appearances on television on an equal basis, revenue from the national television contract would not affect any team's marginal revenue product.

17. Dan Daniel, "Television Clause Snags Player Contract," *TSN,* September 25, 1946, 1–2; Edgar Munzel, "2 Chi Owners Blast Player Bid for TV $s," *TSN,* November 26, 1958, 4.

18. Dave Anderson, "Is Pro Football Heading for a Fall?" *Sport,* July 1964, 16.

19. Dan Daniel, "TV Must Go," *Baseball Magazine,* November 1952, 36.

20. Milt Richman, "War, Weather Cloud 1951 Outlook," *Baseball Digest,* February 1951, 25.

21. Dan Daniel, "TV Must Go," *Baseball Magazine,* November 1952, 6; *TSN,* "Yanks' Televising of Game in Philly Part of Survey of Effect on Gate," October 1, 1952, 8; *NYT,* "Yankees Reducing Home Games on TV," January 28, 1953, 35.

22. Craig, "Organized Baseball," 252; Jordan, "Long-Range Effect," 46–65.

23. Surdam, "Television and Minor League Baseball," 61–77; Surdam, *Postwar Yankees,* 141.

24. *NYT,* "Baltimore Five to Halt Telecasting of Contests," December 23, 1948, 27.

25. U.S. Congress, House, 1957, *OPTS,* 2,524; see also Tex Maule, "Look How the Owners Smile," *Sports Illustrated,* March 10, 1958, 46–47.

26. PFHOFAIC, *NFL LM,* January 21, 1951, 34 and 36. The owners apparently did not note the irony that their recent victory over the AAFC put them over the 75 percent mark; the NFL owners do not appear to have developed a sense of irony.

27. *NYT,* "Bell Loop Faces Anti-Trust Suit," September 28, 1954, 36; *NYT,* "Football League Hits Court Action," January 25, 1955, 12.

28. Quotes from *NYT,* "Radio Big Help to Pro Football, Station Operator Says at Trial," February 10, 1953, 34; *NYT,* "Station Manager Tells of N.F.L. Ban," February 4, 1953, 37; see also *NYT,* "Network Founder Tells in Court How Sports Curbs Hurt Business," February 5, 1953, 28; *NYT,* "Network Founder Tells in Court How Sports Curbs Hurt Business," February 5, 1953, 28. McLendon wanted to be part of the NFL monopoly, demonstrating that most people are not inherently against monopolies, only monopolies that excluded them.

29. *NYT,* "Pro Football Suit Recessed to Feb. 24," February 11, 1953, 41.

30. *NYT,* "Government Establishes Two Important Points During Football Suit," January 28, 1953, 34; see also *NYT,* "Anti-Trust Action Against National Football League Starts at Philadelphia," January 27, 1953, 30.

31. *NYT,* "'Death Knell' of N.F.L. Predicted If Government Wins Court Action," February 25, 1953, 30.

32. Frank Finch, "Ram Playoff Without TV Pulls 83,501," *TSN,* December 27, 1950, Sec. 2, 8; see Frank Finch, "Rams Draw Millions to Games—by Video," *TSN,* September 27, 1950, Sec. 2, 7 for how Rams estimated the contract figures; Peterson, *Pigskin,* 191; MacCambridge, *America's Game,* 67 and 69; *NYT,* "'Death Knell' of N.F.L. Predicted," 30. The Rams' win-loss records were almost the same in 1949 and 1950. Peterson gives an account of this fiasco, claiming that Admiral paid $307,000 to make up the shortfall in attendance; his account's figures do not completely coincide with the attendance figures shown in Maher and Gill's *Pro Football Encyclopedia* (Peterson, *Pigskin,* 197).

33. *Los Angeles Times,* "Rams-Bears Game Drew Record Crowd," December 19, 1950, pt. IV, 2.

34. *NYT,* "Bell Hedges on TV Destroying N.F.L.," February 27, 1953, 29.

35. *NYT,* "Bell Hedges on TV Destroying N.F.L.," February 27, 1953, 29.

36. *NYT,* "Mistrial Motion by N.F.L. Denied," March 3, 1953, 31.

37. *NYT,* "Football Giants Call TV Harmful to Attendance," March 4, 1953, 33; *Chicago Tribune,* "Giants Ask TV Sellout Guarantee," March 4, 1953, Sec. 3, 1.

38. Peterson, *Pigskin,* 198.

39. *NYT,* "Marshall Charges Anti-Trust Suit Is Inspired by Radio, TV Interests," March 5, 1953, 30.

40. The information supplied to Congress in 1957 differs from Kerbawy's figures: $114,754 net income before taxes and $85,980 in radio and television revenues (U.S. Congress, House, 1957, *OPTS,* 2,562–65).

41. *NYT,* "Lion Football Broadcasts Brought $113,000 of $114,000 Profit Last Year, Court Told," March 6, 1953, 31.

42. U.S. Congress, House, 1961, *TPSC,* 16–21 contains a copy of Grim's ruling in "United States v. National Football League;" *NYT,* "Court Limits Pro Football's Control of Television to the Area of Home Games," November 13, 1953, 30.

43. *NYT,* "Court Limits Pro Football's Control of Television to the Area of Home Games," November 13, 1953, 30.

44. PFHOFAIC, *NFL LM,* January 27, 1954, 1–2.

45. PFHOFAIC, *NFL LM,* January 20, 1960, 9.

46. *NYT,* "TV Blackout Rule Kept for Play-Offs," December 26, 1957, 35; *NYT,* "TV Inquiry Requested," January 1, 1958, 34; *NYT,* "Congress Action to Aid Minors in TV Fight Is Held Unlikely," January 15, 1958, 35; *Broadcasting,* "Trouble for Sports Broadcasting," July 21, 1958, 29–31.

47. *Broadcasting,* "Sports Exemption: New measure offered for antitrust relief," August 24, 1959, 70–71.

48. U.S. Congress, Senate, 1959, *OPTS,* 38; see also page 44 for his additional testimony on television blackouts.

49. Tommy Devine, "Television 'Take' Demand for Split, College Problem," *TSN,* October 26, 1949, Sec. 2, 2.

50. U.S. Congress, Senate, 1965, *PSAB-1965,* 117.

51. PFHOFAIC, *NFL LM,* January 21, 1951, 39. As early as 1942, the Redskins suggested that "all contracts for broadcasting and televising of football games shall be made by the Commissioner. The moneys derived from such contract shall be divided equally among the members of the league." The other owners were not enthusiastic, so the Redskins withdrew the motion (PFHOFAIC, *NFL LM,* March 26, 1942, 5). During the 1943 meetings, the NFL's Executive Committee recommended changing the bylaws to define "receipts of the game," for purposes of revenue sharing, to include "any money derived from television;" however, no action was taken on this recommendation (PFHOFAIC, *NFL LM,* April 6, 1943, 2).

52. PFHOFAIC, *NFL LM,* January 20, 1949, 4.

53. Oscar Kahan, "Majors Wrapping 'Attractive Packet' to Boost Air Income," *TSN,* March 14, 1964, 5; Dave Brady, "Rich Clubs Agree to Divvy TV Pot," *TSN,* February 8, 1964, 1 and 4.

54. Shirley Povich, "Lush TV Fees," *Baseball Digest,* March 1965, 34.

55. Roscoe McGowen, "'Pay TV Costly? Bleacher Prices OK'—O'Malley," *TSN,* May 18, 1955, 2.

56. Lowell Reidenbaugh, "Eight Pitchers among Ten Drafted by Majors," *TSN,* December 7, 1955, 12.

57. Clifford Kachline, "Pay-TV of Giant, Dodger Games Likely in '64," *TSN,* August 31, 1963, 1 and 6.

58. *Broadcasting,* "Joker Found in Sports Bill: Eight hidden words would give professional leagues vast control and permit pay-tv," August 17, 1959, 70 and 72; U.S. Congress, Senate, 1958, *OPTS,* 383.

59. U.S. Congress, Senate, 1958, *OPTS,* 139–40; Carl Lundquist, "'Fans Will Never Have to Pay for Series TV' Weaver Says," *TSN,* October 31, 24.

60. Surdam, *Postwar Yankees,* 134–35.

61. U.S. Congress, House, 1957, *OPTS,* 2,525; Bell repeated this refrain in Art Morrow, "N.F.L. Eyeing Gate Record; 1,500,000 in Advance Sale," *TSN,* October 8, 1958, Sec. 2, 9; Jim Beach, "What Pay-TV Means to You," *Sport,* April 1958, 34–35 and 87–88. A year later, the committee again asked Bell what the league's stance on pay television was, perhaps wondering if it had changed, and he related how he wanted to let children attend games for free (U.S. Congress, Senate, 1959, *OPTS,* 47).

62. *NYT,* "Bell Hedges on TV Destroying N.F.L.," February 27, 1953, 29.

63. Joe King, "Bell Opposes Pay-TV for Pro Football Tilts," *TSN,* January 14, 1959, 1 and Sec. 2, 1. Bell informed owners that forty million people watched the 1958 League Championship Game, and that 49 percent of the radios in New York City were tuned to the game (PFHOFAIC, *NFL LM,* January 21, 1959, 5).

64. *Broadcasting,* "Pay TV-Baseball Tie-Up Seen," August 25, 1958, 78. Frick was Bell's match for dire hyperbole.

65. *Broadcasting,* "Celler Hits Sports Bill Lobby," July 28, 1958, 76 and 78.

66. U.S. Congress, Senate, 1958, *OPTS,* 749.

67. U.S. Congress, House, 1966, *PFLM,* 85.

68. U.S. Congress, House, 1966, *PFLM,* 93–94 and 98.

69. U.S. Congress, House, 1966, *PFLM,* 127.

Chapter 11. Baseball and Broadcasting

1. Surdam, "Television and Minor League Baseball," 66–69.

2. U.S. Congress, Senate, 1958, *OPTS,* 105.

3. U.S. Congress, House, 1952, *OB: Hearings,* 1,616 and 1,625.

4. U.S. Congress, House, 1952, *OB: Hearings,* 168, 197–98, 381–82, and 462.

5. U.S. Congress, Senate, 1958, *OPTS,* 185 and 209; U.S. Congress, Senate, 1960, *OPTS,* 139.

6. U.S. Congress, Senate, 1958, *OPTS,* 219; J. G. Spink, "Limit Radio, Drop Farms, Griff Urges," *TSN,* August 4, 1954, 1–2.

7. U.S. Congress, Senate, 1960, *OPTS,* 119 for Frick quote; U.S. Congress, Senate, 1958, *OPTS,* 241 and 244.

8. U.S. Congress, Senate, 1959, *OPTS,* 61.

9. Jack Walsh, "'TV Curb Needed to Save Game'—Frick," *TSN,* July 23, 1958, 7.

10. U.S. Congress, Senate, 1958, *OPTS,* 158–60 and 164; U.S. Congress, Senate, 1959, *OPTS,* 57.

11. U.S. Department of Commerce 1953, *Census of Housing,* Vol. 1, 30.
12. Surdam, "Television and Minor League Baseball," 66–74.
13. U.S. Congress, Senate, 1953, *BTBG,* 5 and 11.
14. U.S. Congress, Senate, 1953, *BTBG,* 14.
15. U.S. Congress, Senate, 1953, *BTBG,* 1.
16. U.S. Congress, Senate, 1953, *BTBG,* 3.
17. U.S. Congress, Senate, 1953, *BTBG,* 4.
18. U.S. Congress, Senate, 1953, *BTBG,* 4–5. Senator Johnson quoted baseball commissioner Ford Frick: "Destroy the minors and you destroy the majors," employing, as many sports officials would, the specter of a dire chain of reactions. Johnson continued in this vein by claimed that if only the Major Leagues survived, "baseball would wither and die on the vine, for baseball is and forever should be an American grassroots institution" (U.S. Congress, Senate, 1953, *BTBG,* 6).
19. U.S. Congress, Senate, 1953, *BTBG,* 2–7.
20. U.S. Congress, Senate, 1953, *BTBG,* 11–12. Frick repeated Johnson's belief a few minutes later, with his statement, "If one club has trouble, the league has trouble; if the league has trouble, the classification is in trouble; if the classification is in trouble, the structure is in trouble" (U.S. Congress, Senate, 1953, *BTBG,* 17).
21. U.S. Congress, Senate, 1953, *BTBG,* 17.
22. U.S. Congress, Senate, 1953, *BTBG,* 20.
23. U.S. Congress, Senate, 1953, *BTBG,* 20.
24. U.S. Congress, Senate, 1953, *BTBG,* 21, 25, 27, and 32.
25. U.S. Congress, Senate, 1953, *BTBG,* 22.
26. U.S. Congress, Senate, 1953, *BTBG,* 28–29.
27. U.S. Congress, Senate, 1953, *BTBG,* 31. Two other minor league presidents testified and provided attendance data (U.S. Congress, Senate, 1953, *BTBG,* 36–37 and 67).
28. U.S. Congress, Senate, 1953, *BTBG,* 32–33. By this point, the reader may marvel at the owners' and their representatives' morbidity.
29. Thomas H. Richardson, president of the Eastern League, also cited the "$7.50 broadcasts" as the culprits. Richardson also made the point that local radio stations, unable to get MLB broadcasts or telecasts then blamed the local club and rule 1(d) (U.S. Congress, Senate, 1953, *BTBG,* 38–39). Senator Warren Magnuson (Wash.) complained, "[Games] are reconstructed, so that when the shortstop makes a catch, the announcer makes it the most spectacular catch of all times. Then they go out and see the [San Francisco] Seals play—and that fellow makes a reasonably good catch, but it is nothing like they heard on the radio from the big leagues" (U.S. Congress, Senate, 1953, *BTBG,* 48).
30. U.S. Congress, Senate, 1953, *BTBG,* 45.
31. U.S. Congress, Senate, 1953, *BTBG,* 46.
32. U.S. Congress, Senate, 1953, *BTBG,* 47.
33. U.S. Congress, Senate, 1953, *BTBG,* 49 and 52. In years to come, Marshall's racist policies would prove an embarrassment to the Kennedy administration. His policies would also, ironically, demonstrate his "stupidity in management," given that the lily-white Redskins sank to the bottom of the NFL for several seasons.

34. U.S. Congress, Senate, 1953, *BTBG*, 52–53. The author would advise any reader, who must testify before Congress, to cultivate his own "Senator Edwin Johnson" as chief inquisitor.

35. U.S. Congress, Senate, 1953, *BTBG*, 60, see 58–59 for other remarks.

36. U.S. Congress, Senate, 1953, *BTBG*, 61.

37. U.S. Congress, Senate, 1953, *BTBG*, 62–63.

38. U.S. Congress, Senate, 1953, *BTBG*, 69–70.

39. U.S. Congress, Senate, 1953, *BTBG*, 70–71.

40. U.S. Congress, Senate, 1953, *BTBG*, 78.

41. U.S. Congress, Senate, 1953, *BTBG*, 86–89, see also 134. Later in the hearings, William Burrow, attorney and ally of McLendon, stated, "The actual happenings of each day, including sporting events, became part of the fact of history immediately upon their happenings. News of them cannot be copyrighted, nor, so far as the public is concerned, can the news itself become the subject of a property right belonging exclusively to any person. To hold otherwise would be to contravene our Constitution, guaranteeing freedom of speech and freedom of the press" (U.S. Congress, Senate, 1953, *BTBG*, 123).

42. U.S. Congress, Senate, 1953, *BTBG*, 95–96.

43. U.S. Congress, Senate, 1953, *BTBG*, 98–101. McLendon was a colorful witness, given to meandering and hyperbole. In a sense, he resembled the owners. He lamented the tamer version of baseball and blamed it, in part, for the faltering attendance (U.S. Congress, Senate, 1953, *BTBG*, 98).

44. U.S. Congress, Senate, 1953, *BTBG*, 135.

45. U.S. Congress, Senate, 1953, *BTBG*, 103, 104, and 114. Johnson was correct that McLendon tended to wander in his testimony, but the senator failed to see the connection McLendon was drawing by likening the reserve clause to the owners' monopoly power. Johnson, however, was getting impatient: "Your long-winded comment is about to get me down" (U.S. Congress, Senate, 1953, *BTBG*, 134, see 125 for McLendon's comment on the reserve clause).

46. U.S. Congress, Senate, 1953, *BTBG*, 107.

47. U.S. Congress, Senate, 1953, *BTBG*, 154.

48. U.S. Congress, Senate, 1953, *BTBG*, 156, see also 142. Economists might raise questions about the selective draft's rationale. If a player, say, Mickey Mantle, was held at a Class C level, even though he was a Class AA talent, the owner of the Class C team was foregoing the opportunity to sell him to an AA team. Economic interest would suggest that few players would languish for very long.

49. U.S. Congress, Senate, 1953, *BTBG*, 167.

50. U.S. Congress, Senate, 1953, *BTBG*, 145.

51. U.S. Congress, Senate, 1953, *BTBG*, 148.

52. U.S. Congress, Senate, 1953, *BTBG*, 168–69. Back in the 1930s, baseball's New York Giants sued the Teleflash Company. The latter company employed a man on property overlooking the ballpark fence. This man transmitted the game's events to a radio broadcast crew. The New York Supreme Court pointed out, "there is no legal barrier to the broadcasting of games from points outside of the park. . . . The ruling that clubs must make their games more

exclusive in order to establish their news value and to prevent indiscriminate broadcasts of the contests, is a particularly interesting point" (*TSN*, "More Static in Radio Problem," March 12, 1936, 4). The FCC stopped unauthorized broadcasts of games by threatening to revoke offending radio stations' licenses (*Broadcasting*, "Rebroadcast of Play-by-Play Baseball Without Permission Criticized/FCC," March 15, 1937, 68).

53. U.S. Congress, Senate, 1953, *BTBG*, 180.

54. Surdam, "Television and Minor League Baseball," 342 (Table 5.5).

55. U.S. Congress, House, 1952, *OB: Hearings*, 1,625.

56. Surdam, "Television and Minor League Baseball," 63–73.

57. Roy Terrell, "Doom Around the Corner," *Sports Illustrated*, December 16, 1957, 36.

58. *NYT*, "Sen. Johnson Still Considering Bill to All Baseball Radio-TV Curb, December 23, 1953, 30; Lowe, *Kid on the Sandlot*, 86–89.

Chapter 12. The NFL's Big Television Score

1. U.S. Congress, House, 1961, *TPSC*, 1–2 and 65.

2. *NYT*, "Foss Predicts $2,500,000 TV Offer: New Football Loop's Head Says 8 Clubs Will Split Take," December 2, 1959, 27; U.S. Congress, House, 1961, *TPSC*, 73; Joe King, "AFL Sets Three-Year Goal for Success," *TSN*, September 7, 1960, 19 and 20.

3. *Broadcasting*, "Football Gets $12 Million From Radio-TV," August 28, 1961, 40–41 and 44.

4. MacCambridge, *America's Game*, 171, cites League Minutes, January 24, 1961.

5. PFHOFAIC, *NFL LM*, March 11, 1960, 33.

6. PFHOFAIC, *NFL LM*, March 12, 1960, 36; March 13, 1960, 38; March 29, 1960, 44–45. MacCambridge claims Baltimore was receiving $600,000 per year from NBC, but this figure is not collaborated by the *Broadcasting* or Rozelle figures; Baltimore's figure might have included radio revenue. MacCambridge and Patton then claim that, in 1960, the revenues with CBS ranged from $75,000 to $175,000, which does not seem too wide a spread between Green Bay and New York, respectively (MacCambridge, *America's Game*, 171 cites Patton, *Razzle-Dazzle*, 53, who does not cite anyone).

7. PFHOFAIC, *NFL LM*, March 12, 1960, 35 and 38. The monopoly aspect was also a major selling point of baseball's John Fetzer's plan to sell a Monday night baseball package in 1965 (Surdam, *Postwar Yankees*, 131–36).

8. MacCambridge, *America's Game*, xvii and 171; Joe King, "Buck Squeeze Forces NFL to Seek Larger Package from Video," *TSN*, February 8, 1961, Sec. 2, 5; MacCambridge, *America's Game*, 171.

9. *NYT*, "Each Club to Get $320,000 a Year," January 11, 1962, 54; *Broadcasting*, "Football Gets $12 Million From Radio-TV," August 28, 1961, 40–41 and 44; Dave Brady, "Congress Learns of Video Role in NFL Club Budgets," *TSN*, September 6, 1961, 14; Richard Shepard, "College Football to Go on C.B.S.-TV," *NYT*, February 16, 1962, 41.

10. Val Adams, N.B.C. Bids Record for Sports Event," *NYT*, April 6, 1961, 67; Val Adams, "C.B.S. Gets Rights to Pro Football," *NYT*, April 27, 1961, 43.

11. Val Adams, "TV Football Pact Voided by Court," *NYT*, July 21, 1961, 1 and 47.

12. Val Adams, "Court Ruling to Cost Football Teams, $2,264,000," *NYT,* July 31, 1961, 41; *NYT,* "National Football League Denied Plea to Delay Voiding TV Pact," July 29, 1961, 39; Dave Brady, "President Signs Package TV Bill; Jackpot for NFL," *TSN,* October 11, 1961, Sec. 2, 6.

13. Harris, *The League,* 15; U.S. Congress, House, 1961, *TPSC,* 71.

14. U.S. Congress, House, 1961, *TPSC,* 5; see also 4 and 9.

15. U.S. Congress, House, 1961, *TPSC,* 6 and 9–10.

16. Coenen, *Sandlots to the Super Bowl,* 202; Harris, *The League,* 14.

17. U.S. Congress, House, 1961, *TPSC,* 1.

18. U.S. Congress, House, 1961, *TPSC,* 10–11.

19. U.S. Congress, House, 1961, *TPSC,* 28.

20. U.S. Congress, House, 1961, *TPSC,* 58 and 73; *Broadcasting,* "Football Gets $12 Million From Radio-TV," August 1961, 40–42.

21. U.S. Congress, House, 1961, *TPSC,* 33.

22. U.S. Congress, House, 1961, *TPSC,* 52 and 61.

23. U.S. Congress, House, 1961, *TPSC,* 69.

24. U.S. Congress, House, 1961, *TPSC,* 35–36

25. U.S. Congress, House, 1961, *TPSC,* 44, and 46.

26. Jack Walsh, "Top Attorney Carries Ball for Pro Gridders," *TSN,* January 6, 1960, Sec. 2, 5 and 6; *NYT,* "N.F.L. Gains Right to Pool TV Pacts," October 1, 1961, S1 and S5.

27. Lowe, *Kid on the Sandlot,* 92; *Broadcasting,* August 21, 1961, 52; July 24, 1961, 61.

28. Joe King, "Pigskin Punts: Green Bay Site for NFL's First Million-Dollar Tilt," *TSN,* December 13, 1961, Sec. 2, 10.

29. For highlights of his statements, see U.S. Congress, Senate, 1964, *PSAB-1964,* 77–78; U.S. Congress, Senate, 1965, *PSAB-1965,* 199.

Chapter 13. Television Blackout Hearings

1. U.S. Congress, Senate, 1972, *BSE,* 166.

2. U.S. Congress, Senate, 1972, *BSE,* 127–28. Government attorney Ellis Rubin told the Senate committee that college bowl games were not usually blacked out (U.S. Congress, Senate, 1972, *BSE,* 102). The comparison with the NFL was not apt, as the bowl games typically brought in large contingents of fans from the communities of the college teams participating in the games.

3. Horowitz, "Sports Telecasts," 161; Daniel, "TV vs. Baseball," 259. Senator William B. Spong Jr. of Virginia expressed his opposition to the bill, claiming that the owners were best situated to make the decision whether to or not to blackout home games (U.S. Congress, Senate, 1972, *BSE,* 120).

4. Horowitz, "Sports Telecasts," 162.

5. Horowitz, "Sports Telecasts," 162.

6. Horowitz, "Sports Telecasts," 165.

7. Horowitz, "Sports Telecasts," 166–67.

8. Horowitz, "Sports Telecasts," 168.

9. U.S. Congress, Senate, 1972, *BSE,* 36.

10. U.S. Congress, Senate, 1972, *BSE,* first quote on 34 and second quote on 31.

11. U.S. Congress, House, 1973, *PSB,* 177.

12. U.S. Congress, House, 1973, *PSB,* 179 and 181. Macdonald suggested that if the NFL stonewalled the networks: "if they got together, NBC, CBS, and ABC, and said to the leagues, we are going to go this far and no further," the NFL might have to accede to the networks' demands. Surprisingly, he did not consider this hypothetical united front by the networks a violation of the antitrust laws (U.S. Congress, House, 1973, *PSB,* 181). Macdonald clearly wanted the legislation to pass; on occasion, he became sarcastic. On the third day of the 1975 hearings, he said, "In fact, just glancing at [Rozelle's] testimony, I am tempted to observe that he appears to be blaming all of the ills of American society on the antiblackout legislation." Rozelle had met his match for hyperbole (U.S. Congress, House, 1975, *SBA75,* 59).

13. U.S. Congress, Senate, 1972, *BSE,* 1. Virginia representative Stanford E. Parris suggested that the antiblackout legislation focused on football and wondered about hockey. Macdonald quipped, "What did the Congress ever do for the National Hockey League?" Parris admitted, "Not a thing of which I am aware." Whereupon Macdonald vented his wrath at the other three sports for all the favors Congress had granted them (U.S. Congress, House, 1973, *PSB,* 24).

14. U.S. Congress, Senate, 1972, *BSE,* 71.

15. U.S. Congress, House, 1975, *SBA75,* 102; for a further example of Brodhead and Rozelle's antagonism, see page 99, where Brodhead accused Rozelle of insensitivity to the economically hard-pressed residents of Detroit and claimed that live attendance at NFL games had "snob appeal," because the average Detroit resident could not afford to attend a games.

16. There was debate over what time limit to enact and how to define "sold out" in such a way to prevent evading the intent of the law by erecting additional seats or standing-room only. Some owners put a limited number of tickets on sale the day of or the day before the game to cultivate a wider fan base, and the legislators were hesitant to discourage this policy (U.S. Congress, House, 1973, *PSB,* 104; for an example of the legislators' suspicions, see Torbert Macdonald's comments during the 1975 hearings, U.S. Congress, House, 1975, *SBA75,* 9).

17. U.S. Congress, House, 1975, *SBA75,* 1–2.

18. U.S. Congress, Senate, 1972, *BSE,* 135; see U.S. Congress, House, 1973, *PSB,* 193.

19. U.S. Congress, Senate, 1972, *BSE,* 50.

20. Quotes from U.S. Congress, House, 1973, *PSB,* 220; U.S. Congress, Senate, 1976, *TARF,* 18; U.S. Congress, Senate, 1978, *FARF,* 9.

21. U.S. Congress, House, 1973, *PSB,* 188 and 190.

22. U.S. Congress, Senate, 1972, *BSE,* 53.

23. U.S. Congress, Senate, 1972, *BSE,* 53; see also U.S. Congress, House, 1975, *SBA75,* 65.

24. U.S. Congress, House, 1975, *SBA75,* 73; U.S. Congress, House, 1973, *PSB,* 192.

25. U.S. Congress, House, 1975, *SBA75,* 70.

26. U.S. Congress, Senate, 1972, *BSE,* 56. Joseph A. Scarmuzzi, president of ARASERVE, Inc., concessionaire to four stadiums hosting NFL games told the committee that he attributed the loss of 1,350 man-days of labor and $165,000 of concessions sales to the lifting of the blackouts at these stadiums (U.S. Congress, House, 1975, *SBA75,* 120).

27. U.S. Congress, Senate, 1972, *BSE,* 98.

28. U.S. Congress, Senate, 1972, *BSE,* 55.

29. U.S. Congress, House, 1975, *SBA75,* 73; U.S. Congress, Senate, 1972, *BSE,* 60. Rozelle and Senator Pastore discussed NFL owners' previous fear of radio broadcasts hurting gate attendance; Rozelle admitted the fears were overblown (U.S. Congress, Senate, 1972, *BSE,* 54).

30. U.S. Congress, House, 1973, *PSB,* 238.

31. U.S. Congress, House, 1975, *SBA75,* 47.

32. U.S. Congress, Senate, 1973, *Federal Sports Act of 1972,* 171. Representative Parris (Va.) presented evidence from a study conducted by the Subcommittee on Investigations that found a majority of Redskins season-ticket holders favored the lifting of the blackout, and the vast majority claimed they would continue to purchase season tickets (U.S. Congress, House, 1973, *PSB,* 22–23).

33. U.S. Congress, House, 1975, *SBA75,* 73. During one of the exchanges between Rozelle and Senator Pastore, the Senator, perhaps in exasperation, blurted out, "The President of the United States has endorsed this bill, yesterday. This has become a national crisis" (U.S. Congress, Senate, 1972, *BSE,* 65).

34. U.S. Congress, Senate, 1972, *BSE,* 57.

35. U.S. Congress, House, 1973, *PSB,* 189.

36. U.S. Congress, House, 1973, *PSB,* 216.

37. U.S. Congress, Senate, 1972, *PB2,* 931, this was an article in an unidentified periodical. Frank made an additional observation: he believed that television provided a better view of the game than even a seat on the fifty-yard line. "Yet fans fight for the privilege of shelling out from $42-$87.50 for a season ticket, bucking traffic and enduring physical discomfort in cold weather."

38. U.S. Congress, House, 1975, *SBA75,* 96.

39. U.S. Congress, House, 1975, *SBA75,* 95.

40. U.S. Congress, House, 1975, *SBA75,* 65 and 93.

41. U.S. Congress, House, 1975, *SBA75,* 66; data on 76–77.

42. U.S. Congress, House, 1975, *SBA75,* quote on 66, see also 131.

43. U.S. Congress, House, 1975, *SBA75,* 71; see also page 20. In earlier testimony, he relied upon attendance figures from isolated games, with vague allusions to weather and other factors (U.S. Congress, Senate, 1972, *BSE,* 58–59).

44. U.S. Congress, House, 1973, *PSB,* 209.

45. U.S. Congress, Senate, 1972, *BSE,* 69 and 123.

46. U.S. Congress, Senate, 1972, *BSE,* 85; U.S. Congress, House, 1973, *PSB,* 39–40.

47. U.S. Congress, Senate, 1972, *BSE,* 86, 92, 138; U.S. Congress, House, 1973, *PSB,* 120–21 and 173; U.S. Congress, House, 1975, *SBA75,* 53.

48. U.S. Congress, Senate, 1972, *BSE,* 143; U.S. Congress, House, 1973, *PSB,* 79 and 95.

49. U.S. Congress, Senate, 1972, *BSE,* 148.
50. U.S. Congress, Senate, 1972, *BSE,* 147.
51. U.S. Congress, House, 1973, *PSB,* 80.
52. U.S. Congress, House, 1973, *PSB,* 82.
53. U.S. Congress, House, 1975, *SBA75,* quote on 23; see also 147.
54. U.S. Congress, House, 1973, *PSB,* 108.
55. U.S. Congress, Senate, 1972, *BSE,* 143.
56. U.S. Congress, Senate, 1972, *BSE,* 154.
57. U.S. Congress, House, 1973, *PSB,* 285.
58. U.S. Congress, Senate, 1973, *Federal Sports Act of 1972,* 276–77.
59. U.S. Congress, Senate, 1972, *BSE,* 152.
60. U.S. Congress, House, 1973, *PSB,* 258.
61. U.S. Congress, House, 1973, *PSB,* 69.
62. U.S. Congress, House, 1973, *PSB,* 71.
63. U.S. Congress, House, 1973, *PSB,* 63.
64. U.S. Congress, Senate, 1974, *Report of the FCC,* 8, 14, and 24.
65. U.S. Congress, Senate, 1976, *TARF,* 265.
66. U.S. Congress, Senate, 1976, *TARF,* 9 and 297. On page 29, the report took a more definite position on the causality: "This is not particularly surprising. The more television exposure a team receives, the greater the interest on the part of the fans. Moreover, since many people prefer to watch games live, that growing interest is translated into increased season ticket sales" (U.S. Congress, Senate, 1976, *TARF,* 29).
67. U.S. Congress, Senate, 1976, *TARF,* 9 and 12.
68. U.S. Congress, Senate, 1976, *TARF,* 27.
69. U.S. Congress, Senate, 1976, *TARF,* 37.
70. Siegfried and Hinshaw, "Professional Football," 172–73.
71. U.S. Congress, Senate, 1977, *Fourth Annual Report of the FCC,* 131.
72. U.S. Congress, Senate, 1977, *Fourth Annual Report of the FCC,* XI. In the *Fourth Annual Report,* the researchers noted, "locally televised home games can have an adverse impact on demand for season tickets. . . . Fortunately, problems created by the sports antiblackout law . . . are not particularly serious in that most teams which are not winning generally do not sell out and locally televise many games" (U.S. Congress, Senate, 1977, *Fourth Annual Report of the FCC,* 14).
73. U.S. Congress, Senate, 1977, *Fourth Annual Report of the FCC,* x.
74. For instance, consider an industry with $10 million in revenues and $6 million in costs, they are currently making $4 million in profits. A 1 percent reduction in revenue would leave the company with $3.9 million in profit, a drop of 2.5 percent.
75. U.S. Congress, Senate, 1977, *Fourth Annual Report of the FCC,* 18.
76. U.S. Congress, Senate, 1978, *FARF,* 4–5 and 14.
77. U.S. Congress, Senate, 1978, *FARF,* 11.
78. U.S. Congress, Senate, 1977, *Fourth Annual Report of the FCC,* 8.
79. "Commission Seeks Comment On Sports Blackout Petition," www.fcc.gov/document/commission-seeks-comment-sports-blackout-petition, viewed July 4, 2013.

80. Ken Belson, "Arctic Temperatures for Players and Fans, but No Blackouts on TV." *NYT*, January 4, 2014, http://www.nytimes.com/2014/01/04/sports/football/nfl-playoffs-cold-with-chance-of-a-tv-blackout.html?_r=0, viewed February 26, 2014.

Chapter 14. The Future Arrives Via Cable Television

1. Though pay television was often discussed as a companion of cable television, this chapter focuses on cable television. In terms of sports, pay television had pretty much been relegated to prominent boxing matches shown in theaters or other venues.

2. U.S. Congress, Senate, 1991, *SPCT*, 237.

3. U.S. Congress, Senate, 1991, *SPCT*, 158.

4. Ross, "Monopoly Sports Leagues," 713.

5. U.S. Congress, Senate, 1991, *SPCT*, 1.

6. U.S. Congress, Senate, 1991, *SPCT*, 3; "National ADS, Wired Cable & Over-the-Air Penetration Trends," www.tvb.org/184839/4729/72512, viewed July 4, 2013; "FCC Adopts Seventh Annual Report on Competition in Video Markets," FCC News, January 8, 2001, transition.fcc.gov/Bureaus/Cable/News_Releases/2001/nrc0101.html, viewed July 4, 2013.

7. U.S. Congress, Senate, 1991, *SPCT*, 98; see 209–10 for a Yankees fan's views on the situation.

8. U.S. Congress, Senate, 1991, *SPCT*, 35 and 134. Padden made the analogy that the MLB/ESPN deal, "would be like prohibiting stations from broadcasting any movie on Wednesday nights because HBO has generic exclusivity for movies" (U.S. Congress, Senate, 1991, *SPCT*, 135). His analogy was inapt, because MLB only controls telecasts of its own product, not all sporting events.

9. U.S. Congress, Senate, 1991, *SPCT*, 19.

10. U.S. Congress, Senate, 1991, *SPCT*, 98.

11. U.S. Congress, Senate, 1991, *SPCT*, 28.

12. U.S. Congress, Senate, 1991, *SPCT*, 41.

13. U.S. Congress, Senate, 1991, *SPCT*, 93.

14. U.S. Congress, Senate, 1991, *SPCT*, 44, 53, and 56.

15. U.S. Congress, Senate, 1991, *SPCT*, 65.

16. U.S. Congress, Senate, 1991, *SPCT*, 83. That Werner was correct can be seen from ESPN's early days, when it showed tractor pulls and became a national target of jokes. Many, if not the vast majority, of Americans wondered about a twenty-four hour sports network.

17. U.S. Congress, Senate, 1991, *SPCT*, 103. Fritts may have exaggerated the cable companies' ability to pass on increased costs to consumers. If customers were very price sensitive, then the cable companies would be unable to pass on a large proportion of any cost increases.

18. The FCC's rules pertaining to siphoning were excerpted in the hearings (U.S. Congress, Senate, 1991, *SPCT*, 176).

19. U.S. Congress, Senate, 1991, *SPCT*, 104, 116, 120–21.

20. U.S. Congress, Senate, 1991, *SPCT*, 148–49, 155, and 169–70.

21. U.S. Congress, Senate, 1991, *SPCT,* 194.

22. U.S. Congress, Senate, 1991, *SPCT,* 226, see also 222–23.

23. Ross, "Monopoly Sports Leagues," 646 and 659–60.

24. Ross, "Monopoly Sports Leagues," 713 and 726. A variation of the natural monopoly idea is that one of the multiple leagues may eventually be seen as superior to the others in the eyes of the patrons, but Ross believes that well-capitalized owners in the eschewed leagues could buy sufficient talent to reverse the perception. Ross, "Monopoly Sports Leagues," 732.

25. U.S. Congress, Senate, 1958, *OPTS,* 383.

Chapter 15. Can't We All Get Along?

1. MacCambridge, *America's Game,* 119–21.

2. U.S. Congress, Senate, 1972, *PB1,* 1,214.

3. U.S. Congress, House, 1966, *PFLM,* 2.

4. U.S. Congress, House, 1966, *PFLM,* 2–3.

5. U.S. Congress, House, 1966, *PFLM,* 7–24.

6. U.S. Congress, House, 1966, *PFLM,* 42–43.

7. U.S. Congress, House, 1966, *PFLM,* 33–34.

8. Both quotes, U.S. Congress, House, 1966, *PFLM,* 34.

9. U.S. Congress, House, 1966, *PFLM,* 34.

10. U.S. Congress, House, 1966, *PFLM,* 34–35.

11. Arthur Daley, "Second Thoughts on Peace," *NYT,* June 10, 1966, 77; excerpt cited in U.S. Congress, House, 1966, *PFLM,* 39.

12. U.S. Congress, House, 1966, *PFLM,* 40 and 100.

13. Daley, "Second Thoughts," *NYT,* June 10, 1966.

14. U.S. Congress, House, 1966, *PFLM,* 51.

15. U.S. Congress, House, 1966, *PFLM,* 51.

16. U.S. Congress, House, 1966, *PFLM,* 52.

17. U.S. Congress, House, 1966, *PFLM,* 106.

18. U.S. Congress, House, 1966, *PFLM,* 107.

19. U.S. Congress, House, 1966, *PFLM,* 53.

20. U.S. Congress, House, 1966, *PFLM,* 66–67.

21. U.S. Congress, House, 1966, *PFLM,* 68.

22. U.S. Congress, House, 1966, *PFLM,* 69–70.

23. U.S. Congress, House, 1966, *PFLM,* 70.

24. U.S. Congress, House, 1966, *PFLM,* 128–29, see also 108. Robert Dole (Kan.) worried that, "Without the plan, it is felt franchise moves and/or franchise failures will occur as a matter of course within the next few years, and a contraction rather than expansion would be the ultimate result" (U.S. Congress, House, 1966, *PFLM,* 109).

25. U.S. Congress, House, 1966, *PFLM,* 102.

26. U.S. Congress, House, 1966, *PFLM,* 103.

27. U.S. Congress, House, 1966, *PFLM,* 105.

28. U.S. Congress, House, 1966, *PFLM,* 115. The NFL owners may have been engaged in sophistry: were there many players in the NFL or the AFL *not* currently making the NFL minimum salary? If the NFL's minimum salary was not a binding constraint upon AFL owners, those owners were giving up very little in terms of player salaries.

29. U.S. Congress, House, 1966, *PFLM,* 116.

30. *Harvard Law Review,* "Super Bowl and the Sherman Act," 431.

31. U.S. Congress, House, 1966, *PFLM,* 116.

32. U.S. Congress, House, 1966, *PFLM,* 116.

33. U.S. Congress, House, 1966, *PFLM,* 116.

34. U.S. Congress, House, 1966, *PFLM,* 117.

35. U.S. Congress, House, 1966, *PFLM,* 118. The reader might note that the owners were pleading for help with their peculiar form of insanity.

36. U.S. Congress, House, 1966, *PFLM,* 118.

37. U.S. Congress, House, 1966, *PFLM,* 118 cites 170 F. Supp. 227 (N.D. Tex. 1059).

38. U.S. Congress, House, 1966, *PFLM,* 119.

39. *American Football League v. National Football League,* 323 F. 2d 124, 131 (4th Cir. 1963).

40. *Harvard Law Review,* "Super Bowl and the Sherman Act," 431.

41. U.S. Congress, House, 1966, *PFLM,* 119.

42. U.S. Congress, House, 1966, *PFLM,* 119. In the accompanying footnote, the proposal stated, "What is often forgotten is that a football club has a very considerable investment in a present or potential player. These and other elements of the situation give a professional football player, like all professional athletes, very considerable leverage in negotiating contract renewals—a leverage which in professional sports generally has produced a growing body of professional athletes with salaries in the six-figure bracket" (U.S. Congress, House, 1966, *PFLM,* 119).

43. U.S. Congress, House, 1966, *PFLM,* 120.

44. Harris, *The League,* 17. Articles in the *New York Times* implied that there was a quid pro quo involved between Rozelle and Boggs/Long (*NYT,* "Football Merger Approval Assured," October 18, 1966, 56; *NYT,* "Measure Will Go to Senate Again," October 21, 1966, 70; *NYT,* "N.F.L. Team Seen for New Orleans," November 1, 1966, 66). Because Celler supported the Investment Tax Credit bill, he ended up voting for both pieces of legislation in the bill, despite his opposition to the football merger (Lowe, *Kid on the Sandlot,* 115–16).

45. *Hecht v. Pro-Football, Inc.,* 444 F. 2d 931-Court of Appeals, District of Columbia).

46. The reversals by the D.C. Circuit are often cited in cases dealing with the "essential facility" doctrine. This doctrine states that a monopolist in an input without a viable substitute is not allowed to restrict access to that input. See http://scholar.google.com/scholar+case?case=46773844347685203148q=en&as+sdt=2&as_vis=18&oi=scholar, viewed July 4, 2013. See also http://scholar_google.com/scholar_case?case=13822243113279057324&hl=en&as_sdt=2&as_vis=1&oi=scholarr, viewed February 17, 2014.

47. According to Peter Chumris, Senator Everett Dirksen and Russell Long introduced a bill approving the merger. After the bill stalled in the House committee, "Time was running out. Congress was trying to adjourn on October 15. So what does Senator Dirksen

do when he heard that the hearing was adjourned . . . and time running out? So Senator Dirksen called up Senator Long and he said, 'Well, we've got to tack this bill on to the tax bill.' That is what was done. The Senate accepted it. It went to the House-Senate conference, the House-Senate conference accepted it, and it became law" (U.S. Congress, Senate, 1972, *PB1*, 755).

Chapter 16. The Proposed NBA/ABA Merger

1. U.S. Congress, House, 1972, *PMABA/NBA*, 201.
2. U.S. Congress, House, 1972, *PMABA/NBA*, 150–51.
3. U.S. Congress, Senate, 1972, *PB2*, 1215.
4. U.S. Congress, Senate, 1972, *PB2*, 855; Leonard Koppett, "Second Thoughts Rise on Merger," *NYT*, March 8, 1972.
5. U.S. Congress, Senate, 1972, *PB2*, 1275; Shirley Povich, "Basketball Owners Run into Ervin Press," *Washington Post*, January 27, 1972.
6. Arlen J. Large, "Blowing the Whistle on Pro Sports," *Wall Street Journal*, October 20, 1971.
7. U.S. Congress, Senate, 1972, *PB1*, 14.
8. U.S. Congress, House, 1972, *PMABA/NBA*, 1.
9. U.S. Congress, House, 1972, *PMABA/NBA*, 243.
10. U.S. Congress, House, 1972, *PMABA/NBA*, 26. Whether Celler understood that legislators were similarly self-interested is an interesting question.
11. U.S. Congress, Senate, 1972, *PB2*, 1233, 1235, 1240, and 1257.
12. U.S. Congress, Senate, 1972, *PB1*, 260.
13. U.S. Congress, Senate, 1972, *PB2*, 1286.
14. U.S. Congress, House, 1972, *PMABA/NBA*, 16.
15. U.S. Congress, Senate, 1972, *PB2*, 1007.
16. U.S. Congress, Senate, 1972, *PB2*, 529 and 536. Two of Ervin's fellow senators on the committee, though, Roman Hruska of Nebraska and John Tunney of California, sided with Kuchel with regard to the request for tax returns.
17. U.S. Congress, Senate, 1972, *PB1*, 368; U.S. Congress, House, 1972, *PMABA/NBA*, 55; see also Ross, "Monopoly Sports Leagues," 728–29.
18. U.S. Congress, House, 1972, *PMABA/NBA*, 55.
19. U.S. Congress, House, 1972, *PMABA/NBA*, 96.
20. U.S. Congress, Senate, 1972, *PB2*, 781.
21. 1968 = 34.8; 1971 = 40.5, www.1.ctdol.state.ct.us/lmi/cpi.asp.
22. U.S. Congress, Senate, 1972, *PB2*, 1,009.
23. U.S. Congress, Senate, 1972, *PB2*, 661.
24. U.S. Congress, Senate, 1972, *PB2*, 611, 633, and 674.
25. U.S. Congress, Senate, 1972, *PB2*, 1004 and 1326, for $25,000 figure and also for ABA franchise "sales."
26. U.S. Congress, Senate, 1972, *PB2*, 577.
27. U.S. Congress, Senate, 1972, *PB2*, 596.

28. U.S. Congress, Senate, 1972, *PB2*, 674.
29. U.S. Congress, Senate, 1972, *PB2*, 1020.
30. U.S. Congress, Senate, 1972, *PB2*, 539.
31. U.S. Congress, Senate, 1972, *PB2*, 988.
32. U.S. Congress, Senate, 1972, *PB2*, 991.
33. U.S. Congress, House, 1972, *PMABA/NBA*, 30–31.
34. U.S. Congress, Senate, 1972, *PB2*, 754.
35. U.S. Congress, Senate, 1972, *PB1*, 345.
36. U.S. Congress, House, 1972, *PMABA/NBA*, 52.
37. U.S. Congress, Senate, 1972, *PB2*, 741–43; Quirk and Fort, *Pay Dirt*, 57–59 and 66. Quirk and Fort show that there was some evidence of a slowing in the appreciation of NBA franchises during the war with the ABA.
38. U.S. Congress, House, 1972, *PMABA/NBA*, 29.
39. U.S. Congress, House, 1972, *PMABA/NBA*, 30.
40. U.S. Congress, House, 1972, *PMABA/NBA*, 153.
41. U.S. Congress, House, 1972, *PMABA/NBA*, 63; U.S. Congress, Senate, 1972, *PB1*, 346 and 364.
42. U.S. Congress, House, 1972, *PMABA/NBA*, 21.
43. U.S. Congress, Senate, 1972, *PB2*, 667.
44. Leonard Koppett, "Congress vs. Sports," *NYT*, November 22, 1971.
45. U.S. Congress, Senate, 1972, *PB2*, 726.
46. U.S. Congress, Senate, 1972, *PB2*, 578; U.S. Congress, House, 1972, *PMABA/NBA*, 20–21.
47. U.S. Congress, House, 1972, *PMABA/NBA*, 19; see also Wendell Cherry's remarks on the issue on page 37 of this hearing.
48. U.S. Congress, Senate, 1972, *PB2*, 670; U.S. Congress, Senate, 1972, *PB1*, 16, 64, and 96.
49. U.S. Congress, Senate, 1972, *PB2*, 728.
50. U.S. Congress, House, 1972, *PMABA/NBA*, 60; U.S. Congress, Senate, 1972, *PB1*, 387.
51. U.S. Congress, Senate, 1972, *PB2*, 870.
52. U.S. Congress, Senate, 1972, *PB2*, 840–41. An economist would ponder why owners would let talented players languish on the bench; would not other owners try to acquire these players?
53. U.S. Congress, Senate, 1972, *PB2*, 561.
54. U.S. Congress, Senate, 1972, *PB2*, 532; Surdam, *Rise of the NBA*, 55–87.
55. U.S. Congress, Senate, 1972, *PB2*, 558.
56. U.S. Congress, Senate, 1972, *PB2*, 1274.
57. U.S. Congress, Senate, 1972, *PB2*, 1213 and 1257.
58. U.S. Congress, Senate, 1972, *Authorizing the Merger of the ABA/NBA*, 13. Lawrence "Larry" Fleisher, NBA Players Association general counsel, echoed Ervin's suspicions pertaining to the ABA's signings of underclassmen (U.S. Congress, Senate, 1972, *PB2*, 1295).
59. U.S. Congress, Senate, 1972, *PB2*, 1059.
60. The Virginia Squires ABA team was to receive an exemption from the $1.25 million entry fee. ABA commissioner Jack Dolph described the situation as "an arrangement" be-

tween the NBA Baltimore Bullets and the ABA Washington Caps (U.S. Congress, Senate, 1972, *PB2*, 750 and 663). The owner of the Caps, Earl Foreman, agreed to relocate his team to Norfolk, although it would also play games in Hampton and Richmond. The struggle between the Baltimore and Washington franchises was reminiscent of the AAFC/NFL struggle two decades earlier.

61. U.S. Congress, Senate, 1972, *PB2*, 1128, Noll quote, and 587.

62. U.S. Congress, House, 1972, *PMABA/NBA*, 252.

63. U.S. Congress, House, 1972, *PMABA/NBA*, 237.

64. U.S. Congress, House, 1972, *PMABA/NBA*, 110–12.

65. U.S. Congress, House, 1972, *PMABA/NBA*, 115–16. Barry testified that he was concerned that the bidding war was deleterious: "I think I am making a lot more money than I should be paid for playing basketball" (U.S. Congress, Senate, 1972, *PB1*, 150).

66. U.S. Congress, House, 1972, *PMABA/NBA*, 62.

67. U.S. Congress, Senate, 1972, *PB2*, 1260.

68. Joe Vila, "Ruppert Belittles Suggestion Yanks Should Aid Weak Clubs," *TSN*, November 10, 1932, 1.

69. U.S. Congress, Senate, 1972, *Authorizing the Merger*, 5.

70. U.S. Congress, Senate, 1972, *Authorizing the Merger*, 6.

71. U.S. Congress, Senate, 1972, *Authorizing the Merger*, 1–4.

72. Jacobs and Winter, "Antitrust Principles and Collective Bargaining."

Bibliography

Areeda, Phillip, and Donald F. Turner. "Predatory Pricing and Related Practices under Section 2 of the Sherman Act." *Harvard Law Review* 88 (1975): 697–733.

Barrow, Ed G., and James M. Kahn. *My Fifty Years in Baseball.* New York: Coward-McCann, 1951.

Barry, Jack. "Pro Basketball's Future Promising." *Boston Garden Arena Sports News* 20(5) (1947–1948): 9 and 11.

Basketball Association of America. *Basketball Association of America League Minutes, 1946–49.* APBR.org/baaminutes.html (April 2, 2010).

Burk, Robert F. *Never Just a Game: Players, Owners, & American Baseball to 1920.* Chapel Hill: University of North Carolina Press, 1994.

———. *Much More than a Game: Players, Owners, & American Baseball Since 1921.* Chapel Hill: University of North Carolina Press, 2001.

Canes, Michael. "The Social Benefits of Restrictions on Team Quality." In *Government and the Sports Business,* edited by Roger G. Noll, 81–113. Washington, D.C.: Brookings Institute, 1974.

Carroll, Bob, Michael Gershman, David Neft, and John Thorn, eds. *Total Football: The Official Encyclopedia of the National Football League.* New York: HarperCollins Publishers, 1997.

Coase, Ronald. "The Problem of Social Cost." *Journal of Law and Economics* 3(1) (1960): 1–44.

Coenen, Craig. *From Sandlots to the Super Bowl.* Knoxville: University of Tennessee Press, 2005.

Cornell Law Review. "Professional Football Telecasts and the Blackout Privilege" 57(2) (January 1972): 297–312.

Craig, Peter. "Organized Baseball: An Industry Study of $100 Spectator Sport." B.A. thesis, Oberlin College, 1950.

Daniel, Dan. "TV vs. Baseball." *Baseball Magazine,* July 1951, 259.

Davis, Jeff. *Papa Bear: The Life and Legacy of George Halas.* New York: McGraw-Hill, 2005.

Davis, Lance. "Self-Regulation in Baseball, 1909–71." In *Government and the Sports Business,* edited by Roger G. Noll, 349–86. Washington, D.C.: Brookings Institution, 1974.

Demmert, Henry. *The Economics of Professional Team Sports.* Lexington, Mass.: Lexington Books, 1973.

Dodd, Donald. *Historical Statistics of the States of the United States: Two Centuries of the Census, 1790–1990.* Westport, Conn.: Greenwood Press, 1993.

Duquette, Jerold J. *Regulating the National Pastime: Baseball and Antitrust.* Westport, Conn.: Praeger, 1999.

Elias, Robert. *The Empire Strikes Out: How Baseball Sold U.S. Foreign Policy and Promoted the American Way Abroad.* New York: New Press, 2010.

Fort, Rodney D. *Sports Economics.*2nd ed. Upper Saddle River, N.J.: Pearson Prentice Hall, 2006.

Fort, Rodney D., and James Quirk. "Cross-subsidization, Incentives, and Outcomes in Professional Team Sports Leagues." *Journal of Economic Literature* 33(3), 1265–99.

Freedman, Warren. *Professional Sports and Antitrust.* Westport, Conn.: Quorum Books, 1987.

Glick, Jeffrey. "Professional Sports Franchise Movements and the Sherman Act: When and Where Teams Should be Able to Move." *Santa Clara Law Review* 23 (Winter 1983): 55–94.

Harris, David. *The League: The Rise and Decline of the NFL.* New York: Bantam Books, 1986.

Harvard Law Review. "The Super Bowl and the Sherman Act: Professional Team Sports and the Antitrust Laws" 81(2) (December 1967):418–34.

Henderson, Cary S. "Los Angeles and the Dodger War, 1957–1962." *Southern California Quarterly* 62 (1980): 261–89.

Horowitz, Ira. "Sports Telecasts: Rights and Regulations." *Journal of Communication* 27(3) (Summer 1977): 160–68.

Isaacs, Neil. *Vintage NBA: The Pioneer Era, 1946–1956.* Indianapolis: Masters Press, 1996.

Jacobs, Michael S., and Ralph K. Winter Jr. "Antitrust Principles and Collective Bargaining by Athletes: Of Superstars in Peonage." *Yale Law Journal* 81(1) (November 1971): 1–29.

Johnson, Arthur T., and James H. Frey, eds. *Government and Sport: The Public Policy Issues.* Totowa, N.J.: Rowman & Allanheld, 1985.

Jordan, Jerry N. "The Long-Range Effect of Television and Other Factors on Sports Attendance." Master's thesis, University of Pennsylvania, 1950.

Kesenne, Stefan. "Revenue Sharing and Competitive Balance in Professional Team Sports." *Journal of Sports Economics* 1(1) (2000): 56–65.

Koller, Roland H., II. "The Myth of Predatory Pricing: An Empirical Study." *Antitrust Law and Economics Review* 4 (1971): 105–23.

Koppett, Leonard. *24 Seconds to Shoot.* Kingston, N.Y.: Total Sports Illustrated Classics, 1999 [1968].

———. *The Essence of the Game Is Deception: Thinking about Basketball.* Boston: Sports Illustrated Books, 1973.

Levin, Richard C., George J. Mitchell, Paul A. Volcker, and George F. Will. *The Report of the Independent Members of the Commissioner's Blue Ribbon Panel on Baseball Economics.* July 2000. www.mlb.com/mlb/downloads/blue_ribbon.pdf.

Levine, Peter. *A.G. Spalding and the Rise of Baseball: The Promise of American Sport.* New York: Oxford University Press, 1985.

Lowe, Stephen R. *The Kid on the Sandlot: Congress and Professional Sports, 1910–1992.* Bowling Green, Ohio: Bowling Green State University, 1995.

MacCambridge, Michael. *America's Game: The Epic Story of How Pro Football Captured a Nation.* New York: Random House, 2004.

Maher, Tod, and Bob Gill. *The Pro Football Encyclopedia: The Complete and Definitive Record of Professional Football.* New York: Macmillan USA, 1997.

Maine Law Review. "The Balance of Power in Professional Sports" 22(2) (1970): 459–80.

Miller, Marvin. *A Whole Different Ball Game: The Inside Story of Baseball's New Deal.* New York: Fireside, 1991.

Nathanson, Mitchell. "The Sovereign Nation of Baseball: Why Federal Law Does Not Apply to 'America's Game' and How It Got That Way." *Villanova Sports & Entertainment Law Journal* 16 (2009): 49–98.

National Basketball Association. Bulletins and other materials. Housed at Joseph M. O'Brien Historical Resource Center (JMOHRC), Naismith Memorial Basketball Hall of Fame.

National League and American Association of Professional Baseball Clubs. 1901. *Annual Meeting of the National League and American Association of Professional Baseball Clubs, December 10 to 14, 1901.*

Neale, Walter. "The Peculiar Economics of Professional Sports." *Quarterly Journal of Economics* 78(1) (February 1964): 1–14.

Nelson, Murry. *The National Basketball League: A History, 1935–1949.* Jefferson, N.C.: McFarland, 2009.

New York Yankee Base Ball Club, *Yankee Baseball Collection,* "Minutes of a Special Meeting of the Board of Directors, October 24, 1939," and "Minutes of February 20, 1941 Meeting."

Noll, Roger, ed. *Government and the Sports Business.* Washington, D.C.: Brookings Institution, 1974.

Noll, Roger, and Andrew Zimbalist, eds. *Sports, Jobs, and Taxes: The Economic Impact of Sports Teams and Stadiums.* Washington, D.C.: Brookings Institution, 1997.

Palmer, Harry. "Consolidation: A League Official's Views Upon the Subject." *Sporting Life,* June 8, 1887, 2.

Parente, Donald E. "The Interdependence of Sports and Television." *Journal of Communication* 27(3) (Summer 1977): 128–32.

Patton, Phil. *Razzle-Dazzle: The Curious Marriage of Television and Professional Football.* Garden City, N.Y.: The Dial Press, 1984.

Peterson, Robert W. *Cages to Jump Shots: Pro Basketball's Early Years.* New York: Oxford University Press, 1990.

———. *Pigskin: The Early Years of Pro Football.* New York: Oxford University Press, 1997.

Pietrusza, David. *Major Leagues: The Formation, Sometimes Absorption and Mostly Inevitable Demise of 18 Professional Baseball Organizations, 1871 to Present.* Jefferson, N.C.: McFarland, 1991.

Pluto, Terry. *Tall Tales: The Glory Years of the NBA.* New York: Simon & Schuster, 1992.

Poggi, Jack. *Theater in America: The Impact of Economic Forces, 1870–1967.* Ithaca, N.Y.: Cornell University Press, 1968.

Pro Football Hall of Fame Archives and Information Center. NFL League Minutes, 1945–60; AFL League Minutes, 1959–60.

Quinn, Kevin, and David Surdam. Unpublished. "Case of the Missing Fans: Did Major League Baseball Owners Act Opportunistically?"

Quirk, Charles E., ed. *Sports and the Law: Major Legal Cases.* New York: Garland Publishing, 1996.

Quirk, James. "An Economic Analysis of Team Movements in Professional Sports." *Law and Contemporary Problems* 38 (Winter-Spring 1973): 42–66.

Quirk, James, and Rodney Fort. *Pay Dirt: The Business of Professional Team Sports.* Princeton, N.J.: Princeton University Press, 1992.

———. *Hard Ball: The Abuse of Power in Pro Team Sports.* Princeton, N.J.: Princeton University Press, 1999.

Roberts, Gary. "The Antitrust Status of Sports Leagues Revisited." *Tulane Law Review* 64 (November 1989): 117–45.

———. "Sports Leagues and the Sherman Act: The Use and Abuse of Section 1 to Regulate Restraints on Intraleague Rivalry." *UCLA Law Review* 32 (December 1984): 219–301.

Ross, Stephen F. "Monopoly Sports Leagues." *Minnesota Law Review* 73(3) (February 1989): 647–761.

Rottenberg, Simon. "The Baseball Players' Labor Market." *Journal of Political Economy* 64 (1956): 242–58.

Salzberg, Charles. *From Set Shot to Slam Dunk: The Glory Days of Basketball in the Words of Those Who Played It.* Lincoln: University of Nebraska Press, originally E.P. Dutton of New York, 1998 [1987].

Scherer, F. M., and David Ross. *Industrial Market Structure and Economic Performance.* 3rd ed. Boston: Houghton Mifflin, 1990.

Seymour, Harold. *Baseball: The Early Years.* New York: Oxford University Press, 1960.

———. *Baseball: The Golden Age.* New York: Oxford University Press, 1971.

Siegfried, John J., and C. Elton Hinshaw. "Professional Football and the Anti-Blackout Law." *Journal of Communication* 27(3) (Summer 1977): 169–74.

Smiley, Robert. "Empirical Evidence on Strategic Entry Deterrence." *International Journal of Industrial Organization* 6 (1988): 167–80.

Sporting News. *The Sporting News Official NBA Guide, 2002–2003 Edition.* St. Louis: The Sporting News, 2002.

Supreme Court of the United States. *American Needle, Inc. v. National Football League et al.*

Surdam, David. "Television and Minor League Baseball: Changing Patterns of Leisure in Postwar America." *Journal of Sports Economics* 6 (February 2005): 61–77.

———. "The Coase Theorem and Player Movement in Major League Baseball." *Journal of Sports Economics* 7 (May 2006): 201–21.
———. "A Tale of Two Gate-Sharing Plans: The National Football League and the National League, 1952–56." *Southern Economic Journal* 73 (April 2007): 931–46.
———. *The Postwar Yankees: Baseball's Golden Age Revisited.* Lincoln: University of Nebraska Press, 2008.
———. "What Brings Fans to the Ball Park? Evidence from New York Yankees' and Philadelphia Phillies' Financial Records." *Journal of Economics* 35 (2009): 35–48.
———. *Wins, Losses, & Empty Seats: How Baseball Outlasted the Great Depression.* Lincoln: University of Nebraska Press, 2011.
———. *The Rise of the National Basketball Association.* Champaign and Urbana: University of Illinois Press, 2012.
———. *Run to Glory and Profits: The Economic Rise of the NFL during the 1950s.* Lincoln: University of Nebraska Press, 2013.
Szymanski, Stefan, and Stefan Kesenne. "Competitive Balance and Gate Revenue Sharing in Team Sports." *Journal of Industrial Economics* 52(1) (2004): 165–77.
Thomas, David C. "Baseball's Amateur Draft—An Abstract Analysis." *Baseball Research Journal* 23 (1994): 92–96.
Thorn, John, Pete Palmer, and Michael Gershman, eds. *The Official Encyclopedia of Major League Baseball: Total Baseball.* 7th ed. New York: Viking 2001.
Topkis, Jay H. "Monopoly in Professional Sports." *Yale Law Review* 58 (1949): 691–712.
Truman, David. *The Governmental Process: Political Interests and Public Opinion.* New York: Alfred A. Knopf, 1971 [1957].
U.S. Congress, House of Representatives. *Organized Baseball: Hearings before the Subcommittee on the Study of Monopoly Power of the Committee of the Judiciary.* House Report No. 2002, 82nd Cong., 1st Sess. Washington, D.C.: Government Printing Office, 1952.
———. *Organized Baseball: Report of the Subcommittee on the Study of Monopoly Power of the Committee of the Judiciary.* House Report No. 2002, 82nd Cong., 1st Sess. Washington, D.C.: Government Printing Office, 1952.
———. *Organized Professional Team Sports. Hearings before the Antitrust Subcommittee of the Committee on the Judiciary.* Serial no. 8. 85th Cong., 1st Sess. Washington, D.C.: Government Printing Office, 1957.
———. *Telecasting of Professional Sports Contests. Hearings before the Antitrust Subcommittee of the Committee on the Judiciary.* Serial no. 13. 87th Cong., 1st Sess. Washington, D.C.: Government Printing Office, 1961.
———. *Professional Football League Merger. Hearings before Antitrust Subcommittee of the Committee on the Judiciary.* Serial no. 22. 89th Cong., 2nd Sess. Washington, D.C.: Government Printing Office, 1966.
———. *The Antitrust Laws and Organized Professional Team Sports Including Consideration of the Proposed Merger of the American and National Basketball Associations.* 92nd Cong., 2nd Sess. Washington, D.C.: Government Printing Office, 1972.
———. *Professional Sports Blackouts: Hearings before the Subcommittee on Communications and Power of the Committee on Interstate and Foreign Commerce.* 93rd Cong., 1st Sess. Washington, D.C.: Government Printing Office, 1973.

———. *Sports Broadcasting Act of 1975. Hearings before the Subcommittee on Communications of the Committee on Interstate and Foreign Commerce.* 94th Cong., 1st Sess. Washington, D.C.: Government Printing Office 1975.

———. *Inquiry into Professional Sports. Final Report of the Select Committee on Professional Sports.* House Report No. 94-1786. 94th Congress, 2nd Session. Washington, D.C.: Government Printing Office, 1977.

———. *Professional Sports Team Community Protection Act: Hearings before the Subcommittee on Commerce, and Transportation and Tourism.* 98th Cong., 2nd Sess. Washington, D.C.: Government Printing Office, 1984.

———. Committee on Education and the Workforce. Subcommittee on Employer-Employee Relations. *Pension Fairness for NBA Pioneers.* 105th Congress, 2nd Sess. Washington, D.C.: Government Printing Office. 1998.

U.S. Congress, Senate. *Broadcasting and Televising Baseball Games. Hearings Before a Subcommittee of the Committee on Interstate and Foreign Commerce.* 83rd Cong., 1st Sess. Washington, D.C.: Government Printing Office, 1953.

———. *Organized Professional Team Sports. Hearings before the Subcommittee on Antitrust and Monopoly of the Committee on the Judiciary.* 85th Cong., 2nd Sess. Washington, D.C.: Government Printing Office, 1958.

———. *Organized Professional Team Sports. Hearings before the Subcommittee on Antitrust and Monopoly of the Committee on the Judiciary.* 86th Cong., 1st Sess. Washington, D.C.: Government Printing Office, 1959.

———. *Organized Professional Team Sports. Hearings before the Subcommittee on Antitrust and Monopoly of the Committee on the Judiciary.* 86th Cong., 2nd Sess. Washington, D.C.: Government Printing Office, 1960.

———. *Professional Sports Antitrust Bill—1964. Hearings before the Subcommittee on Antitrust and Monopoly of the Committee on the Judiciary.* 88th Cong., 2nd Sess. Washington, D.C.: Government Printing Office, 1964.

———. *Professional Sports Antitrust Bill—1965. Hearings before the Subcommittee on Antitrust and Monopoly of the Committee on the Judiciary.* 89th Cong., 1st Sess. Washington D.C.: Government Printing Office, 1965.

———. *Professional Basketball: A Bill to Allow the Merger of Two or More Professional Basketball Leagues. Hearing before the Subcommittee on Antitrust and Monopoly of the Committee on the Judiciary.* 92nd Cong., 1st Sess. Washington, D.C.: Government Printing Office, 1972.

———. *Professional Basketball: A Bill to Allow the Merger of Two or More Professional Basketball Leagues. Part 2. Hearing before the Subcommittee on Antitrust and Monopoly of the Committee on the Judiciary.* 92nd Cong., 1st Sess. Washington, D.C.: Government Printing Office, 1972.

———. *Blackout of Sporting Events on TV. Hearings before the Subcommittee on Communications. Committee on Commerce.* 92nd Cong., 2nd Sess. Washington, D.C.: Government Printing Office 1972.

———. *Authorizing the Merger of Two or More Professional Basketball Leagues, and for Other Purposes. Report to the Committee on the Judiciary.* 92nd Cong., 2nd Sess. Washington, D.C.: Government Printing Office, 1972.

———. *Federal Sports Act of 1972: Hearings before the Committee on Commerce United States Senate*. 92nd Cong. 2nd Sess. Washington, D.C.: Government Printing Office 1973.

———. *Report of the Federal Communications Commission on the Effect of Public Law 93-107, the Sports Anti-Blackout Law on the Broadcasting of Sold-Out Home Games of Professional Football, Baseball, Basketball, and Hockey*. 93d Cong., 2nd Sess. Washington, D.C.: Government Printing Office, 1974.

———. *Third Annual Report of the FCC on the Effect of P.L. 93-107, the Sports Anti-Blackout Law, On the Broadcasting of Sold-Out Home Games of Professional Football, Baseball, Basketball, and Hockey: Committee on Commerce, Science, and Transportation*. 94th Cong., 2nd Sess. Washington, D.C.: Government Printing Office, 1976.

———. *Fourth Annual Report of the Federal Communications Commission on the Effect of P.L. 93-107, the Sports Anti-Blackout Law, On the Broadcasting of Sold-Out Home Games of Professional Football, Baseball, Basketball, and Hockey: Committee on Commerce, Science, and Transportation*. 94th Cong., 2nd Sess. Washington, D.C.: Government Printing Office, 1977.

———. *Fifth Annual Report of the FCC on the Effect of P.L. 93-107, the Sports Anti-Blackout Law, On the Broadcasting of Sold-Out Home Games of Professional Football, Baseball, Basketball, and Hockey: Committee on Commerce, Science, and Transportation*. 95th Cong., 2nd Sess. Washington, D.C.: Government Printing Office, 1978.

———. *Professional Sports Team Community Protection Act: Hearings before the Committee on Commerce, Science, and Transportation*. 98th Cong., 2nd Sess. Washington, D.C.: Government Printing Office, 1984.

———. *Professional Sports Community Protection Act of 1985: Hearings before the Committee on Commerce, Science, and Transportation*. 99th Cong., 1st Sess. Washington, D.C.: Government Printing Office, 1985.

———. *Professional Sports Antitrust Immunity: Hearings before the Committee on the Judiciary*. 99th Cong., 1st Sess. Washington, D.C.: 1986.

———. *Sports Programming and Cable Television: Hearing before the Subcommittee on Antitrust, Monopolies and Business Rights of the Committee on the Judiciary*. 101st Cong., 1st Sess. Washington, D.C.: 1991.

U.S. Department of Commerce. Bureau of the Census. *Census of Housing: 1950. Vol. I. General Characteristics, pt. 1, United States Summary*. Washington, D.C.: GPO, 1953.

———. Bureau of the Census. *Statistical Abstract of the United States, 1952*. Washington, D.C.: Government Printing Office, 1952.

———. Bureau of the Census. *Historical Statistics of the United States: Colonial Times to 1970*. 2 vols. Washington, D.C.: Government Printing Office, 1975.

U.S. Department of Justice. Federal Trade Commission. *Horizontal Merger Guidelines*, issued August 19, 2010. www.justice.gov/atr/public/guidelines/hmg-2010.html, viewed March 3, 2014.

Veeck, Bill. *Veeck as in Wreck*. New York: Putnam, 1962.

———. *The Hustler's Handbook*. New York: Putnam, 1965.

Voigt, David Q. *American Baseball: From Gentleman's Sport to the Commissioner System*. Norman: University of Oklahoma Press, 1966.

———. *American Baseball: From the Commissioners to Continental Expansion.* Reprint: University Park: Pennsylvania State University Press, 1983 [1970].

———. *American Baseball: From Postwar Expansion to the Electronic Age.* University Park: Pennsylvania State University Press, 1983.

Vrooman, John. "A General Theory of Sports Leagues." *Southern Journal of Economics* 61(April 1995): 971–90.

White, G. Edward. *Creating the National Pastime: Baseball Transforms Itself, 1903–1953.* Princeton, N.J.: Princeton University Press, 1996.

Wolohan, John. "The Curt Flood Act of 1998 and Major League Baseball's Federal Antitrust Exemption." *Marquette Sports Law Journal* 9(2) (Spring 1999): 347–77.

Index

DAVID GEORGE SURDAM is an associate professor of economics at the University of Northern Iowa. He is the author of *Wins, Losses, and Empty Seats: How Baseball Outlasted the Great Depression.*